THE BLITHEDALE ROMANCE

AN AUTHORITATIVE TEXT
BACKGROUNDS AND SOURCES
CRITICISM

W.W. NORTON & COMPANY, INC.
also publishes

THE NORTON ANTHOLOGY OF AMERICAN LITERATURE
edited by Nina Baym et al.

THE NORTON ANTHOLOGY OF ENGLISH LITERATURE
edited by M. H. Abrams et al.

THE NORTON ANTHOLOGY OF LITERATURE BY WOMEN
edited by Sandra M. Gilbert and Susan Gubar

THE NORTON ANTHOLOGY OF MODERN POETRY
edited by Richard Ellmann and Robert O'Clair

THE NORTON ANTHOLOGY OF POETRY
edited by Alexander W. Allison et al.

THE NORTON ANTHOLOGY OF SHORT FICTION
edited by R. V. Cassill

THE NORTON ANTHOLOGY OF WORLD MASTERPIECES
edited by Maynard Mack et al.

THE NORTON FACSIMILE OF
THE FIRST FOLIO OF SHAKESPEARE
prepared by Charlton Hinman

THE NORTON INTRODUCTION TO LITERATURE
edited by Carl E. Bain, Jerome Beaty, and J. Paul Hunter

THE NORTON INTRODUCTION TO THE SHORT NOVEL
edited by Jerome Beaty

THE NORTON READER
edited by Arthur M. Eastman et al.

THE NORTON SAMPLER
edited by Thomas Cooley

NATHANIEL HAWTHORNE

THE BLITHEDALE ROMANCE

AN AUTHORITATIVE TEXT
BACKGROUNDS AND SOURCES
CRITICISM

Edited by

SEYMOUR GROSS
THE UNIVERSITY OF DETROIT

and

ROSALIE MURPHY
SWEET BRIAR COLLEGE

W · W · NORTON & COMPANY
New York · London

W. W. Norton & Company, Inc., 500 Fifth Avenue, New York, N.Y. 10110
W. W. Norton & Company Ltd., 37 Great Russell Street, London WC1B 3NU

CENTER FOR EDITIONS OF
AMERICAN AUTHORS

AN APPROVED TEXT

MODERN LANGUAGE
ASSOCIATION OF AMERICA

®

Since this page cannot legibly accommodate all the copyright notices,
the page that follows constitutes an extension of the copyright page.

Library of Congress Cataloging in Publication Data
Hawthorne, Nathaniel, 1804–1864.
    The Blithedale romance.
    (A Norton critical edition)
    Bibliography: p.
    1. Hawthorne, Nathaniel, 1804–1864. The Blithedale
romance. I. Gross, Seymour Lee, 1926–   II. Murphy,
Rosalie. III. Title.
PZ3.H318Bl 1977 [PS1855] 813′.3 77–24887
ISBN 0-393-04449-1
ISBN 0-393-09150-3 pbk.

9

For
Elaine and Brian

Contents

MODERN ESSAYS IN CRITICISM

Introduction

No shift in the concerns of society at large or in the emphases of literary criticism will ever dislodge *The Scarlet Letter* from its pre-eminent place among Hawthorne's novels. It will remain what it has been almost from its publication in 1850—the Hawthorne novel of most interest to both general reader and specialist. Second place, however, is less certain. There is growing evidence that *The Blithedale Romance* (1852), after a long period of neglect, is gradually coming to occupy that position. After an initial flurry of interest in the novel, nineteenth- and early twentieth-century critics—with the notable exceptions of Henry James and William Dean Howells—tended to brush the work aside. Typical is Paul Elmer More's comment at the turn of the century that a study of Hawthorne need not include a discussion of *The Blithedale Romance*, "the slightest and most colourless of the novels."

Beginning in the 1950s, however, interest in *The Blithedale Romance* gathered such momentum that analyses of the novel have numerically outstripped those of any of Hawthorne's other longer works, with (of course) the exception of *The Scarlet Letter*. The reasons for this shift are clear: the subject matter of the novel and the form in which the story is told coincided with certain cultural and critical concerns. *The Blithedale Romance* is about "a knot of dreamers" who withdraw from society in search of a better American way of life. That the 1950s and 60s should have been drawn to such a novel (as they were drawn to *Walden*) was inevitable, for not since the 1840s—which saw the formation of more than fifty communities, at least twenty-five of which were Fourierist phalanxes—had a period in American history displayed such a passionate interest in radically idealistic communitarian movements and ideas. It is possible to see now that an early signal of this change in the critical fortunes of the novel was Irving Howe's serious treatment of *Blithedale* in *Politics and the Novel* (1957)—alongside such monuments of social fiction as Dostoevsky's *The Possessed*, Conrad's *Under Western Eyes*, Malraux's *Man's Fate*, Koestler's *Darkness at Noon*, and Orwell's *1984*. An interest in first-person point of view narratives made it equally inevitable that a problematic narrator like Coverdale would compel substantial critical response. Coverdale's mind, the ambiguous perspective from which the story is told, determines the meaning of the novel as surely as does the mind of Ishmael in *Moby-Dick*, Nick Carraway in *The Great Gatsby*, or Jack Burden in *All the King's Men*.

The choice and organization of the materials in the Modern

Essays in Criticism section of this book reflect the cultural and critical concerns of recent scholarship. The essays are presented chronologically within, roughly, three thematic categories. The first five (Howe, Male, Kaul, Levy, and Lang) focus primarily on *The Blithedale Romance* as a cultural document, either as a revelation of Hawthorne's America or as an exploration of certain ongoing American cultural concerns. The following three essays (Rahv, the Lefcowitzes, Baym) are concerned with the nature of woman, either as a psychological problem for the author and/or in American society, their critical strategies mediating between the issue of feminism and formalistic matters. The final six essays (Waggoner, Crews, Griffith, Auchincloss, Justus, and Bales) treat such artistic matters as imagery, structure, and point of view, most especially the last.

The choice and organization of the materials in the Contemporary Reviews section reflect the cultural and critical concerns of the early criticism. One of the pieties frequently encountered in Hawthorne criticism is that it all began with James. It is our view, however, that the criticism of *The Blithedale Romance*, whatever the truth may be about Hawthorne's other novels, began at the beginning, with the contemporary reviews. We have therefore not followed the usual practice of including a few of these for their antiquarian interest. We have, instead, selected and arranged numerous excerpts to display how the contemporary reviewers, in our view rather extraordinarily, located the problems of the novel which later criticism pursues in more detailed and sophisticated fashion. The selections in the Modern Essay section support this thesis. The Contemporary Reviews section does, however, include material on the work as a "romance" (the place of fact in fiction as an artistic and historical problem) and on the possible real-life models for the characters of the work. Given the limitations of space, we did not feel that modern criticism in these areas (the biographical interest being most characteristic of the 1930s) warranted inclusion. The substantial Backgrounds and Sources section does, however, offer a clear indication of Hawthorne's use of primary materials. And the annotations of the text offer many of the speculations and insights of biographical criticism.

For their assistance in the preparation of this volume, we would like to thank Professors Dolores Burdick and Steve Schucard of Oakland University, Rochester; Professors James Wey, Richard Kowalczyk, and Gene Montague and Mrs. Aline Smith of the University of Detroit; and—with special personal feeling—Lois Mastrangelo, Thomas Gross, Claire Tanase, and John and Mark Murphy.

SEYMOUR GROSS
ROSALIE MURPHY

The Text of
The Blithedale Romance

A Note on the Text

The text of *The Blithedale Romance* is that of the Centenary Edition of the Works of Nathaniel Hawthorne, a publication of the Ohio State University Center for Textual Studies and the Ohio State University Press.

PREFACE

IN THE 'BLITHEDALE' of this volume, many readers will
probably suspect a faint and not very faithful shadowing
of BROOK FARM, in Roxbury, which (now a little more
than ten years ago) was occupied and cultivated by a company
of socialists.[1] The Author does not wish to deny, that he had
this Community in his mind, and that (having had the good
fortune, for a time, to be personally connected with it) he
has occasionally availed himself of his actual reminiscences,
in the hope of giving a more lifelike tint to the fancy-sketch
in the following pages. He begs it to be understood, however,
that he has considered the Institution itself as not less fairly
the subject of fictitious handling, than the imaginary personages whom he has introduced there. His whole treatment of
the affair is altogether incidental to the main purpose of the
Romance; nor does he put forward the slightest pretensions
to illustrate a theory, or elicit a conclusion, favorable or otherwise, in respect to Socialism.

In short, his present concern with the Socialist Community
is merely to establish a theatre, a little removed from the

1. Brook Farm (1841–47), situated about
nine miles from Boston, was the most famous cooperative community of the nineteenth century. It began as an attempt to
put into practice some of the idealistic
social ideas of Transcendentalism, a romantic New England movement which intended the regeneration of the entire
quality of American life. Hawthorne, although not a Transcendentalist, lived at
Brook Farm (in which he owned stock)
from April to November of 1841. For the
uses he made of that experience in *Blithedale*, see the section entitled "Hawthorne
and Brook Farm," below.

1

highway of ordinary travel, where the creatures of his brain may play their phantasmagorical antics, without exposing them to too close a comparison with the actual events of real lives. In the old countries, with which Fiction has long been conversant, a certain conventional privilege seems to be awarded to the romancer; his work is not put exactly side by side with nature; and he is allowed a license with regard to every-day Probability, in view of the improved effects which he is bound to produce thereby. Among ourselves, on the contrary, there is as yet no such Faery Land, so like the real world, that, in a suitable remoteness, one cannot well tell the difference, but with an atmosphere of strange enchantment, beheld through which the inhabitants have a propriety of their own. This atmosphere is what the American romancer needs. In its absence, the beings of imagination are compelled to show themselves in the same category as actually living mortals; a necessity that generally renders the paint and pasteboard of their composition but too painfully discernible. With the idea of partially obviating this difficulty, (the sense of which has always pressed very heavily upon him,) the Author has ventured to make free with his old, and affectionately remembered home, at BROOK FARM, as being, certainly, the most romantic episode of his own life—essentially a day-dream, and yet a fact—and thus offering an available foothold between fiction and reality. Furthermore, the scene was in good keeping with the personages whom he desired to intro-duce.

These characters, he feels it right to say, are entirely fictitious. It would, indeed, (considering how few amiable qualities he distributes among his imaginary progeny,) be a most grievous wrong to his former excellent associates, were the Author to allow it to be supposed that he has been sketching any of their likenesses. Had he attempted it, they would at least have recognized the touches of a friendly pencil. But he has done nothing of the kind. The self-concentrated Philanthropist; the high-spirited Woman, bruising herself against the narrow limitations of her sex; the weakly Maiden, whose tremulous nerves endow her with Sibylline[2] attributes; the Minor Poet, beginning life with strenuous aspirations, which die out with his youthful fervor —all these might have been looked for, at BROOK FARM, but, by some accident, never made their appearance there.

The Author cannot close his reference to this subject, without expressing a most earnest wish that some one of the many cultivated and philosophic minds, which took an interest in that enterprise, might now give the world its history. Ripley, with whom rests the honorable paternity of the Institution, Dana, Dwight, Channing, Burton, Parker,[3] for instance—with others, whom he dares not name, because they veil themselves from the public eye—among these is the ability to convey both the outward narrative and the inner truth and spirit of the whole affair, together with the lessons which those years of thought and toil must have elaborated, for the behoof of future experimentalists. Even the brilliant Howadji[4] might find as rich a theme in his youthful reminiscenses of BROOK FARM, and a more novel one—close at hand as it lies—than those which he has since made so distant a pilgrimage to seek, in Syria, and along the current of the Nile.

CONCORD (Mass.), May, 1852.

2. Characteristic of sibyls, women regarded as prophetesses by the ancient Greeks and Romans.
3. George Ripley (1802–80), Unitarian minister (resigned), literary critic and social reformer, was organizer and head of Brook Farm. Charles Anderson Dana (1819–97), newspaper editor, lived there from 1841–46; John Sullivan Dwight (1813–93), music critic, from 1841–47; Warren Burton (1800–1866), Unitarian minister and educator, from 1841–44. William Henry Channing (1810–84), Unitarian minister and social reformer, and Theodore Parker (1810–60), Unitarian minister whose parish in West Roxbury included many Brook Farmers, were frequent visitors to the Farm. None of these men wrote a history of Brook Farm, although Ripley died while writing a short account for Justin Winsor's *The Memorial History of Boston* (1881) and Dana gave a lecture-tribute to Brook Farm at the University of Michigan in 1895.
4. George William Curtis (1824–92), a student at Brook Farm from 1842 to 1843, wrote two *Impressions de voyage* entitled "Nile Notes of a Howadji" (1851), that is, of a "traveller," and "Howadji in Syria" (1852). Late in life he wrote a short essay, "Hawthorne and Brook Farm," for *Harper's New Monthly Magazine*.

I

OLD MOODIE

THE EVENING before my departure for Blithedale,[5] I
was returning to my bachelor-apartments, after attend-
ing the wonderful exhibition of the Veiled Lady, when
an elderly-man of rather shabby appearance met me in an
obscure part of the street.

"Mr. Coverdale,"[6] said he, softly, "can I speak with you
a moment?"

As I have casually alluded to the Veiled Lady, it may not
be amiss to mention, for the benefit of such of my readers as
are unacquainted with her now forgotten celebrity, that she
was a phenomenon in the mesmeric line;[7] one of the earliest
that had indicated the birth of a new science, or the revival
of an old humbug. Since those times, her sisterhood have
grown too numerous to attract much individual notice; nor,
in fact, has any one of them ever come before the public
under such skilfully contrived circumstances of stage-effect,
as those which at once mystified and illuminated the remarkable performances of the lady in question. Now-a-days, in
the management of his 'subject,' 'clairvoyant,' or 'medium,'
the exhibitor affects the simplicity and openness of scientific

5. Happy Valley.

6. Miles Coverdale (1488–1569) did the
first translation into English of the whole
Bible with Apocrypha (1535). For a discussion of the novel and the Bible, see
Joan Magretta, "The Coverdale Translation: *Blithedale* and the Bible," *Nathaniel
Hawthorne Journal* (1974), 250–56.

7. By 1789 any contribution which Franz
Mesmer (1734–1815) made to Vitalistic
philosophy or to curative medicine, with
his theory of an invisible universal fluid
which penetrated and surrounded all bodies, had been obscured by an eclectic, spiritualist form of mesmerism which entertained the public with magic, seances,
hypnotism, somnambulism, and exhibitions similar to that described by Coverdale in Chapter XXIII. For Hawthorne's
attitude toward mesmerism, see his letters, below.

experiment; and even if he profess to tread a step or two across the boundaries of the spiritual world, yet carries with him the laws of our actual life, and extends them over his preternatural conquests. Twelve or fifteen years ago, on the contrary, all the arts of mysterious arrangement, of picturesque disposition, and artistically contrasted light and shade, were made available in order to set the apparent miracle in the strongest attitude of opposition to ordinary facts. In the case of the Veiled Lady, moreover, the interest of the spectator was further wrought up by the enigma of her identity, and an absurd rumor (probably set afloat by the exhibitor, and at one time very prevalent) that a beautiful young lady, of family and fortune, was enshrouded within the misty drapery of the veil. It was white, with somewhat of a subdued silver sheen, like the sunny side of a cloud; and falling over the wearer, from head to foot, was supposed to insulate her from the material world, from time and space, and to endow her with many of the privileges of a disembodied spirit.

Her pretensions, however, whether miraculous or otherwise, have little to do with the present narrative; except, indeed, that I had propounded, for the Veiled Lady's prophetic solution, a query as to the success of our Blithedale enterprise. The response, by-the-by, was of the true Sibylline stamp, nonsensical in its first aspect, yet, on closer study, unfolding a variety of interpretations, one of which has certainly accorded with the event. I was turning over this riddle in my mind, and trying to catch its slippery purport by the tail, when the old man, above-mentioned, interrupted me.

"Mr. Coverdale!—Mr. Coverdale!" said he, repeating my name twice, in order to make up for the hesitating and ineffectual way in which he uttered it—"I ask your pardon, sir—but I hear you are going to Blithedale tomorrow?"

I knew the pale, elderly face, with the red-tipt nose, and the patch over one eye, and likewise saw something characteristic in the old fellow's way of standing under the arch of a gate, only revealing enough of himself to make me recognize him as an acquaintance. He was a very shy personage, this Mr. Moodie; and the trait was the more singular, as his mode of getting his bread necessarily brought him into the stir and hubbub of the world, more than the generality of men.

"Yes, Mr. Moodie," I answered, wondering what interest he could take in the fact, "it is my intention to go to Blithedale tomorrow. Can I be of any service to you, before my departure?"

"If you pleased, Mr. Coverdale," said he, "you might do me a very great favor."

"A very great one!" repeated I, in a tone that must have expressed but little alacrity of beneficence, although I was ready to do the old man any amount of kindness involving no special trouble to myself. "A very great favor, do you say? My time is brief, Mr. Moodie, and I have a good many preparations to make. But be good enough to tell me what you wish."

"Ah, sir," replied old Moodie, "I don't quite like to do that; and, on further thoughts, Mr. Coverdale, perhaps I had better apply to some older gentleman, or to some lady, if you would have the kindness to make me known to one, who may happen to be going to Blithedale. You are a young man, sir!"

"Does that fact lessen my availability for your purpose?" asked I. "However, if an older man will suit you better, there is Mr. Hollingsworth,[8] who has three or four years the advantage of me in age, and is a much more solid character, and a philanthropist to boot. I am only a poet, and, so the critics tell me, no great affair at that! But what can this business be, Mr. Moodie? It begins to interest me; especially since your hint that a lady's influence might be found desirable. Come; I am really anxious to be of service to you."

8. In *"The Blithedale Romance:* A History of Ideas Approach" (reprinted below), Hans-Joachim Lang speculates on Hawthorne's choice of the name *Hollingsworth*, with its suggestion of "the arch radical of that time," Thomas Holcroft.

But the old fellow, in his civil and demure manner, was both freakish and obstinate; and he had now taken some notion or other into his head that made him hesitate in his former design.

"I wonder, sir," said he, "whether you know a lady whom they call Zenobia?"

"Not personally," I answered, "although I expect that pleasure tomorrow, as she has got the start of the rest of us, and is already a resident at Blithedale. But have you a literary turn, Mr. Moodie?—or have you taken up the advocacy of women's rights?—or what else can have interested you in this lady? Zenobia, by-the-by, as I suppose you know, is merely her public name;[9] a sort of mask in which she comes before the world, retaining all the privileges of privacy—a contrivance, in short, like the white drapery of the Veiled Lady, only a little more transparent. But it is late! Will you tell me what I can do for you?"

"Please to excuse me to-night, Mr. Coverdale," said Moodie. "You are very kind; but I am afraid I have troubled you, when, after all, there may be no need. Perhaps, with your good leave, I will come to your lodgings tomorrow-morning, before you set out for Blithedale. I wish you a good-night, sir, and beg pardon for stopping you."

And so he slipt away; and, as he did not show himself, the next morning, it was only through subsequent events that I ever arrived at a plausible conjecture as to what his business could have been. Arriving at my room, I threw a lump of cannel coal[1] upon the grate, lighted a cigar, and spent an hour in musings of every hue, from the brightest to the most sombre; being, in truth, not so very confident as at some former periods, that this final step, which would mix me up irrevocably with the Blithedale affair, was the wisest that could possibly be taken. It was nothing short of midnight

---

9. The historical Zenobia was the third-century Queen of Palmyra who defied the Roman empire and was defeated by the emperor Aurelian. For the possible influence of William Ware's *Zenobia, or The Fall of Palmyra* (1837), see John C. Hirsh, "Zenobia as Queen: The Background Sources to Hawthorne's *The Blithedale Romance*," *Nathaniel Hawthorne Journal* (1971), 182–90.

1. A brightly burning but exceedingly smoky fuel.

when I went to bed, after drinking a glass of particularly
fine Sherry, on which I used to pride myself, in those days.
It was the very last bottle; and I finished it, with a friend, the
next forenoon, before setting out for Blithedale.

II

BLITHEDALE

THERE can hardly remain for me, (who am really
getting to be a frosty bachelor, with another white hair,
every week or so, in my moustache,) there can hardly
flicker up again so cheery a blaze upon the hearth, as that
which I remember, the next day, at Blithedale. It was a
wood-fire, in the parlor of an old farm-house, on an April
afternoon,[2] but with the fitful gusts of a wintry snow-storm
roaring in the chimney. Vividly does that fireside re-create
itself, as I rake away the ashes from the embers in my memory, and blow them up with a sigh, for lack of more inspiring
breath. Vividly, for an instant, but, anon, with the dimmest
gleam, and with just as little fervency for my heart as for my
finger-ends! The staunch oaken-logs were long ago burnt out.
Their genial glow must be represented, if at all, by the merest
phosphoric glimmer, like that which exudes, rather than
shines, from damp fragments of decayed trees, deluding the
benighted wanderer through a forest. Around such chill mockery of a fire, some few of us might sit on the withered leaves,
spreading out each a palm towards the imaginary warmth, and
talk over our exploded scheme for beginning the life of
Paradise anew.

2. John W. Shroeder parallels the sea-
sonal structure of *Blithedale* with that of
Edmund Spenser's *The Faerie Queene*;
he further argues that four episodes in
the novel are based on eclogues in Spenser's *The Shepheardes Calendar:* pp. 58–
59 on "April"; pp. 75–78 on "May"; pp.
232–37 on "November"; and Chapter
XXIX on "December." ("Miles Coverdale's Calendar," *Essex Institute Historical Collections*, 103 [1967], 353–64.)

Paradise, indeed! Nobody else in the world, I am bold to affirm—nobody, at least, in our bleak little world of New England—had dreamed of Paradise, that day, except as the pole suggests the tropic. Nor, with such materials as were at hand, could the most skilful architect have constructed any better imitation of Eve's bower, than might be seen in the snow-hut of an Esquimaux. But we made a summer of it, in spite of the wild drifts.

It was an April day, as already hinted, and well towards the middle of the month. When morning dawned upon me, in town, its temperature was mild enough to be pronounced even balmy, by a lodger—like myself—in one of the midmost houses of a brick-block; each house partaking of the warmth of all the rest, besides the sultriness of its individual furnace-heat. But, towards noon, there had come snow, driven along the street by a north-easterly blast, and whitening the roofs and sidewalks with a business-like perseverance that would have done credit to our severest January tempest. It set about its task, apparently as much in earnest as if it had been guaranteed from a thaw, for months to come. The greater, surely, was my heroism, when, puffing out a final whiff of cigar-smoke, I quitted my cosey pair of bachelor-rooms—with a good fire burning in the grate, and a closet right at hand, where there was still a bottle or two in the champagne-basket, and a residuum of claret in a box, and somewhat of proof in the concavity of a big demijohn[3] —quitted, I say, these comfortable quarters, and plunged into the heart of the pitiless snow-storm, in quest of a better life.

The better life! Possibly, it would hardly look so, now; it is enough if it looked so, then. The greatest obstacle to being heroic, is the doubt whether one may not be going to prove one's self a fool; the truest heroism is, to resist the

---

3. Some whiskey in a multi-gallon wicker-encased bottle; "and somewhat of proof in the concavity of a big demijohn" was deleted in the manuscript of *Blithedale*. The editors of the Centenary Edition decided to restore the phrase because the deletion was most probably due only to Mrs. Hawthorne's notorious prudishness. Two other excised passages, one a sexual reference (p. 17, lines 4 and 5) and the other a lengthy defense of liquor (p. 160, line 28, through p. 161, line 19) were restored for the same reason.

doubt—and the profoundest wisdom, to know when it ought to be resisted, and when to be obeyed.

Yet, after all, let us acknowledge it wiser, if not more sagacious, to follow out one's day-dream to its natural consummation, although, if the vision have been worth the having, it is certain never to be consummated otherwise than by a failure. And what of that! Its airiest fragments, impalpable as they may be, will possess a value that lurks not in the most ponderous realities of any practicable scheme. They are not the rubbish of the mind. Whatever else I may repent of, therefore, let it be reckoned neither among my sins nor follies, that I once had faith and force enough to form generous hopes of the world's destiny—yes!—and to do what in me lay for their accomplishment; even to the extent of quitting a warm fireside, flinging away a freshly lighted cigar, and travelling far beyond the strike of city-clocks, through a drifting snow-storm.

There were four of us who rode together through the storm; and Hollingsworth, who had agreed to be of the number, was accidentally delayed, and set forth at a later hour, alone. As we threaded the streets, I remember how the buildings, on either side, seemed to press too closely upon us, insomuch that our mighty hearts found barely room enough to throb between them. The snow-fall, too, looked inexpressibly dreary, (I had almost called it dingy,) coming down through an atmosphere of city-smoke, and alighting on the sidewalk, only to be moulded into the impress of somebody's patched boot or over-shoe. Thus, the track of an old conventionalism was visible on what was freshest from the sky. But—when we left the pavements, and our muffled hoof-tramps beat upon a desolate extent of country-road, and were effaced by the unfettered blast, as soon as stamped—then, there was better air to breathe. Air, that had not been breathed, once and again! Air, that had not been spoken into words of falsehood, formality, and error, like all the air of the dusky city!

"How pleasant it is!" remarked I, while the snow-flakes flew into my mouth, the moment it was opened. "How very mild and balmy is this country-air!"

"Ah, Coverdale, don't laugh at what little enthusiasm you have left," said one of my companions. "I maintain that this nitrous atmosphere[4] is really exhilarating; and, at any rate, we can never call ourselves regenerated men, till a February north-easter shall be as grateful to us as the softest breeze of June."

So we all of us took courage, riding fleetly and merrily along, by stone-fences that were half-buried in the wave-like drifts; and through patches of woodland, where the tree-trunks opposed a snow-encrusted side towards the north-east; and within ken of deserted villas, with no foot-prints in their avenues; and past scattered dwellings, whence puffed the smoke of country fires, strongly impregnated with the pungent aroma of burning peat. Sometimes, encountering a traveller, we shouted a friendly greeting; and he, unmuffling his ears to the bluster and the snow-spray, and listening eagerly, appeared to think our courtesy worth less than the trouble which it cost him. The churl! He understood the shrill whistle of the blast, but had no intelligence for our blithe tones of brotherhood. This lack of faith in our cordial sympathy, on the traveller's part, was one among the innumerable tokens how difficult a task we had in hand, for the reformation of the world. We rode on, however, with still unflagging spirits, and made such good companionship with the tempest, that, at our journey's end, we professed ourselves almost loth to bid the rude blusterer good bye. But, to own the truth, I was little better than an icicle, and began to be suspicious that I had caught a fearful cold.

And, now, we were seated by the brisk fireside of the old farm-house; the same fire that glimmers so faintly among my reminiscences, at the beginning of this chapter. There we sat, with the snow melting out of our hair and beards, and our

4. An epithet for air, stemming from the belief that the air was charged with particles of nitre.

faces all a-blaze, what with the past inclemency and present warmth. It was, indeed, a right good fire that we found awaiting us, built up of great, rough logs, and knotty limbs, and splintered fragments of an oak-tree, such as farmers are wont to keep for their own hearths; since these crooked and unmanageable boughs could never be measured into merchantable cords for the market. A family of the old Pilgrims might have swung their kettle over precisely such a fire as this, only, no doubt, a bigger one; and, contrasting it with my coal-grate, I felt, so much the more, that we had transported ourselves a world-wide distance from the system of society that shackled us at breakfast-time.

Good, comfortable Mrs. Foster (the wife of stout Silas Foster, who was to manage the farm, at a fair stipend, and be our tutor in the art of husbandry) bade us a hearty welcome. At her back—a back of generous breadth—appeared two young women, smiling most hospitably, but looking rather awkward withal, as not well knowing what was to be their position in our new arrangement of the world. We shook hands affectionately, all round, and congratulated ourselves that the blessed state of brotherhood and sisterhood, at which we aimed, might fairly be dated from this moment. Our greetings were hardly concluded, when the door opened, and Zenobia—whom I had never before seen, important as was her place in our enterprise—Zenobia entered the parlor.

This (as the reader, if at all acquainted with our literary biography, need scarcely be told) was not her real name. She had assumed it, in the first instance, as her magazine-signature; and as it accorded well with something imperial which her friends attributed to this lady's figure and deportment, they, half-laughingly, adopted it in their familiar intercourse with her. She took the appellation in good part, and even encouraged its constant use, which, in fact, was thus far appropriate, that our Zenobia—however humble looked her new philosophy—had as much native pride as any queen would have known what to do with.

III

A KNOT OF DREAMERS

ZENOBIA bade us welcome, in a fine, frank, mellow voice, and gave each of us her hand, which was very soft and warm. She had something appropriate, I recollect, to say to every individual; and what she said to myself was this:—

"I have long wished to know you, Mr. Coverdale, and to thank you for your beautiful poetry, some of which I have learned by heart;—or, rather, it has stolen into my memory, without my exercising any choice or volition about the matter. Of course—permit me to say—you do not think of relinquishing an occupation in which you have done yourself so much credit. I would almost rather give you up, as an associate, than that the world should lose one of its true poets!"

"Ah, no; there will not be the slightest danger of that, especially after this inestimable praise from Zenobia!" said I, smiling and blushing, no doubt, with excess of pleasure. "I hope, on the contrary, now, to produce something that shall really deserve to be called poetry—true, strong, natural, and sweet, as is the life which we are going to lead—something that shall have the notes of wild-birds twittering through it, or a strain like the wind-anthems in the woods, as the case may be!"

"Is it irksome to you to hear your own verses sung?" asked Zenobia, with a gracious smile. "If so, I am very sorry; for you will certainly hear me singing them, sometimes, in the summer evenings."

"Of all things," answered I, "that is what will delight me most."

While this passed, and while she spoke to my companions, I was taking note of Zenobia's aspect; and it impressed itself on me so distinctly, that I can now summon her up like a ghost, a little wanner than the life, but otherwise identical with it. She was dressed as simply as possible, in an American print, (I think the dry-goods people call it so,) but with a silken kerchief, between which and her gown there was one glimpse of a white shoulder. It struck me as a great piece of good-fortune that there should be just that glimpse. Her hair —which was dark, glossy, and of singular abundance—was put up rather soberly and primly, without curls, or other ornament, except a single flower. It was an exotic, of rare beauty, and as fresh as if the hot-house gardener had just clipt it from the stem. That flower has struck deep root into my memory. I can both see it and smell it, at this moment. So brilliant, so rare, so costly as it must have been, and yet enduring only for a day, it was more indicative of the pride and pomp, which had a luxuriant growth in Zenobia's character, than if a great diamond had sparkled among her hair.

Her hand, though very soft, was larger than most women would like to have—or than they could afford to have—though not a whit too large in proportion with the spacious plan of Zenobia's entire development. It did one good to see a fine intellect (as hers really was, although its natural tendency lay in another direction than towards literature) so fitly cased. She was, indeed, an admirable figure of a woman, just on the hither verge of her richest maturity, with a combination of features which it is safe to call remarkably beautiful, even if some fastidious persons might pronounce them a little deficient in softness and delicacy. But we find enough of those attributes, everywhere. Preferable—by way of variety, at least —was Zenobia's bloom, health, and vigor, which she possessed in such overflow that a man might well have fallen in love with her for their sake only. In her quiet moods, she seemed rather indolent; but when really in earnest, particularly if there were a spice of bitter feeling, she grew all alive, to her finger-tips.

"I am the first-comer," Zenobia went on to say, while her smile beamed warmth upon us all; "so I take the part of hostess, for to-day, and welcome you as if to my own fireside. You shall be my guests, too, at supper. Tomorrow, if you please, we will be brethren and sisters, and begin our new life from day-break."

"Have we our various parts assigned?" asked some one.

"Oh, we of the softer sex," responded Zenobia, with her mellow, almost broad laugh—most delectable to hear, but not in the least like an ordinary woman's laugh—"we women (there are four of us here, already) will take the domestic and indoor part of the business, as a matter of course. To bake, to boil, to roast, to fry, to stew—to wash, and iron, and scrub, and sweep, and, at our idler intervals, to repose ourselves on knitting and sewing—these, I suppose, must be feminine occupations for the present. By-and-by, perhaps, when our individual adaptations begin to develop themselves, it may be that some of us, who wear the petticoat, will go afield, and leave the weaker brethren to take our places in the kitchen!"

"What a pity," I remarked, "that the kitchen, and the house-work generally, cannot be left out of our system altogether! It is odd enough, that the kind of labor which falls to the lot of women is just that which chiefly distinguishes artificial life—the life of degenerated mortals—from the life of Paradise. Eve had no dinner-pot, and no clothes to mend, and no washing-day."

"I am afraid," said Zenobia, with mirth gleaming out of her eyes, "we shall find some difficulty in adopting the Paradisiacal system, for at least a month to come. Look at that snow-drift sweeping past the window! Are there any figs ripe, do you think? Have the pine-apples been gathered, to-day? Would you like a bread-fruit, or a cocoa-nut? Shall I run out and pluck you some roses? No, no, Mr. Coverdale, the only flower hereabouts is the one in my hair, which I got out of a green-house, this morning. As for the garb of Eden," added she, shivering playfully, "I shall not assume it till after May-day!"

Assuredly, Zenobia could not have intended it—the fault

must have been entirely in my imagination—but these last words, together with something in her manner, irresistibly brought up a picture of that fine, perfectly developed figure, in Eve's earliest garment. I almost fancied myself actually beholding it. Her free, careless, generous modes of expression often had this effect of creating images which, though pure, are hardly felt to be quite decorous, when born of a thought that passes between man and woman. I imputed it, at that time, to Zenobia's noble courage, conscious of no harm, and scorning the petty restraints which take the life and color out of other women's conversation. There was another peculiarity about her. We seldom meet with women, now-a-days, and in this country, who impress us as being women at all; their sex fades away and goes for nothing, in ordinary intercourse. Not so with Zenobia. One felt an influence breathing out of her, such as we might suppose to come from Eve, when she was just made, and her Creator brought her to Adam, saying— 'Behold, here is a woman!' Not that I would convey the idea of especial gentleness, grace, modesty, and shyness, but of a certain warm and rich characteristic, which seems, for the most part, to have been refined away out of the feminine system.

"And now," continued Zenobia, "I must go and help get supper. Do you think you can be content—instead of figs, pine-apples, and all the other delicacies of Adam's supper-table—with tea and toast, and a certain modest supply of ham and tongue, which, with the instinct of a housewife, I brought hither in a basket? And there shall be bread-and-milk, too, if the innocence of your taste demands it."

The whole sisterhood now went about their domestic avocations, utterly declining our offers to assist, farther than by bringing wood, for the kitchen-fire, from a huge pile in the back-yard. After heaping up more than a sufficient quantity, we returned to the sitting-room, drew our chairs closer to the hearth, and began to talk over our prospects. Soon, with a tremendous stamping in the entry, appeared Silas Foster, lank, stalwart, uncouth, and grisly-bearded. He came from foddering the cattle, in the barn, and from the field, where he had been ploughing, until the depth of the snow rendered it impossible to draw a furrow. He greeted us in pretty much the same tone as if he were speaking to his oxen, took a quid [5] from his iron tobacco-box, pulled off his wet cow-hide boots, and sat down before the fire in his stocking-feet. The steam arose from his soaked garments, so that the stout yeoman looked vaporous and spectre-like.

"Well, folks," remarked Silas, "you'll be wishing yourselves back to town again, if this weather holds!"

And, true enough, there was a look of gloom, as the twilight fell silently and sadly out of the sky, its gray or sable flakes intermingling themselves with the fast descending snow. The storm, in its evening aspect, was decidedly dreary. It seemed to have arisen for our especial behoof; a symbol of the cold, desolate, distrustful phantoms that invariably haunt the mind, on the eve of adventurous enterprises, to warn us back within the boundaries of ordinary life.

But our courage did not quail. We would not allow ourselves to be depressed by the snow-drift, trailing past the window, any more than if it had been the sigh of a summer wind among rustling boughs. There have been few brighter seasons for us, than that. If ever men might lawfully dream awake, and give utterance to their wildest visions, without dread of laughter or scorn on the part of the audience—yes, and speak of earthly happiness, for themselves and mankind, as an object to be hopefully striven for, and probably attained —we, who made that little semi-circle round the blazing fire, were those very men. We had left the rusty iron frame-work of society behind us. We had broken through many hindrances that are powerful enough to keep most people on the weary tread-mill of the established system, even while they feel its irksomeness almost as intolerable as we did. We had stept down from the pulpit; we had flung aside the pen; we had shut up the ledger; we had thrown off that sweet, bewitching, enervating indolence, which is better, after all, than

5. A wad of tobacco for chewing.

most of the enjoyments within mortal grasp. It was our purpose—a generous one, certainly, and absurd, no doubt, in full
proportion with its generosity—to give up whatever we had
heretofore attained, for the sake of showing mankind the
example of a life governed by other than the false and cruel
principles, on which human society has all along been based.

And, first of all, we had divorced ourselves from Pride, and
were striving to supply its place with familiar love. We meant
to lessen the laboring man's great burthen of toil, by performing our due share of it at the cost of our own thews[6] and
sinews. We sought our profit by mutual aid, instead of wrest-
ing it by the strong hand from an enemy, or filching it craftily
from those less shrewd than ourselves, (if, indeed, there were
any such, in New England,) or winning it by selfish competition with a neighbor; in one or another of which fashions,
every son of woman both perpetrates and suffers his share
of the common evil, whether he chooses it or no. And, as the
basis of our institution, we purposed to offer up the earnest
toil of our bodies, as a prayer, no less than an effort, for the
advancement of our race.

Therefore, if we built splendid castles (phalansteries,[7]
perhaps, they might be more fitly called,) and pictured beautiful scenes, among the fervid coals of the hearth around
which we were clustering—and if all went to rack with the
crumbling embers, and have never since arisen out of the
ashes—let us take to ourselves no shame. In my own behalf,
I rejoice that I could once think better of the world's improv-
ability than it deserved. It is a mistake into which men seldom
fall twice, in a lifetime; or, if so, the rarer and higher is the
nature that can thus magnanimously persist in error.

Stout Silas Foster mingled little in our conversation; but
when he did speak, it was very much to some practical purpose. For instance:—

"Which man among you," quoth he, "is the best judge of

6. Muscles.
7. A phalanstery was the huge and elaborate building which contained a variety
of apartments, dining rooms, and activity
rooms to meet the desires of all the types
of personalities found among 1,620 members of a phalanx, the basic social unit of
Charles Fourier's utopian society.

swine? Some of us must go to the next Brighton fair, and buy half-a-dozen pigs!"

Pigs! Good heavens, had we come out from among the swinish multitude, for this? And again, in reference to some discussion about raising early vegetables for the market:—

"We shall never make any hand at market-gardening," said Silas Foster, "unless the women-folks will undertake to do all the weeding. We haven't team enough for that and the regular farm-work, reckoning three of you city-folks as worth one common field-hand. No, no, I tell you, we should have to get up a little too early in the morning, to compete with the market-gardeners round Boston!"

It struck me as rather odd, that one of the first questions raised, after our separation from the greedy, struggling, self-seeking world, should relate to the possibility of getting the advantage over the outside barbarians, in their own field of labor. But, to own the truth, I very soon became sensible, that, as regarded society at large, we stood in a position of new hostility, rather than new brotherhood. Nor could this fail to be the case, in some degree, until the bigger and better half of society should range itself on our side. Constituting so pitiful a minority as now, we were inevitably estranged from the rest of mankind, in pretty fair proportion with the strictness of our mutual bond among ourselves.

This dawning idea, however, was driven back into my inner consciousness by the entrance of Zenobia. She came with the welcome intelligence that supper was on the table. Looking at herself in the glass, and perceiving that her one magnificent flower had grown rather languid, (probably by being exposed to the fervency of the kitchen-fire,) she flung it on the floor, as unconcernedly as a village-girl would throw away a faded violet. The action seemed proper to her character; although, methought, it would still more have befitted the bounteous nature of this beautiful woman to scatter fresh flowers from her hand, and to revive faded ones by her touch. Nevertheless—it was a singular, but irresistible effect—the presence of Zenobia caused our heroic enterprise to show like an illusion, a masquerade, a pastoral, a counterfeit Arcadia,[8] in which we grown-up men and women were making a play-day of the years that were given us to live in. I tried to analyze this impression, but not with much success.

"It really vexes me," observed Zenobia, as we left the room, "that Mr. Hollingsworth should be such a laggard. I should not have thought him at all the sort of person to be turned back by a puff of contrary wind, or a few snow-flakes drifting into his face."

"Do you know Hollingsworth personally?" I inquired.

"No; only as an auditor—auditress, I mean—of some of his lectures," said she. "What a voice he has! And what a man he is! Yet not so much an intellectual man, I should say, as a great heart; at least, he moved me more deeply than I think myself capable of being moved, except by the stroke of a true, strong heart against my own. It is a sad pity that he should have devoted his glorious powers to such a grimy, unbeautiful, and positively hopeless object as this reformation of criminals, about which he makes himself and his wretchedly small audiences so very miserable. To tell you a secret, I never could tolerate a philanthropist, before. Could you?"

"By no means," I answered; "neither can I now!"

"They are, indeed, an odiously disagreeable set of mortals," continued Zenobia. "I should like Mr. Hollingsworth a great deal better, if the philanthropy had been left out. At all events, as a mere matter of taste, I wish he would let the bad people alone, and try to benefit those who are not already past his help. Do you suppose he will be content to spend his life—or even a few months of it—among tolerably virtuous and comfortable individuals, like ourselves?"

"Upon my word, I doubt it," said I. "If we wish to keep him with us, we must systematically commit at least one crime apiece! Mere peccadillos will not satisfy him."

---

8. A place epitomizing pastoral simplicity and harmony.

Zenobia turned, sidelong, a strange kind of a glance upon me; but, before I could make out what it meant, we had entered the kitchen, where, in accordance with the rustic simplicity of our new life, the supper-table was spread.

IV

THE SUPPER-TABLE

THE PLEASANT firelight! I must still keep harping on it.

The kitchen-hearth had an old-fashioned breadth, depth, and spaciousness, far within which lay what seemed the butt of a good-sized oak-tree, with the moisture bubbling merrily out of both ends. It was now half-an-hour beyond dusk. The blaze from an armfull of substantial sticks, rendered more combustible by brush-wood and pine, flickered powerfully on the smoke-blackened walls, and so cheered our spirits that we cared not what inclemency might rage and roar, on the other side of our illuminated windows. A yet sultrier warmth was bestowed by a goodly quantity of peat, which was crumbling to white ashes among the burning brands, and incensed the kitchen with its not ungrateful fragrance. The exuberance of this household fire would alone have sufficed to bespeak us no true farmers; for the New England yeoman, if he have the misfortune to dwell within practicable distance of a wood-market, is as niggardly of each stick as if it were a bar of California gold.

But it was fortunate for us, on that wintry eve of our untried life, to enjoy the warm and radiant luxury of a somewhat too abundant fire. If it served no other purpose, it made the men look so full of youth, warm blood, and hope, and the women— such of them, at least, as were anywise convertible by its magic —so very beautiful, that I would cheerfully have spent my

last dollar to prolong the blaze. As for Zenobia, there was a
glow in her cheeks that made me think of Pandora, fresh
from Vulcan's workshop, and full of the celestial warmth by
dint of which he had tempered and moulded her.[9]

"Take your places, my dear friends all," cried she; "seat
yourselves without ceremony—and you shall be made happy
with such tea as not many of the world's working-people,
except yourselves, will find in their cups to-night. After this
one supper, you may drink butter-milk, if you please.
To-night, we will quaff this nectar, which, I assure you,
could not be bought with gold."

We all sat down—grisly Silas Foster, his rotund helpmate,
and the two bouncing handmaidens, included—and looked at
one another in a friendly, but rather awkward way. It was the
first practical trial of our theories of equal brotherhood and
sisterhood; and we people of superior cultivation and refinement (for as such, I presume, we unhesitatingly reckoned
ourselves) felt as if something were already accomplished
towards the millennium of love. The truth is, however, that
the laboring oar was with our unpolished companions; it being
far easier to condescend, than to accept of condescension.
Neither did I refrain from questioning, in secret, whether
some of us—and Zenobia among the rest—would so quietly
have taken our places among these good people, save for the
cherished consciousness that it was not by necessity, but
choice. Though we saw fit to drink our tea out of earthen
cups to-night, and in earthen company, it was at our own
option to use pictured porcelain and handle silver forks again,
tomorrow. This same salvo, as to the power of regaining our
former position, contributed much, I fear, to the equanimity
with which we subsequently bore many of the hardships and
humiliations of a life of toil. If ever I have deserved—(which
has not often been the case, and, I think, never)—but if ever
I did deserve to be soundly cuffed by a fellow-mortal, for

9. After Prometheus stole the gift of fire
from Zeus for man, Zeus punished mankind by having the blacksmith of the
gods, Vulcan, create the first woman,
Pandora; although endowed with beauty
and grace, Pandora's curiosity led her
to open the box in which all the world's
pain and evil had been confined.

secretly putting weight upon some imaginary social advantage, it must have been while I was striving to prove myself ostentatiously his equal, and no more. It was while I sat beside him on his cobbler's bench, or clinked my hoe against his own, in the cornfield, or broke the same crust of bread, my earth-grimed hand to his, at our noontide lunch. The poor, proud man should look at both sides of sympathy like this.

The silence, which followed upon our sitting down to table, grew rather oppressive; indeed, it was hardly broken by a word, during the first round of Zenobia's fragrant tea.

"I hope," said I, at last, "that our blazing windows will be visible a great way off. There is nothing so pleasant and encouraging to a solitary traveller, on a stormy night, as a flood of firelight, seen amid the gloom. These ruddy window-panes cannot fail to cheer the hearts of all that look at them. Are they not warm and bright with the beacon-fire which we have kindled for humanity?"

"The blaze of that brush-wood will only last a minute or two longer," observed Silas Foster; but whether he meant to insinuate that our moral illumination would have as brief a term, I cannot say.

"Meantime," said Zenobia, "it may serve to guide some wayfarer to a shelter."

And, just as she said this, there came a knock at the house-door.

"There is one of the world's wayfarers!" said I.

"Aye, aye, just so!" quoth Silas Foster. "Our firelight will draw stragglers, just as a candle draws dor-bugs,[1] on a summer night."

Whether to enjoy a dramatic suspense, or that we were selfishly contrasting our own comfort with the chill and dreary situation of the unknown person at the threshold—or that some of us city-folk felt a little startled at the knock which came so unseasonably, through night and storm, to the door of the lonely farm-house—so it happened, that nobody, for an

1. Beetles.

instant or two, arose to answer the summons. Pretty soon, there came another knock. The first had been moderately loud; the second was smitten so forcibly that the knuckles of the applicant must have left their mark in the door-panel.

"He knocks as if he had a right to come in," said Zenobia, laughing. "And what are we thinking of? It must be Mr. Hollingsworth!"

Hereupon, I went to the door, unbolted, and flung it wide open. There, sure enough, stood Hollingsworth, his shaggy great-coat all covered with snow; so that he looked quite as much like a polar bear as a modern philanthropist.

"Sluggish hospitality, this!" said he, in those deep tones of his, which seemed to come out of a chest as capacious as a barrel. "It would have served you right if I had lain down and spent the night on the door-step, just for the sake of putting you to shame. But here is a guest, who will need a warmer and softer bed."

And stepping back to the wagon, in which he had journeyed hither, Hollingsworth received into his arms, and deposited on the door-step, a figure enveloped in a cloak. It was evidently a woman; or rather—judging from the ease with which he lifted her, and the little space which she seemed to fill in his arms—a slim and unsubstantial girl. As she showed some hesitation about entering the door, Hollingsworth, with his usual directness and lack of ceremony, urged her forward, not merely within the entry, but into the warm and strongly lighted kitchen.

"Who is this?" whispered I, remaining behind with him, while he was taking off his great-coat.

"Who? Really, I don't know," answered Hollingsworth, looking at me with some surprise. "It is a young person who belongs here, however; and, no doubt, she has been expected. Zenobia, or some of the women-folks, can tell you all about it."

"I think not," said I, glancing towards the new-comer and the other occupants of the kitchen. "Nobody seems to welcome her. I should hardly judge that she was an expected guest."

"Well, well," said Hollingsworth, quietly. "We'll make it right."

The stranger, or whatever she were, remained standing precisely on that spot of the kitchen-floor, to which Hollingsworth's kindly hand had impelled her. The cloak falling partly off, she was seen to be a very young woman, dressed in a poor, but decent gown, made high in the neck, and without any regard to fashion or smartness. Her brown hair fell down from beneath a hood, not in curls, but with only a slight wave; her face was of a wan, almost sickly hue, betokening habitual seclusion from the sun and free atmosphere, like a flower-shrub that had done its best to blossom in too scanty light. To complete the pitiableness of her aspect, she shivered either with cold, or fear, or nervous excitement, so that you might have beheld her shadow vibrating on the fire-lighted wall. In short, there has seldom been seen so depressed and sad a figure as this young girl's; and it was hardly possible to help being angry with her, from mere despair of doing anything for her comfort. The fantasy occurred to me, that she was some desolate kind of a creature, doomed to wander about in snow-storms, and that, though the ruddiness of our window-panes had tempted her into a human dwelling, she would not remain long enough to melt the icicles out of her hair.

Another conjecture likewise came into my mind. Recollecting Hollingsworth's sphere of philanthropic action, I deemed it possible that he might have brought one of his guilty patients, to be wrought upon, and restored to spiritual health, by the pure influences which our mode of life would create.

As yet, the girl had not stirred. She stood near the door, fixing a pair of large, brown, melancholy eyes upon Zenobia—only upon Zenobia!—she evidently saw nothing else in the room, save that bright, fair, rosy, beautiful woman. It was the strangest look I ever witnessed; long a mystery to me, and forever a memory. Once, she seemed about to move forward and greet her—I know not with what warmth, or with what words;—but, finally, instead of doing so, she drooped down upon her knees, clasped her hands, and gazed piteously into Zenobia's face. Meeting no kindly reception, her head fell on her bosom.

I never thoroughly forgave Zenobia for her conduct on this occasion. But women are always more cautious, in their casual hospitalities, than men.

"What does the girl mean?" cried she, in rather a sharp tone. "Is she crazy? Has she no tongue?"

And here Hollingsworth stept forward.

"No wonder if the poor child's tongue is frozen in her mouth," said he—and I think he positively frowned at Zenobia —"The very heart will be frozen in her bosom, unless you women can warm it, among you, with the warmth that ought to be in your own!"

Hollingsworth's appearance was very striking, at this moment. He was then about thirty years old, but looked several years older, with his great shaggy head, his heavy brow, his dark complexion, his abundant beard, and the rude strength with which his features seemed to have been hammered out of iron, rather than chiselled or moulded from any finer or softer material. His figure was not tall, but massive and brawny, and well befitting his original occupation, which —as the reader probably knows—was that of a blacksmith. As for external polish, or mere courtesy of manner, he never possessed more than a tolerably educated bear; although, in his gentler moods, there was a tenderness in his voice, eyes, mouth, in his gesture, and in every indescribable manifestation, which few men could resist, and no woman. But he now looked stern and reproachful; and it was with that inauspicious meaning in his glance, that Hollingsworth first met Zenobia's eyes, and began his influence upon her life.

To my surprise, Zenobia—of whose haughty spirit I had been told so many examples—absolutely changed color, and seemed mortified and confused.

"You do not quite do me justice, Mr. Hollingsworth," said she, almost humbly. "I am willing to be kind to the poor girl.

Is she a protégée of yours? What can I do for her?"

"Have you anything to ask of this lady?" said Hollingsworth, kindly, to the girl. "I remember you mentioned her name, before we left town."

"Only that she will shelter me," replied the girl, tremulously. "Only that she will let me be always near her!"

"Well, indeed," exclaimed Zenobia, recovering herself, and laughing, "this is an adventure, and well worthy to be the first incident in our life of love and free-heartedness! But I accept it, for the present, without further question—only," added she, "it would be a convenience if we knew your name!"

"Priscilla," said the girl; and it appeared to me that she hesitated whether to add anything more, and decided in the negative. "Pray do not ask me my other name—at least, not yet—if you will be so kind to a forlorn creature."

Priscilla! Priscilla! I repeated the name to myself, three or four times; and, in that little space, this quaint and prim cognomen had so amalgamated itself with my idea of the girl, that it seemed as if no other name could have adhered to her for a moment. Heretofore, the poor thing had not shed any tears; but now that she found herself received, and at least temporarily established, the big drops began to ooze out from beneath her eyelids, as if she were full of them. Perhaps it showed the iron substance of my heart, that I could not help smiling at this odd scene of unknown and unaccountable calamity, into which our cheerful party had been entrapped, without the liberty of choosing whether to sympathize or no. Hollingsworth's behavior was certainly a great deal more creditable than mine.

"Let us not pry farther into her secrets," he said to Zenobia and the rest of us, apart—and his dark, shaggy face looked really beautiful with its expression of thoughtful benevolence —"Let us conclude that Providence has sent her to us, as the first fruits of the world, which we have undertaken to make happier than we find it. Let us warm her poor, shivering body with this good fire, and her poor, shivering heart with our best

kindness. Let us feed her, and make her one of us. As we do
by this friendless girl, so shall we prosper! And, in good time,
whatever is desirable for us to know will be melted out of
her, as inevitably as those tears which we see now."

"At least," remarked I, "you may tell us how and where
you met with her."

"An old man brought her to my lodgings," answered
Hollingsworth, "and begged me to convey her to Blithedale,
where—so I understood him—she had friends. And this is
positively all I know about the matter."

Grim Silas Foster, all this while, had been busy at the
supper-table, pouring out his own tea, and gulping it down
with no more sense of its exquisiteness than if it were a
decoction of catnip; helping himself to pieces of dipt toast on
the flat of his knife-blade, and dropping half of it on the
table-cloth; using the same serviceable implement to cut slice
after slice of ham; perpetrating terrible enormities with the
butter-plate; and, in all other respects, behaving less like a
civilized Christian than the worst kind of an ogre. Being, by
this time, fully gorged, he crowned his amiable exploits with a
draught from the water-pitcher, and then favored us with his
opinion about the business in hand. And, certainly, though
they proceeded out of an unwiped mouth, his expressions
did him honor.

"Give the girl a hot cup of tea, and a thick slice of this first-
rate bacon," said Silas, like a sensible man as he was. "That's
what she wants. Let her stay with us as long as she likes, and
help in the kitchen, and take the cow-breath at milking-time;
and, in a week or two, she'll begin to look like a creature
of this world!"

So we sat down again to supper, and Priscilla along with us.

V

UNTIL BEDTIME

SILAS FOSTER, by the time we concluded our meal, had
stript off his coat and planted himself on a low chair
by the kitchen-fire, with a lap-stone, a hammer, a piece
of sole-leather, and some waxed ends, in order to cobble an
old pair of cow-hide boots; he being, in his own phrase,
'something of a dab' (whatever degree of skill that may imply)
at the shoemaking-business. We heard the tap of his hammer,
at intervals, for the rest of the evening. The remainder of the
party adjourned to the sitting-room. Good Mrs. Foster took
her knitting-work, and soon fell fast asleep, still keeping her
needles in brisk movement, and, to the best of my observation,
absolutely footing a stocking out of the texture of a dream.
And a very substantial stocking it seemed to be. One of the
two handmaidens hemmed a towel, and the other appeared
to be making a ruffle, for her Sunday's wear, out of a little
bit of embroidered muslin, which Zenobia had probably
given her.

It was curious to observe how trustingly, and yet how
timidly, our poor Priscilla betook herself into the shadow of
Zenobia's protection. She sat beside her on a stool, looking
up, every now and then, with an expression of humble
delight at her new friend's beauty. A brilliant woman is
often an object of the devoted admiration—it might almost be
termed worship, or idolatry—of some young girl, who perhaps
beholds the cynosure only at an awful distance, and has as
little hope of personal intercourse as of climbing among the
stars of heaven. We men are too gross to comprehend it. Even
a woman, of mature age, despises or laughs at such a passion.
There occurred to me no mode of accounting for Priscilla's
behavior, except by supposing that she had read some of
Zenobia's stories, (as such literature goes everywhere,) or

her tracts in defence of the sex, and had come hither with the one purpose of being her slave. There is nothing parallel to this, I believe—nothing so foolishly disinterested, and hardly anything so beautiful—in the masculine nature, at whatever epoch of life; or, if there be, a fine and rare development of character might reasonably be looked for, from the youth who should prove himself capable of such self-forgetful affection.

Zenobia happening to change her seat, I took the opportunity, in an under tone, to suggest some such notion as the above.

"Since you see the young woman in so poetical a light," replied she, in the same tone, "you had better turn the affair into a ballad. It is a grand subject, and worthy of supernatural machinery. The storm, the startling knock at the door, the entrance of the sable knight Hollingsworth and this shadowy snow-maiden, who, precisely at the stroke of midnight, shall melt away at my feet, in a pool of ice-cold water, and give me my death with a pair of wet slippers! And when the verses are written, and polished quite to your mind, I will favor you with my idea as to what the girl really is."

"Pray let me have it now," said I. "It shall be woven into the ballad."

"She is neither more nor less," answered Zenobia, "than a seamstress from the city, and she has probably no more transcendental purpose than to do my miscellaneous sewing; for I suppose she will hardly expect to make my dresses."

"How can you decide upon her so easily?" I inquired.

"Oh, we women judge one another by tokens that escape the obtuseness of masculine perceptions," said Zenobia. "There is no proof, which you would be likely to appreciate, except the needle marks on the tip of her forefinger. Then, my supposition perfectly accounts for her paleness, her nervousness, and her wretched fragility. Poor thing! She has been stifled with the heat of a salamander-stove,[2] in a small, close room, and has drunk coffee, and fed upon dough-nuts, raisins, candy, and all such trash, till she is scarcely half-alive;

2. A portable stove used to dry buildings under construction.

and so, as she has hardly any physique, a poet, like Mr. Miles Coverdale, may be allowed to think her spiritual!"

"Look at her now!" whispered I.

Priscilla was gazing towards us, with an inexpressible sorrow in her wan face, and great tears running down her cheeks. It was difficult to resist the impression, that, cautiously as we had lowered our voices, she must have overheard and been wounded by Zenobia's scornful estimate of her character and purposes.

"What ears the girl must have!" whispered Zenobia, with a look of vexation, partly comic and partly real. "I will confess to you that I cannot quite make her out. However, I am positively not an ill-natured person, unless when very grievously provoked; and as you, and especially Mr. Hollingsworth, take so much interest in this odd creature—and as she knocks, with a very slight tap, against my own heart, likewise—why, I mean to let her in! From this moment, I will be reasonably kind to her. There is no pleasure in tormenting a person of one's own sex, even if she do favor one with a little more love than one can conveniently dispose of;—and that, let me say, Mr. Coverdale, is the most troublesome offence you can offer to a woman."

"Thank you!" said I, smiling. "I don't mean to be guilty of it."

She went towards Priscilla, took her hand, and passed her own rosy finger-tips, with a pretty, caressing movement, over the girl's hair. The touch had a magical effect. So vivid a look of joy flushed up beneath those fingers, that it seemed as if the sad and wan Priscilla had been snatched away, and another kind of creature substituted in her place. This one caress, bestowed voluntarily by Zenobia, was evidently received as a pledge of all that the stranger sought from her, whatever the unuttered boon might be. From that instant, too, she melted in quietly amongst us, and was no longer a foreign element. Though always an object of peculiar interest, a riddle, and a theme of frequent discussion, her tenure at Blithedale was thenceforth fixed; we no more thought of questioning it, than if Priscilla had been recognized as a domestic sprite, who had haunted the rustic fireside, of old, before we had ever been warmed by its blaze.

She now produced, out of a work-bag that she had with her, some little wooden instruments, (what they are called, I never knew,) and proceeded to knit, or net, an article which ultimately took the shape of a silk purse. As the work went on, I remembered to have seen just such purses, before. Indeed, I was the possessor of one. Their peculiar excellence, besides the great delicacy and beauty of the manufacture, lay in the almost impossibility that any uninitiated person should discover the aperture; although, to a practised touch, they would open as wide as charity or prodigality might wish. I wondered if it were not a symbol of Priscilla's own mystery.

Notwithstanding the new confidence with which Zenobia had inspired her, our guest showed herself disquieted by the storm. When the strong puffs of wind spattered the snow against the windows, and made the oaken frame of the farmhouse creak, she looked at us apprehensively, as if to inquire whether these tempestuous outbreaks did not betoken some unusual mischief in the shrieking blast. She had been bred up, no doubt, in some close nook, some inauspiciously sheltered court of the city, where the uttermost rage of a tempest, though it might scatter down the slates of the roof into the bricked area, could not shake the casement of her little room. The sense of vast, undefined space, pressing from the outside against the black panes of our uncurtained windows, was fearful to the poor girl, heretofore accustomed to the narrowness of human limits, with the lamps of neighboring tenements glimmering across the street. The house probably seemed to her adrift on the great ocean of the night. A little parallelogram of sky was all that she had hitherto known of nature; so that she felt the awfulness that really exists in its limitless extent. Once, while the blast was bellowing, she caught hold of Zenobia's robe, with precisely the air of one who hears her own name spoken, at a distance, but is unutterably reluctant to obey the call.

We spent rather an incommunicative evening. Hollingsworth hardly said a word, unless when repeatedly and pertinaciously addressed. Then, indeed, he would glare upon us from the thick shrubbery of his meditations, like a tiger out of a jungle, make the briefest reply possible, and betake himself back into the solitude of his heart and mind. The poor fellow had contracted this ungracious habit from the intensity with which he contemplated his own ideas, and the infrequent sympathy which they met with from his auditors; a circumstance that seemed only to strengthen the implicit confidence that he awarded to them. His heart, I imagine, was never really interested in our socialist scheme, but was forever busy with his strange, and, as most people thought it, impracticable plan for the reformation of criminals, through an appeal to their higher instincts. Much as I liked Hollingsworth, it cost me many a groan to tolerate him on this point. He ought to have commenced his investigation of the subject by perpetrating some huge sin, in his proper person, and examining the condition of his higher instincts, afterwards.

The rest of us formed ourselves into a committee for providing our infant Community with an appropriate name; a matter of greatly more difficulty than the uninitiated reader would suppose. Blithedale was neither good nor bad. We should have resumed the old Indian name of the premises, had it possessed the oil-and-honey flow which the aborigines were so often happy in communicating to their local appellations; but it chanced to be a harsh, ill-connected, and interminable word, which seemed to fill the mouth with a mixture of very stiff clay and very crumbly pebbles.[3] Zenobia suggested 'Sunny Glimpse,' as expressive of a vista into a better system of society. This we turned over and over, for awhile, acknowledging its prettiness, but concluded it to be rather too fine and sentimental a name (a fault inevitable by literary ladies, in such attempts) for sun-burnt men to work under. I ventured to whisper 'Utopia,' which, however, was unanimously

3. Although no Indian name for Roxbury has been discovered, Hawthorne may here have in mind one of the three Indian names for a larger area which included Roxbury: Accomonticus, Amaganset, Mashawmut.

scouted down, and the proposer very harshly maltreated, as if he had intended a latent satire. Some were for calling our institution 'The Oasis,' in view of its being the one green spot in the moral sand-waste of the world; but others insisted on a proviso for reconsidering the matter, at a twelvemonth's end; when a final decision might be had, whether to name it 'The Oasis,' or 'Saharah.' So, at last, finding it impracticable to hammer out anything better, we resolved that the spot should still be Blithedale, as being of good augury enough.

The evening wore on, and the outer solitude looked in upon us through the windows, gloomy, wild, and vague, like another state of existence, close beside the littler sphere of warmth and light in which we were the prattlers and bustlers of a moment. By-and-by, the door was opened by Silas Foster, with a cotton handkerchief about his head, and a tallow candle in his hand.

"Take my advice, brother-farmers," said he, with a great, broad, bottomless yawn, "and get to bed as soon as you can. I shall sound the horn at day-break; and we've got the cattle to fodder, and nine cows to milk, and a dozen other things to do, before breakfast."

Thus ended the first evening at Blithedale. I went shivering to my fireless chamber, with the miserable consciousness (which had been growing upon me for several hours past) that I had caught a tremendous cold, and should probably awaken, at the blast of the horn, a fit subject for a hospital. The night proved a feverish one. During the greater part of it, I was in that vilest of states when a fixed idea remains in the mind, like the nail in Sisera's brain,[4] while innumerable other ideas go and come, and flutter to-and-fro, combining constant transition with intolerable sameness. Had I made a record of that night's half-waking dreams, it is my belief that it would have anticipated several of the chief incidents of this narrative, including a dim shadow of its catastrophe. Starting up in bed, at length, I saw that the storm was past,

4. In the Bible, Sisera, commander of the army of the Canaanites, after being defeated by the Israelites takes refuge with Jael, wife of Heber; she, however, treacherously kills him by driving a tent nail through his head (Judges IV).

and the moon was shining on the snowy landscape, which looked like a lifeless copy of the world in marble.

From the bank of the distant river, which was shimmering in the moonlight, came the black shadow of the only cloud in heaven, driven swiftly by the wind, and passing over meadow and hillock—vanishing amid tufts of leafless trees, but reappearing on the hither side—until it swept across our door-step.

How cold an Arcadia was this!

VI

COVERDALE'S SICK-CHAMBER

THE HORN sounded at day-break, as Silas Foster had forewarned us, harsh, uproarious, inexorably drawn out, and as sleep-dispelling as if this hard-hearted old yeoman had got hold of the trump of doom.

On all sides, I could hear the creaking of the bedsteads, as the brethren of Blithedale started from slumber, and thrust themselves into their habiliments, all awry, no doubt, in their haste to begin the reformation of the world. Zenobia put her head into the entry, and besought Silas Foster to cease his clamor, and to be kind enough to leave an armful of firewood and a pail of water at her chamber-door. Of the whole household—unless, indeed, it were Priscilla, for whose habits, in this particular, I cannot vouch—of all our apostolic society, whose mission was to bless mankind, Hollingsworth, I apprehend, was the only one who began the enterprise with prayer. My sleeping-room being but thinly partitioned from his, the solemn murmur of his voice made its way to my ears, compelling me to be an auditor of his awful privacy with the Creator. It affected me with a deep reverence for Hollingsworth, which no familiarity then existing, or that afterwards grew more intimate between us—no, nor my subsequent perception of his own great errors—ever quite effaced. It is so rare, in these times, to meet with a man of prayerful habits, (except, of course, in the pulpit,) that such an one is decidedly marked out by a light of transfiguration, shed upon him in the divine interview from which he passes into his daily life.

As for me, I lay abed, and, if I said my prayers, it was backward, cursing my day as bitterly as patient Job himself. The truth was, the hot-house warmth of a town-residence, and the luxurious life in which I indulged myself, had taken much of the pith out of my physical system; and the wintry blast of the preceding day, together with the general chill of our airy old farm-house, had got fairly into my heart and the marrow of my bones. In this predicament, I seriously wished—selfish as it may appear—that the reformation of society had been postponed about half-a-century, or at all events, to such a date as should have put my intermeddling with it entirely out of the question.

What, in the name of common-sense, had I to do with any better society than I had always lived in! It had satisfied me well enough. My pleasant bachelor-parlor, sunny and shadowy, curtained and carpeted, with the bed-chamber adjoining; my centre-table, strewn with books and periodicals; my writing-desk, with a half-finished poem in a stanza of my own contrivance; my morning lounge at the reading-room or picture-gallery; my noontide walk along the cheery pavement, with the suggestive succession of human faces, and the brisk throb of human life, in which I shared; my dinner at the Albion, where I had a hundred dishes at command, and could banquet as delicately as the wizard Michael Scott,[5] when the devil fed him from the King of France's kitchen; my evening at the billiard-club, the concert, the theatre, or at somebody's party, if I pleased:—what could be better than all this? Was it better to hoe, to mow, to toil and moil amidst

5. Michael Scott (c. 1175–c. 1235), a medieval scholar, alchemist and reputed magician, whose most famous legendary trick was to entertain his friends with a feast composed of dishes brought by devils from the kitchens of European royalty.

the accumulations of a barn-yard, to be the chambermaid of two yoke of oxen and a dozen cows, to eat salt-beef and earn it with the sweat of my brow, and thereby take the tough morsel out of some wretch's mouth, into whose vocation I had thrust myself? Above all, was it better to have a fever, and die blaspheming, as I was like to do?

In this wretched plight, with a furnace in my heart, and another in my head, by the heat of which I was kept constantly at the boiling point—yet shivering at the bare idea of extruding so much as a finger into the icy atmosphere of the room—I kept my bed until breakfast-time, when Hollingsworth knocked at the door, and entered.

"Well, Coverdale," cried he, "you bid fair to make an admirable farmer! Don't you mean to get up to-day?"

"Neither to-day nor tomorrow," said I, hopelessly. "I doubt if I ever rise again!"

"What is the matter now?" he asked.

I told him my piteous case, and besought him to send me back to town, in a close carriage.

"No, no!" said Hollingsworth, with kindly seriousness. "If you are really sick, we must take care of you."

Accordingly, he built a fire in my chamber, and having little else to do while the snow lay on the ground, established himself as my nurse. A doctor was sent for, who, being homeopathic, gave me as much medicine, in the course of a fortnight's attendance, as would have lain on the point of a needle. They fed me on water-gruel, and I speedily became a skeleton above ground. But, after all, I have many precious recollections connected with that fit of sickness.

Hollingsworth's more than brotherly attendance gave me inexpressible comfort. Most men—and, certainly, I could not always claim to be one of the exceptions—have a natural indifference, if not an absolutely hostile feeling, towards those whom disease, or weakness, or calamity of any kind, causes to faulter and faint amid the rude jostle of our selfish existence. The education of Christianity, it is true, the sympathy of a like experience, and the example of women, may soften, and possibly subvert, this ugly characteristic of our sex. But it is originally there, and has likewise its analogy in the practice of our brute brethren, who hunt the sick or disabled member of the herd from among them, as an enemy. It is for this reason that the stricken deer goes apart, and the sick lion grimly withdraws himself into his den. Except in love, or the attachments of kindred, or other very long and habitual affection, we really have no tenderness. But there was something of the woman moulded into the great, stalwart frame of Hollingsworth; nor was he ashamed of it, as men often are of what is best in them, nor seemed ever to know that there was such a soft place in his heart. I knew it well, however, at that time; although, afterwards, it came nigh to be forgotten. Methought there could not be two such men alive, as Hollingsworth. There never was any blaze of a fireside that warmed and cheered me, in the down-sinkings and shiverings of my spirit, so effectually as did the light out of those eyes, which lay so deep and dark under his shaggy brows.

Happy the man that has such a friend beside him, when he comes to die! And unless a friend like Hollingsworth be at hand, as most probably there will not, he had better make up his mind to die alone. How many men, I wonder, does one meet with, in a lifetime, whom he would choose for his death-bed companions! At the crisis of my fever, I besought Hollingsworth to let nobody else enter the room, but continually to make me sensible of his own presence by a grasp of the hand, a word—a prayer, if he thought good to utter it—and that then he should be the witness how courageously I would encounter the worst. It still impresses me as almost a matter of regret, that I did not die, then, when I had tolerably made up my mind to it; for Hollingsworth would have gone with me to the hither verge of life, and have sent his friendly and hopeful accents far over on the other side, while I should be treading the unknown path. Now, were I to send for him, he would hardly come to my bedside; nor should I depart the easier, for his presence.

"You are not going to die, this time," said he, gravely smiling. "You know nothing about sickness, and think your case a great deal more desperate than it is."

"Death should take me while I am in the mood," replied I, with a little of my customary levity.

"Have you nothing to do in life," asked Hollingsworth, "that you fancy yourself so ready to leave it?"

"Nothing," answered I—"nothing, that I know of, unless to make pretty verses, and play a part, with Zenobia and the rest of the amateurs, in our pastoral. It seems but an unsubstantial sort of business, as viewed through a mist of fever. But, dear Hollingsworth, your own vocation is evidently to be a priest, and to spend your days and nights in helping your fellow-creatures to draw peaceful dying-breaths."

"And by which of my qualities," inquired he, "can you suppose me fitted for this awful ministry?"

"By your tenderness," I said. "It seems to me the reflection of God's own love."

"And you call me tender!" repeated Hollingsworth, thoughtfully. "I should rather say, that the most marked trait in my character is an inflexible severity of purpose. Mortal man has no right to be so inflexible, as it is my nature and necessity to be!"

"I do not believe it," I replied.

But, in due time, I remembered what he said.

Probably, as Hollingsworth suggested, my disorder was never so serious as, in my ignorance of such matters, I was inclined to consider it. After so much tragical preparation, it was positively rather mortifying to find myself on the mending hand.

All the other members of the Community showed me kindness, according to the full measure of their capacity. Zenobia brought me my gruel, every day, made by her own hands, (not very skilfully, if the truth must be told,) and, whenever I seemed inclined to converse, would sit by my bedside, and talk with so much vivacity as to add several gratuitous throbs to my pulse. Her poor little stories and tracts never half did justice to her intellect; it was only the lack of a fitter avenue that drove her to seek development in literature. She was made (among a thousand other things that she might have been) for a stump-oratress. I recognized no severe culture in Zenobia; her mind was full of weeds. It startled me, sometimes, in my state of moral, as well as bodily faint-heartedness, to observe the hardihood of her philosophy; she made no scruple of oversetting all human institutions, and scattering them as with a breeze from her fan. A female reformer, in her attacks upon society, has an instinctive sense of where the life lies, and is inclined to aim directly at that spot. Especially, the relation between the sexes is naturally among the earliest to attract her notice.

Zenobia was truly a magnificent woman. The homely simplicity of her dress could not conceal, nor scarcely diminish, the queenliness of her presence. The image of her form and face should have been multiplied all over the earth. It was wronging the rest of mankind, to retain her as the spectacle of only a few. The stage would have been her proper sphere. She should have made it a point of duty, moreover, to sit endlessly to painters and sculptors, and preferably to the latter; because the cold decorum of the marble would consist with the utmost scantiness of drapery, so that the eye might chastely be gladdened with her material perfection, in its entireness. I know not well how to express, that the native glow of coloring in her cheeks, and even the flesh-warmth over her round arms, and what was visible of her full bust—in a word, her womanliness incarnated—compelled me sometimes to close my eyes, as if it were not quite the privilege of modesty to gaze at her. Illness and exhaustion, no doubt, had made me morbidly sensitive.

I noticed—and wondered how Zenobia contrived it—that she had always a new flower in her hair. And still it was a hot-house flower—an outlandish flower—a flower of the tropics, such as appeared to have sprung passionately out of a soil, the very weeds of which would be fervid and spicy. Unlike as was the flower of each successive day to the preceding one, it yet so assimilated its richness to the rich beauty of the woman, that I thought it the only flower fit to be worn; so fit, indeed, that Nature had evidently created this floral gem, in a happy exuberance, for the one purpose of worthily adorning Zenobia's head. It might be, that my feverish fantasies clustered themselves about this peculiarity, and caused it to look more gorgeous and wonderful than if beheld with temperate eyes. In the height of my illness, as I well recollect, I went so far as to pronounce it preternatural.

"Zenobia is an enchantress!" whispered I once to Hollingsworth. "She is a sister of the Veiled Lady! That flower in her hair is a talisman. If you were to snatch it away, she would vanish, or be transformed into something else!"

"What does he say?" asked Zenobia.

"Nothing that has an atom of sense in it," answered Hollingsworth. "He is a little beside himself, I believe, and talks about your being a witch, and of some magical property in the flower that you wear in your hair."

"It is an idea worthy of a feverish poet," said she, laughing, rather compassionately, and taking out the flower. "I scorn to owe anything to magic. Here, Mr. Hollingsworth:—you may keep the spell, while it has any virtue in it; but I cannot promise you not to appear with a new one, tomorrow. It is the one relic of my more brilliant, my happier days!"

The most curious part of the matter was, that, long after my slight delirium had passed away—as long, indeed, as I continued to know this remarkable woman—her daily flower affected my imagination, though more slightly, yet in very much the same way. The reason must have been, that, whether intentionally on her part, or not, this favorite ornament was actually a subtle expression of Zenobia's character.

One subject, about which—very impertinently, moreover—I perplexed myself with a great many conjectures, was, whether Zenobia had ever been married. The idea, it must be understood, was unauthorized by any circumstance or suggestion that had made its way to my ears. So young as I beheld her, and the freshest and rosiest woman of a thousand, there was certainly no need of imputing to her a destiny already accomplished; the probability was far greater, that her coming years had all life's richest gifts to bring. If the great event of a woman's existence had been consummated, the world knew nothing of it, although the world seemed to know Zenobia well. It was a ridiculous piece of romance, undoubtedly, to imagine that this beautiful personage, wealthy as she was, and holding a position that might fairly enough be called distinguished, could have given herself away so privately, but that some whisper and suspicion, and, by degrees, a full understanding of the fact, would eventually be blown abroad. But, then, as I failed not to consider, her original home was at a distance of many hundred miles. Rumors might fill the social atmosphere, or might once have filled it, there, which would travel but slowly, against the wind, towards our north-eastern metropolis, and perhaps melt into thin air before reaching it.

There was not, and I distinctly repeat it, the slightest foundation in my knowledge for any surmise of the kind. But there is a species of intuition—either a spiritual lie, or the subtle recognition of a fact—which comes to us in a reduced state of the corporeal system. The soul gets the better of the body, after wasting illness, or when a vegetable diet may have mingled too much ether in the blood.[6] Vapors then rise up to the brain, and take shapes that often image falsehood, but sometimes truth. The spheres of our companions have, at such periods, a vastly greater influence upon our own, than when robust health gives us a repellent and self-defensive energy. Zenobia's sphere, I imagine, impressed itself powerfully on mine, and transformed me, during this period of my weakness, into something like a mesmerical clairvoyant.

Then, also, as anybody could observe, the freedom of her deportment (though, to some tastes, it might commend itself as the utmost perfection of manner, in a youthful widow, or a blooming matron) was not exactly maidenlike. What

6. According to various contemporary theories of nutrition, meatless diets generated ether in the body and made one less carnal and more "ethereal."

girl had ever laughed as Zenobia did! What girl had ever spoken in her mellow tones! Her unconstrained and inevitable manifestation, I said often to myself, was that of a woman to whom wedlock had thrown wide the gates of mystery. Yet, sometimes, I strove to be ashamed of these conjectures. I acknowledged it as a masculine grossness—a sin of wicked interpretation, of which man is often guilty towards the other sex—thus to mistake the sweet, liberal, but womanly frankness of a noble and generous disposition. Still, it was of no avail to reason with myself, nor to upbraid myself. Pertinaciously the thought—'Zenobia is a wife! Zenobia has lived, and loved! There is no folded petal, no latent dew-drop, in this perfectly developed rose!'—irresistibly that thought drove out all other conclusions, as often as my mind reverted to the subject.

Zenobia was conscious of my observation, though not, I presume, of the point to which it led me.

"Mr. Coverdale," said she, one day, as she saw me watching her, while she arranged my gruel on the table, "I have been exposed to a great deal of eye-shot in the few years of my mixing in the world, but never, I think, to precisely such glances as you are in the habit of favoring me with. I seem to interest you very much; and yet—or else a woman's instinct is for once deceived—I cannot reckon you as an admirer. What are you seeking to discover in me?"

"The mystery of your life," answered I, surprised into the truth by the unexpectedness of her attack. "And you will never tell me."

She bent her head towards me, and let me look into her eyes, as if challenging me to drop a plummet-line down into the depths of her consciousness.

"I see nothing now," said I, closing my own eyes, "unless it be the face of a sprite, laughing at me from the bottom of a deep well."

A bachelor always feels himself defrauded, when he knows, or suspects, that any woman of his acquaintance has given herself away. Otherwise, the matter could have been no concern of mine. It was purely speculative; for I should not, under any circumstances, have fallen in love with Zenobia. The riddle made me so nervous, however, in my sensitive condition of mind and body, that I most ungratefully began to wish that she would let me alone. Then, too, her gruel was very wretched stuff, with almost invariably the smell of pine-smoke upon it, like the evil taste that is said to mix itself up with a witch's best concocted dainties. Why could not she have allowed one of the other women to take the gruel in charge? Whatever else might be her gifts, Nature certainly never intended Zenobia for a cook. Or, if so, she should have meddled only with the richest and spiciest dishes, and such as are to be tasted at banquets, between draughts of intoxicating wine.

VII

THE CONVALESCENT

AS SOON as my incommodities allowed me to think of past occurrences, I failed not to inquire what had become of the odd little guest, whom Hollingsworth had been the medium of introducing among us. It now appeared, that poor Priscilla had not so literally fallen out of the clouds, as we were at first inclined to suppose. A letter, which should have introduced her, had since been received from one of the city-missionaries, containing a certificate of character, and an allusion to circumstances which, in the writer's judgment, made it especially desirable that she should find shelter in our Community. There was a hint, not very intelligible, implying either that Priscilla had recently escaped from some particular peril, or irksomeness of position, or else that she was still liable to this danger or difficulty, whatever it might be. We should ill have deserved the reputation of a

benevolent fraternity, had we hesitated to entertain a peti-
tioner in such need, and so strongly recommended to our
kindness; not to mention, moreover, that the strange maiden
had set herself diligently to work, and was doing good service
with her needle. But a slight mist of uncertainty still floated
about Priscilla, and kept her, as yet, from taking a very
decided place among creatures of flesh and blood.

The mysterious attraction, which, from her first entrance
on our scene, she evinced for Zenobia, had lost nothing of its
force. I often heard her footsteps, soft and low, accompanying
the light, but decided tread of the latter, up the staircase,
stealing along the passage-way by her new friend's side, and
pausing while Zenobia entered my chamber. Occasionally,
Zenobia would be a little annoyed by Priscilla's too close
attendance. In an authoritative and not very kindly tone, she
would advise her to breathe the pleasant air in a walk, or to
go with her work into the barn, holding out half a promise to
come and sit on the hay with her, when at leisure. Evidently,
Priscilla found but scanty requital for her love. Hollingsworth
was likewise a great favorite with her. For several minutes
together, sometimes, while my auditory nerves retained the
susceptibility of delicate health, I used to hear a low, pleasant
murmur, ascending from the room below, and at last ascertained it to be Priscilla's voice, babbling like a little brook to
Hollingsworth. She talked more largely and freely with him
than with Zenobia, towards whom, indeed, her feelings
seemed not so much to be confidence, as involuntary affection.
I should have thought all the better of my own qualities, had
Priscilla marked me out for the third place in her regards.
But, though she appeared to like me tolerably well, I could
never flatter myself with being distinguished by her, as
Hollingsworth and Zenobia were.

One forenoon, during my convalescence, there came a
gentle tap at my chamber-door. I immediately said—"Come
in, Priscilla!"—with an acute sense of the applicant's identity.
Nor was I deceived. It was really Priscilla, a pale, large-eyed
little woman, (for she had gone far enough into her teens

to be, at least, on the outer limit of girlhood,) but much less wan than at my previous view of her, and far better conditioned both as to health and spirits. As I first saw her, she had reminded me of plants that one sometimes observes doing their best to vegetate among the bricks of an enclosed court, where there is scanty soil, and never any sunshine. At present, though with no approach to bloom, there were indications that the girl had human blood in her veins.

Priscilla came softly to my bedside, and held out an article of snow-white linen, very carefully and smoothly ironed. She did not seem bashful, nor anywise embarrassed. My weakly condition, I suppose, supplied a medium in which she could approach me.

"Do not you need this?" asked she. "I have made it for you."

It was a night-cap!

"My dear Priscilla," said I, smiling, "I never had on a night-cap in my life! But perhaps it will be better for me to wear one, now that I am a miserable invalid. How admirably you have done it! No, no; I never can think of wearing such an exquisitely wrought night-cap as this, unless it be in the day-time, when I sit up to receive company!"

"It is for use, not beauty," answered Priscilla. "I could have embroidered it and made it much prettier, if I pleased."

While holding up the night-cap, and admiring the fine needle-work, I perceived that Priscilla had a sealed letter, which she was waiting for me to take. It had arrived from the village post-office, that morning. As I did not immediately offer to receive the letter, she drew it back, and held it against her bosom, with both hands clasped over it, in a way that had probably grown habitual to her. Now, on turning my eyes from the night-cap to Priscilla, it forcibly struck me that her air, though not her figure, and the expression of her face, but not its features, had a resemblance to what I had often seen in a friend of mine, one of the most gifted women of the age. I cannot describe it. The points, easiest to convey to the reader, were, a certain curve of the shoulders, and a partial closing of the eyes, which seemed to look more penetratingly into my own eyes, through the narrowed apertures, than if they had been open at full width. It was a singular anomaly of likeness co-existing with perfect dissimilitude.

"Will you give me the letter, Priscilla?" said I.

She started, put the letter into my hand, and quite lost the look that had drawn my notice.

"Priscilla," I inquired, "did you ever see Miss Margaret Fuller?"[7]

"No," she answered.

"Because," said I, "you reminded me of her, just now, and it happens, strangely enough, that this very letter is from her!"

Priscilla, for whatever reason, looked very much discomposed.

"I wish people would not fancy such odd things in me!" she said, rather petulantly. "How could I possibly make myself resemble this lady, merely by holding her letter in my hand?"

"Certainly, Priscilla, it would puzzle me to explain it," I replied. "Nor do I suppose that the letter had anything to do with it. It was just a coincidence—nothing more."

She hastened out of the room; and this was the last that I saw of Priscilla, until I ceased to be an invalid.

Being much alone, during my recovery, I read interminably in Mr. Emerson's Essays, the Dial, Carlyle's works, George Sand's romances,[8] (lent me by Zenobia,) and other books which one or another of the brethren or sisterhood had brought with them. Agreeing in little else, most of these utterances were like the cry of some solitary sentinel, whose station was on the outposts of the advance-guard of human progression; or, sometimes, the voice came sadly from among the shattered ruins of the past, but yet had a hopeful echo in

7. The most famous woman Transcendentalist and a frequent visitor to Brook Farm; see note 1, p. 1.
8. Emerson's *Essays* (1841, 1844); *The Dial* (1840–44), magazine of the Transcendental Club; and Thomas Carlyle (1795–1881), British man of letters, attacked the empiricism and materialism of modern society. George Sand, pseudonym of Aurore Dupin (1804–76), French woman novelist, championed women's rights and defended unconventional sexual relationships.

the future. They were well adapted (better, at least, than any other intellectual products, the volatile essence of which had heretofore tinctured a printed page) to pilgrims like ourselves, whose present bivouâc was considerably farther into the waste of chaos than any mortal army of crusaders had ever marched before. Fourier's works, also, in a series of horribly tedious volumes,[9] attracted a good deal of my attention, from the analogy which I could not but recognize between his system and our own. There was far less resemblance, it is true, than the world chose to imagine; inasmuch as the two theories differed, as widely as the zenith from the nadir, in their main principles.

I talked about Fourier to Hollingsworth, and translated, for his benefit, some of the passages that chiefly impressed me.

"When, as a consequence of human improvement," said I, "the globe shall arrive at its final perfection, the great ocean is to be converted into a particular kind of lemonade, such as was fashionable at Paris in Fourier's time. He calls it *limonade à cèdre.*[1] It is positively a fact! Just imagine the city-docks filled, every day, with a flood-tide of this delectable beverage!"

"Why did not the Frenchman make punch of it, at once?" asked Hollingsworth. "The jack-tars would be delighted to go down in ships, and do business in such an element."

I further proceeded to explain, as well as I modestly could, several points of Fourier's system, illustrating them with here and there a page or two, and asking Hollingsworth's opinion as to the expediency of introducing these beautiful peculiarities into our own practice.

---

9. Charles Fourier (1772–1837) published six volumes criticizing present conditions in the world and offering projects for its reformation. Basically, he called for co-operative units large enough and scientifically structured according to personality types to provide for the agricultural, industrial and social needs of the group and to gratify the basic passions of the individual members.

1. The French is inaccurate. What Fourier wrote was "*Ce fluide* ['*un acide ci-trique boréal*'] *combiné avec le sel don-nera à l'eau de mer le goût d'une sorte de limonade que nous nommons aigre 'de cèdre'.*" ("This fluid ['a borealic citric acid'] combined with salt will give sea-water the taste of a kind of lemonade known to us as *aigre 'de cèdre'* " [a tart citrus drink made from the lemon-fla-vored fruit of the citron tree].) (*Théorie des quatre Mouvements et des Destinées Générales* [Paris, 1946], p. 45n.)

"Let me hear no more of it!" cried he, in utter disgust. "I never will forgive this fellow! He has committed the Unpardonable Sin! For what more monstrous iniquity could the Devil himself contrive, than to choose the selfish principle —the principle of all human wrong, the very blackness of man's heart, the portion of ourselves which we shudder at, and which it is the whole aim of spiritual discipline to eradicate—to choose it as the master-workman of his system? To seize upon and foster whatever vile, petty, sordid, filthy, bestial, and abominable corruptions have cankered into our nature, to be the efficient instruments of his infernal regeneration! And his consummated Paradise, as he pictures it, would be worthy of the agency which he counts upon for establishing it. The nauseous villain!"

"Nevertheless," remarked I, "in consideration of the promised delights of his system—so very proper, as they certainly are, to be appreciated by Fourier's countrymen—I cannot but wonder that universal France did not adopt his theory, at a moment's warning. But is there not something very characteristic of his nation in Fourier's manner of putting forth his views? He makes no claim to inspiration. He has not persuaded himself—as Swedenborg[2] did, and as any other than a Frenchman would, with a mission of like importance to communicate—that he speaks with authority from above. He promulgates his system, so far as I can perceive, entirely on his own responsibility. He has searched out and discovered the whole counsel of the Almighty, in respect to mankind, past, present, and for exactly seventy thousand years to come, by the mere force and cunning of his individual intellect!"

"Take the book out of my sight!" said Hollingsworth, with great virulence of expression, "or, I tell you fairly, I shall fling it in the fire! And as for Fourier, let him make a Paradise, if he can, of Gehenna,[3] where, as I conscientiously believe, he is floundering at this moment!"

2. Emanuel Swedenborg (1688–1772), Swedish theologian whose several experiences of divine revelation convinced him that he was a direct instrument of God; his belief that every natural object has a spiritual cause influenced American Transcendentalism.

3. A place of torment (Hell).

"And bellowing, I suppose," said I—not that I felt any ill-will towards Fourier, but merely wanted to give the finishing touch to Hollingsworth's image—"bellowing for the least drop of his beloved *limonade à cèdre!*"

There is but little profit to be expected in attempting to argue with a man who allows himself to declaim in this manner; so I dropt the subject, and never took it up again.

But had the system, at which he was so enraged, combined almost any amount of human wisdom, spiritual insight, and imaginative beauty, I question whether Hollingsworth's mind was in a fit condition to receive it. I began to discern that he had come among us, actuated by no real sympathy with our feelings and our hopes, but chiefly because we were estranging ourselves from the world, with which his lonely and exclusive object in life had already put him at odds. Hollingsworth must have been originally endowed with a great spirit of benevolence, deep enough, and warm enough, to be the source of as much disinterested good, as Providence often allows a human being the privilege of conferring upon his fellows. This native instinct yet lived within him. I myself had profited by it, in my necessity. It was seen, too, in his treatment of Priscilla. Such casual circumstances, as were here involved, would quicken his divine power of sympathy, and make him seem, while their influence lasted, the tenderest man and the truest friend on earth. But, by-and-by, you missed the tenderness of yesterday, and grew drearily conscious that Hollingsworth had a closer friend than ever you could be. And this friend was the cold, spectral monster which he had himself conjured up, and on which he was wasting all the warmth of his heart, and of which, at last—as these men of a mighty purpose so invariably do—he had grown to be the bond-slave. It was his philanthropic theory!

This was a result exceedingly sad to contemplate, considering that it had been mainly brought about by the very ardor and exuberance of his philanthropy. Sad, indeed, but by no means unusual. He had taught his benevolence to pour its warm tide exclusively through one channel; so that there was nothing to spare for other great manifestations of love to man, nor scarcely for the nutriment of individual attachments, unless they could minister, in some way, to the terrible egotism which he mistook for an angel of God. Had Hollingsworth's education been more enlarged, he might not so inevitably have stumbled into this pit-fall. But this identical pursuit had educated him. He knew absolutely nothing, except in a single direction, where he had thought so energetically, and felt to such a depth, that, no doubt, the entire reason and justice of the universe appeared to be concentrated thitherward.

It is my private opinion, that, at this period of his life, Hollingsworth was fast going mad; and, as with other crazy people, (among whom I include humorists of every degree,) it required all the constancy of friendship to restrain his associates from pronouncing him an intolerable bore. Such prolonged fiddling upon one string; such multiform presentation of one idea! His specific object (of which he made the public more than sufficiently aware, through the medium of lectures and pamphlets) was to obtain funds for the construction of an edifice, with a sort of collegiate endowment. On this foundation, he purposed to devote himself and a few disciples to the reform and mental culture of our criminal brethren. His visionary edifice was Hollingsworth's one castle in the air; it was the material type, in which his philanthropic dream strove to embody itself; and he made the scheme more definite, and caught hold of it the more strongly, and kept his clutch the more pertinaciously, by rendering it visible to the bodily eye. I have seen him, a hundred times, with a pencil and sheet of paper, sketching the façade, the side-view, or the rear of the structure, or planning the internal arrangements, as lovingly as another man might plan those of the projected home, where he meant to be happy with his wife and children. I have known him to begin a model of the building with little stones, gathered at the brookside, whither we had gone to cool ourselves in the sultry noon of haying-time. Unlike all other ghosts, his spirit haunted an edifice which, instead of being time-worn, and full of storied love, and joy, and sorrow, had never yet come into existence.

"Dear friend," said I, once, to Hollingsworth, before leaving my sick-chamber, "I heartily wish that I could make your schemes my schemes, because it would be so great a happiness to find myself treading the same path with you. But I am afraid there is not stuff in me stern enough for a philanthropist —or not in this peculiar direction—or, at all events, not solely in this. Can you bear with me, if such should prove to be the case?"

"I will, at least, wait awhile," answered Hollingsworth, gazing at me sternly and gloomily. "But how can you be my life-long friend, except you strive with me towards the great object of my life?"

Heaven forgive me! A horrible suspicion crept into my heart, and stung the very core of it as with the fangs of an adder. I wondered whether it were possible that Hollings-worth could have watched by my bedside, with all that devoted care, only for the ulterior purpose of making me a proselyte to his views!

VIII

A MODERN ARCADIA

MAY-DAY[4]—I forget whether by Zenobia's sole decree, or by the unanimous vote of our Community—had been declared a moveable festival. It was deferred until the sun should have had a reasonable time to clear away the snow-drifts, along the lee of the stone-walls, and bring out a few of the readiest wild-flowers. On the forenoon

4. First day of the month; originally a pagan festival for Maia, mother of Mercury; in Medieval and Tudor England, a public holiday in which young and old went "a-Maying," crowned a May queen, and danced around a Maypole.

of the substituted day, after admitting some of the balmy air into my chamber, I decided that it was nonsense and effeminacy to keep myself a prisoner any longer. So I descended to the sitting-room, and finding nobody there, proceeded to the barn, whence I had already heard Zenobia's voice, and along with it a girlish laugh, which was not so certainly recognizable. Arriving at the spot, it a little surprised me to discover that these merry outbreaks came from Priscilla.

The two had been a-maying together. They had found anemones in abundance, houstonias by the handfull, some columbines, a few long-stalked violets, and a quantity of white everlasting-flowers, and had filled up their basket with the delicate spray of shrubs and trees. None were prettier than the maple-twigs, the leaf of which looks like a scarlet-bud, in May, and like a plate of vegetable gold in October. Zenobia—who showed no conscience in such matters—had also rifled a cherry-tree of one of its blossomed boughs; and, with all this variety of sylvan ornament, had been decking out Priscilla. Being done with a good deal of taste, it made her look more charming than I should have thought possible, with my recollection of the wan, frost-nipt girl, as heretofore described. Nevertheless, among those fragrant blossoms, and conspicuously, too, had been stuck a weed of evil odor and ugly aspect, which, as soon as I detected it, destroyed the effect of all the rest. There was a gleam of latent mischief— not to call it deviltry—in Zenobia's eye, which seemed to indicate a slightly malicious purpose in the arrangement.

As for herself, she scorned the rural buds and leaflets, and wore nothing but her invariable flower of the tropics.

"What do you think of Priscilla now, Mr. Coverdale?" asked she, surveying her as a child does its doll. "Is not she worth a verse or two?"

"There is only one thing amiss," answered I.

Zenobia laughed, and flung the malignant weed away.

"Yes; she deserves some verses now," said I, "and from a better poet than myself. She is the very picture of the New England spring, subdued in tint, and rather cool, but with a capacity of sunshine, and bringing us a few alpine blossoms, as earnest of something richer, though hardly more beautiful, hereafter. The best type of her is one of those anemones."

"What I find most singular in Priscilla, as her health improves," observed Zenobia, "is her wildness. Such a quiet little body as she seemed, one would not have expected that! Why, as we strolled the woods together, I could hardly keep her from scrambling up the trees like a squirrel! She has never before known what it is to live in the free air, and so it intoxicates her as if she were sipping wine. And she thinks it such a Paradise here, and all of us, particularly Mr. Hollingsworth and myself, such angels! It is quite ridiculous, and provokes one's malice, almost, to see a creature so happy—especially a feminine creature."

"They are always happier than male creatures," said I.

"You must correct that opinion, Mr. Coverdale," replied Zenobia, contemptuously, "or I shall think you lack the poetic insight. Did you ever see a happy woman in your life? Of course, I do not mean a girl—like Priscilla, and a thousand others, for they are all alike, while on the sunny side of experience—but a grown woman. How can she be happy, after discovering that fate has assigned her but one single event, which she must contrive to make the substance of her whole life? A man has his choice of innumerable events."

"A woman, I suppose," answered I, "by constant repetition of her one event, may compensate for the lack of variety."

"Indeed!" said Zenobia.

While we were talking, Priscilla caught sight of Hollingsworth, at a distance, in a blue frock[5] and with a hoe over his shoulder, returning from the field. She immediately set out to meet him, running and skipping, with spirits as light as the breeze of the May-morning, but with limbs too little exercised to be quite responsive; she clapt her hands, too, with great exuberance of gesture, as is the custom of young girls, when their electricity overcharges them. But, all at once, midway to Hollingsworth, she paused, looked round

5. A workman's outer shirt.

about her, towards the river, the road, the woods, and back towards us, appearing to listen, as if she heard some one calling her name, and knew not precisely in what direction.

"Have you bewitched her?" I exclaimed.

"It is no sorcery of mine," said Zenobia. "But I have seen the girl do that identical thing, once or twice before. Can you imagine what is the matter with her?"

"No; unless," said I, "she has the gift of hearing those 'airy tongues that syllable men's names'—which Milton tells about."[6]

From whatever cause, Priscilla's animation seemed entirely to have deserted her. She seated herself on a rock, and remained there until Hollingsworth came up; and when he took her hand and led her back to us, she rather resembled my original image of the wan and spiritless Priscilla, than the flowery May Queen of a few moments ago. These sudden transformations, only to be accounted for by an extreme nervous susceptibility, always continued to characterize the girl, though with diminished frequency, as her health progressively grew more robust.

I was now on my legs again. My fit of illness had been an avenue between two existences; the low-arched and darksome doorway, through which I crept out of a life of old conventionalisms, on my hands and knees, as it were, and gained admittance into the freer region that lay beyond. In this respect, it was like death. And, as with death, too, it was good to have gone through it. No otherwise could I have rid myself of a thousand follies, fripperies, prejudices, habits, and other such worldly dust as inevitably settles upon the crowd along the broad highway, giving them all one sordid aspect, before noontime, however freshly they may have begun their pilgrimage, in the dewy morning. The very substance upon my bones had not been fit to live with, in any better, truer, or more energetic mode than that to which I was accustomed. So it was taken off me and flung aside,

6. Line 207 of John Milton's *Comus* (1634), a masque in which the chaste young woman who speaks these lines is safe from the enchantment of Comus ("reveling") because of her "virtuous mind."

like any other worn out or unseasonable garment; and, after shivering a little while in my skeleton, I began to be clothed anew, and much more satisfactorily than in my previous suit. In literal and physical truth, I was quite another man. I had a lively sense of the exultation with which the spirit will enter on the next stage of its eternal progress, after leaving the heavy burthen of its mortality in an earthly grave, with as little concern for what may become of it, as now affected me for the flesh which I had lost.[7]

Emerging into the genial sunshine, I half fancied that the labors of the brotherhood had already realized some of Fourier's predictions. Their enlightened culture of the soil, and the virtues with which they sanctified their life, had begun to produce an effect upon the material world and its climate. In my new enthusiasm, man looked strong and stately!—and woman, oh, how beautiful!—and the earth, a green garden, blossoming with many-colored delights! Thus Nature, whose laws I had broken in various artificial ways, comported herself towards me as a strict, but loving mother, who uses the rod upon her little boy for his naughtiness, and then gives him a smile, a kiss, and some pretty playthings, to console the urchin for her severity.

In the interval of my seclusion, there had been a number of recruits to our little army of saints and martyrs. They were mostly individuals who had gone through such an experience as to disgust them with ordinary pursuits, but who were not yet so old, nor had suffered so deeply, as to lose their faith in the better time to come. On comparing their minds, one with another, they often discovered that this idea of a Community had been growing up, in silent and unknown sympathy, for years. Thoughtful, strongly-lined faces were among them, sombre brows, but eyes that did not require spectacles, unless prematurely dimmed by the student's lamplight, and hair that seldom showed a thread of silver. Age, wedded to the past, incrusted over with a stony layer of habits, and

7. This paragraph echoes John Bunyan's *Pilgrim's Progress* (1678) in its vocabulary and in its use of clothing and loss- of-mortality images. (See Robert Stanton, "Hawthorne, Bunyan, and the American Romances," *PMLA*, 71 [1956], 155–65.)

retaining nothing fluid in its possibilities, would have been absurdly out of place in an enterprise like this. Youth, too, in its early dawn, was hardly more adapted to our purpose; for it would behold the morning radiance of its own spirit beaming over the very same spots of withered grass and barren sand, whence most of us had seen it vanish. We had very young people with us, it is true—downy lads, rosy girls in their first teens, and children of all heights above one's knee;—but these had chiefly been sent hither for education, which it was one of the objects and methods of our institution to supply. Then we had boarders, from town and elsewhere, who lived with us in a familiar way, sympathized more or less in our theories, and sometimes shared in our labors.

On the whole, it was a society such as has seldom met together; nor, perhaps, could it reasonably be expected to hold together long. Persons of marked individuality—crooked sticks, as some of us might be called—are not exactly the easiest to bind up into a faggot. But, so long as our union should subsist, a man of intellect and feeling, with a free nature in him, might have sought far and near, without finding so many points of attraction as would allure him hitherward. We were of all creeds and opinions, and generally tolerant of all, on every imaginable subject. Our bond, it seems to me, was not affirmative, but negative. We had individually found one thing or another to quarrel with, in our past life, and were pretty well agreed as to the inexpediency of lumbering along with the old system any farther. As to what should be substituted, there was much less unanimity. We did not greatly care—at least, I never did— for the written constitution under which our millennium had commenced. My hope was, that, between theory and practice, a true and available mode of life might be struck out, and that, even should we ultimately fail, the months or years spent in the trial would not have been wasted, either as regarded passing enjoyment, or the experience which makes men wise.

Arcadians though we were, our costume bore no resem-

blance to the be-ribboned doublets, silk breeches and stockings, and slippers fastened with artificial roses, that distinguish
the pastoral people of poetry and the stage. In outward show,
I humbly conceive, we looked rather like a gang of beggars
or banditti, than either a company of honest laboring men or
a conclave of philosophers. Whatever might be our points
of difference, we all of us seemed to have come to Blithedale
with the one thrifty and laudable idea of wearing out our old
clothes. Such garments as had an airing, whenever we strode
afield! Coats with high collars, and with no collars, broad-
skirted or swallow-tailed, and with the waist at every point
between the hip and armpit; pantaloons of a dozen successive
epochs, and greatly defaced at the knees by the humiliations
of the wearer before his lady-love;—in short, we were a living
epitome of defunct fashions, and the very raggedest presentment of men who had seen better days. It was gentility in
tatters. Often retaining a scholarlike or clerical air, you might
have taken us for the denizens of Grub-street,[8] intent on
getting a comfortable livelihood by agricultural labor; or
Coleridge's projected Pantisocracy,[9] in full experiment; or
Candide and his motley associates, at work in their cabbage-
garden;[1] or anything else that was miserably out at elbows, and
most clumsily patched in the rear. We might have been
sworn comrades to Falstaff's ragged regiment.[2] Little skill as
we boasted in other points of husbandry, every mother's son
of us would have served admirably to stick up for a scarecrow.
And the worst of the matter was, that the first energetic movement, essential to one downright stroke of real labor, was
sure to put a finish to these poor habiliments. So we gradually
flung them all aside, and took to honest homespun and linsey-
woolsey, as preferable, on the whole, to the plan recommended, I think, by Virgil—'*Ara nudus; sere nudus*'[3]—which,

8. A London street occupied by hack
writers.
9. A Utopian scheme ("all-equal rule")
headed by Samuel Taylor Coleridge
(1772–1834) and Robert Southey (1774–
1843), who planned to establish it in
Pennsylvania.
1. In Voltaire's *Candide* (1759), a satiric
novel, the characters retire to their own
garden after incredible misfortunes in the
world.
2. Refers to the 150 "tattered prodigals"
that Falstaff takes into battle in Shakespeare's *Henry IV, Part I*, IV, ii.
3. "Strip to plow, strip to sow " (*Geor-
gics*, I, 299).

as Silas Foster remarked when I translated the maxim, would be apt to astonish the women-folks.

After a reasonable training, the yeoman-life throve well with us. Our faces took the sunburn kindly; our chests gained in compass, and our shoulders in breadth and squareness; our great brown fists looked as if they had never been capable of kid gloves. The plough, the hoe, the scythe, and the hay-fork, grew familiar to our grasp. The oxen responded to our voices. We could do almost as fair a day's work as Silas Foster himself, sleep dreamlessly after it, and awake at daybreak with only a little stiffness of the joints, which was usually quite gone by breakfast-time.

To be sure, our next neighbors pretended to be incredulous as to our real proficiency in the business which we had taken in hand. They told slanderous fables about our inability to yoke our own oxen, or to drive them afield, when yoked, or to release the poor brutes from their conjugal bond at nightfall. They had the face to say, too, that the cows laughed at our awkwardness at milking-time, and invariably kicked over the pails; partly in consequence of our putting the stool on the wrong side, and partly because, taking offence at the whisking of their tails, we were in the habit of holding these natural flyflappers with one hand, and milking with the other. They further averred, that we hoed up whole acres of Indian corn and other crops, and drew the earth carefully about the weeds; and that we raised five hundred tufts of burdock,[4] mistaking them for cabbages; and that, by dint of unskilful planting, few of our seeds ever came up at all, or if they did come up, it was stern foremost, and that we spent the better part of the month of June in reversing a field of beans, which had thrust themselves out of the ground in this unseemly way. They quoted it as nothing more than an ordinary occurrence for one or other of us to crop off two or three fingers, of a morning, by our clumsy use of the hay-cutter. Finally, and as an ultimate catastrophe, these mendacious rogues circulated a report that we Communitarians were exter-

4. Coarse, prickly plants.

minated, to the last man, by severing ourselves asunder with the sweep of our own scythes!—and that the world had lost nothing by this little accident.

But this was pure envy and malice on the part of the neighboring farmers. The peril of our new way of life was not lest we should fail in becoming practical agriculturalists, but that we should probably cease to be anything else. While our enterprise lay all in theory, we had pleased ourselves with delectable visions of the spiritualization of labor. It was to be our form of prayer, and ceremonial of worship. Each stroke of the hoe was to uncover some aromatic root of wisdom, heretofore hidden from the sun. Pausing in the field, to let the wind exhale the moisture from our foreheads, we were to look upward, and catch glimpses into the far-off soul of truth. In this point of view, matters did not turn out quite so well as we anticipated. It is very true, that, sometimes, gazing casually around me, out of the midst of my toil, I used to discern a richer picturesqueness in the visible scene of earth and sky. There was, at such moments, a novelty, an unwonted aspect on the face of Nature, as if she had been taken by surprise and seen at unawares, with no opportunity to put off her real look, and assume the mask with which she mysteriously hides herself from mortals. But this was all. The clods of earth, which we so constantly belabored and turned over and over, were never etherealized into thought. Our thoughts, on the contrary, were fast becoming cloddish. Our labor symbolized nothing, and left us mentally sluggish in the dusk of the evening. Intellectual activity is incompatible with any large amount of bodily exercise. The yeoman and the scholar— the yeoman and the man of finest moral culture, though not the man of sturdiest sense and integrity—are two distinct individuals, and can never be melted or welded into one substance.

Zenobia soon saw this truth, and gibed me about it, one evening, as Hollingsworth and I lay on the grass, after a hard day's work.

"I am afraid you did not make a song, to-day, while

loading the hay-cart," said she, "as Burns did, when he was reaping barley."[5]

"Burns never made a song in haying-time," I answered, very positively. "He was no poet while a farmer, and no farmer while a poet."

"And, on the whole, which of the two characters do you like best?" asked Zenobia. "For I have an idea that you cannot combine them, any better than Burns did. Ah, I see, in my mind's eye, what sort of an individual you are to be, two or three years hence! Grim Silas Foster is your prototype, with his palm of sole-leather, and his joints of rusty iron, (which, all through summer, keep the stiffness of what he calls his winter's rheumatize,) and his brain of—I don't know what his brain is made of, unless it be a Savoy cabbage;[6] but yours may be cauliflower, as a rather more delicate variety. Your physical man will be transmuted into salt-beef and fried pork, at the rate, I should imagine, of a pound and a half a day; that being about the average which we find necessary in the kitchen. You will make your toilet for the day (still like this delightful Silas Foster) by rinsing your fingers and the front part of your face in a little tin-pan of water, at the door-step, and teasing your hair with a wooden pocket-comb, before a seven-by-nine-inch looking-glass. Your only pastime will be, to smoke some very vile tobacco in the black stump of a pipe!"

"Pray spare me!" cried I. "But the pipe is not Silas's only mode of solacing himself with the weed."

"Your literature," continued Zenobia, apparently delighted with her description, "will be the Farmer's Almanac;[7] for, I observe, our friend Foster never gets so far as the newspaper. When you happen to sit down, at odd moments, you will fall asleep, and make nasal proclamation of the fact, as he does; and invariably you must be jogged out of a nap, after supper,

---

5. Robert Burns (1759–96) combined an impoverished life as a farmer in Scotland with a career as a poet.
6. A rough variety of common cabbage grown for winter use.
7. Massachusetts almanac begun by Robert Bailey Thomas in 1793 and still published today.

by the future Mrs. Coverdale, and persuaded to go regularly to bed. And on Sundays; when you put on a blue coat with brass buttons, you will think of nothing else to do, but to go and lounge over the stone-walls and rail-fences, and stare at the corn growing. And you will look with a knowing eye at oxen, and will have a tendency to clamber over into pig-sties, and feel of the hogs, and give a guess how much they will weigh, after you shall have stuck and dressed·them. Already, I have noticed, you begin to speak through your nose, and with a drawl. Pray, if you really did make any poetry to-day, let us hear it in that kind of utterance!"

"Coverdale has given up making verses, now," said Hollingsworth, who never had the slightest appreciation of my poetry. "Just think of him penning a sonnet, with a fist like that! There is at least this good in a life of toil, that it takes the nonsense and fancy-work out of a man, and leaves nothing but what truly belongs to him. If a farmer can make poetry at the plough-tail, it must be because his nature insists on it; and if that be the case, let him make it, in Heaven's name!"

"And how is it with you?" asked Zenobia, in a different voice; for she never laughed at Hollingsworth, as she often did at me.—"You, I think, cannot have ceased to live a life of thought and feeling."

"I have always been in earnest," answered Hollingsworth. "I have hammered thought out of iron, after heating the iron in my heart! It matters little what my outward toil may be. Were I a slave at the bottom of a mine, I should keep the same purpose—the same faith in its ultimate accomplishment—that I do now. Miles Coverdale is not in earnest, either as a poet or a laborer."

"You give me hard measure, Hollingsworth," said I, a little hurt. "I have kept pace with you in the field; and my bones feel as if I had been in earnest, whatever may be the case with my brain!"

"I cannot conceive," observed Zenobia, with great emphasis—and, no doubt, she spoke fairly the feeling of the moment—"I cannot conceive of being, so continually as Mr. Coverdale is, within the sphere of a strong and noble nature, without being strengthened and enobled by its influence!"

This amiable remark of the fair Zenobia confirmed me in what I had already begun to suspect—that Hollingsworth, like many other illustrious prophets, reformers, and philanthropists, was likely to make at least two proselytes, among the women, to one among the men. Zenobia and Priscilla! These, I believe, (unless my unworthy self might be reckoned for a third,) were the only disciples of his mission; and I spent a great deal of time, uselessly, in trying to conjecture what Hollingsworth meant to do with them—and they with him!

IX

HOLLINGSWORTH, ZENOBIA, PRISCILLA

IT IS not, I apprehend, a healthy kind of mental occupation, to devote ourselves too exclusively to the study of individual men and women. If the person under examination be one's self, the result is pretty certain to be diseased action of the heart, almost before we can snatch a second glance. Or, if we take the freedom to put a friend under our microscope, we thereby insulate him from many of his true relations, magnify his peculiarities, inevitably tear him into parts, and, of course, patch him very clumsily together again. What wonder, then, should we be frightened by the aspect of a monster, which, after all—though we can point to every feature of his deformity in the real personage— may be said to have been created mainly by ourselves!

Thus, as my conscience has often whispered me, I did Hollingsworth a great wrong by prying into his character, and am perhaps doing him as great a one, at this moment, by putting faith in the discoveries which I seemed to make. But I could not help it. Had I loved him less, I might have used him better. He—and Zenobia and Priscilla, both for their own sakes and as connected with him—were separated from the rest of the Community, to my imagination, and stood forth as the indices of a problem which it was my business to solve. Other associates had a portion of my time; other matters amused me; passing occurrences carried me along with them, while they lasted. But here was the vortex of my meditations around which they revolved, and whitherward they too continually tended. In the midst of cheerful society, I had often a feeling of loneliness. For it was impossible not to be sensible, that, while these three characters figured so largely on my private theatre, I—though probably reckoned as a friend by all—was at best but a secondary or tertiary personage with either of them.

I loved Hollingsworth, as has already been enough expressed. But it impressed me, more and more, that there was a stern and dreadful peculiarity in this man, such as could not prove otherwise than pernicious to the happiness of those who should be drawn into too intimate a connection with him. He was not altogether human. There was something else in Hollingsworth, besides flesh and blood, and sympathies and affections, and celestial spirit.

This is always true of those men who have surrendered themselves to an over-ruling purpose. It does not so much impel them from without, nor even operate as a motive power within, but grows incorporate with all that they think and feel, and finally converts them into little else save that one principle. When such begins to be the predicament, it is not cowardice, but wisdom, to avoid these victims. They have no heart, no sympathy, no reason, no conscience. They will keep no friend, unless he make himself the mirror of their purpose; they will smite and slay you, and trample your dead corpse under foot, all the more readily, if you take the first step with them, and cannot take the second, and the third, and every other step of their terribly straight path. They have an idol, to which they consecrate themselves high-priest, and deem it holy work to offer sacrifices of whatever is most precious, and never once seem to suspect—so cunning has the Devil been with them—that this false deity, in whose iron features, immitigable to all the rest of mankind, they see only benignity and love, is but a spectrum of the very priest himself, projected upon the surrounding darkness. And the higher and purer the original object, and the more unselfishly it may have been taken up, the slighter is the probability that they can be led to recognize the process, by which godlike benevolence has been debased into all-devouring egotism.

Of course, I am perfectly aware that the above statement is exaggerated, in the attempt to make it adequate. Professed philanthropists have gone far; but no originally good man, I presume, ever went quite so far as this. Let the reader abate whatever he deems fit. The paragraph may remain, however, both for its truth and its exaggeration, as strongly expressive of the tendencies which were really operative in Hollingsworth, and as exemplifying the kind of error into which my mode of observation was calculated to lead me. The issue was, that, in solitude, I often shuddered at my friend. In my recollection of his dark and impressive countenance, the features grew more sternly prominent than the reality, duskier in their depth and shadow, and more lurid in their light; the frown, that had merely flitted across his brow, seemed to have contorted it with an adamantine wrinkle. On meeting him again, I was often filled with remorse, when his deep eyes beamed kindly upon me, as with the glow of a household fire that was burning in a cave.—"He is a man, after all!" thought I—"his Maker's own truest image, a philanthropic man!—not that steel engine of the Devil's contrivance, a philanthropist!"—But, in my wood-walks, and in my silent chamber, the dark face frowned at me again.

When a young girl comes within the sphere of such a man, she is as perilously situated as the maiden whom, in the old classical myths, the people used to expose to a dragon. If I had any duty whatever, in reference to Hollingsworth, it was, to endeavor to save Priscilla from that kind of personal worship which her sex is generally prone to lavish upon saints and heroes. It often requires but one smile, out of the hero's eyes into the girl's or woman's heart, to transform this devotion, from a sentiment of the highest approval and confidence, into passionate love. Now, Hollingsworth smiled much upon Priscilla; more than upon any other person. If she thought him beautiful, it was no wonder. I often thought him so, with the expression of tender, human care, and gentlest sympathy, which she alone seemed to have power to call out upon his features. Zenobia, I suspect, would have given her eyes, bright as they were, for such a look; it was the least that our poor Priscilla could do, to give her heart for a great many of them. There was the more danger of this, inasmuch as the footing, on which we all associated at Blithedale, was widely different from that of conventional society. While inclining us to the soft affections of the Golden Age,[8] it seemed to authorize any individual, of either sex, to fall in love with any other, regardless of what would elsewhere be judged suitable and prudent. Accordingly, the tender passion was very rife among us, in various degrees of mildness or virulence, but mostly passing away with the state of things that had given it origin. This was all well enough; but, for a girl like Priscilla, and a woman like Zenobia, to jostle one another in their love of a man like Hollingsworth, was likely to be no child's play.

Had I been as cold-hearted as I sometimes thought myself, nothing would have interested me more than to witness the play of passions that must thus have been evolved. But, in honest truth, I would really have gone far to save Priscilla, at least, from the catastrophe in which such a drama would be apt to terminate.

Priscilla had now grown to be a very pretty girl, and still kept budding and blossoming, and daily putting on some new charm, which you no sooner became sensible of, than you thought it worth all that she had previously possessed. So unformed, vague, and without substance, as she had come to us, it seemed as if we could see Nature shaping out a woman

---

8. The first age of the world, a period of perfect peace and happiness in which Saturn ruled, only men were upon the earth, and women had not yet been created.

before our very eyes, and yet had only a more reverential sense of the mystery of a woman's soul and frame. Yesterday, her cheek was pale; to-day, it had a bloom. Priscilla's smile, like a baby's first one, was a wondrous novelty. Her imperfections and short-comings affected me with a kind of playful pathos, which was as absolutely bewitching a sensation as ever I experienced. After she had been a month or two at Blithedale, her animal spirits waxed high, and kept her pretty constantly in a state of bubble and ferment, impelling her to far more bodily activity than she had yet strength to endure. She was very fond of playing with the other girls, out-of-doors. There is hardly another sight in the world so pretty, as that of a company of young girls, almost women grown, at play, and so giving themselves up to their airy impulse that their tiptoes barely touch the ground.

Girls are incomparably wilder and more effervescent than boys, more untameable, and regardless of rule and limit, with an ever-shifting variety, breaking continually into new modes of fun, yet with a harmonious propriety through all. Their steps, their voices, appear free as the wind, but keep consonance with a strain of music, inaudible to us. Young men and boys, on the other hand, play according to recognized law, old, traditionary games, permitting no caprioles of fancy, but with scope enough for the outbreak of savage instincts. For, young or old, in play or in earnest, man is prone to be a brute.

Especially is it delightful to see a vigorous young girl run a race, with her head thrown back, her limbs moving more friskily than they need, and an air between that of a bird and a young colt. But Priscilla's peculiar charm, in a foot-race, was the weakness and irregularity with which she ran. Growing up without exercise, except to her poor little fingers, she had never yet acquired the perfect use of her legs. Setting buoyantly forth, therefore, as if no rival less swift than Atalanta[9] could compete with her, she ran faulteringly, and often tumbled on the grass. Such an incident—though it

9. According to Ovid's *Metamorphoses*, a beautiful woman who could outrun any man in the world.

seems too slight to think of—was a thing to laugh at, but which brought the water into one's eyes, and lingered in the memory after far greater joys and sorrows were swept out of it, as antiquated trash. Priscilla's life, as I beheld it, was full of trifles that affected me in just this way.

When she had come to be quite at home among us, I used to fancy that Priscilla played more pranks, and perpetrated more mischief, than any other girl in the Community. For example, I once heard Silas Foster, in a very gruff voice, threatening to rivet three horse-shoes round Priscilla's neck and chain her to a post, because she, with some other young people, had clambered upon a load of hay and caused it to slide off the cart. How she made her peace, I never knew; but very soon afterwards, I saw old Silas, with his brawny hands round Priscilla's waist, swinging her to-and-fro and finally depositing her on one of the oxen, to take her first lesson in riding. She met with terrible mishaps in her efforts to milk a cow; she let the poultry into the garden; she generally spoilt whatever part of the dinner she took in charge; she broke crockery; she dropt our biggest pitcher into the well; and—except with her needle, and those little wooden instruments for purse-making—was as unserviceable a member of society as any young lady in the land. There was no other sort of efficiency about her. Yet everybody was kind to Priscilla; everybody loved her, and laughed at her, to her face, and did not laugh, behind her back; everybody would have given her half of his last crust, or the bigger share of his plum-cake. These were pretty certain indications that we were all conscious of a pleasant weakness in the girl, and considered her not quite able to look after her own interests, or fight her battle with the world. And Hollingsworth—perhaps because he had been the means of introducing Priscilla to her new abode—appeared to recognize her as his own especial charge.

Her simple, careless, childish flow of spirits often made me sad. She seemed to me like a butterfly, at play in a flickering bit of sunshine, and mistaking it for a broad and eternal summer. We sometimes hold mirth to a stricter accountability than sorrow; it must show good cause, or the echo of its laughter comes back drearily. Priscilla's gaiety, moreover, was of a nature that showed me how delicate an instrument she was, and what fragile harp-strings were her nerves. As they made sweet music at the airiest touch, it would require but a stronger one to burst them all asunder. Absurd as it might be, I tried to reason with her, and persuade her not to be so joyous, thinking that, if she would draw less lavishly upon her fund of happiness, it would last the longer. I remember doing so, one summer evening, when we tired laborers sat looking on, like Goldsmith's old folks under the village thorn-tree, while the young people were at their sports.[1]

"What is the use or sense of being so very gay?" I said to Priscilla, while she was taking breath after a great frolic. "I love to see a sufficient cause for everything; and I can see none for this. Pray tell me, now, what kind of a world you imagine this to be, which you are so merry in?"

"I never think about it at all," answered Priscilla, laughing. "But this I am sure of—that it is a world where everybody is kind to me, and where I love everybody. My heart keeps dancing within me; and all the foolish things, which you see me do, are only the motions of my heart. How can I be dismal, if my heart will not let me?"

"Have you nothing dismal to remember?" I suggested. "If not, then, indeed, you are very fortunate!"

"Ah!" said Priscilla, slowly.

And then came that unintelligible gesture, when she seemed to be listening to a distant voice.

"For my part," I continued, beneficently seeking to over-shadow her with my own sombre humor, "my past life has been a tiresome one enough; yet I would rather look backward ten times, than forward once. For, little as we know of our life to come, we may be very sure, for one thing, that the good we aim at will not be attained. People never do get just the good they seek. If it come at all, it is something else,

1. A reference to ll. 13–24 of "The Deserted Village" (1770) by Oliver Goldsmith; "thorntree" is another name for the "hawthorn bush" Goldsmith mentions in l. 13.

which they never dreamed of, and did not particularly want. Then, again, we may rest certain that our friends of to-day will not be our friends of a few years hence; but, if we keep one of them, it will be at the expense of the others—and, most probably, we shall keep none. To be sure, there are more to be had! But who cares about making a new set of friends, even should they be better than those around us?"

"Not I!" said Priscilla. "I will live and die with these!"

"Well; but let the future go!" resumed I. "As for the present moment, if we could look into the hearts where we wish to be most valued, what should you expect to see? One's own likeness, in the innermost, holiest niche? Ah, I don't know! It may not be there at all. It may be a dusty image, thrust aside into a corner, and by-and-by to be flung out-of-doors, where any foot may trample upon it. If not to-day, then tomorrow! And so, Priscilla, I do not see much wisdom in being so very merry in this kind of a world!"

It had taken me nearly seven years of worldly life, to hive up the bitter honey which I here offered to Priscilla. And she rejected it!

"I don't believe one word of what you say!" she replied, laughing anew. "You made me sad, for a minute, by talking about the past. But the past never comes back again. Do we dream the same dream twice? There is nothing else that I am afraid of."

So away she ran, and fell down on the green grass, as it was often her luck to do, but got up again without any harm.

"Priscilla, Priscilla!" cried Hollingsworth, who was sitting on the door-step. "You had better not run any more to-night. You will weary yourself too much. And do not sit down out of doors; for there is a heavy dew beginning to fall!"

At his first word, she went and sat down under the porch, at Hollingsworth's feet, entirely contented and happy. What charm was there, in his rude massiveness, that so attracted and soothed this shadowlike girl? It appeared to me—who have always been curious in such matters—that Priscilla's vague and seemingly causeless flow of felicitous feeling was that with which love blesses inexperienced hearts, before they begin to suspect what is going on within them. It transports them to the seventh heaven;[2] and if you ask what brought them thither, they neither can tell nor care to learn, but cherish an ecstatic faith that there they shall abide forever.

Zenobia was in the door-way, not far from Hollingsworth. She gazed at Priscilla, in a very singular way. Indeed, it was a sight worth gazing at, and a beautiful sight too, as the fair girl sat at the feet of that dark, powerful figure. Her air, while perfectly modest, delicate, and virginlike, denoted her as swayed by Hollingsworth, attracted to him, and unconsciously seeking to rest upon his strength. I could not turn away my own eyes, but hoped that nobody, save Zenobia and myself, were witnessing this picture. It is before me now, with the evening twilight a little deepened by the dusk of memory.

"Come hither, Priscilla!" said Zenobia. "I have something to say to you!"

She spoke in little more than a whisper. But it is strange how expressive of moods a whisper may often be. Priscilla felt at once that something had gone wrong.

"Are you angry with me?" she asked, rising slowly and standing before Zenobia in a drooping attitude. "What have I done? I hope you are not angry!"

"No, no, Priscilla!" said Hollingsworth, smiling. "I will answer for it, she is not. You are the one little person in the world, with whom nobody can be angry!"

"Angry with you, child? What a silly idea!" exclaimed Zenobia, laughing. "No, indeed! But, my dear Priscilla, you are getting to be so very pretty that you absolutely need a duenna;[3] and as I am older than you, and have had my own little experience of life, and think myself exceedingly sage, I intend to fill the place of a maiden-aunt. Every day, I shall give you a lecture, a quarter-of-an-hour in length, on the morals, manners, and proprieties of social life. When our pas-

2. The dwelling place of God and the angels in the Moslem religious system.
3. An elderly lady with a position some-where between that of a governess and that of a companion.

toral shall be quite played out, Priscilla, my worldly wisdom
may stand you in good stead!"

"I am afraid you are angry with me," repeated Priscilla,
sadly; for, while she seemed as impressible as wax, the girl
often showed a persistency in her own ideas, as stubborn
as it was gentle.

"Dear me, what can I say to the child!" cried Zenobia, in
a tone of humorous vexation. "Well, well; since you insist
on my being angry, come to my room, this moment, and let
me beat you!"

Zenobia bade Hollingsworth good night very sweetly, and
nodded to me with a smile. But, just as she turned aside with
Priscilla into the dimness of the porch, I caught another
glance at her countenance. It would have made the fortune
of a tragic actress, could she have borrowed it for the moment
when she fumbles in her bosom for the concealed dagger, or
the exceedingly sharp bodkin,[4] or mingles the ratsbane[5] in her
lover's bowl of wine, or her rival's cup of tea. Not that I
in the least anticipated any such catastrophe; it being a
remarkable truth, that custom has in no one point a greater
sway than over our modes of wreaking our wild passions.
And, besides, had we been in Italy, instead of New England,
it was hardly yet a crisis for the dagger or the bowl.

It often amazed me, however, that Hollingsworth should
show himself so recklessly tender towards Priscilla, and never
once seem to think of the effect which it might have upon her
heart. But the man, as I have endeavored to explain, was
thrown completely off his moral balance, and quite bewildered as to his personal relations, by his great excrescence
of a philanthropic scheme. I used to see, or fancy, indications
that he was not altogether obtuse to Zenobia's influence as a
woman. No doubt, however, he had a still more exquisite
enjoyment of Priscilla's silent sympathy with his purposes, so
unalloyed with criticism, and therefore more grateful than
any intellectual approbation, which always involves a pos-

4. A small pointed instrument for mak-   5. Arsenic.
ing holes in leather.

sible reserve of latent censure. A man—poet, prophet, or whatever he may be—readily persuades himself of his right to all the worship that is voluntarily tendered. In requital of so rich benefits as he was to confer upon mankind, it would have been hard to deny Hollingsworth the simple solace of a young girl's heart, which he held in his hand, and smelled to,[6] like a rosebud. But what if, while pressing out its fragrance, he should crush the tender rosebud in his grasp!

As for Zenobia, I saw no occasion to give myself any trouble. With her native strength, and her experience of the world, she could not be supposed to need any help of mine. Nevertheless, I was really generous enough to feel some little interest likewise for Zenobia. With all her faults, (which might have been a great many, besides the abundance that I knew of,) she possessed noble traits, and a heart which must at least have been valuable while new. And she seemed ready to fling it away, as uncalculatingly as Priscilla herself. I could not but suspect, that, if merely at play with Hollingsworth, she was sporting with a power which she did not fully estimate. Or, if in earnest, it might chance, between Zenobia's passionate force and his dark, self-delusive egotism, to turn out such earnest as would develop itself in some sufficiently tragic catastrophe, though the dagger and the bowl should go for nothing in it.

Meantime, the gossip of the Community set them down as a pair of lovers. They took walks together, and were not seldom encountered in the wood-paths; Hollingsworth deeply discoursing, in tones solemn and sternly pathetic. Zenobia, with a rich glow on her cheeks, and her eyes softened from their ordinary brightness, looked so beautiful, that, had her companion been ten times a philanthropist, it seemed impossible but that one glance should melt him back into a man. Oftener than anywhere else, they went to a certain point on the slope of a pasture, commanding nearly the whole of our

6. To "smell to" the "young girl's heart": intransitive usage of the verb *smell*, meaning to make use of the sense of smell in relation to a specified object; possible prepositions are *at*, *of* (especially U.S.) or *to*. Hollingsworth smelled the heart as though it were a rosebud.

own domain, besides a view of the river and an airy prospect of many distant hills. The bond of our Community was such, that the members had the privilege of building cottages for their own residence, within our precincts, thus laying a hearth-stone and fencing in a home, private and peculiar, to all desirable extent; while yet the inhabitants should continue to share the advantages of an associated life. It was inferred, that Hollingsworth and Zenobia intended to rear their dwelling on this favorite spot.

I mentioned these rumors to Hollingsworth in a playful way.

"Had you consulted me," I went on to observe, "I should have recommended a site further to the left, just a little withdrawn into the wood, with two or three peeps at the prospect, among the trees. You will be in the shady vale of years, long before you can raise any better kind of shade around your cottage, if you build it on this bare slope."

"But I offer my edifice as a spectacle to the world," said Hollingsworth, "that it may take example and build many another like it. Therefore I mean to set it on the open hill-side."

Twist these words how I might, they offered no very satisfactory import. It seemed hardly probable that Hollingsworth should care about educating the public taste in the department of cottage-architecture, desirable as such improvement certainly was.

X

A VISITOR FROM TOWN

HOLLINGSWORTH and I—we had been hoeing potatoes, that forenoon, while the rest of the fraternity were engaged in a distant quarter of the farm —sat under a clump of maples, eating our eleven o'clock lunch, when we saw a stranger approaching along the edge of the field. He had admitted himself from the road-side, through a turnstile, and seemed to have a purpose of speaking with us.

And, by-the-by, we were favored with many visits at Blithedale; especially from people who sympathized with our theories, and perhaps held themselves ready to unite in our actual experiment, as soon as there should appear a reliable promise of its success. It was rather ludicrous, indeed, (to me, at least, whose enthusiasm had insensibly been exhaled, together with the perspiration of many a hard day's toil,) it was absolutely funny, therefore, to observe what a glory was shed about our life and labors, in the imagination of these longing proselytes. In their view, we were as poetical as Arcadians, besides being as practical as the hardest-fisted husbandmen in Massachusetts. We did not, it is true, spend much time in piping to our sheep, or warbling our innocent loves to the sisterhood. But they gave us credit for imbuing the ordinary rustic occupations with a kind of religious poetry, insomuch that our very cow-yards and pig-sties were as delightfully fragrant as a flower-garden. Nothing used to please me more than to see one of these lay enthusiasts snatch up a hoe, as they were very prone to do, and set to work with a vigor that perhaps carried him through about a dozen ill-directed strokes. Men are wonderfully soon satisfied, in this day of shameful bodily enervation, when, from one end of life to the other, such multitudes never taste the sweet weariness that follows accustomed toil. I seldom saw the new enthusiasm that did not grow as flimsy and flaccid as the proselyte's moistened shirt-collar, with a quarter-of-an-hour's active labor, under a July sun.

But the person, now at hand, had not at all the air of one of these amiable visionaries. He was an elderly man, dressed rather shabbily, yet decently enough, in a gray frock-coat, faded towards a brown hue, and wore a broad-brimmed white hat, of the fashion of several years gone by. His hair was perfect silver, without a dark thread in the whole of it; his nose, though it had a scarlet tip, by no means indicated the jollity of which a red nose is the generally admitted symbol. He was a subdued, undemonstrative old man, who would doubtless drink a glass of liquor, now and then, and probably more than was good for him; not, however, with a purpose of undue exhilaration, but in the hope of bringing his spirits up to the ordinary level of the world's cheerfulness. Drawing nearer, there was a shy look about him, as if he were ashamed of his poverty, or, at any rate, for some reason or other, would rather have us glance at him sidelong than take a full-front view. He had a queer appearance of hiding himself behind the patch on his left eye.

"I know this old gentleman," said I to Hollingsworth, as we sat observing him—"that is, I have met him a hundred times, in town, and have often amused my fancy with wondering what he was, before he came to be what he is. He haunts restaurants and such places, and has an odd way of lurking in corners or getting behind a door, whenever practicable, and holding out his hand, with some little article in it, which he wishes you to buy. The eye of the world seems to trouble him, although he necessarily lives so much in it. I never expected to see him in an open field."

"Have you learned anything of his history?" asked Hollingsworth.

"Not a circumstance," I answered. "But there must be something curious in it. I take him to be a harmless sort of a person, and a tolerably honest one; but his manners, being so furtive, remind me of those of a rat—a rat without the mischief, the fierce eye, the teeth to bite with, or the desire to bite. See, now! He means to skulk along that fringe of bushes, and approach us on the other side of our clump of maples."

We soon heard the old man's velvet tread on the grass, indicating that he had arrived within a few feet of where we sat.

"Good morning, Mr. Moodie," said Hollingsworth, addressing the stranger as an acquaintance. "You must have had a hot and tiresome walk from the city. Sit down, and take a morsel of our bread and cheese!"

The visitor made a grateful little murmur of acquiescence, and sat down in a spot somewhat removed; so that, glancing round, I could see his gray pantaloons and dusty shoes, while his upper part was mostly hidden behind the shrubbery. Nor did he come forth from this retirement during the whole of the interview that followed. We handed him such food as we had, together with a brown jug of molasses-and-water, (would that it had been brandy, or something better, for the sake of his chill old heart!) like priests offering dainty sacrifice to an enshrined and invisible idol. I have no idea that he really lacked sustenance; but it was quite touching, nevertheless, to hear him nibbling away at our crusts.

"Mr. Moodie," said I, "do you remember selling me one of those very pretty little silk purses, of which you seem to have a monopoly in the market? I keep it, to this day, I can assure you."

"Ah, thank you!" said our guest. "Yes, Mr. Coverdale, I used to sell a good many of those little purses."

He spoke languidly, and only those few words, like a watch with an inelastic spring, that just ticks, a moment or two, and stops again. He seemed a very forlorn old man. In the wantonness of youth, strength, and comfortable condition—making my prey of people's individualities, as my custom was—I tried to identify my mind with the old fellow's, and take his view of the world, as if looking through a smoke-blackened glass at the sun. It robbed the landscape of all its life. Those pleasantly swelling slopes of our farm, descending towards the wide meadows, through which sluggishly circled the brimfull tide of the Charles, bathing the long sedges on its hither and farther shores; the broad, sunny gleam over the winding water; that peculiar picturesqueness of the scene, where capes and headlands put themselves boldly forth upon the perfect level of the meadow, as into a green lake, with inlets between the promontories; the shadowy woodland, with twinkling showers of light falling into its depths; the sultry

heat-vapor, which rose everywhere like incense, and in which
my soul delighted, as indicating so rich a fervor in the passionate day, and in the earth that was burning with its love:—I
beheld all these things as through old Moodie's eyes. When
my eyes are dimmer than they have yet come to be, I will go
thither again, and see if I did not catch the tone of his mind
aright, and if the cold and lifeless tint of his perceptions be
not then repeated in my own.

Yet it was unaccountable to myself, the interest that I
felt in him.

"Have you any objection," said I, "to telling me who made
those little purses?"

"Gentlemen have often asked me that," said Moodie,
slowly; "but I shake my head, and say little or nothing, and
creep out of the way, as well as I can. I am a man of few
words; and if gentlemen were to be told one thing, they would
be very apt, I suppose, to ask me another. But it happens,
just now, Mr. Coverdale, that you can tell me more about
the maker of those little purses, than I can tell you."

"Why do you trouble him with needless questions, Coverdale?" interrupted Hollingsworth. "You must have known,
long ago, that it was Priscilla. And so, my good friend, you
have come to see her? Well, I am glad of it. You will find
her altered very much for the better, since that wintry evening
when you put her into my charge. Why, Priscilla has a bloom
in her cheeks, now!"

"Has my pale little girl a bloom?" repeated Moodie, with a
kind of slow wonder. "Priscilla with a bloom in her cheeks!
Ah, I am afraid I shall not know my little girl. And is she
happy?"

"Just as happy as a bird," answered Hollingsworth.

"Then, gentlemen," said our guest, apprehensively, "I
don't think it well for me to go any further. I crept hitherward only to ask about Priscilla; and now that you have told
me such good news, perhaps I can do no better than to creep
back again. If she were to see this old face of mine, the
child would remember some very sad times which we have

spent together. Some very sad times indeed! She has forgotten them, I know—them and me—else she could not be so
happy, nor have a bloom in her cheeks. Yes—yes—yes," continued he, still with the same torpid utterance; "with many
thanks to you, Mr. Hollingsworth, I will creep back to town
again."

"You shall do no such thing, Mr. Moodie!" said Hollingsworth, bluffly. "Priscilla often speaks of you; and if there
lacks anything to make her cheeks bloom like two damask[7]
roses, I'll venture to say, it is just the sight of your face. Come;
we will go and find her."

"Mr. Hollingsworth!" said the old man, in his hesitating
way.

"Well!" answered Hollingsworth.

"Has there been any call for Priscilla?" asked Moodie; and
though his face was hidden from us, his tone gave a sure
indication of the mysterious nod and wink with which he
put the question. "You know, I think, sir, what I mean."

"I have not the remotest suspicion what you mean, Mr.
Moodie," replied Hollingsworth. "Nobody, to my knowledge,
has called for Priscilla, except yourself. But, come; we are
losing time, and I have several things to say to you, by the
way."

"And, Mr. Hollingsworth!" repeated Moodie.

"Well, again!" cried my friend, rather impatiently. "What
now?"

"There is a lady here," said the old man; and his voice lost
some of its wearisome hesitation. "You will account it a very
strange matter for me to talk about; but I chanced to know
this lady, when she was but a little child. If I am rightly
informed, she has grown to be a very fine woman, and
makes a brilliant figure in the world, with her beauty, and
her talents, and her noble way of spending her riches. I
should recognize this lady, so people tell me, by a magnificent flower in her hair!"

7. Pink.

"What a rich tinge it gives to his colorless ideas, when he speaks of Zenobia!" I whispered to Hollingsworth. "But how can there possibly be any interest or connecting link between him and her?"

"The old man, for years past," whispered Hollingsworth, "has been a little out of his right mind, as you probably see."

"What I would inquire," resumed Moodie, "is, whether this beautiful lady is kind to my poor Priscilla."

"Very kind," said Hollingsworth.

"Does she love her?" asked Moodie.

"It should seem so," answered my friend. "They are always together."

"Like a gentlewoman and her maid servant, I fancy?" suggested the old man.

There was something so singular in his way of saying this, that I could not resist the impulse to turn quite round, so as to catch a glimpse of his face; almost imagining that I should see another person than old Moodie. But there he sat, with the patched side of his face towards me.

"Like an elder and younger sister, rather," replied Hollingsworth.

"Ah," said Moodie, more complaisantly—for his latter tones had harshness and acidity in them—"it would gladden my old heart to witness that. If one thing would make me happier than another, Mr. Hollingsworth, it would be, to see that beautiful lady holding my little girl by the hand."

"Come along," said Hollingsworth, "and perhaps you may."

After a little more delay on the part of our freakish visitor, they set forth together; old Moodie keeping a step or two ˙ behind Hollingsworth, so that the latter could not very conveniently look him in the face. I remained under the tuft of maples, doing my utmost to draw an inference from the scene that had just passed. In spite of Hollingsworth's offhand explanation, it did not strike me that our strange guest was really beside himself, but only that his mind needed screwing up, like an instrument long out of tune, the strings of which have ceased to vibrate smartly and sharply. Methought it would be profitable for us, projectors of a happy life, to welcome this old gray shadow, and cherish him as one of us, and let him creep about our domain, in order that he might be a little merrier for our sakes, and we, sometimes, a little sadder for his. Human destinies look ominous, without some perceptible intermixture of the sable or the gray. And then, too, should any of our fraternity grow feverish with an over-exulting sense of prosperity, it would be a sort of cooling regimen to slink off into the woods, and spend an hour, or a day, or as many days as might be requisite to the cure, in uninterrupted communion with this deplorable old Moodie!

Going homeward to dinner, I had a glimpse of him behind the trunk of a tree, gazing earnestly towards a particular window of the farm-house. And, by-and-by, Priscilla appeared at this window, playfully drawing along Zenobia, who looked as bright as the very day that was blazing down upon us, only not, by many degrees, so well advanced towards her noon. I was convinced that this pretty sight must have been purposely arranged by Priscilla, for the old man to see. But either the girl held her too long, or her fondness was resented as too great a freedom; for Zenobia suddenly put Priscilla decidedly away, and gave her a haughty look, as from a mistress to a dependant. Old Moodie shook his head—and again, and again, I saw him shake it, as he withdrew along the road—and, at the last point whence the farm-house was visible, he turned, and shook his uplifted staff.

XI

THE WOOD-PATH

NOT LONG after the preceding incident, in order to get the ache of too constant labor out of my bones, and to relieve my spirit of the irksomeness of a settled routine, I took a holiday. It was my purpose to spend it, all alone, from breakfast-time till twilight, in the deepest wood-seclusion that lay anywhere around us. Though fond of society, I was so constituted as to need these occasional retirements, even in a life like that of Blithedale, which was itself characterized by a remoteness from the world. Unless renewed by a yet farther withdrawal towards the inner circle of self-communion, I lost the better part of my individuality. My thoughts became of little worth, and my sensibilities grew as arid as a tuft of moss, (a thing whose life is in the shade, the rain, or the noontide dew,) crumbling in the sunshine, after long expectance of a shower. So, with my heart full of a drowsy pleasure, and cautious not to dissipate my mood by previous intercourse with any one, I hurried away, and was soon pacing a wood-path, arched overhead with boughs, and dusky brown beneath my feet.

At first, I walked very swiftly, as if the heavy floodtide of social life were roaring at my heels, and would outstrip and overwhelm me, without all the better diligence in my escape. But, threading the more distant windings of the track, I abated my pace and looked about me for some side-aisle, that should admit me into the innermost sanctuary of this green cathedral; just as, in human acquaintanceship, a casual opening sometimes lets us, all of a sudden, into the long-sought intimacy of a mysterious heart. So much was I absorbed in my reflections—or rather, in my mood, the substance of which was as yet too shapeless to be called thought—that footsteps rustled on the leaves, and a figure passed me by, almost without impressing either the sound or sight upon my consciousness.

A moment afterwards, I heard a voice at a little distance behind me, speaking so sharply and impertinently that it made a complete discord with my spiritual state, and caused the latter to vanish, as abruptly as when you thrust a finger into a soap-bubble.

"Halloo, friend!" cried this most unseasonable voice. "Stop a moment, I say! I must have a word with you!"

I turned about, in a humor ludicrously irate. In the first place, the interruption, at any rate, was a grievous injury; then, the tone displeased me. And, finally, unless there be real affection in his heart, a man cannot—such is the bad state to which the world has brought itself—cannot more effectually show his contempt for a brother-mortal, nor more gallingly assume a position of superiority, than by addressing him as 'friend.' Especially does the misapplication of this phrase bring out that latent hostility, which is sure to animate peculiar sects, and those who, with however generous a purpose, have sequestered themselves from the crowd; a feeling, it is true, which may be hidden in some dog-kennel of the heart, grumbling there in the darkness, but is never quite extinct, until the dissenting party have gained power and scope enough to treat the world generously. For my part, I should have taken it as far less an insult to be styled 'fellow,' 'clown,' or 'bumpkin.' To either of these appellations, my rustic garb (it was a linen blouse, with checked shirt and striped pantaloons, a chip-hat[8] on my head, and a rough hickory-stick in my hand) very fairly entitled me. As the case stood, my temper darted at once to the opposite pole; not friend, but enemy!

"What do you want with me?" said I, facing about.

"Come a little nearer, friend!" said the stranger, beckoning.

"No," answered I. "If I can do anything for you, without too much trouble to myself, say so. But recollect, if you

---

8. A hat made of thin strips of woody fiber.

please, that you are not speaking to an acquaintance, much less a friend!"

"Upon my word, I believe not!" retorted he, looking at me with some curiosity; and lifting his hat, he made me a salute, which had enough of sarcasm to be offensive, and just enough of doubtful courtesy to render any resentment of it absurd.— "But I ask your pardon! I recognize a little mistake. If I may take the liberty to suppose it, you, sir, are probably one of the Æsthetic—or shall I rather say ecstatic?—laborers, who have planted themselves hereabouts. This is your forest of Arden; and you are either the banished Duke, in person, or one of the chief nobles in his train. The melancholy Jacques, perhaps?[9] Be it so! In that case, you can probably do me a favor."

I never, in my life, felt less inclined to confer a favor on any man.

"I am busy!" said I.

So unexpectedly had the stranger made me sensible of his presence, that he had almost the effect of an apparition, and certainly a less appropriate one (taking into view the dim woodland solitude about us) than if the salvage man of antiquity, hirsute and cinctured with a leafy girdle, had started out of a thicket.[1] He was still young, seemingly a little under thirty, of a tall and well-developed figure, and as handsome a man as ever I beheld. The style of his beauty, however, though a masculine style, did not at all commend itself to my taste. His countenance—I hardly know how to describe the peculiarity—had an indecorum in it, a kind of rudeness, a hard, coarse, forth-putting freedom of expression, which no degree of external polish could have abated, one single jot. Not that it was vulgar. But he had no fineness of nature; there was in his eyes (although they might have artifice enough of another sort) the naked exposure of something that ought not to be left prominent. With these vague allu-

9. In Shakespeare's *As You Like It*, the forest of Arden offers a romantic pastoral existence to such melancholy realists as the banished duke, his nobles, and the mournful courtier Jacques.

1. In medieval mumming and Elizabethan pageantry, the Green Man, one covered with hair and clothed in ivy to represent a savage.

sions to what I have seen in other faces, as well as his, I leave the quality to be comprehended best—because with an intuitive repugnance—by those who possess least of it.

His hair, as well as his beard and moustache, was coal-black; his eyes, too, were black and sparkling, and his teeth remarkably brilliant. He was rather carelessly, but well and fashionably dressed, in a summer-morning costume. There was a gold chain, exquisitely wrought, across his vest. I never saw a smoother or whiter gloss than that upon his shirt-bosom, which had a pin in it, set with a gem that glimmered, in the leafy shadow where he stood, like a living tip of fire. He carried a stick with a wooden head, carved in vivid imitation of that of a serpent. I hated him, partly, I do believe, from a comparison of my own homely garb with his well-ordered foppishness.

"Well, sir," said I, a little ashamed of my first irritation, but still with no waste of civility, "be pleased to speak at once, as I have my own business in hand."

"I regret that my mode of addressing you was a little unfortunate," said the stranger, smiling; for he seemed a very acute sort of person, and saw, in some degree, how I stood affected towards him. "I intended no offence, and shall certainly comport myself with due ceremony hereafter. I merely wish to make a few inquiries respecting a lady, formerly of my acquaintance, who is now resident in your Community, and, I believe, largely concerned in your social enterprise. You call her, I think, Zenobia."

"That is her name in literature," observed I—"a name, too, which possibly she may permit her private friends to know and address her by;—but not one which they feel at liberty to recognize, when used of her, personally, by a stranger or casual acquaintance."

"Indeed!" answered this disagreeable person; and he turned aside his face, for an instant, with a brief laugh, which struck me as a noteworthy expression of his character. "Perhaps I might put forward a claim, on your own grounds, to call the lady by a name so appropriate to her splendid qualities. But

I am willing to know her by any cognomen that you may suggest."

Heartily wishing that he would be either a little more offensive, or a good deal less so, or break off our intercourse altogether, I mentioned Zenobia's real name.

"True," said he; "and, in general society, I have never heard her called otherwise. And, after all, our discussion of the point has been gratuitous. My object is only to inquire when, where, and how, this lady may most conveniently be seen?"

"At her present residence, of course," I replied. "You have but to go thither and ask for her. This very path will lead you within sight of the house;—so I wish you good morning."

"One moment, if you please," said the stranger. "The course you indicate would certainly be the proper one, in an ordinary morning-call. But my business is private, personal, and somewhat peculiar. Now, in a Community like this, I should judge that any little occurrence is likely to be discussed rather more minutely than would quite suit my views. I refer solely to myself, you understand, and without intimating that it would be other than a matter of entire indifference to the lady. In short, I especially desire to see her in private. If her habits are such as I have known them, she is probably often to be met with in the woods, or by the river-side; and I think you could do me the favor to point out some favorite walk, where, about this hour, I might be fortunate enough to gain an interview."

I reflected, that it would be quite a super-erogatory piece of quixotism, in me, to undertake the guardianship of Zenobia, who, for my pains, would only make me the butt of endless ridicule, should the fact ever come to her knowledge. I therefore described a spot which, as often as any other, was Zenobia's resort, at this period of the day; nor was it so remote from the farm-house as to leave her in much peril, whatever might be the stranger's character.

"A single word more!" said he; and his black eyes sparkled at me, whether with fun or malice I knew not, but certainly as if the Devil were peeping out of them. "Among your fraternity, I understand, there is a certain holy and benevolent blacksmith; a man of iron, in more senses than one; a rough, cross-grained, well-meaning individual, rather boorish in his manners—as might be expected—and by no means of the highest intellectual cultivation. He is a philanthropical lecturer, with two or three disciples, and a scheme of his own, the preliminary step in which involves a large purchase of land, and the erection of a spacious edifice, at an expense considerably beyond his means; inasmuch as these are to be reckoned in copper or old iron, much more conveniently than in gold or silver. He hammers away upon his one topic, as lustily as ever he did upon a horse-shoe! Do you know such a person?"

I shook my head, and was turning away.

"Our friend," he continued, "is described to me as a brawny, shaggy, grim, and ill-favored personage, not particularly well-calculated, one would say, to insinuate himself with the softer sex. Yet, so far has this honest fellow succeeded with one lady, whom we wot[2] of, that he anticipates, from her abundant resources, the necessary funds for realizing his plan in brick and mortar!"

Here the stranger seemed to be so much amused with his sketch of Hollingsworth's character and purposes, that he burst into a fit of merriment, of the same nature as the brief, metallic laugh already alluded to, but immensely prolonged and enlarged. In the excess of his delight, he opened his mouth wide, and disclosed a gold band around the upper part of his teeth; thereby making it apparent that every one of his brilliant grinders and incisors was a sham. This discovery affected me very oddly. I felt as if the whole man were a moral and physical humbug; his wonderful beauty of face, for aught I knew, might be removeable like a mask; and, tall and comely as his figure looked, he was perhaps but a wizened little elf, gray and decrepit, with nothing genuine about him,

2. Know.

save the wicked expression of his grin. The fantasy of his spectral character so wrought upon me, together with the contagion of his strange mirth on my sympathies, that I soon began to laugh as loudly as himself.

By-and-by, he paused, all at once; so suddenly, indeed, that my own cachinnation[3] lasted a moment longer.

"Ah, excuse me!" said he. "Our interview seems to proceed more merrily than it began."

"It ends here," answered I. "And I take shame to myself, that my folly has lost me the right of resenting your ridicule of a friend."

"Pray allow me," said the stranger, approaching a step nearer, and laying his gloved hand on my sleeve. "One other favor I must ask of you. You have a young person, here at Blithedale, of whom I have heard—whom, perhaps, I have known—and in whom, at all events, I take a peculiar interest. She is one of those delicate, nervous young creatures, not uncommon in New England, and whom I suppose to have become what we find them by the gradual refining away of the physical system, among your women. Some philosophers choose to glorify this habit of body by terming it spiritual; but, in my opinion, it is rather the effect of unwholesome food, bad air, lack of out-door exercise, and neglect of bathing, on the part of these damsels and their female progenitors; all resulting in a kind of hereditary dyspepsia. Zenobia, even with her uncomfortable surplus of vitality, is far the better model of womanhood. But—to revert again to this young person—she goes among you by the name of Priscilla. Could you possibly afford me the means of speaking with her?"

"You have made so many inquiries of me," I observed, "that I may at least trouble you with one. What is your name?"

He offered me a card, with 'Professor Westervelt' engraved on it. At the same time, as if to vindicate his claim to the professorial dignity, so often assumed on very questionable

3. Convulsive laughter.

grounds, he put on a pair of spectacles, which so altered the character of his face that I hardly knew him again. But I liked the present aspect no better than the former one.

"I must decline any further connection with your affairs," said I, drawing back. "I have told you where to find Zenobia. As for Priscilla, she has closer friends than myself, through whom, if they see fit, you can gain access to her."

"In that case," returned the Professor, ceremoniously raising his hat, "good morning to you."

He took his departure, and was soon out of sight among the windings of the wood-path. But, after a little reflection, I could not help regretting that I had so peremptorily broken off the interview, while the stranger seemed inclined to continue it. His evident knowledge of matters, affecting my three friends, might have led to disclosures, or inferences, that would perhaps have been serviceable. I was particularly struck with the fact, that, ever since the appearance of Priscilla, it had been the tendency of events to suggest and establish a connection between Zenobia and her. She had come, in the first instance, as if with the sole purpose of claiming Zenobia's protection. Old Moodie's visit, it appeared, was chiefly to ascertain whether this object had been accomplished. And here, to-day, was the questionable Professor, linking one with the other in his inquiries, and seeking communication with both.

Meanwhile, my inclination for a ramble having been baulked, I lingered in the vicinity of the farm, with perhaps a vague idea that some new event would grow out of Wester-velt's proposed interview with Zenobia. My own part, in these transactions, was singularly subordinate. It resembled that of the Chorus in a classic play, which seems to be set aloof from the possibility of personal concernment, and be-stows the whole measure of its hope or fear, its exultation or sorrow, on the fortunes of others, between whom and itself this sympathy is the only bond. Destiny, it may be—the most skilful of stage-managers—seldom chooses to arrange its scenes, and carry forward its drama, without securing the presence of at least one calm observer. It is his office to give applause, when due, and sometimes an inevitable tear, to detect the final fitness of incident to character, and distil, in his long-brooding thought, the whole morality of the performance.

Not to be out of the way, in case there were need of me in my vocation, and, at the same time, to avoid thrusting myself where neither Destiny nor mortals might desire my presence, I remained pretty near the verge of the woodlands. My position was off the track of Zenobia's customary walk, yet not so remote but that a recognized occasion might speedily have brought me thither.

XII

COVERDALE'S HERMITAGE

LONG since, in this part of our circumjacent wood, I had found out for myself a little hermitage. It was a kind of leafy cave, high upward into the air, among the midmost branches of a white-pine tree. A wild grape-vine, of unusual size and luxuriance, had twined and twisted itself up into the tree, and, after wreathing the entanglement of its tendrils around almost every bough, had caught hold of three or four neighboring trees, and married the whole clump with a perfectly inextricable knot of polygamy. Once, while sheltering myself from a summer shower, the fancy had taken me to clamber up into this seemingly impervious mass of foliage. The branches yielded me a passage, and closed again, beneath, as if only a squirrel or a bird had passed. Far aloft, around the stem of the central pine, behold, a perfect nest for Robinson Crusoe or King Charles![4] A hollow chamber, of rare seclusion, had been formed by the decay

4. In Daniel Defoe's *Robinson Crusoe* (1719), the title character looks for ships from a platform in a tree; Charles II, after losing the battle of Worcester (September 3, 1651), escaped Cromwell's troops by hiding in an oak tree.

of some of the pine-branches, which the vine had lovingly strangled with its embrace, burying them from the light of day in an aerial sepulchre of its own leaves. It cost me but little ingenuity to enlarge the interior, and open loop-holes through the verdant walls. Had it ever been my fortune to spend a honey-moon, I should have thought seriously of inviting my bride up thither, where our next neighbors would have been two orioles in another part of the clump.

It was an admirable place to make verses, tuning the rhythm to the breezy symphony that so often stirred among the vine-leaves; or to meditate an essay for the Dial, in which the many tongues of Nature whispered mysteries, and seemed to ask only a little stronger puff of wind, to speak out the solution of its riddle. Being so pervious to air-currents, it was just the nook, too, for the enjoyment of a cigar. This hermitage was my one exclusive possession, while I counted myself a brother of the socialists. It symbolized my individuality, and aided me in keeping it inviolate. None ever found me out in it, except, once, a squirrel. I brought thither no guest, because, after Hollingsworth failed me, there was no longer the man alive with whom I could think of sharing all. So there I used to sit, owl-like, yet not without liberal and hospitable thoughts. I counted the innumerable clusters of my vine, and fore-reckoned the abundance of my vintage. It gladdened me to anticipate the surprise of the Community, when, like an allegorical figure of rich October, I should make my appearance, with shoulders bent beneath the burthen of ripe grapes, and some of the crushed ones crimsoning my brow as with a blood-stain.[5]

Ascending into this natural turret, I peeped, in turn, out of several of its small windows. The pine-tree, being ancient, rose high above the rest of the wood, which was of comparatively recent growth. Even where I sat, about midway between the root and the topmost bough, my position was

5. Alludes to the figure of October in   (1590, 1596), VII, vii, 39.
Edmund Spenser's *The Faerie Queen*

lofty enough to serve as an observatory, not for starry investigations, but for those sublunary matters in which lay a lore as infinite as that of the planets. Through one loop-hole, I saw the river lapsing calmly onward, while, in the meadow near its brink, a few of the brethren were digging peat for our winter's fuel. On the interior cart-road of our farm, I discerned Hollingsworth, with a yoke of oxen hitched to a drag of stones, that were to be piled into a fence, on which we employed ourselves at the odd intervals of other labor. The harsh tones of his voice, shouting to the sluggish steers, made me sensible, even at such a distance, that he was ill at ease, and that the baulked philanthropist had the battle-spirit in his heart.

"Haw Buck!" quoth he. "Come along there, ye lazy ones! What are ye about now? Gee!"

"Mankind, in Hollingsworth's opinion," thought I, "is but another yoke of oxen, as stubborn, stupid, and sluggish, as our old Brown and Bright. He vituperates us aloud, and curses us in his heart, and will begin to prick us with the goad stick, by-and-by. But, are we his oxen? And what right has he to be the driver? And why, when there is enough else to do, should we waste our strength in dragging home the ponderous load of his philanthropic absurdities? At my height above the earth, the whole matter looks ridiculous!"

Turning towards the farm-house, I saw Priscilla (for, though a great way off, the eye of faith assured me that it was she) sitting at Zenobia's window, and making little purses, I suppose, or perhaps mending the Community's old linen. A bird flew past my tree; and as it clove its way onward into the sunny atmosphere, I flung it a message for Priscilla.

"Tell her," said I, "that her fragile thread of life has inextricably knotted itself with other and tougher threads, and most likely it will be broken. Tell her that Zenobia will not be long her friend. Say that Hollingsworth's heart is on fire with his own purpose, but icy for all human affection, and that, if she has given him her love, it is like casting a flower into a sepulchre. And say, that, if any mortal really cares for her, it is myself, and not even I, for her realities—poor little seamstress, as Zenobia rightly called her!—but for the fancy-work with which I have idly decked her out!"

The pleasant scent of the wood, evolved by the hot sun, stole up to my nostrils, as if I had been an idol in its niche. Many trees mingled their fragrance into a thousand-fold odor. Possibly, there was a sensual influence in the broad light of noon that lay beneath me. It may have been the cause, in part, that I suddenly found myself possessed by a mood of disbelief in moral beauty or heroism, and a conviction of the folly of attempting to benefit the world. Our especial scheme of reform, which, from my observatory, I could take in with the bodily eye, looked so ridiculous that it was impossible not to laugh aloud.

"But the joke is a little too heavy," thought I. "If I were wise, I should get out of the scrape, with all diligence, and then laugh at my companions for remaining in it!"

While thus musing, I heard, with perfect distinctness, somewhere in the wood beneath, the peculiar laugh, which I have described as one of the disagreeable characteristics of Professor Westervelt. It brought my thoughts back to our recent interview. I recognized, as chiefly due to this man's influence, the sceptical and sneering view which, just now, had filled my mental vision in regard to all life's better purposes. And it was through his eyes, more than my own, that I was looking at Hollingsworth, with his glorious, if impracticable dream, and at the noble earthliness of Zenobia's character, and even at Priscilla, whose impalpable grace lay so singularly between disease and beauty. The essential charm of each had vanished. There are some spheres, the contact with which inevitably degrades the high, debases the pure, deforms the beautiful. It must be a mind of uncommon strength, and little impressibility, that can permit itself the habit of such intercourse, and not be permanently deterio-rated; and yet the Professor's tone represented that of worldly society at large, where a cold scepticism smothers what it can of our spiritual aspirations, and makes the rest ridiculous. I detested this kind of man, and all the more, because a part of my own nature showed itself responsive to him.

Voices were now approaching, through the region of the wood which lay in the vicinity of my tree. Soon, I caught glimpses of two figures—a woman and a man—Zenobia and the stranger—earnestly talking together as they advanced.

Zenobia had a rich, though varying color. It was, most of the while, a flame, and anon a sudden paleness. Her eyes glowed, so that their light sometimes flashed upward to me, as when the sun throws a dazzle from some bright object on the ground. Her gestures were free, and strikingly impressive. The whole woman was alive with a passionate intensity, which I now perceived to be the phase in which her beauty culminated. Any passion would have become her well, and passionate love, perhaps, the best of all. This was not love, but anger, largely intermixed with scorn. Yet the idea strangely forced itself upon me, that there was a sort of familiarity between these two companions, necessarily the result of an intimate love—on Zenobia's part, at least—in days gone by, but which had prolonged itself into as intimate a hatred, for all futurity. As they passed among the trees, reckless as her movement was, she took good heed that even the hem of her garment should not brush against the stranger's person. I wondered whether there had always been a chasm, guarded so religiously, betwixt these two.

As for Westervelt, he was not a whit more warmed by Zenobia's passion, than a salamander by the heat of its native furnace.[6] He would have been absolutely statuesque, save for a look of slight perplexity tinctured strongly with derision. It was a crisis in which his intellectual perceptions could not altogether help him out. He failed to comprehend, and cared but little for comprehending, why Zenobia should put herself

6. Refers to the ancient belief that sala-   could withstand the action of fire.
manders were so cold-blooded that they

into such a fume; but satisfied his mind that it was all folly, and only another shape of a woman's manifold absurdity, which men can never understand. How many a woman's evil fate has yoked her with a man like this! Nature thrusts some of us into the world miserably incomplete, on the emotional side, with hardly any sensibilities except what pertain to us as animals. No passion, save of the senses; no holy tenderness, nor the delicacy that results from this. Externally, they bear a close resemblance to other men, and have perhaps all save the finest grace; but when a woman wrecks herself on such a being, she ultimately finds that the real womanhood, within her, has no corresponding part in him. Her deepest voice lacks a response; the deeper her cry, the more dead his silence. The fault may be none of his; he cannot give her what never lived within his soul. But the wretchedness, on her side, and the moral deterioration attendant on a false and shallow life, without strength enough to keep itself sweet, are among the most pitiable wrongs that mortals suffer.

Now, as I looked down from my upper region at this man and woman—outwardly so fair a sight, and wandering like two lovers in the wood—I imagined that Zenobia, at an earlier period of youth, might have fallen into the misfortune above indicated. And when her passionate womanhood, as was inevitable, had discovered its mistake, there had ensued the character of eccentricity and defiance, which distinguished the more public portion of her life.

Seeing how aptly matters had chanced, thus far, I began to think it the design of fate to let me into all Zenobia's secrets, and that therefore the couple would sit down beneath my tree, and carry on a conversation which would leave me nothing to inquire. No doubt, however, had it so happened, I should have deemed myself honorably bound to warn them of a listener's presence by flinging down a handful of unripe grapes; or by sending an unearthly groan out of my hiding-

place, as if this were one of the trees of Dante's ghostly forest.[7]
But real life never arranges itself exactly like a romance.
In the first place, they did not sit down at all. Secondly,
even while they passed beneath the tree, Zenobia's utterance
was so hasty and broken, and Westervelt's so cool and low,
that I hardly could make out an intelligible sentence, on
either side. What I seem to remember, I yet suspect may
have been patched together by my fancy, in brooding over
the matter, afterwards.

"Why not fling the girl off," said Westervelt, "and let
her go?"

"She clung to me from the first," replied Zenobia. "I neither
know nor care what it is in me that so attaches her. But she
loves me, and I will not fail her."

"She will plague you, then," said he, "in more ways
than one."

"The poor child!" exclaimed Zenobia. "She can do me
neither good nor harm. How should she?"

I know not what reply Westervelt whispered; nor did
Zenobia's subsequent exclamation give me any clue, except
that it evidently inspired her with horror and disgust.

"With what kind of a being am I linked!" cried she. "If
my Creator cares aught for my soul, let him release me from
this miserable bond!"

"I did not think it weighed so heavily," said her companion.

"Nevertheless," answered Zenobia, "it will strangle me
at last!"

And then I heard her utter a helpless sort of moan; a sound
which, struggling out of the heart of a person of her pride
and strength, affected me more than if she had made the
wood dolorously vocal with a thousand shrieks and wails.

Other mysterious words, besides what are above-written,

7. The "dark wood" in which Dante wanders at the opening of the *Inferno*.

they spoke together; but I understood no more, and even question whether I fairly understood so much as this. By long brooding over our recollections, we subtilize them into something akin to imaginary stuff, and hardly capable of being distinguished from it. In a few moments, they were completely beyond ear-shot. A breeze stirred after them, and awoke the leafy tongues of the surrounding trees, which forthwith began to babble, as if innumerable gossips had all at once got wind of Zenobia's secret. But, as the breeze grew stronger, its voice among the branches was as if it said—'Hush! Hush!'—and I resolved that to no mortal would I disclose what I had heard. And, though there might be room for casuistry, such, I conceive, is the most equitable rule in all similar conjunctures.

XIII

ZENOBIA'S LEGEND

THE illustrious Society of Blithedale, though it toiled in downright earnest for the good of mankind, yet not unfrequently illuminated its laborious life with an afternoon or evening of pastime. Pic-nics under the trees were considerably in vogue; and, within doors, fragmentary bits of theatrical performance, such as single acts of tragedy or comedy, or dramatic proverbs and charades. Zenobia, besides, was fond of giving us readings from Shakspeare, and often with a depth of tragic power, or breadth of comic effect, that made one feel it an intolerable wrong to the world, that she did not at once go upon the stage. *Tableaux vivants*[8] were another of our occasional modes of amusement, in which scarlet shawls, old silken robes, ruffs, velvets, furs, and all kinds of miscellaneous trumpery, converted our familiar companions into the people of a pictorial world. We had been

8. A static depiction of a scene.

thus engaged, on the evening after the incident narrated in the last chapter. Several splendid works of art—either arranged after engravings from the Old Masters,[9] or original illustrations of scenes in history or romance—had been presented, and we were earnestly entreating Zenobia for more.

She stood, with a meditative air, holding a large piece of gauze, or some such ethereal stuff, as if considering what picture should next occupy the frame; while at her feet lay a heap of many-colored garments, which her quick fancy and magic skill could so easily convert into gorgeous draperies for heroes and princesses.

"I am getting weary of this," said she, after a moment's thought. "Our own features, and our own figures and airs, show a little too intrusively through all the characters we assume. We have so much familiarity with one another's realities, that we cannot remove ourselves, at pleasure, into an imaginary sphere. Let us have no more pictures, to-night; but, to make you what poor amends I can, how would you like to have me trump up a wild, spectral legend, on the spur of the moment?"

Zenobia had the gift of telling a fanciful little story, off hand, in a way that made it greatly more effective, than it was usually found to be, when she afterwards elaborated the same production with her pen. Her proposal, therefore, was greeted with acclamation.

"Oh, a story, a story, by all means!" cried the young girls. "No matter how marvellous, we will believe it, every word! And let it be a ghost-story, if you please!"

"No; not exactly a ghost-story," answered Zenobia; "but something so nearly like it that you shall hardly tell the difference. And, Priscilla, stand you before me, where I may look at you, and get my inspiration out of your eyes. They are very deep and dreamy, to-night!"

I know not whether the following version of her story will retain any portion of its pristine character. But, as Zenobia told it, wildly and rapidly, hesitating at no extravagance, and

9. Distinguished European artists who lived before the eighteenth century.

dashing at absurdities which I am too timorous to repeat—
giving it the varied emphasis of her inimitable voice, and the
pictorial illustration of her mobile face, while, through it all,
we caught the freshest aroma of the thoughts, as they came
bubbling out of her mind—thus narrated, and thus heard,
the legend seemed quite a remarkable affair. I scarcely knew,
at the time, whether she intended us to laugh, or be more
seriously impressed. From beginning to end it was undeniable
nonsense, but not necessarily the worse for that.

THE SILVERY VEIL

You have heard, my dear friends, of the Veiled Lady,
who grew suddenly so very famous, a few months ago. And
have you never thought how remarkable it was, that this
marvellous creature should vanish, all at once, while her
renown was on the increase, before the public had grown
weary of her, and when the enigma of her character, instead
of being solved, presented itself more mystically at every exhibition? Her last appearance, as you know, was before a
crowded audience. The next evening—although the bills
had announced her, at the corner of every street, in red letters
of a gigantic size—there was no Veiled Lady to be seen! Now,
listen to my simple little tale; and you shall hear the very
latest incident in the known life—(if life it may be called,
which seemed to have no more reality than the candlelight
image of one's self, which peeps at us outside of a dark
window-pane)—the life of this shadowy phenomenon.

A party of young gentlemen, you are to understand, were
enjoying themselves, one afternoon, as young gentlemen are
sometimes fond of doing, over a bottle or two of champagne;
and—among other ladies less mysterious—the subject of the
Veiled Lady, as was very natural, happened to come up before
them for discussion. She rose, as it were, with the sparkling
effervescence of their wine, and appeared in a more airy and
fantastic light, on account of the medium through which they
saw her. They repeated to one another, between jest and
earnest, all the wild stories that were in vogue; nor, I presume,

did they hesitate to add any small circumstance that the inventive whim of the moment might suggest, to heighten the marvellousness of their theme.

"But what an audacious report was that," observed one, "which pretended to assert the identity of this strange creature with a young lady"—and here he mentioned her name—"the daughter of one of our most distinguished families!"

"Ah, there is more in that story than can well be accounted for!" remarked another. "I have it on good authority, that the young lady in question is invariably out of sight, and not to be traced, even by her own family, at the hours when the Veiled Lady is before the public; nor can any satisfactory explanation be given of her disappearance. And just look at the thing! Her brother is a young fellow of spirit. He cannot but be aware of these rumors in reference to his sister. Why, then, does he not come forward to defend her character, unless he is conscious that an investigation would only make the matter worse?"

It is essential to the purposes of my legend to distinguish one of these young gentlemen from his companions; so, for the sake of a soft and pretty name, (such as we, of the literary sisterhood, invariably bestow upon our heroes,) I deem it fit to call him 'Theodore.'

"Pshaw!" exclaimed Theodore. "Her brother is no such fool! Nobody, unless his brain be as full of bubbles as this wine, can seriously think of crediting that ridiculous rumor. Why, if my senses did not play me false, (which never was the case yet,) I affirm that I saw that very lady, last evening, at the exhibition, while this veiled phenomenon was playing off her juggling tricks! What can you say to that?"

"Oh, it was a spectral illusion that you saw!" replied his friends, with a general laugh. "The Veiled Lady is quite up to such a thing."

However, as the above-mentioned fable could not hold its ground against Theodore's downright refutation, they went on to speak of other stories, which the wild babble of the town had set afloat. Some upheld, that the veil covered the most beautiful countenance in the world; others—and certainly with more reason, considering the sex of the Veiled Lady—that the face was the most hideous and horrible, and that this was her sole motive for hiding it. It was the face of a corpse; it was the head of a skeleton; it was a monstrous visage, with snaky locks, like Medusa's,[1] and one great red eye in the centre of the forehead. Again, it was affirmed, that there was no single and unchangeable set of features, beneath the veil, but that whosoever should be bold enough to lift it, would behold the features of that person, in all the world, who was destined to be his fate; perhaps he would be greeted by the tender smile of the woman whom he loved; or, quite as probably, the deadly scowl of his bitterest enemy would throw a blight over his life. They quoted, moreover, this startling explanation of the whole affair:—that the Magician (who exhibited the Veiled Lady, and who, by-the-by, was the handsomest man in the whole world) had bartered his own soul for seven years' possession of a familiar fiend, and that the last year of the contract was wearing towards its close.

If it were worth our while, I could keep you till an hour beyond midnight, listening to a thousand such absurdities as these. But, finally, our friend Theodore, who prided himself upon his common-sense, found the matter getting quite beyond his patience.

"I offer any wager you like," cried he, setting down his glass so forcibly as to break the stem of it, "that, this very evening, I find out the mystery of the Veiled Lady!"

Young men, I am told, boggle at nothing, over their wine. So, after a little more talk, a wager of considerable amount was actually laid, the money staked, and Theodore left to choose his own method of settling the dispute.

How he managed it, I know not, nor is it of any great importance to this veracious legend; the most natural way, to be sure, was by bribing the door-keeper, or, possibly, he pre-

1. A terrible monster in Greek mythology who had snakes instead of hair on her head.

ferred clambering in at the window. But, at any rate, that very evening, while the exhibition was going forward in the hall, Theodore contrived to gain admittance into the private with-drawing-room, whither the Veiled Lady was accustomed to retire, at the close of her performances. There he waited, listening, I suppose, to the stifled hum of the great audience; and, no doubt, he could distinguish the deep tones of the Magician, causing the wonders that he wrought to appear more dark and intricate, by his mystic pretence of an explana-tion; perhaps, too, in the intervals of the wild, breezy music which accompanied the exhibition, he might hear the low voice of the Veiled Lady, conveying her Sibylline responses. Firm as Theodore's nerves might be, and much as he prided himself on his sturdy perception of realities, I should not be surprised if his heart throbbed at a little more than its ordinary rate!

Theodore concealed himself behind a screen. In due time, the performance was brought to a close; and whether the door was softly opened, or whether her bodiless presence came through the wall, is more than I can say; but, all at once, without the young man's knowing how it happened, a veiled figure stood in the centre of the room. It was one thing to be in presence of this mystery, in the hall of exhibition, where the warm, dense life of hundreds of other mortals kept up the beholder's courage, and distributed her influence among so many; it was another thing to be quite alone with her, and that, too, with a hostile, or, at least, an unauthorized and unjustifiable purpose. I rather imagine that Theodore now began to be sensible of something more serious in his enterprise than he had been quite aware of, while he sat with his boon-companions over their sparkling wine.

Very strange, it must be confessed, was the movement with which the figure floated to-and-fro over the carpet, with the silvery veil covering her from head to foot; so impalpable, so ethereal, so without substance, as the texture seemed, yet hiding her every outline in an impenetrability like that of midnight. Surely, she did not walk! She floated, and flitted, and hovered about the room;—no sound of a footstep, no perceptible motion of a limb;—it was as if a wandering breeze wafted her before it, at its own wild and gentle pleasure. But, by-and-by, a purpose began to be discernible, throughout the seeming vagueness of her unrest. She was in quest of something! Could it be, that a subtile presentiment had informed her of the young man's presence? And, if so, did the Veiled Lady seek, or did she shun him? The doubt in Theodore's mind was speedily resolved; for, after a moment or two of these erratic flutterings, she advanced, more decidedly, and stood motionless before the screen.

"Thou art here!" said a soft, low voice. "Come forth, Theodore!"

Thus summoned by his name, Theodore, as a man of courage, had no choice. He emerged from his concealment, and presented himself before the Veiled Lady, with the wine-flush, it may be, quite gone out of his cheeks.

"What wouldst thou with me?" she inquired, with the same gentle composure that was in her former utterance.

"Mysterious creature," replied Theodore, "I would know who and what you are!"

"My lips are forbidden to betray the secret!" said the Veiled Lady.

"At whatever risk, I must discover it!" rejoined Theodore.

"Then," said the Mystery, "there is no way, save to lift my veil!"

And Theodore, partly recovering his audacity, stept forward, on the instant, to do as the Veiled Lady had suggested. But she floated backward to the opposite side of the room, as if the young man's breath had possessed power enough to waft her away.

"Pause, one little instant," said the soft, low voice, "and learn the conditions of what thou art so bold to undertake! Thou canst go hence, and think of me no more; or, at thy option, thou canst lift this mysterious veil, beneath which I am a sad and lonely prisoner, in a bondage which is worse to me than death. But, before raising it, I entreat thee, in all maiden modesty, to bend forward, and impress a kiss, where my breath stirs the veil; and my virgin lips shall come forward to meet thy lips; and from that instant, Theodore, thou shalt be mine, and I thine, with never more a veil between us! And all the felicity of earth and of the future world shall be thine and mine together. So much may a maiden say behind the veil! If thou shrinkest from this, there is yet another way."

"And what is that?" asked Theodore.

"Dost thou hesitate," said the Veiled Lady, "to pledge thyself to me, by meeting these lips of mine, while the veil yet hides my face? Has not thy heart recognized me? Dost thou come hither, not in holy faith, nor with a pure and generous purpose, but in scornful scepticism and idle curiosity? Still, thou mayst lift the veil! But from that instant, Theodore, I am doomed to be thy evil fate; nor wilt thou ever taste another breath of happiness!"

There was a shade of inexpressible sadness in the utterance of these last words. But Theodore, whose natural tendency was towards scepticism, felt himself almost injured and insulted by the Veiled Lady's proposal that he should pledge himself, for life and eternity, to so questionable a creature as herself; or even that she should suggest an inconsequential kiss, taking into view the probability that her face was none of the most bewitching. A delightful idea, truly, that he should salute the lips of a dead girl, or the jaws of a skeleton, or the grinning cavity of a monster's mouth! Even should she prove a comely maiden enough, in other respects, the odds were ten to one that her teeth were defective; a terrible drawback on the delectableness of a kiss!

"Excuse me, fair lady," said Theodore—and I think he nearly burst into a laugh—"if I prefer to lift the veil first; and for this affair of the kiss, we may decide upon it, afterwards!"

"Thou hast made thy choice," said the sweet, sad voice, behind the veil; and there seemed a tender, but unresentful sense of wrong done to womanhood by the young man's contemptuous interpretation of her offer. "I must not counsel thee to pause; although thy fate is still in thine own hand!"

Grasping at the veil, he flung it upward, and caught a glimpse of a pale, lovely face, beneath; just one momentary glimpse; and then the apparition vanished, and the silvery veil fluttered slowly down, and lay upon the floor. Theodore was alone. Our legend leaves him there. His retribution was, to pine, forever and ever, for another sight of that dim, mournful face—which might have been his life-long, household, fireside joy—to desire, and waste life in a feverish quest, and never meet it more!

But what, in good sooth, had become of the Veiled Lady? Had all her existence been comprehended within that mysterious veil, and was she now annihilated? Or was she a spirit, with a heavenly essence, but which might have been tamed down to human bliss, had Theodore been brave and true enough to claim her? Hearken, my sweet friends—and hearken, dear Priscilla—and you shall learn the little more that Zenobia can tell you!

Just at the moment, so far as can be ascertained, when the Veiled Lady vanished, a maiden, pale and shadowy, rose up amid a knot of visionary people, who were seeking for the better life. She was so gentle and so sad—a nameless melancholy gave her such hold upon their sympathies—that they never thought of questioning whence she came. She might have heretofore existed; or her thin substance might have been moulded out of air, at the very instant when they first beheld her. It was all one to them; they took her to their hearts. Among them was a lady, to whom, more than to all the rest, this pale, mysterious girl attached herself.

But, one morning, the lady was wandering in the woods, and there met her a figure in an Oriental robe, with a dark beard, and holding in his hand a silvery veil. He motioned her to stay. Being a woman of some nerve, she did not shriek, nor run away, nor faint, as many ladies would have been apt to do, but stood quietly, and bade him speak. The truth was, she had seen his face before, but had never feared it, although she knew him to be a terrible magician.

"Lady," said he, with a warning gesture, "you are in peril!"

"Peril!" she exclaimed. "And of what nature?"

"There is a certain maiden," replied the Magician, "who has come out of the realm of Mystery, and made herself your most intimate companion. Now, the fates have so ordained it, that, whether by her own will, or no, this stranger is your deadliest enemy. In love, in worldly fortune, in all your pursuit of happiness, she is doomed to fling a blight over your prospects. There is but one possibility of thwarting her disastrous influence."

"Then, tell me that one method," said the lady.

"Take this veil!" he answered, holding forth the silvery texture. "It is a spell; it is a powerful enchantment, which I wrought for her sake, and beneath which she was once my prisoner. Throw it, at unawares, over the head of this secret foe, stamp your foot, and cry—'Arise, Magician, here is the Veiled Lady'—and immediately I will rise up through the earth, and seize her. And from that moment, you are safe!"

So the lady took the silvery veil, which was like woven air, or like some substance airier than nothing, and that would float upward and be lost among the clouds, were she once to let it go. Returning homeward, she found the shadowy girl, amid the knot of visionary transcendentalists, who were still seeking for the better life. She was joyous, now, and had a rose-bloom in her cheeks, and was one of the prettiest creatures, and seemed one of the happiest, that the world could show. But the lady stole noiselessly behind her, and threw the veil over her head. As the slight, ethereal texture sank inevitably down over her figure, the poor girl strove to raise it, and met her dear friend's eyes with one glance of mortal terror, and deep, deep reproach. It could not change her purpose.

"Arise, Magician!" she exclaimed, stamping her foot upon the earth. "Here is the Veiled Lady!"

At the word, uprose the bearded man in the Oriental robes—the beautiful!—the dark Magician, who had bartered away his soul! He threw his arms around the Veiled Lady; and she was his bond-slave, forever more!

Zenobia, all this while, had been holding the piece of gauze, and so managed it as greatly to increase the dramatic effect of the legend, at those points where the magic veil was to be described. Arriving at the catastrophe, and uttering the fatal words, she flung the gauze over Priscilla's head; and, for an instant, her auditors held their breath, half expecting, I verily believe, that the Magician would start up through the floor, and carry off our poor little friend, before our eyes.

As for Priscilla, she stood, droopingly, in the midst of us, making no attempt to remove the veil.

"How do you find yourself, my love?" said Zenobia, lifting a corner of the gauze, and peeping beneath it, with a mischievous smile. "Ah, the dear little soul! Why, she is really going to faint! Mr. Coverdale, Mr. Coverdale, pray bring a glass of water!"

Her nerves being none of the strongest, Priscilla hardly recovered her equanimity during the rest of the evening. This, to be sure, was a great pity; but, nevertheless, we thought it a very bright idea of Zenobia's, to bring her legend to so effective a conclusion.

XIV

ELIOT'S PULPIT

OUR SUNDAYS, at Blithedale, were not ordinarily kept with such rigid observance as might have befitted the descendants of the Pilgrims, whose high enterprise, as we sometimes flattered ourselves, we had taken up, and were carrying it onward and aloft, to a point which they never dreamed of attaining.

On that hallowed day, it is true, we rested from our labors. Our oxen, relieved from their week-day yoke, roamed at large through the pasture; each yoke-fellow, however, keeping close beside his mate, and continuing to acknowledge, from the force of habit and sluggish sympathy, the union which the taskmaster had imposed for his own hard ends. As for us, human yoke-fellows, chosen companions of toil, whose hoes had clinked together throughout the week, we wandered off, in various directions, to enjoy our interval of repose. Some, I believe, went devoutly to the village-church. Others, it may be, ascended a city or a country-pulpit, wearing the clerical robe with so much dignity that you would scarcely have suspected the yeoman's frock to have been flung off, only since milking-time. Others took long rambles among the rustic lanes and by-paths, pausing to look at black, old farm-houses, with their sloping roofs; and at the modern cottage, so like a plaything that it seemed as if real joy or sorrow could have no scope within; and at the more pretending villa, with its range of wooden columns, supporting the needless insolence of a great portico. Some betook themselves into the wide, dusky barn, and lay there, for hours together, on the odorous hay; while the sunstreaks and the shadows strove together— these to make the barn solemn, those to make it cheerful—and both were conquerors; and the swallows twittered a cheery anthem, flashing into sight, or vanishing, as they darted to-and-fro among the golden rules of sunshine. And others went a little way into the woods, and threw themselves on Mother Earth, pillowing their heads on a heap of moss, the green decay of an old log; and dropping asleep, the humble-bees and musquitoes sung and buzzed about their ears, causing the slumberers to twitch and start, without awakening.

With Hollingsworth, Zenobia, Priscilla, and myself, it grew to be a custom to spend the Sabbath-afternoon at a certain rock. It was known to us under the name of Eliot's pulpit, from a tradition that the venerable Apostle Eliot[2] had preached

2. John Eliot (1604–90), "teacher" at the church at Roxbury for almost sixty years, was known as the "Apostle to the Indians" because he preached to them in their native tongue and translated the Bible into the language of the Massachusetts Indians.

there, two centuries gone by, to an Indian auditory. The old pine-forest, through which the Apostle's voice was wont to sound, had fallen, an immemorial time ago. But the soil, being of the rudest and most broken surface, had apparently never been brought under tillage; other growths, maple, and beech, and birch, had succeeded to the primeval trees; so that it was still as wild a tract of woodland as the great-great-great-great grandson of one of Eliot's Indians (had any such posterity been in existence) could have desired, for the site and shelter of his wigwam. These after-growths, indeed, lose the stately solemnity of the original forest. If left in due neglect, however, they run into an entanglement of softer wildness, among the rustling leaves of which the sun can scatter cheerfulness, as it never could among the dark-browed pines.

The rock itself rose some twenty or thirty feet, a shattered granite boulder, or heap of boulders, with an irregular outline and many fissures, out of which sprang shrubs, bushes, and even trees; as if the scanty soil, within those crevices, were sweeter to their roots than any other earth. At the base of the pulpit, the broken boulders inclined towards each other, so as to form a shallow cave, within which our little party had sometimes found protection from a summer shower. On the threshold, or just across it, grew a tuft of pale columbines, in their season, and violets, sad and shadowy recluses, such as Priscilla was, when we first knew her; children of the sun, who had never seen their father, but dwelt among damp mosses, though not akin to them. At the summit, the rock was overshadowed by the canopy of a birch-tree, which served as a sounding-board for the pulpit. Beneath this shade, (with my eyes of sense half shut, and those of the imagination widely opened,) I used to see the holy Apostle of the Indians, with the sunlight flickering down upon him through the leaves, and glorifying his figure as with the half-perceptible glow of a transfiguration.

I the more minutely describe the rock, and this little Sabbath solitude, because Hollingsworth, at our solicitation, often ascended Eliot's pulpit, and—not exactly preached—but talked to us, his few disciples, in a strain that rose and fell as naturally as the wind's breath among the leaves of the birch-tree. No other speech of man has ever moved me like some of those discourses. It seemed most pitiful—a positive calamity to the world—that a treasury of golden thoughts should thus be scattered, by the liberal handful, down among us three, when a thousand hearers might have been the richer for them; and Hollingsworth the richer, likewise, by the sympathy of multitudes. After speaking much or little, as might happen, he would descend from his gray pulpit, and generally fling himself at full length on the ground, face downward. Meanwhile, we talked around him, on such topics as were suggested by the discourse.

Since her interview with Westervelt, Zenobia's continual inequalities of temper had been rather difficult for her friends to bear. On the first Sunday after that incident, when Hollingsworth had clambered down from Eliot's pulpit, she declaimed with great earnestness and passion, nothing short of anger, on the injustice which the world did to women, and equally to itself, by not allowing them, in freedom and honor, and with the fullest welcome, their natural utterance in public.

"It shall not always be so!" cried she. "If I live another year, I will lift up my own voice, in behalf of woman's wider liberty."

She, perhaps, saw me smile.

"What matter of ridicule do you find in this, Miles Coverdale?" exclaimed Zenobia, with a flash of anger in her eyes. "That smile, permit me to say, makes me suspicious of a low tone of feeling, and shallow thought. It is my belief—yes, and my prophecy, should I die before it happens—that, when my sex shall achieve its rights, there will be ten eloquent women, where there is now one eloquent man. Thus far, no woman in the world has ever once spoken out her whole heart and her whole mind. The mistrust and disapproval of the vast bulk of society throttles us, as with two gigantic hands at our throats! We mumble a few weak words, and leave a thousand better ones unsaid. You let us write a little, it is true, on a limited range of subjects. But the pen is not for woman. Her power is too natural and immediate. It is with the living voice, alone, that she can compel the world to recognize the light of her intellect and the depth of her heart!"

Now—though I could not well say so to Zenobia—I had not smiled from any unworthy estimate of woman, or in denial of the claims which she is beginning to put forth. What amused and puzzled me, was the fact, that women, however intellectually superior, so seldom disquiet themselves about the rights or wrongs of their sex, unless their own individual affections chance to lie in idleness, or to be ill at ease. They are not natural reformers, but become such by the pressure of exceptional misfortune. I could measure Zenobia's inward trouble, by the animosity with which she now took up the general quarrel of woman against man.

"I will give you leave, Zenobia," replied I, "to fling your utmost scorn upon me, if you ever hear me utter a sentiment unfavorable to the widest liberty which woman has yet dreamed of. I would give her all she asks, and add a great deal more, which she will not be the party to demand, but which men, if they were generous and wise, would grant of their own free motion. For instance, I should love dearly—for the next thousand years, at least—to have all government devolve into the hands of women. I hate to be ruled by my own sex; it excites my jealousy and wounds my pride. It is the iron sway of bodily force, which abases us, in our com- pelled submission. But, how sweet the free, generous courtesy, with which I would kneel before a woman-ruler!"

"Yes; if she were young and beautiful," said Zenobia, laughing. "But how if she were sixty, and a fright?"

"Ah; it is you that rate womanhood low," said I. "But let me go on. I have never found it possible to suffer a bearded priest so near my heart and conscience, as to do me any spiritual good. I blush at the very thought! Oh, in the better order of things, Heaven grant that the ministry of souls may be left in charge of women! The gates of the Blessed City will be thronged with the multitude that enter in, when that day comes! The task belongs to woman. God meant it for her. He has endowed her with the religious sentiment in its utmost depth and purity, refined from that gross, intellectual alloy, with which every masculine theologist—save only One, who merely veiled Himself in mortal and masculine shape, but was, in truth, divine—has been prone to mingle it. I have always envied the Catholics their faith in that sweet, sacred Virgin Mother, who stands between them and the Deity, intercepting somewhat of His awful splendor, but permitting His love to stream upon the worshipper, more intelligibly to human comprehension, through the medium of a woman's tenderness. Have I not said enough, Zenobia?"

"I cannot think that this is true," observed Priscilla, who had been gazing at me with great, disapproving eyes. "And I am sure I do not wish it to be true!"

"Poor child!" exclaimed Zenobia, rather contemptuously. "She is the type of womanhood, such as man has spent centuries in making it. He is never content, unless he can degrade himself by stooping towards what he loves. In denying us our rights, he betrays even more blindness to his own interests, than profligate disregard of ours!"

"Is this true?" asked Priscilla, with simplicity, turning to Hollingsworth. "Is it all true that Mr. Coverdale and Zenobia have been saying?"

"No, Priscilla," answered Hollingsworth, with his customary bluntness. "They have neither of them spoken one true word yet."

"Do you despise woman?" said Zenobia. "Ah, Hollingsworth, that would be most ungrateful!"

"Despise her?—No!" cried Hollingsworth, lifting his great shaggy head and shaking it at us, while his eyes glowed almost fiercely. "She is the most admirable handiwork of God, in her true place and character. Her place is at man's side. Her office, that of the Sympathizer; the unreserved, unquestioning Believer; the Recognition, withheld in every other manner, but given, in pity, through woman's heart, lest man should utterly lose faith in himself; the Echo of God's own voice, pronouncing—'It is well done!' All the separate action of woman is, and ever has been, and always shall be, false, foolish, vain, destructive of her own best and holiest qualities, void of every good effect, and productive of intolerable mischiefs! Man is a wretch without woman; but woman is a monster—and, thank Heaven, an almost impossible and hitherto imaginary monster—without man, as her acknowledged principal! As true as I had once a mother, whom I loved, were there any possible prospect of woman's taking the social stand which some of them—poor, miserable, abortive creatures, who only dream of such things because they have missed woman's peculiar happiness, or because Nature made them really neither man nor woman!—if there were a chance of their attaining the end which these petticoated monstrosities have in view, I would call upon my own sex to use its physical force, that unmistakeable evidence of sovereignty, to scourge them back within their proper bounds! But it will not be needful. The heart of true womanhood knows where its own sphere is, and never seeks to stray beyond it!"

Never was mortal blessed—if blessing it were—with a glance of such entire acquiescence and unquestioning faith, happy in its completeness, as our little Priscilla unconsciously bestowed on Hollingsworth. She seemed to take the sentiment from his lips into her heart, and brood over it in perfect content. The very woman whom he pictured—the gentle parasite, the soft reflection of a more powerful existence—sat there at his feet.

I looked at Zenobia, however, fully expecting her to resent —as I felt, by the indignant ebullition of my own blood, that she ought—this outrageous affirmation of what struck me as the intensity of masculine egotism. It centred everything in itself, and deprived woman of her very soul, her inexpressible and unfathomable all, to make it a mere incident in the great sum of man. Hollingsworth had boldly uttered what he, and millions of despots like him, really felt. Without intending it, he had disclosed the well-spring of all these troubled waters. Now, if ever, it surely behoved Zenobia to be the champion of her sex.

But, to my surprise, and indignation too, she only looked humbled. Some tears sparkled in her eyes, but they were wholly of grief, not anger.

"Well; be it so," was all she said. "I, at least, have deep cause to think you right. Let man be but manly and godlike, and woman is only too ready to become to him what you say!"

I smiled—somewhat bitterly, it is true—in contemplation of my own ill-luck. How little did these two women care for me, who had freely conceded all their claims, and a great deal more, out of the fulness of my heart; while Hollingsworth, by some necromancy of his horrible injustice, seemed to have brought them both to his feet!

"Women almost invariably behave thus!" thought I. "What does the fact mean? Is it their nature? Or is it, at last, the result of ages of compelled degradation? And, in either case, will it be possible ever to redeem them?"

An intuition now appeared to possess all the party, that, for this time, at least, there was no more to be said. With one accord, we arose from the ground, and made our way through the tangled undergrowth towards one of those pleasant wood-paths, that wound among the over-arching trees. Some of the branches hung so low as partly to conceal the figures that went before, from those who followed. Priscilla had leaped up more lightly than the rest of us, and ran along in advance, with as much airy activity of spirit as was typified in the motion of a bird, which chanced to be flitting from tree to tree, in the same direction as herself. Never did she seem so happy as that afternoon. She skipt, and could not help it, from very playfulness of heart.

Zenobia and Hollingsworth went next, in close contiguity, but not with arm in arm. Now, just when they had passed the impending bough of a birch-tree, I plainly saw Zenobia take the hand of Hollingsworth in both her own, press it to her bosom, and let it fall again!

The gesture was sudden and full of passion; the impulse had evidently taken her by surprise; it expressed all! Had Zenobia knelt before him, or flung herself upon his breast, and gasped out—'I love you, Hollingsworth!'—I could not have been more certain of what it meant. They then walked onward, as before. But, methought, as the declining sun threw Zenobia's magnified shadow along the path, I beheld it tremulous; and the delicate stem of the flower, which she wore in her hair, was likewise responsive to her agitation.

Priscilla—through the medium of her eyes, at least—could not possibly have been aware of the gesture above-described. Yet, at that instant, I saw her droop. The buoyancy, which just before had been so birdlike, was utterly departed; the life seemed to pass out of her, and even the substance of her figure to grow thin and gray. I almost imagined her a shadow, fading gradually into the dimness of the wood. Her pace became so slow, that Hollingsworth and Zenobia passed by, and I, without hastening my footsteps, overtook her.

"Come, Priscilla," said I, looking her intently in the face, which was very pale and sorrowful, "we must make haste after our friends. Do you feel suddenly ill? A moment ago, you flitted along so lightly that I was comparing you to a bird. Now, on the contrary, it is as if you had a heavy heart, and very little strength to bear it with. Pray take my arm!"

"No," said Priscilla, "I do not think it would help me. It is my heart, as you say, that makes me heavy; and I know not why. Just now, I felt very happy."

No doubt, it was a kind of sacrilege in me to attempt to come within her maidenly mystery. But as she appeared to be tossed aside by her other friends, or carelessly let fall, like a flower which they had done with, I could not resist the impulse to take just one peep beneath her folded petals.

"Zenobia and yourself are dear friends, of late," I remarked.

"At first—that first evening when you came to us—she did not receive you quite so warmly as might have been wished."

"I remember it," said Priscilla. "No wonder she hesitated to love me, who was then a stranger to her, and a girl of no grace or beauty; she being herself so beautiful!"

"But she loves you now, of course," suggested I. "And, at this very instant, you feel her to be your dearest friend?"

"Why do you ask me that question?" exclaimed Priscilla, as if frightened at the scrutiny into her feelings which I compelled her to make. "It somehow puts strange thoughts into my mind. But I do love Zenobia dearly! If she only loves me half as well, I shall be happy!"

"How is it possible to doubt that, Priscilla?" I rejoined. "But, observe how pleasantly and happily Zenobia and Hollingsworth are walking together! I call it a delightful spectacle. It truly rejoices me that Hollingsworth has found so fit and affectionate a friend! So many people in the world mistrust him—so many disbelieve and ridicule, while hardly any do him justice, or acknowledge him for the wonderful man he is—that it is really a blessed thing for him to have won the sympathy of such a woman as Zenobia. Any man might be proud of that. Any man, even if he be as great as Hollingsworth, might love so magnificent a woman. How very beautiful Zenobia is! And Hollingsworth knows it, too!"

There may have been some petty malice in what I said. Generosity is a very fine thing, at a proper time, and within due limits. But it is an insufferable bore, to see one man engrossing every thought of all the women, and leaving his friend to shiver in outer seclusion, without even the alternative of solacing himself with what the more fortunate individual has rejected. Yes; it was out of a foolish bitterness of heart that I had spoken.

"Go on before!" said Priscilla, abruptly, and with true feminine imperiousness, which heretofore I had never seen her exercise. "It pleases me best to loiter along by myself. I do not walk so fast as you."

With her hand, she made a little gesture of dismissal. It provoked me, yet, on the whole, was the most bewitching thing that Priscilla had ever done. I obeyed her, and strolled moodily homeward, wondering—as I had wondered a thousand times, already—how Hollingsworth meant to dispose of these two hearts, which (plainly to my perception, and, as I could not but now suppose, to his) he had engrossed into his own huge egotism.

There was likewise another subject, hardly less fruitful of speculation. In what attitude did Zenobia present herself to Hollingsworth? Was it in that of a free woman, with no mortgage on her affections nor claimant to her hand, but fully at liberty to surrender both, in exchange for the heart and hand which she apparently expected to receive? But, was it a vision that I had witnessed in the wood? Was Westervelt a goblin? Were those words of passion and agony, which Zenobia had uttered in my hearing, a mere stage-declamation? Were they formed of a material lighter than common air? Or, supposing them to bear sterling weight, was it not a perilous and dreadful wrong, which she was meditating towards herself and Hollingsworth?

Arriving nearly at the farm-house, I looked back over the long slope of pasture-land, and beheld them standing together, in the light of sunset, just on the spot where, according to the gossip of the Community, they meant to build their cottage. Priscilla, alone and forgotten, was lingering in the shadow of the wood.

XV

A CRISIS

THUS the summer was passing away; a summer of toil, of interest, of something that was not pleasure, but which went deep into my heart, and there became a rich experience. I found myself looking forward to years, if not to a lifetime, to be spent on the same system. The Community were now beginning to form their permanent plans. One of our purposes was to erect a Phalanstery (as I think we called it, after Fourier; but the phraseology of those days is not very fresh in my remembrance) where the great and general family should have its abiding-place. Individual members, too, who made it a point of religion to preserve the sanctity of an exclusive home, were selecting sites for their cottages, by the wood-side, or on the breezy swells, or in the sheltered nook of some little valley, according as their taste might lean towards snugness or the picturesque. Altogether, by projecting our minds outward, we had imparted a show of novelty to existence, and contemplated it as hopefully as if the soil, beneath our feet, had not been fathom-deep with the dust of deluded generations, on every one of which, as on ourselves, the world had imposed itself as a hitherto unwedded bride.

Hollingsworth and myself had often discussed these prospects. It was easy to perceive, however, that he spoke with little or no fervor, but either as questioning the fulfilment of our anticipations, or, at any rate, with a quiet consciousness that it was no personal concern of his. Shortly after the scene at Eliot's pulpit, while he and I were repairing an old stone-fence, I amused myself with sallying forward into the future time.

"When we come to be old men," I said, "they will call us Uncles, or Fathers—Father Hollingsworth and Uncle Coverdale—and we will look back cheerfully to these early days, and make a romantic story for the young people (and if a little more romantic than truth may warrant, it will be no harm) out of our severe trials and hardships. In a century or two, we shall every one of us be mythical personages, or exceedingly picturesque and poetical ones, at all events. They will have a great public hall, in which your portrait, and mine, and twenty other faces that are living now, shall be hung up; and as for me, I will be painted in my shirt-sleeves, and with the sleeves rolled up, to show my muscular development. What stories will be rife among them about our mighty strength," continued I, lifting a big stone and putting it into its place; "though our posterity will really be far stronger than ourselves, after several generations of a simple, natural, and active life! What legends of Zenobia's beauty, and Priscilla's slender and shadowy grace, and those mysterious qualities which make her seem diaphanous with spiritual light! In due course of ages, we must all figure heroically in an Epic Poem; and we will ourselves—at least, I will—bend unseen over the future poet, and lend him inspiration, while he writes it."

"You seem," said Hollingsworth, "to be trying how much nonsense you can pour out in a breath."

"I wish you would see fit to comprehend," retorted I, "that the profoundest wisdom must be mingled with nine-tenths of nonsense; else it is not worth the breath that utters it. But I do long for the cottages to be built, that the creeping plants may begin to run over them, and the moss to gather on the walls, and the trees—which we will set out—to cover them with a breadth of shadow. This spick-and-span novelty does not quite suit my taste. It is time, too, for children to be born among us. The first-born child is still to come! And I shall never feel as if this were a real, practical, as well as poetical, system of human life, until somebody has sanctified it by death."

"A pretty occasion for martyrdom, truly!" said Hollingsworth.

"As good as any other!" I replied. "I wonder, Hollingsworth, who, of all these strong men, and fair women and maidens, is doomed the first to die. Would it not be well, even before we have absolute need of it, to fix upon a spot for a cemetery? Let us choose the rudest, roughest, most uncultivable spot, for Death's garden-ground; and Death shall teach us to beautify it, grave by grave. By our sweet, calm way of dying, and the airy elegance out of which we will shape our funeral rites, and the cheerful allegories[3] which we will model into tombstones, the final scene shall lose its terrors; so that, hereafter, it may be happiness to live, and bliss to die. None of us must die young. Yet, should Providence ordain it so, the event shall not be sorrowful, but affect us with a tender, delicious, only half-melancholy, and almost smiling pathos!"

"That is to say," muttered Hollingsworth, "you will die like a Heathen, as you certainly live like one! But, listen to me, Coverdale. Your fantastic anticipations make me discern, all the more forcibly, what a wretched, unsubstantial scheme is this, on which we have wasted a precious summer of our lives. Do you seriously imagine that any such realities as you, and many others here, have dreamed of, will ever be brought to pass?"

"Certainly, I do," said I. "Of course, when the reality comes, it will wear the every-day, common-place, dusty, and rather homely garb, that reality always does put on. But, setting aside the ideal charm, I hold, that our highest anticipations have a solid footing on common-sense."

"You only half believe what you say," rejoined Hollingsworth; "and as for me, I neither have faith in your dream, nor would care the value of this pebble for its realization, were that possible. And what more do you want of it? It has given you a theme for poetry. Let that content you. But, now, I ask you to be, at last, a man of sobriety and earnestness, and aid me in an enterprise which is worth all our strength, and the strength of a thousand mightier than we!"

3. Emblems; drawings or pictures expressing moral fables or allegories.

There can be no need of giving, in detail, the conversation that ensued. It is enough to say, that Hollingsworth once more brought forward his rigid and unconquerable idea; a scheme for the reformation of the wicked by methods moral, intellectual, and industrial, by the sympathy of pure, humble, and yet exalted minds, and by opening to his pupils the possibility of a worthier life than that which had become their fate. It appeared, unless he over-estimated his own means, that Hollingsworth held it at his choice (and he did so choose) to obtain possession of the very ground on which we had planted our Community, and which had not yet been made irrevocably ours, by purchase. It was just the foundation that he desired. Our beginnings might readily be adapted to his great end. The arrangements, already completed, would work quietly into his system. So plausible looked his theory, and, more than that, so practical; such an air of reasonableness had he, by patient thought, thrown over it; each segment of it was contrived to dove-tail into all the rest, with such a complicated applicability; and so ready was he with a response for every objection—that, really, so far as logic and argument went, he had the matter all his own way.

"But," said I, "whence can you, having no means of your own, derive the enormous capital which is essential to this experiment? State-street,[4] I imagine, would not draw its purse-strings very liberally, in aid of such a speculation."

"I have the funds—as much, at least, as is needed for a commencement—at command," he answered. "They can be produced within a month, if necessary."

My thoughts reverted to Zenobia. It could only be her wealth which Hollingsworth was appropriating so lavishly. And on what conditions was it to be had? Did she fling it into the scheme, with the uncalculating generosity that characterizes a woman, when it is her impulse to be generous at all? And did she fling herself along with it? But Hollingsworth did not volunteer an explanation.

4. The financial center of Boston.

"And have you no regrets," I inquired, "in overthrowing this fair system of our new life, which has been planned so deeply, and is now beginning to flourish so hopefully around us? How beautiful it is, and, so far as we can yet see, how practicable! The Ages have waited for us, and here we are— the very first that have essayed to carry on our mortal exist- ence, in love, and mutual help! Hollingsworth, I would be loth to take the ruin of this enterprise upon my conscience!"

"Then let it rest wholly upon mine!" he answered, knit- ting his black brows. "I see through the system. It is full of defects—irremediable and damning ones!—from first to last, there is nothing else! I grasp it in my hand, and find no substance whatever. There is not human nature in it!"

"Why are you so secret in your operations?" I asked. "God forbid that I should accuse you of intentional wrong; but the besetting sin of a philanthropist, it appears to me, is apt to be a moral obliquity. His sense of honor ceases to be the sense of other honorable men. At some point of his course—I know not exactly when nor where—he is tempted to palter with the right, and can scarcely forbear persuading himself that the importance of his public ends renders it allowable to throw aside his private conscience. Oh, my dear friend, beware this error! If you meditate the overthrow of this establishment, call together our companions, state your design, support it with all your eloquence, but allow them an opportunity of defending themselves!"

"It does not suit me," said Hollingsworth. "Nor is it my duty to do so."

"I think it is!" replied I.

Hollingsworth frowned; not in passion, but like Fate, inexorably.

"I will not argue the point," said he. "What I desire to know of you is—and you can tell me in one word—whether I am to look for your co-operation in this great scheme of good. Take it up with me! Be my brother in it! It offers you (what you have told me, over and over again, that you most need) a purpose in life, worthy of the extremest self-devotion

—worthy of martyrdom, should God so order it! In this view, I present it to you. You can greatly benefit mankind. Your peculiar faculties, as I shall direct them, are capable of being so wrought into this enterprise, that not one of them need lie idle. Strike hands with me; and, from this moment, you shall never again feel the languor and vague wretchedness of an indolent or half-occupied man! There may be no more aimless beauty in your life; but, in its stead, there shall be strength, courage, immitigable will—everything that a manly and generous nature should desire! We shall succeed! We shall have done our best for this miserable world; and happiness (which never comes but incidentally) will come to us unawares!"

It seemed his intention to say no more. But, after he had quite broken off, his deep eyes filled with tears, and he held out both his hands to me.

"Coverdale," he murmured, "there is not the man in this wide world, whom I can love as I could you. Do not forsake me!"

As I look back upon this scene, through the coldness and dimness of so many years, there is still a sensation as if Hollingsworth had caught hold of my heart, and were pulling it towards him with an almost irresistible force. It is a mystery to me, how I withstood it. But, in truth, I saw in his scheme of philanthropy nothing but what was odious. A loathsomeness that was to be forever in my daily work! A great, black ugliness of sin, which he proposed to collect out of a thousand human hearts, and that we should spend our lives in an experiment of transmuting it into virtue! Had I but touched his extended hand, Hollingsworth's magnetism would perhaps have penetrated me with his own conception of all these matters. But I stood aloof. I fortified myself with doubts whether his strength of purpose had not been too gigantic for his integrity, impelling him to trample on considerations that should have been paramount to every other.

"Is Zenobia to take a part in your enterprise?" I asked.

"She is," said Hollingsworth.

"She!—the beautiful!—the gorgeous!" I exclaimed. "And how have you prevailed with such a woman to work in this squalid element?"

"Through no base methods, as you seem to suspect," he answered, "but by addressing whatever is best and noblest in her."

Hollingsworth was looking on the ground. But, as he often did so—generally, indeed, in his habitual moods of thought—I could not judge whether it was from any special unwillingness now to meet my eyes. What it was that dictated my next question, I cannot precisely say. Nevertheless, it rose so inevitably into my mouth, and, as it were, asked itself, so involuntarily, that there must needs have been an aptness in it.

"What is to become of Priscilla?"

Hollingsworth looked at me fiercely, and with glowing eyes. He could not have shown any other kind of expression than that, had he meant to strike me with a sword.

"Why do you bring in the names of these women?" said he, after a moment of pregnant silence. "What have they to do with the proposal which I make you? I must have your answer! Will you devote yourself, and sacrifice all to this great end, and be my friend of friends, forever?"

"In Heaven's name, Hollingsworth," cried I, getting angry, and glad to be angry, because so only was it possible to oppose his tremendous concentrativeness and indomitable will, "cannot you conceive that a man may wish well to the world, and struggle for its good, on some other plan than precisely that which you have laid down? And will you cast off a friend, for no unworthiness, but merely because he stands upon his right, as an individual being, and looks at matters through his own optics, instead of yours?"

"Be with me," said Hollingsworth, "or be against me! There is no third choice for you."

"Take this, then, as my decision," I answered. "I doubt the wisdom of your scheme. Furthermore, I greatly fear that the methods, by which you allow yourself to pursue it, are such as cannot stand the scrutiny of an unbiassed conscience."

"And you will not join me?"

"No!"

I never said the word—and certainly can never have it to say, hereafter—that cost me a thousandth part so hard an effort as did that one syllable. The heart-pang was not merely figurative, but an absolute torture of the breast. I was gazing steadfastly at Hollingsworth. It seemed to me that it struck him, too, like a bullet. A ghastly paleness—always so terrific on a swarthy face—overspread his features. There was a convulsive movement of his throat, as if he were forcing down some words that struggled and fought for utterance. Whether words of anger, or words of grief, I cannot tell; although, many and many a time, I have vainly tormented myself with conjecturing which of the two they were. One other appeal to my friendship—such as once, already, Hollingsworth had made—taking me in the revulsion that followed a strenuous exercise of opposing will, would completely have subdued me. But he left the matter there.

"Well!" said he.

And that was all! I should have been thankful for one word more, even had it shot me through the heart, as mine did him. But he did not speak it; and, after a few moments, with one accord, we set to work again, repairing the stone-fence. Hollingsworth, I observed, wrought like a Titan;[5] and, for my own part, I lifted stones which, at this day—or, in a calmer mood, at that one—I should no more have thought it possible to stir, than to carry off the gates of Gaza on my back.[6]

5. One of the primordial gods (children of Father Heaven and Mother Earth) who were deposed by the Olympian gods led by Zeus.
6. When Samson, ruler of Israel, visited a harlot in Gaza, the Philistines locked the city gates so they could kill him in the morning; at midnight, however, Samson simply picked up the gates and carried them to the top of a nearby hill (Judges XVI, 1–3).

XVI

LEAVE-TAKINGS

A FEW DAYS after the tragic passage-at-arms between Hollingsworth and me, I appeared at the dinner-table, actually dressed in a coat, instead of my customary blouse; with a satin cravat, too, a white vest, and several other things that made me seem strange and outlandish to myself. As for my companions, this unwonted spectacle caused a great stir upon the wooden benches, that bordered either side of our homely board.

"What's in the wind now, Miles?" asked one of them. "Are you deserting us?"

"Yes, for a week or two," said I. "It strikes me that my health demands a little relaxation of labor, and a short visit to the seaside, during the dog-days."

"You look like it!" grumbled Silas Foster, not greatly pleased with the idea of losing an efficient laborer, before the stress of the season was well over. "Now, here's a pretty fellow! His shoulders have broadened, a matter of six inches, since he came among us; he can do his day's work, if he likes, with any man or ox on the farm;—and yet he talks about going to the seashore for his health! Well, well, old woman," added he to his wife, "let me have a platefull of that pork and cabbage! I begin to feel in a very weakly way. When the others have had their turn, you and I will take a jaunt to Newport or Saratoga!"[7]

"Well, but, Mr. Foster," said I, "you must allow me to take a little breath."

"Breath!" retorted the old yeoman. "Your lungs have the play of a pair of blacksmith's bellows, already. What on earth

7. Newport (Rhode Island) and Saratoga (New York) were popular health spas and resorts in the nineteenth century.

do you want more? But go along! I understand the business. We shall never see your face here again. Here ends the reformation of the world, so far as Miles Coverdale has a hand in it!"

"By no means," I replied. "I am resolute to die in the last ditch, for the good of the cause."

"Die in a ditch!" muttered gruff Silas, with genuine Yankee intolerance of any intermission of toil, except on Sunday, the Fourth of July, the autumnal Cattle-show, Thanksgiving, or the annual Fast.[8] "Die in a ditch! I believe in my conscience you would, if there were no steadier means than your own labor to keep you out of it!"

The truth was, that an intolerable discontent and irksomeness had come over me. Blithedale was no longer what it had been. Everything was suddenly faded. The sun-burnt and arid aspect of our woods and pastures, beneath the August sky, did but imperfectly symbolize the lack of dew and moisture that, since yesterday, as it were, had blighted my fields of thought, and penetrated to the innermost and shadiest of my contemplative recesses. The change will be recognized by many, who, after a period of happiness, have endeavored to go on with the same kind of life, in the same scene, in spite of the alteration or withdrawal of some principal circumstance. They discover (what heretofore, perhaps, they had not known) that it was this which gave the bright color and vivid reality to the whole affair.

I stood on other terms than before, not only with Hollingsworth, but with Zenobia and Priscilla. As regarded the two latter, it was that dreamlike and miserable sort of change that denies you the privilege to complain, because you can assert no positive injury, nor lay your finger on anything tangible. It is a matter which you do not see, but feel, and which, when you try to analyze it, seems to lose its very existence, and resolve itself into a sickly humor of your own. Your understanding, possibly, may put faith in this denial. But your

---

8. A day set aside by some New England colonies and states as a holiday for fasting and prayer.

heart will not so easily rest satisfied. It incessantly remon-
strates, though, most of the time, in a bass-note, which you do
not separately distinguish; but, now-and-then, with a sharp
cry, importunate to be heard, and resolute to claim belief.
'Things are not as they were!'—it keeps saying—'You shall not
impose on me! I will never be quiet! I will throb painfully!
I will be heavy, and desolate, and shiver with cold! For I, your
deep heart, know when to be miserable, as once I knew when
to be happy! All is changed for us! You are beloved no more!'
And, were my life to be spent over again, I would invariably
lend my ear to this Cassandra[9] of the inward depths, however
clamorous the music and the merriment of a more superficial region.

My outbreak with Hollingsworth, though never definitely
known to our associates, had really an effect upon the moral
atmosphere of the Community. It was incidental to the closeness of relationship, into which we had brought ourselves,
that an unfriendly state of feeling could not occur between
any two members, without the whole society being more or
less commoted[1] and made uncomfortable thereby. This species
of nervous sympathy (though a pretty characteristic enough,
sentimentally considered, and apparently betokening an actual
bond of love among us) was yet found rather inconvenient in
its practical operation; mortal tempers being so infirm and
variable as they are. If one of us happened to give his neighbor a box on the ear, the tingle was immediately felt, on the
same side of everybody's head. Thus, even on the supposition
that we were far less quarrelsome than the rest of the world,
a great deal of time was necessarily wasted in rubbing our ears.

Musing on all these matters, I felt an inexpressible longing
for at least a temporary novelty. I thought of going across the
Rocky Mountains, or to Europe, or up the Nile—of offering
myself a volunteer on the Exploring Expedition—of taking a
ramble of years, no matter in what direction, and coming back
on the other side of the world. Then, should the colonists of

9. In Greek legend, the Trojan prophetess (usually of doom) who was never
believed.
1. Agitated.

Blithedale have established their enterprise on a permanent basis, I might fling aside my pilgrim-staff and dusty shoon,[2] and rest as peacefully here as elsewhere. Or, in case Hollingsworth should occupy the ground with his School of Reform, as he now purposed, I might plead earthly guilt enough, by that time, to give me what I was inclined to think the only trustworthy hold on his affections. Meanwhile, before deciding on any ultimate plan, I determined to remove myself to a little distance, and take an exterior view of what we had all been about.

In truth, it was dizzy work, amid such fermentation of opinions as was going on in the general brain of the Community. It was a kind of Bedlam,[3] for the time being; although, out of the very thoughts that were wildest and most destructive, might grow a wisdom, holy, calm, and pure, and that should incarnate itself with the substance of a noble and happy life. But, as matters now were, I felt myself (and having a decided tendency towards the actual, I never liked to feel it) getting quite out of my reckoning, with regard to the existing state of the world. I was beginning to lose the sense of what kind of a world it was, among innumerable schemes of what it might or ought to be. It was impossible, situated as we were, not to imbibe the idea that everything in nature and human existence was fluid, or fast becoming so; that the crust of the Earth, in many places, was broken, and its whole surface portentously upheaving; that it was a day of crisis, and that we ourselves were in the critical vortex. Our great globe floated in the atmosphere of infinite space like an unsubstantial bubble. No sagacious man will long retain his sagacity, if he live exclusively among reformers and progressive people, without periodically returning into the settled system of things, to correct himself by a new observation from that old stand-point.

It was now time for me, therefore, to go and hold a little

2. Archaic plural of "shoe."
3. Madhouse, from St. Mary of Bethlehem, a hospital for the insane in London.

talk with the conservatives, the writers of the North American Review,[4] the merchants, the politicians, the Cambridge men, and all those respectable old blockheads, who still, in this intangibility and mistiness of affairs, kept a death-grip on one or two ideas which had not come into vogue since yesterday-morning.

The brethren took leave of me with cordial kindness; and as for the sisterhood, I had serious thoughts of kissing them all round, but forbore to do so, because, in all such general salutations, the penance is fully equal to the pleasure. So I kissed none of them, and nobody, to say the truth, seemed to expect it.

"Do you wish me," I said to Zenobia, "to announce, in town, and at the watering-places, your purpose to deliver a course of lectures on the rights of women?"

"Women possess no rights," said Zenobia, with a half-melancholy smile; "or, at all events, only little girls and grandmothers would have the force to exercise them."

She gave me her hand, freely and kindly, and looked at me, I thought, with a pitying expression in her eyes; nor was there any settled light of joy in them, on her own behalf, but a troubled and passionate flame, flickering and fitful.

"I regret, on the whole, that you are leaving us," she said; "and all the more, since I feel that this phase of our life is finished, and can never be lived over again. Do you know, Mr. Coverdale, that I have been several times on the point of making you my confidant, for lack of a better and wiser one? But you are too young to be my Father Confessor; and you would not thank me for treating you like one of those good little handmaidens, who share the bosom-secrets of a tragedy-queen!"

"I would at least be loyal and faithful," answered I, "and would counsel you with an honest purpose, if not wisely."

---

4. A literary and historical quarterly (1815–1939) closely associated with Harvard and the intellectual aristocracy of Boston.

"Yes," said Zenobia, "you would be only too wise—too honest. Honesty and wisdom are such a delightful pastime, at another person's expense!"

"Ah, Zenobia," I exclaimed, "if you would but let me speak!"

"By no means," she replied; "especially when you have just resumed the whole series of social conventionalisms, together with that straight-bodied coat. I would as lief open my heart to a lawyer or a clergyman! No, no, Mr. Coverdale; if I choose a counsellor, in the present aspect of my affairs, it must be either an angel or a madman; and I rather apprehend that the latter would be likeliest of the two to speak the fitting word. It needs a wild steersman when we voyage through Chaos![5] The anchor is up! Farewell!"

Priscilla, as soon as dinner was over, had betaken herself into a corner, and set to work on a little purse. As I approached her, she let her eyes rest on me, with a calm, serious look; for, with all her delicacy of nerves, there was a singular self-possession in Priscilla, and her sensibilities seemed to lie sheltered from ordinary commotion, like the water in a deep well.

"Will you give me that purse, Priscilla," said I, "as a parting keepsake?"

"Yes," she answered; "if you will wait till it is finished."

"I must not wait, even for that," I replied. "Shall I find you here, on my return?"

"I never wish to go away," said she.

"I have sometimes thought," observed I, smiling, "that you, Priscilla, are a little prophetess; or, at least, that you have spiritual intimations respecting matters which are dark to us grosser people. If that be the case, I should like to ask you what is about to happen. For I am tormented with a strong foreboding, that, were I to return even so soon as tomorrow morning, I should find everything changed. Have you any impressions of this nature?"

5. In Greek mythology, the formless nothingness of primordial matter which preceded the emergence of Night and Erebus (a division of the underworld).

"Ah, no!" said Priscilla, looking at me apprehensively. "If any such misfortune is coming, the shadow has not reached me yet. Heaven forbid! I should be glad if there might never be any change, but one summer follow another, and all just like this!"

"No summer ever came back, and no two summers ever were alike," said I, with a degree of Orphic[6] wisdom that astonished myself. "Times change, and people change; and if our hearts do not change as readily, so much the worse for us! Good bye, Priscilla!"

I gave her hand a pressure, which, I think, she neither resisted nor returned. Priscilla's heart was deep, but of small compass; it had room but for a very few dearest ones, among whom she never reckoned me.

On the door-step, I met Hollingsworth. I had a momentary impulse to hold out my hand, or, at least, to give a parting nod, but resisted both. When a real and strong affection has come to an end, it is not well to mock the sacred past with any show of those common-place civilities that belong to ordinary intercourse. Being dead henceforth to him, and he to me, there could be no propriety in our chilling one another with the touch of two corpse-like hands, or playing at looks of courtesy with eyes that were impenetrable beneath the glaze and the film. We passed, therefore, as if mutually invisible.

I can nowise explain what sort of whim, prank, or perversity it was, that, after all these leave-takings, induced me to go to the pig-stye and take leave of the swine! There they lay, buried as deeply among the straw as they could burrow, four huge black grunters, the very symbols of slothful ease and sensual comfort. They were asleep, drawing short and heavy breaths, which heaved their big sides up and down. Unclosing their eyes, however, at my approach, they looked dimly forth at the outer world, and simultaneously uttered a gentle grunt; not putting themselves to the trouble of an

6. Originally in reference to Orphism, the first Greek religion with a (real or myth-ical) founder and a written literature; here in the popular sense of oracular.

additional breath for that particular purpose, but grunting with their ordinary inhalation. They were involved, and almost stifled, and buried alive, in their own corporeal substance. The very unreadiness and oppression, wherewith these greasy citizens gained breath enough to keep their life-machinery in sluggish movement, appeared to make them only the more sensible of the ponderous and fat satisfaction of their existence. Peeping at me, an instant, out of their small, red, hardly perceptible eyes, they dropt asleep again; yet not so far asleep but that their unctuous bliss was still present to them, betwixt dream and reality.

"You must come back in season to eat part of a spare-rib," said Silas Foster, giving my hand a mighty squeeze. "I shall have these fat fellows hanging up by the heels, heads downward, pretty soon, I tell you!"

"Oh, cruel Silas, what a horrible idea!" cried I. "All the rest of us, men, women, and live-stock, save only these four porkers, are bedevilled with one grief or another; they alone are happy—and you mean to cut their throats, and eat them! It would be more for the general comfort to let them eat us; and bitter and sour morsels we should be!"

XVII

THE HOTEL

ARRIVING in town, (where my bachelor-rooms, long before this time, had received some other occupant,) I established myself, for a day or two, in a certain respectable hotel. It was situated somewhat aloof from my former track in life; my present mood inclining me to avoid most of my old companions, from whom I was now sundered by other interests, and who would have been likely enough to amuse themselves at the expense of the amateur working-man. The hotel-keeper put me into a back-room of the third story of his spacious establishment. The day was lowering, with occasional gusts of rain, and an ugly-tempered east-wind, which seemed to come right off the chill and melancholy sea, hardly mitigated by sweeping over the roofs, and amalgamating itself with the dusky element of city-smoke. All the effeminacy of past days had returned upon me at once. Summer as it still was, I ordered a coal-fire in the rusty grate, and was glad to find myself growing a little too warm with an artificial temperature.

My sensations were those of a traveller, long sojourning in remote regions, and at length sitting down again amid customs once familiar. There was a newness and an oldness, oddly combining themselves into one impression. It made me acutely sensible how strange a piece of mosaic-work had lately been wrought into my life. True; if you look at it in one way, it had been only a summer in the country. But, considered in a profounder relation, it was part of another age, a different state of society, a segment of an existence peculiar in its aims and methods, a leaf of some mysterious volume, interpolated into the current history which Time was writing off. At one moment, the very circumstances now surrounding me—my coal-fire, and the dingy room in the bustling hotel—appeared far off and intangible. The next instant, Blithedale looked vague, as if it were at a distance both in time and space, and so shadowy, that a question might be raised whether the whole affair had been anything more than the thoughts of a speculative man. I had never before experienced a mood that so robbed the actual world of its solidity. It nevertheless involved a charm, on which—a devoted epicure of my own emotions—I resolved to pause, and enjoy the moral sillabub[7] until quite dissolved away.

Whatever had been my taste for solitude and natural scenery, yet the thick, foggy, stifled element of cities, the entangled life of many men together, sordid as it was, and empty of the beautiful, took quite as strenuous a hold upon my mind. I felt

7. Literally a dessert made of wine and curdled cream; here something deliciously sweet.

as if there could never be enough of it. Each characteristic sound was too suggestive to be passed over, unnoticed. Beneath and around me, I heard the stir of the hotel; the loud voices of guests, landlord, or barkeeper; steps echoing on the staircase; the ringing of a bell, announcing arrivals or departures; the porter lumbering past my door with baggage, which he thumped down upon the floors of neighboring chambers; the lighter feet of chamber-maids scudding along the passages;—it is ridiculous to think what an interest they had for me. From the street, came the tumult of the pavements, pervading the whole house with a continual uproar, so broad and deep that only an unaccustomed ear would dwell upon it. A company of the city-soldiery, with a full military band, marched in front of the hotel, invisible to me, but stirringly audible both by its foot-tramp and the clangor of its instruments. Once or twice, all the city-bells jangled together, announcing a fire, which brought out the engine-men and their machines, like an army with its artillery rushing to battle. Hour by hour, the clocks in many steeples responded one to another. In some public hall, not a great way off, there seemed to be an exhibition of a mechanical diorama;[8] for, three times during the day, occurred a repetition of obstreperous music, winding up with the rattle of imitative cannon and musketry, and a huge final explosion. Then ensued the applause of the spectators, with clap of hands, and thump of sticks, and the energetic pounding of their heels. All this was just as valuable, in its way, as the sighing of the breeze among the birch-trees, that overshadowed Eliot's pulpit.

Yet I felt a hesitation about plunging into this muddy tide of human activity and pastime. It suited me better, for the present, to linger on the brink, or hover in the air above it. So I spent the first day, and the greater part of the second, in the laziest manner possible, in a rocking-chair, inhaling the fragrance of a series of cigars, with my legs and slippered feet horizontally disposed, and in my hand a novel, purchased

8. A scene, viewed through a small open-   changing effects.
ing, in which various lights produce

of a railroad bibliopolist.[9] The gradual waste of my cigar
accomplished itself with an easy and gentle expenditure of
breath. My book was of the dullest, yet had a sort of sluggish
flow, like that of a stream in which your boat is as often
aground as afloat. Had there been a more impetuous rush, a
more absorbing passion of the narrative, I should the sooner
have struggled out of its uneasy current, and have given myself up to the swell and subsidence of my thoughts. But, as
it was, the torpid life of the book served as an unobtrusive
accompaniment to the life within me and about me. At intervals, however, when its effect grew a little too soporific—not
for my patience, but for the possibility of keeping my eyes
open—I bestirred myself, started from the rocking-chair, and
looked out of the window.

A gray sky; the weathercock of a steeple, that rose beyond
the opposite range of buildings, pointing from the eastward;
a sprinkle of small, spiteful-looking raindrops on the window-
pane! In that ebb-tide of my energies, had I thought of ven-
turing abroad, these tokens would have checked the abortive
purpose.

After several such visits to the window, I found myself
getting pretty well acquainted with that little portion of the
backside of the universe which it presented to my view. Over
against the hotel and its adjacent houses, at the distance of
forty or fifty yards, was the rear of a range of buildings, which
appeared to be spacious, modern, and calculated for fashionable residences. The interval between was apportioned into
grass-plots, and here and there an apology for a garden, per-
taining severally to these dwellings. There were apple-trees,
and pear and peach-trees, too, the fruit on which looked
singularly large, luxuriant, and abundant; as well it might,
in a situation so warm and sheltered, and where the soil had
doubtless been enriched to a more than natural fertility. In
two or three places, grape-vines clambered upon trellises, and
bore clusters already purple, and promising the richness of

9. Bookseller.

Malta or Madeira[1] in their ripened juice. The blighting winds of our rigid climate could not molest these trees and vines; the sunshine, though descending late into this area, and too early intercepted by the height of the surrounding houses, yet lay tropically there, even when less than temperate in every other region. Dreary as was the day, the scene was illuminated by not a few sparrows and other birds, which spread their wings, and flitted and fluttered, and alighted now here, now there, and busily scratched their food out of the wormy earth. Most of these winged people seemed to have their domicile in a robust and healthy buttonwood-tree. It aspired upward, high above the roof of the houses, and spread a dense head of foliage half across the area.

There was a cat—as there invariably is, in such places—who evidently thought herself entitled to all the privileges of forest-life, in this close heart of city-conventionalisms. I watched her creeping along the low, flat roofs of the offices, descending a flight of wooden steps, gliding among the grass, and besieging the buttonwood-tree, with murderous purpose against its feathered citizens. But, after all, they were birds of city-breeding, and doubtless knew how to guard themselves against the peculiar perils of their position.

Bewitching to my fancy are all those nooks and crannies, where Nature, like a stray partridge, hides her head among the long-established haunts of men! It is likewise to be remarked, as a general rule, that there is far more of the picturesque, more truth to native and characteristic tendencies, and vastly greater suggestiveness, in the back view of a residence, whether in town or country, than in its front. The latter is always artificial; it is meant for the world's eye, and is therefore a veil and a concealment. Realities keep in the rear, and put forward an advance-guard of show and humbug. The posterior aspect of any old farm-house, behind which a railroad has unexpectedly been opened, is so different from that

---

1. Malta, an island in the Mediterranean, and Madeira, a group of islands off   Africa, are producers of fine wines.

looking upon the immemorial highway, that the spectator gets new ideas of rural life and individuality, in the puff or two of steam-breath which shoots him past the premises. In a city, the distinction between what is offered to the public, and what is kept for the family, is certainly not less striking.

But, to return to my window, at the back of the hotel. Together with a due contemplation of the fruit-trees, the grape-vines, the buttonwood-tree, the cat, the birds, and many other particulars, I failed not to study the row of fashionable dwellings to which all these appertained. Here, it must be confessed, there was a general sameness. From the upper-story to the first floor, they were so much alike that I could only conceive of the inhabitants as cut out on one identical pattern, like little wooden toy-people of German manufacture. One long, united roof, with its thousands of slates glittering in the rain, extended over the whole. After the distinctness of separate characters, to which I had recently been accustomed, it perplexed and annoyed me not to be able to resolve this combination of human interests into well-defined elements. It seemed hardly worth while for more than one of those families to be in existence; since they all had the same glimpse of the sky, all looked into the same area, all received just their equal share of sunshine through the front windows, and all listened to precisely the same noises of the street on which they bordered. Men are so much alike, in their nature, that they grow intolerable unless varied by their circumstances.

Just about this time, a waiter entered my room. The truth was, I had rung the bell and ordered a sherry-cobbler.[2]

"Can you tell me," I inquired, "what families reside in any of those houses opposite?"

"The one right opposite is a rather stylish boarding-house," said the waiter. "Two of the gentlemen-boarders keep horses at the stable of our establishment. They do things in very good style, sir, the people that live there."

I might have found out nearly as much for myself, on

---

2. A drink made with sherry, citrus juice, sugar, and cracked ice.

examining the house a little more closely. In one of the upper chambers, I saw a young man in a dressing-gown, standing before the glass and brushing his hair, for a quarter-of-an-hour together. He then spent an equal space of time in the elaborate arrangement of his cravat, and finally made his appearance in a dress-coat, which I suspected to be newly come from the tailor's, and now first put on for a dinner-party. At a window of the next story below, two children, prettily dressed, were looking out. By-and-by, a middle-aged gentleman came softly behind them, kissed the little girl, and playfully pulled the little boy's ear. It was a papa, no doubt, just come in from his counting-room or office; and anon appeared mamma, stealing as softly behind papa, as he had stolen behind the children, and laying her hand on his shoulder to surprise him. Then followed a kiss between papa and mamma, but a noiseless one; for the children did not turn their heads.

"I bless God for these good folks!" thought I to myself. "I have not seen a prettier bit of nature, in all my summer in the country, than they have shown me here in a rather stylish boarding-house. I will pay them a little more attention, by-and-by."

On the first floor, an iron balustrade ran along in front of the tall, and spacious windows, evidently belonging to a back drawing-room; and, far into the interior, through the arch of the sliding-doors, I could discern a gleam from the windows of the front apartment. There were no signs of present occupancy in this suite of rooms; the curtains being enveloped in a protective covering, which allowed but a small portion of their crimson material to be seen. But two housemaids were industriously at work; so that there was good prospect that the boarding-house might not long suffer from the absence of its most expensive and profitable guests. Meanwhile, until they should appear, I cast my eyes downward to the lower regions. There, in the dusk that so early settles into such places, I saw the red glow of the kitchen-range; the hot cook, or one of her subordinates, with a ladle in her hand, came to draw a cool breath at the back-door; as soon as she disappeared, an Irish man-servant, in a white jacket, crept slily forth and threw away the fragments of a china-dish, which unquestionably he had just broken. Soon afterwards, a lady, showily dressed, with a curling front of what must have been false hair, and reddish brown, I suppose, in hue—though my remoteness allowed me only to guess at such particulars—this respectable mistress of the boarding-house made a momentary transit across the kitchen-window, and appeared no more. It was her final, comprehensive glance, in order to make sure that soup, fish, and flesh, were in a proper state of readiness, before the serving up of dinner.

There was nothing else worth noticing about the house; unless it be, that, on the peak of one of the dormer-windows, which opened out of the roof, sat a dove, looking very dreary and forlorn; insomuch that I wondered why she chose to sit there, in the chilly rain, while her kindred were doubtless nestling in a warm and comfortable dove-cote. All at once, this dove spread her wings, and launching herself in the air, came flying so straight across the intervening space, that I fully expected her to alight directly on my window-sill. In the latter part of her course, however, she swerved aside, flew upward, and vanished, as did likewise the slight, fantastic pathos with which I had invested her.

XVIII

THE BOARDING-HOUSE

THE NEXT day, as soon as I thought of looking again towards the opposite house, there sat the dove again, on the peak of the same dormer-window!

It was by no means an early hour; for, the preceding evening, I had ultimately mustered enterprise enough to visit the theatre, had gone late to bed, and slept beyond all limit, in my remoteness from Silas Foster's awakening horn. Dreams had tormented me, throughout the night. The train of thoughts which, for months past, had worn a track through my mind, and to escape which was one of my chief objects in leaving Blithedale, kept treading remorselessly to-and-fro, in their old footsteps, while slumber left me impotent to regulate them. It was not till I had quitted my three friends that they first began to encroach upon my dreams. In those of the last night, Hollingsworth and Zenobia, standing on either side of my bed, had bent across it to exchange a kiss of passion. Priscilla, beholding this—for she seemed to be peeping in at the chamber-window—had melted gradually away, and left only the sadness of her expression in my heart. There it still lingered, after I awoke; one of those unreasonable sadnesses that you know not how to deal with, because it involves nothing for common-sense to clutch.

It was a gray and dripping forenoon; gloomy enough in town, and still gloomier in the haunts to which my recollections persisted in transporting me. For, in spite of my efforts to think of something else, I thought how the gusty rain was drifting over the slopes and valleys of our farm; how wet must be the foliage that overshadowed the pulpit-rock; how cheerless, in such a day, my hermitage—the tree-solitude of my owl-like humors—in the vine-encircled heart of the tall pine! It was a phase of home-sickness. I had wrenched myself too suddenly out of an accustomed sphere. There was no choice now, but to bear the pang of whatever heart-strings were snapt asunder, and that illusive torment (like the ache of a limb long ago cut off) by which a past mode of life prolongs itself into the succeeding one. I was full of idle and shapeless regrets. The thought impressed itself upon me, that I had left duties unperformed. With the power, perhaps, to act in the place of destiny, and avert misfortune from my friends, I had resigned them to their fate. That cold tendency, between instinct and intellect, which made me pry with a speculative interest into people's passions and impulses, appeared to have gone far towards unhumanizing my heart.

But a man cannot always decide for himself whether his

own heart is cold or warm. It now impresses me, that, if I erred at all, in regard to Hollingsworth, Zenobia, and Priscilla, it was through too much sympathy, rather than too little.

To escape the irksomeness of these meditations, I resumed my post at the window. At first sight, there was nothing new to be noticed. The general aspect of affairs was the same as yesterday, except that the more decided inclemency of to-day had driven the sparrows to shelter, and kept the cat within doors, whence, however, she soon emerged, pursued by the cook, and with what looked like the better half of a roast chicken in her mouth. The young man in the dress-coat was invisible; the two children, in the story below, seemed to be romping about the room, under the superintendence of a nursery-maid. The damask curtains of the drawing-room, on the first floor, were now fully displayed, festooned gracefully from top to bottom of the windows, which extended from the ceiling to the carpet. A narrower window, at the left of the drawing-room, gave light to what was probably a small boudoir, within which I caught the faintest imaginable glimpse of a girl's figure, in airy drapery. Her arm was in regular movement, as if she were busy with her German worsted, or some other such pretty and unprofitable handiwork.

While intent upon making out this girlish shape, I became sensible that a figure had appeared at one of the windows of the drawing-room. There was a presentiment in my mind; or perhaps my first glance, imperfect and sidelong as it was, had sufficed to convey subtle information of the truth. At any rate, it was with no positive surprise, but as if I had all along expected the incident, that, directing my eyes thitherward, I beheld—like a full-length picture, in the space between the heavy festoons of the window-curtains—no other than Zenobia! At the same instant, my thoughts made sure of the identity of the figure in the boudoir. It could only be Priscilla.

Zenobia was attired, not in the almost rustic costume which she had heretofore worn, but in a fashionable morning-dress.

There was, nevertheless, one familiar point. She had, as usual, a flower in her hair, brilliant, and of a rare variety, else it had not been Zenobia. After a brief pause at the window, she turned away, exemplifying, in the few steps that removed her out of sight, that noble and beautiful motion which character- ized her as much as any other personal charm. Not one woman in a thousand could move so admirably as Zenobia. Many women can sit gracefully; some can stand gracefully; and a few, perhaps, can assume a series of graceful positions. But natural movement is the result and expression of the whole being, and cannot be well and nobly performed, unless responsive to something in the character. I often used to think that music—light and airy, wild and passionate, or the full harmony of stately marches, in accordance with her vary- ing mood—should have attended Zenobia's footsteps.

I waited for her re-appearance. It was one peculiarity, dis- tinguishing Zenobia from most of her sex, that she needed for her moral well-being, and never would forego, a large amount of physical exercise. At Blithedale, no inclemency of sky or muddiness of earth had ever impeded her daily walks. Here, in town, she probably preferred to tread the extent of the two drawing-rooms, and measure out the miles by spaces of forty feet, rather than bedraggle her skirts over the sloppy pavements. Accordingly, in about the time requisite to pass through the arch of the sliding-doors to the front window, and to return upon her steps, there she stood again, between the festoons of the crimson curtains. But another personage was now added to the scene. Behind Zenobia ap- peared that face which I had first encountered in the wood- path; the man who had passed, side by side with her, in such mysterious familiarity and estrangement, beneath my vine- curtained hermitage in the tall pine-tree. It was Westervelt. And though he was looking closely over her shoulder, it still seemed to me, as on the former occasion, that Zenobia repelled him—that, perchance, they mutually repelled each other—by some incompatibility of their spheres.

This impression, however, might have been altogether the result of fancy and prejudice, in me. The distance was so great as to obliterate any play of feature, by which I might otherwise have been made a partaker of their counsels.

There now needed only Hollingsworth and old Moodie to complete the knot of characters, whom a real intricacy of events, greatly assisted by my method of insulating them from other relations, had kept so long upon my mental stage, as actors in a drama. In itself, perhaps, it was no very remarkable event, that they should thus come across me, at the moment when I imagined myself free. Zenobia, as I well knew, had retained an establishment in town, and had not unfrequently withdrawn herself from Blithedale, during brief intervals, on one of which occasions she had taken Priscilla along with her. Nevertheless, there seemed something fatal in the coincidence that had borne me to this one spot, of all others in a great city, and transfixed me there, and compelled me again to waste my already wearied sympathies on affairs which were none of mine, and persons who cared little for me. It irritated my nerves; it affected me with a kind of heart-sickness. After the effort which it cost me to fling them off— after consummating my escape, as I thought, from these goblins of flesh and blood, and pausing to revive myself with a breath or two of an atmosphere in which they should have no share—it was a positive despair, to find the same figures arraying themselves before me, and presenting their old problem in a shape that made it more insoluble than ever.

I began to long for a catastrophe. If the noble temper of Hollingsworth's soul were doomed to be utterly corrupted by the too powerful purpose, which had grown out of what was noblest in him; if the rich and generous qualities of Zenobia's womanhood might not save her; if Priscilla must perish by her tenderness and faith, so simple and so devout;— then be it so! Let it all come! As for me, I would look on, as it seemed my part to do, understandingly, if my intellect could fathom the meaning and the moral, and, at all events, reverently and sadly. The curtain fallen, I would pass onward with my poor individual life, which was now attenuated of much of its proper substance, and diffused among many alien interests.

Meanwhile, Zenobia and her companion had retreated from the window. Then followed an interval, during which I directed my eyes towards the figure in the boudoir. Most certainly it was Priscilla, although dressed with a novel and fanciful elegance. The vague perception of it, as viewed so far off, impressed me as if she had suddenly passed out of a chrysalis state and put forth wings. Her hands were not now in motion. She had dropt her work, and sat with her head thrown back, in the same attitude that I had seen several times before, when she seemed to be listening to an imperfectly distinguished sound.

Again the two figures in the drawing-room became visible. They were now a little withdrawn from the window, face to face, and, as I could see by Zenobia's emphatic gestures, were discussing some subject in which she, at least, felt a passionate concern. By-and-by, she broke away, and vanished beyond my ken. Westervelt approached the window, and leaned his forehead against a pane of glass, displaying the sort of smile on his handsome features which, when I before met him, had let me into the secret of his gold-bordered teeth. Every human being, when given over to the Devil, is sure to have the wizard mark upon him, in one form or another. I fancied that this smile, with its peculiar revelation, was the Devil's signet on the Professor.

This man, as I had soon reason to know, was endowed with a cat-like circumspection; and though precisely the most unspiritual quality in the world, it was almost as effective as spiritual insight, in making him acquainted with whatever it suited him to discover. He now proved it, considerably to my discomfiture, by detecting and recognizing me, at my post of observation. Perhaps I ought to have blushed at being caught in such an evident scrutiny of Professor Westervelt and his affairs. Perhaps I did blush. Be that as it might, I retained presence of mind enough not to make my position yet more irksome, by the poltroonery of drawing back.

Westervelt looked into the depths of the drawing-room, and beckoned. Immediately afterwards, Zenobia appeared at the window, with color much heightened, and eyes which, as my conscience whispered me, were shooting bright arrows, barbed with scorn, across the intervening space, directed full at my sensibilities as a gentleman. If the truth must be told, far as her flight-shot was, those arrows hit the mark. She signified her recognition of me by a gesture with her head and hand, comprising at once a salutation and dismissal. The next moment, she administered one of those pitiless rebukes which a woman always has at hand, ready for an offence, (and which she so seldom spares, on due occasion,) by letting down a white linen curtain between the festoons of the damask ones. It fell like the drop-curtain of a theatre, in the interval between the acts.

Priscilla had disappeared from the boudoir. But the dove still kept her desolate perch, on the peak of the attic-window.

XIX

ZENOBIA'S DRAWING-ROOM

THE REMAINDER of the day, so far as I was concerned, was spent in meditating on these recent incidents. I contrived, and alternately rejected, innumerable methods of accounting for the presence of Zenobia and Priscilla, and the connection of Westervelt with both. It must be owned, too, that I had a keen, revengeful sense of the insult inflicted by Zenobia's scornful recognition, and more particularly by her letting down the curtain; as if such were the proper barrier to be interposed between a character like hers, and a perceptive faculty like mine. For, was mine a mere vulgar curiosity? Zenobia should have known me better than to suppose it. She should have been able to appreciate that quality of the intellect and the heart, which impelled me (often against my own will, and to the detriment of my own comfort) to live in other lives, and to endeavor— by generous sympathies, by delicate intuitions, by taking note of things too slight for record, and by bringing my human spirit into manifold accordance with the companions whom God assigned me—to learn the secret which was hidden even from themselves.

Of all possible observers, methought, a woman, like Zenobia, and a man, like Hollingsworth, should have selected me. And, now, when the event has long been past, I retain the same opinion of my fitness for the office. True; I might have condemned them. Had I been judge, as well as witness, my sentence might have been stern as that of Destiny itself. But, still, no trait of original nobility of character; no struggle against temptation; no iron necessity of will, on the one hand, nor extenuating circumstance to be derived from passion and despair, on the other; no remorse that might co-exist with error, even if powerless to prevent it; no proud repentance, that should claim retribution as a meed—would go unappreciated. True, again, I might give my full assent to the punishment which was sure to follow. But it would be given mournfully, and with undiminished love. And, after all was finished, I would come, as if to gather up the white ashes of those who had perished at the stake, and to tell the world— the wrong being now atoned for—how much had perished there, which it had never yet known how to praise.

I sat in my rocking-chair, too far withdrawn from the window to expose myself to another rebuke, like that already inflicted. My eyes still wandered towards the opposite house, but without effecting any new discoveries. Late in the afternoon, the weathercock on the church-spire indicated a change of wind; the sun shone dimly out, as if the golden wine of its beams were mingled half-and-half with water. Nevertheless, they kindled up the whole range of edifices, threw a glow over the windows, glistened on the wet roofs, and, slowly withdrawing upward, perched upon the chimney-tops; thence they took a higher flight, and lingered an instant on the tip of the spire, making it the final point of more cheerful light in the whole sombre scene. The next moment, it was all gone. The twilight fell into the area like a shower of dusky snow; and before it was quite dark, the gong of the hotel summoned me to tea.

When I returned to my chamber, the glow of an astral lamp was penetrating mistily through the white curtain of Zenobia's drawing-room. The shadow of a passing figure was now-and-then cast upon this medium, but with too vague an outline for even my adventurous conjectures to read the hieroglyphic that it presented.

All at once, it occurred to me how very absurd was my behavior, in thus tormenting myself with crazy hypotheses as to what was going on within that drawing-room, when it was at my option to be personally present there. My relations with Zenobia, as yet unchanged—as a familiar friend, and associated in the same life-long enterprise—gave me the right, and made it no more than kindly courtesy demanded, to call on her. Nothing, except our habitual independence of conventional rules, at Blithedale, could have kept me from sooner recognizing this duty. At all events, it should now be performed.

In compliance with this sudden impulse, I soon found myself actually within the house, the rear of which, for two days past, I had been so sedulously watching. A servant took my card, and immediately returning, ushered me up-stairs. On the way, I heard a rich, and, as it were, triumphant burst of music from a piano, in which I felt Zenobia's character, although heretofore I had known nothing of her skill upon the instrument. Two or three canary-birds, excited by this gush of sound, sang piercingly, and did their utmost to produce a kindred melody. A bright illumination streamed through the door of the front drawing-room; and I had barely stept across the threshold before Zenobia came forward to meet me, laughing, and with an extended hand.

"Ah, Mr. Coverdale," said she, still smiling, but, as I thought, with a good deal of scornful anger underneath, "it has gratified me to see the interest which you continue to take in my affairs! I have long recognized you as a sort of transcendental Yankee, with all the native propensity of your countrymen to investigate matters that come within their range, but rendered almost poetical, in your case, by the refined methods which you adopt for its gratification. After all, it was an unjustifiable stroke, on my part—was it not?— to let down the window-curtain!"

"I cannot call it a very wise one," returned I, with a secret bitterness which, no doubt, Zenobia appreciated. "It is really impossible to hide anything, in this world, to say nothing of the next. All that we ought to ask, therefore, is, that the witnesses of our conduct, and the speculators on our motives, should be capable of taking the highest view which the circumstances of the case may admit. So much being secured, I, for one, would be most happy in feeling myself followed, everywhere, by an indefatigable human sympathy."

"We must trust for intelligent sympathy to our guardian angels, if any there be," said Zenobia. "As long as the only spectator of my poor tragedy is a young man, at the window of his hotel, I must still claim the liberty to drop the curtain."

While this passed, as Zenobia's hand was extended, I had applied the very slightest touch of my fingers to her own. In spite of an external freedom, her manner made me sensible that we stood upon no real terms of confidence. The thought came sadly across me, how great was the contrast betwixt this interview and our first meeting. Then, in the warm light of the country fireside, Zenobia had greeted me cheerily and hopefully, with a full sisterly grasp of the hand, conveying as much kindness in it as other women could have evinced by the pressure of both arms around my neck, or by yielding a cheek to the brotherly salute. The difference was as complete as between her appearance, at that time—so simply attired, and with only the one superb flower in her hair—and now, when her beauty was set off by all that dress and ornament could do for it. And they did much. Not, indeed, that they created, or added anything to what Nature had lavishly done for Zenobia. But, those costly robes which she had on, those flaming jewels on her neck, served as lamps to display the personal advantages which required nothing less than such an illumination, to be fully seen. Even her characteristic flower, though it seemed to be still there, had undergone a cold and bright transfiguration; it was a flower exquisitely imitated in jeweller's work, and imparting the last touch that transformed Zenobia into a work of art.

"I scarcely feel," I could not forbear saying, "as if we had ever met before. How many years ago it seems, since we last sat beneath Eliot's pulpit, with Hollingsworth extended on the fallen leaves, and Priscilla at his feet! Can it be, Zenobia, that you ever really numbered yourself with our little band of earnest, thoughtful, philanthropic laborers?"

"Those ideas have their time and place," she answered, coldly. "But, I fancy, it must be a very circumscribed mind that can find room for no others."

Her manner bewildered me. Literally, moreover, I was dazzled by the brilliancy of the room. A chandelier hung down in the centre, glowing with I know not how many lights; there were separate lamps, also, on two or three tables, and on marble brackets, adding their white radiance to that of the chandelier. The furniture was exceedingly rich. Fresh from our old farm-house, with its homely board and benches in the dining-room, and a few wicker-chairs in the best parlor, it struck me that here was the fulfilment of every fantasy of an imagination, revelling in various methods of costly self-indulgence and splendid ease. Pictures, marbles, vases; in brief, more shapes of luxury than there could be any object in enumerating, except for an auctioneer's advertisement—and the whole repeated and doubled by the reflection of a great mirror, which showed me Zenobia's proud figure, like-

wise, and my own. It cost me, I acknowledge, a bitter sense
of shame, to perceive in myself a positive effort to bear up
against the effect which Zenobia sought to impose on me. I
reasoned against her, in my secret mind, and strove so to keep
my footing. In the gorgeousness with which she had surrounded herself—in the redundance of personal ornament,
which the largeness of her physical nature and the rich type
of her beauty caused to seem so suitable—I malevolently
beheld the true character of the woman, passionate, luxurious,
lacking simplicity, not deeply refined, incapable of pure
and perfect taste.

But, the next instant, she was too powerful for all my
opposing struggles. I saw how fit it was that she should make
herself as gorgeous as she pleased, and should do a thousand
things that would have been ridiculous in the poor, thin,
weakly characters of other women. To this day, however, I
hardly know whether I then beheld Zenobia in her truest
attitude, or whether that were the truer one in which she
had presented herself at Blithedale. In both, there was something like the illusion which a great actress flings around her.

"Have you given up Blithedale forever?" I inquired.

"Why should you think so?" asked she.

"I cannot tell," answered I; "except that it appears all like
a dream that we were ever there together."

"It is not so to me," said Zenobia. "I should think it a
poor and meagre nature, that is capable of but one set of
forms, and must convert all the past into a dream, merely
because the present happens to be unlike it. Why should we
be content with our homely life of a few months past, to the
exclusion of all other modes? It was good; but there are other
lives as good or better. Not, you will understand, that I
condemn those who give themselves up to it more entirely
than I, for myself, should deem it wise to do."

It irritated me, this self-complacent, condescending, qualified approval and criticism of a system to which many
individuals—perhaps as highly endowed as our gorgeous
Zenobia—had contributed their all of earthly endeavor, and

their loftiest aspirations. I determined to make proof if there were any spell that would exorcise her out of the part which she seemed to be acting. She should be compelled to give me a glimpse of something true; some nature, some passion, no matter whether right or wrong, provided it were real.

"Your allusion to that class of circumscribed characters, who can live only in one mode of life," remarked I, coolly, "reminds me of our poor friend Hollingsworth. Possibly, he was in your thoughts, when you spoke thus. Poor fellow! It is a pity that, by the fault of a narrow education, he should have so completely immolated himself to that one idea of his; especially as the slightest modicum of common-sense would teach him its utter impracticability. Now that I have returned into the world, and can look at his project from a distance, it requires quite all my real regard for this respectable and well-intentioned man to prevent me laughing at him—as, I find, society at large does!"

Zenobia's eyes darted lightning; her cheeks flushed; the vividness of her expression was like the effect of a powerful light, flaming up suddenly within her. My experiment had fully succeeded. She had shown me the true flesh and blood of her heart, by thus involuntarily resenting my slight, pitying, half-kind, half-scornful mention of the man who was all in all with her. She herself, probably, felt this; for it was hardly a moment before she tranquillized her uneven breath, and seemed as proud and self-possessed as ever.

"I rather imagine," said she, quietly, "that your appreciation falls short of Mr. Hollingsworth's just claims. Blind enthusiasm, absorption in one idea, I grant, is generally ridiculous, and must be fatal to the respectability of an ordinary man; it requires a very high and powerful character, to make it otherwise. But a great man—as, perhaps, you do not know—attains his normal condition only through the inspiration of one great idea. As a friend of Mr. Hollingsworth, and, at the same time, a calm observer, I must tell you that he seems to me such a man. But you are very pardonable for fancying him ridiculous. Doubtless, he is so—to you! There can be no truer test of the noble and heroic, in any individual, than the degree in which he possesses the faculty of distinguishing heroism from absurdity."

I dared make no retort to Zenobia's concluding apothegm. In truth, I admired her fidelity. It gave me a new sense of Hollingsworth's native power, to discover that his influence was no less potent with this beautiful woman, here, in the midst of artificial life, than it had been, at the foot of the gray rock, and among the wild birch-trees of the wood-path, when she so passionately pressed his hand against her heart. The great, rude, shaggy, swarthy man! And Zenobia loved him!

"Did you bring Priscilla with you?" I resumed. "Do you know, I have sometimes fancied it not quite safe, considering the susceptibility of her temperament, that she should be so constantly within the sphere of a man like Hollingsworth? Such tender and delicate natures, among your sex, have often, I believe, a very adequate appreciation of the heroic element in men. But, then, again, I should suppose them as likely as any other women to make a reciprocal impression. Hollingsworth could hardly give his affections to a person capable of taking an independent stand, but only to one whom he might absorb into himself. He has certainly shown great tenderness for Priscilla."

Zenobia had turned aside. But I caught the reflection of her face in the mirror, and saw that it was very pale;—as pale, in her rich attire, as if a shroud were round her.

"Priscilla is here," said she, her voice a little lower than usual. "Have not you learnt as much, from your chamber-window? Would you like to see her?"

She made a step or two into the back drawing-room, and called:—

"Priscilla! Dear Priscilla!"

XX

THEY VANISH

PRISCILLA immediately answered the summons, and made her appearance through the door of the boudoir. I had conceived the idea—which I now recognized as a very foolish one—that Zenobia would have taken measures to debar me from an interview with this girl, between whom and herself there was so utter an opposition of their dearest interests, that, on one part or the other, a great grief, if not likewise a great wrong, seemed a matter of necessity. But, as Priscilla was only a leaf, floating on the dark current of events, without influencing them by her own choice or plan—as she probably guessed not whither the stream was bearing her, nor perhaps even felt its inevitable movement—there could be no peril of her communicating to me any intelligence with regard to Zenobia's purposes.

On perceiving me, she came forward with great quietude of manner; and when I held out my hand, her own moved slightly towards it, as if attracted by a feeble degree of magnetism.

"I am glad to see you, my dear Priscilla," said I, still holding her hand. "But everything that I meet with, now-a-days, makes me wonder whether I am awake. You, especially, have always seemed like a figure in a dream—and now more than ever."

"Oh, there is substance in these fingers of mine!" she answered, giving my hand the faintest possible pressure, and then taking away her own. "Why do you call me a dream? Zenobia is much more like one than I; she is so very, very beautiful! And, I suppose," added Priscilla, as if thinking aloud, "everybody sees it, as I do."

But, for my part, it was Priscilla's beauty, not Zenobia's, of which I was thinking, at that moment. She was a person who could be quite obliterated, so far as beauty went, by anything unsuitable in her attire; her charm was not positive and material enough to bear up against a mistaken choice of color, for instance, or fashion. It was safest, in her case, to attempt no art of dress; for it demanded the most perfect taste, or else the happiest accident in the world, to give her precisely the adornment which she needed. She was now dressed in pure white, set off with some kind of a gauzy fabric, which—as I bring up her figure in my memory, with a faint gleam on her shadowy hair, and her dark eyes bent shyly on mine, through all the vanished years—seems to be floating about her like a mist. I wondered what Zenobia meant by evolving so much loveliness out of this poor girl. It was what few women could afford to do; for, as I looked from one to the other, the sheen and splendor of Zenobia's presence took nothing from Priscilla's softer spell, if it might not rather be thought to add to it.

"What do you think of her?" asked Zenobia.

I could not understand the look of melancholy kindness with which Zenobia regarded her. She advanced a step, and beckoning Priscilla near her, kissed her cheek; then, with a slight gesture of repulse, she moved to the other side of the room. I followed.

"She is a wonderful creature," I said. "Ever since she came among us, I have been dimly sensible of just this charm which you have brought out. But it was never absolutely visible till now. She is as lovely as a flower!"

"Well; say so, if you like," answered Zenobia. "You are a poet—at least, as poets go, now-a-days—and must be allowed to make an opera-glass of your imagination, when you look at women. I wonder, in such Arcadian freedom of falling in love as we have lately enjoyed, it never occurred to you to fall in love with Priscilla! In society, indeed, a genuine American never dreams of stepping across the inappreciable air-line which separates one class from another. But what was rank to the colonists of Blithedale?"

"There were other reasons," I replied, "why I should

have demonstrated myself an ass, had I fallen in love with
Priscilla. By-the-by, has Hollingsworth ever seen her in
this dress?"

"Why do you bring up his name, at every turn?" asked
Zenobia, in an undertone, and with a malign look which
wandered from my face to Priscilla's. "You know not what
you do! It is dangerous, sir, believe me, to tamper thus with
earnest human passions, out of your own mere idleness, and
for your sport. I will endure it no longer! Take care that it
does not happen again! I warn you!"

"You partly wrong me, if not wholly," I responded. "It
is an uncertain sense of some duty to perform, that brings
my thoughts, and therefore my words, continually to that
one point."

"Oh, this stale excuse of duty!" said Zenobia, in a whisper so full of scorn that it penetrated me like the hiss of
a serpent. "I have often heard it before, from those who
sought to interfere with me, and I know precisely what
it signifies. Bigotry; self-conceit; an insolent curiosity; a
meddlesome temper; a cold-blooded criticism, founded on a
shallow interpretation of half-perceptions; a monstrous scepticism in regard to any conscience or any wisdom, except one's
own; a most irreverent propensity to thrust Providence aside,
and substitute one's self in its awful place—out of these, and
other motives as miserable as these, comes your idea of duty!
But beware, sir! With all your fancied acuteness, you step
blindfold into these affairs. For any mischief that may follow
your interference, I hold you responsible!"

It was evident, that, with but a little further provocation,
the lioness would turn to bay; if, indeed, such were not her
attitude, already. I bowed, and, not very well knowing what
else to do, was about to withdraw. But, glancing again
towards Priscilla, who had retreated into a corner, there fell
upon my heart an intolerable burthen of despondency, the
purport of which I could not tell, but only felt it to bear
reference to her. I approached her, and held out my hand;
a gesture, however, to which she made no response. It was

always one of her peculiarities that she seemed to shrink from even the most friendly touch, unless it were Zenobia's or Hollingsworth's. Zenobia, all this while, stood watching us, but with a careless expression, as if it mattered very little what might pass.

"Priscilla," I inquired, lowering my voice, "when do you go back to Blithedale?"

"Whenever they please to take me," said she.

"Did you come away of your own free-will?" I asked.

"I am blown about like a leaf," she replied. "I never have any free-will."

"Does Hollingsworth know that you are here?" said I.

"He bade me come," answered Priscilla.

She looked at me, I thought, with an air of surprise, as if the idea were incomprehensible, that she should have taken this step without his agency.

"What a gripe this man has laid upon her whole being!" muttered I, between my teeth. "Well; as Zenobia so kindly intimates, I have no more business here. I wash my hands of it all. On Hollingsworth's head be the consequences! Priscilla," I added, aloud, "I know not that ever we may meet again. Farewell!"

As I spoke the word, a carriage had rumbled along the street, and stopt before the house. The door-bell rang, and steps were immediately afterwards heard on the staircase. Zenobia had thrown a shawl over her dress.

"Mr. Coverdale," said she, with cool courtesy, "you will perhaps excuse us. We have an engagement, and are going out."

"Whither?" I demanded.

"Is not that a little more than you are entitled to inquire?" said she, with a smile. "At all events, it does not suit me to tell you."

The door of the drawing-room opened, and Westervelt appeared. I observed that he was elaborately dressed, as if for some grand entertainment. My dislike for this man was infinite. At that moment, it amounted to nothing less than a creeping of the flesh, as when, feeling about in a dark place, one touches something cold and slimy, and questions what the secret hatefulness may be. And, still, I could not but acknowledge, that, for personal beauty, for polish of manner, for all that externally befits a gentleman, there was hardly another like him. After bowing to Zenobia, and graciously saluting Priscilla in her corner, he recognized me by a slight, but courteous inclination.

"Come, Priscilla," said Zenobia, "it is time. Mr. Coverdale, good evening!"

As Priscilla moved slowly forward, I met her in the middle of the drawing-room.

"Priscilla," said I, in the hearing of them all, "do you know whither you are going?"

"I do not know," she answered.

"Is it wise to go?—and is it your choice to go?" I asked. "If not—I am your friend, and Hollingsworth's friend—tell me so, at once!"

"Possibly," observed Westervelt, smiling, "Priscilla sees in me an older friend than either Mr. Coverdale or Mr. Hollingsworth. I shall willingly leave the matter at her option."

While thus speaking, he made a gesture of kindly invitation; and Priscilla passed me, with the gliding movement of a sprite, and took his offered arm. He offered the other to Zenobia. But she turned her proud and beautiful face upon him, with a look which—judging from what I caught of it in profile—would undoubtedly have smitten the man dead, had he possessed any heart, or had this glance attained to it. It seemed to rebound, however, from his courteous visage, like an arrow from polished steel. They all three descended the stairs; and when I likewise reached the street-door, the carriage was already rolling away.

XXI

AN OLD ACQUAINTANCE

THUS excluded from everybody's confidence, and attaining no further, by my most earnest study, than to an uncertain sense of something hidden from me, it would appear reasonable that I should have flung off all these alien perplexities. Obviously, my best course was, to betake myself to new scenes. Here, I was only an intruder. Elsewhere, there might be circumstances in which I could establish a personal interest, and people who would respond, with a portion of their sympathies, for so much as I should bestow of mine.

Nevertheless, there occurred to me one other thing to be done. Remembering old Moodie, and his relationship with Priscilla, I determined to seek an interview, for the purpose of ascertaining whether the knot of affairs was as inextricable, on that side, as I found it on all others. Being tolerably well acquainted with the old man's haunts, I went, the next day, to the saloon of a certain establishment about which he often lurked. It was a reputable place enough, affording good entertainment in the way of meat, drink, and fumigation; and there, in my young and idle days and nights, when I was neither nice nor wise, I had often amused myself with watching the staid humors and sober jollities of the thirsty souls around me.

At my first entrance, old Moodie was not there. The more patiently to await him, I lighted a cigar, and establishing myself in a corner, took a quiet, and, by sympathy, a boozy kind of pleasure in the customary life that was going forward. Human nature, in my opinion, has a naughty instinct that approves of wine, at least, if not of stronger liquor. The temperance-men may preach till doom's day; and still this cold and barren world will look warmer, kindlier, mellower, through the medium of a toper's[3] glass; nor can they, with all their efforts, really spill his draught upon the floor, until some hitherto unthought-of discovery shall supply him with a truer element of joy. The general atmosphere of life must first be rendered so inspiriting that he will not need his delirious solace. The custom of tippling has its defensible side, as well as any other question. But these good people snatch at the old, time-honored demijohn, and offer nothing—either sensual or moral—nothing whatever to supply its place; and human life, as it goes with a multitude of men, will not endure so great a vacuum as would be left by the withdrawal of that big-bellied convexity. The space, which it now occupies, must somehow or other be filled up. As for the rich, it would be little matter if a blight fell upon their vineyards; but the poor man—whose only glimpse of a better state is through the muddy medium of his liquor—what is to be done for him? The reformers should make their efforts positive, instead of negative; they must do away with evil by substituting good.

The saloon was fitted up with a good deal of taste. There were pictures on the walls, and among them an oil-painting of a beef-steak, with such an admirable show of juicy tenderness, that the beholder sighed to think it merely visionary, and incapable of ever being put upon a gridiron. Another work of high art was the lifelike representation of a noble sirloin; another, the hind-quarters of a deer, retaining the hoofs and tawny fur; another, the head and shoulders of a salmon; and, still more exquisitely finished, a brace of canvass-back ducks, in which the mottled feathers were depicted with the accuracy of a daguerreotype.[4] Some very hungry painter, I suppose, had wrought these subjects of still life, heightening his imagination with his appetite, and earning, it is to be hoped, the privilege of a daily dinner off whichever of his pictorial viands he liked best. Then there was a fine old

3. A toper is a hard drinker.
4. The product of an early form of photography invented by Louis-Jacques-Mandé Daguerre (1789–1851), who revealed the process to the public on August 19, 1839.

cheese, in which you could almost discern the mites; and some sardines, on a small plate, very richly done, and looking as if oozy with the oil in which they had been smothered. All these things were so perfectly imitated, that you seemed to have the genuine article before you, and yet with an indescribable, ideal charm; it took away the grossness from what was fleshiest and fattest, and thus helped the life of man, even in its earthliest relations, to appear rich and noble, as well as warm, cheerful, and substantial. There were pictures, too, of gallant revellers, those of the old time, Flemish, apparently, with doublets and slashed sleeves, drinking their wine out of fantastic, long-stemmed glasses; quaffing joyously, quaffing forever, with inaudible laughter and song; while the champagne bubbled immortally against their moustaches, or the purple tide of Burgundy ran inexhaustibly down their throats.

But, in an obscure corner of the saloon, there was a little picture—excellently done, moreover—of a ragged, bloated, New England toper, stretched out on a bench, in the heavy, apoplectic sleep of drunkenness. The death-in-life was too well portrayed. You smelt the fumy liquor that had brought on this syncope. Your only comfort lay in the forced reflection, that, real as he looked, the poor caitiff was but imaginary, a bit of painted canvass, whom no delirium tremens, nor so much as a retributive headache, awaited, on the morrow.

By this time, it being past eleven o'clock, the two bar-keepers of the saloon were in pretty constant activity. One of these young men had a rare faculty in the concoction of gin-cocktails. It was a spectacle to behold, how, with a tumbler in each hand, he tossed the contents from one to the other. Never conveying it awry, nor spilling the least drop, he compelled the frothy liquor, as it seemed to me, to spout forth from one glass and descend into the other, in a great parabolic curve, as well-defined and calculable as a planet's orbit. He had a good forehead, with a particularly large development just above the eyebrows; fine intellectual gifts, no doubt, which he had educated to this profitable end; being

famous for nothing but gin-cocktails, and commanding a fair
salary by his one accomplishment. These cocktails, and other
artificial combinations of liquor, (of which there were at
least a score, though mostly, I suspect, fantastic in their
differences,) were much in favor with the younger class of
customers, who, at farthest, had only reached the second stage
of potatory life. The staunch, old soakers, on the other hand—
men who, if put on tap, would have yielded a red alcoholic
liquor, by way of blood—usually confined themselves to plain
brandy-and-water, gin, or West India rum; and, oftentimes,
they prefaced their dram with some medicinal remark as to
the wholesomeness and stomachic qualities of that particular
drink. Two or three appeared to have bottles of their own,
behind the counter; and winking one red eye to the barkeeper, he forthwith produced these choicest and peculiar
cordials, which it was a matter of great interest and favor,
among their acquaintances, to obtain a sip of.

Agreeably to the Yankee habit, under whatever circumstances, the deportment of all these good fellows, old or
young, was decorous and thoroughly correct. They grew only
the more sober in their cups; there was no confused babble,
nor boisterous laughter. They sucked in the joyous fire of
the decanters, and kept it smouldering in their inmost recesses,
with a bliss known only to the heart which it warmed and
comforted. Their eyes twinkled a little, to be sure; they
hemmed vigorously, after each glass, and laid a hand upon
the pit of the stomach, as if the pleasant titillation, there, was
what constituted the tangible part of their enjoyment. In
that spot, unquestionably, and not in the brain, was the acme
of the whole affair. But the true purpose of their drinking—
and one that will induce men to drink, or do something
equivalent, as long as this weary world shall endure—was
the renewed youth and vigor, the brisk, cheerful sense of
things present and to come, with which, for about a quarter-
of-an-hour, the dram permeated their systems. And when
such quarters-of-an-hour can be obtained in some mode less
baneful to the great sum of a man's life—but, nevertheless,

with a little spice of impropriety, to give it a wild flavor—we temperance-people may ring out our bells for victory!

The prettiest object in the saloon was a tiny fountain, which threw up its feathery jet, through the counter, and sparkled down again into an oval basin, or lakelet, containing several gold-fishes. There was a bed of bright sand, at the bottom, strewn with coral and rock-work; and the fishes went gleaming about, now turning up the sheen of a golden side, and now vanishing into the shadows of the water, like the fanciful thoughts that coquet with a poet in his dream. Never before, I imagine, did a company of water-drinkers remain so entirely uncontaminated by the bad example around them; nor could I help wondering that it had not occurred to any freakish inebriate, to empty a glass of liquor into their lakelet. What a delightful idea! Who would not be a fish, if he could inhale jollity with the essential element of his existence!

I had begun to despair of meeting old Moodie, when, all at once, I recognized his hand and arm, protruding from behind a screen that was set up for the accommodation of bashful topers. As a matter of course, he had one of Priscilla's little purses, and was quietly insinuating it under the notice of a person who stood near. This was always old Moodie's way. You hardly ever saw him advancing towards you, but became aware of his proximity without being able to guess how he had come thither. He glided about like a spirit, assuming visibility close to your elbow, offering his petty trifles of merchandise, remaining long enough for you to purchase, if so disposed, and then taking himself off, between two breaths, while you happened to be thinking of something else.

By a sort of sympathetic impulse that often controlled me, in those more impressible days of my life, I was induced to approach this old man in a mode as undemonstrative as his own. Thus, when, according to his custom, he was probably just about to vanish, he found me at his elbow.

"Ah!" said he, with more emphasis than was usual with him. "It is Mr. Coverdale!"

"Yes, Mr. Moodie, your old acquaintance," answered I. "It is some time now since we ate our luncheon together, at Blithedale, and a good deal longer since our little talk together, at the street-corner."

"That was a good while ago," said the old man.

And he seemed inclined to say not a word more. His existence looked so colorless and torpid—so very faintly shadowed on the canvass of reality—that I was half afraid lest he should altogether disappear, even while my eyes were fixed full upon his figure. He was certainly the wretchedest old ghost in the world, with his crazy hat, the dingy handkerchief about his throat, his suit of threadbare gray, and especially that patch over his right eye,[5] behind which he always seemed to be hiding himself. There was one method, however, of bringing him out into somewhat stronger relief. A glass of brandy would effect it. Perhaps the gentler influence of a bottle of claret might do the same. Nor could I think it a matter for the recording angel to write down against me, if—with my painful consciousness of the frost in this old man's blood, and the positive ice that had congealed about his heart—I should thaw him out, were it only for an hour, with the summer warmth of a little wine. What else could possibly be done for him? How else could he be imbued with energy enough to hope for a happier state, hereafter? How else be inspirited to say his prayers? For there are states of our spiritual system, when the throb of the soul's life is too faint and weak to render us capable of religious aspiration.

"Mr. Moodie," said I, "shall we lunch together? And would you like to drink a glass of wine?"

His one eye gleamed. He bowed; and it impressed me

5. Earlier (p. 77), Moodie wears the patch on his left eye. Roy Male argues that this is not an oversight but a part of Hawthorne's "examination of what happens to personal identity in a culture that demands constant change" (*Explicator*, 28 [1970], item 56).

that he grew to be more of a man at once, either in anticipation of the wine, or as a grateful response to my good-
fellowship in offering it.

"With pleasure," he replied.

The barkeeper, at my request, showed us into a private
room, and, soon afterwards, set some fried oysters and a
bottle of claret on the table; and I saw the old man glance
curiously at the label of the bottle, as if to learn the brand.

"It should be good wine," I remarked, "if it have any
right to its label."

"You cannot suppose, sir," said Moodie, with a sigh, "that
a poor old fellow, like me, knows any difference in wines."

And yet, in his way of handling the glass, in his preliminary
snuff at the aroma, in his first cautious sip of the wine, and
the gustatory skill with which he gave his palate the full
advantage of it, it was impossible not to recognize the con-
noisseur.

"I fancy, Mr. Moodie," said I, "you are a much better judge
of wines than I have yet learned to be. Tell me fairly—
did you never drink it where the grape grows?"

"How should that have been, Mr. Coverdale?" answered
old Moodie, shyly; but then he took courage, as it were, and
uttered a feeble little laugh. "The flavor of this wine," added
he, "and its perfume, still more than its taste, makes me
remember that I was once a young man!"

"I wish, Mr. Moodie," suggested I—not that I greatly cared
about it, however, but was only anxious to draw him into
some talk about Priscilla and Zenobia—"I wish, while we
sit over our wine, you would favor me with a few of those
youthful reminiscences."

"Ah," said he, shaking his head, "they might interest you
more than you suppose. But I had better be silent, Mr.
Coverdale. If this good wine—though claret, I suppose, is
not apt to play such a trick—but if it should make my tongue
run too freely, I could never look you in the face again."

"You never did look me in the face, Mr. Moodie," I replied,
"until this very moment."

"Ah!" sighed old Moodie.

It was wonderful, however, what an effect the mild grape-juice wrought upon him. It was not in the wine, but in the associations which it seemed to bring up. Instead of the mean, slouching, furtive, painfully depressed air of an old city-vagabond, more like a gray kennel-rat than any other living thing, he began to take the aspect of a decayed gentleman. Even his garments—especially after I had myself quaffed a glass or two—looked less shabby than when we first sat down. There was, by-and-by, a certain exuberance and elaborateness of gesture, and manner, oddly in contrast with all that I had hitherto seen of him. Anon, with hardly any impulse from me, old Moodie began to talk. His communications referred exclusively to a long past and more fortunate period of his life, with only a few unavoidable allusions to the circumstances that had reduced him to his present state. But, having once got the clue, my subsequent researches acquainted me with the main facts of the following narrative; although, in writing it out, my pen has perhaps allowed itself a trifle of romantic and legendary license, worthier of a small poet than of a grave biographer.

XXII

FAUNTLEROY

FIVE-AND-TWENTY years ago, at the epoch of this story, there dwelt, in one of the middle states, a man whom we shall call Fauntleroy; a man of wealth, and magnificent tastes, and prodigal expenditure. His home might almost be styled a palace; his habits, in the ordinary sense, princely. His whole being seemed to have crystallized itself into an external splendor, wherewith he glittered in the eyes of the world, and had no other life than upon this gaudy surface. He had married a lovely woman, whose nature was deeper than his own. But his affection for her, though it showed largely, was superficial, like all his other manifestations and developments; he did not so truly keep this noble creature in his heart, as wear her beauty for the most brilliant ornament of his outward state. And there was born to him a child, a beautiful daughter, whom he took from the beneficent hand of God with no just sense of her immortal value, but as a man, already rich in gems, would receive another jewel. If he loved her, it was because she shone.

After Fauntleroy had thus spent a few empty years, corruscating continually an unnatural light, the source of it—which was merely his gold—began to grow more shallow, and finally became exhausted. He saw himself in imminent peril of losing all that had heretofore distinguished him; and, conscious of no innate worth to fall back upon, he recoiled from this calamity, with the instinct of a soul shrinking from annihilation. To avoid it—wretched man!—or, rather, to defer it, if but for a month, a day, or only to procure himself the life of a few breaths more, amid the false glitter which was now less his own than ever—he made himself guilty of a crime. It was just the sort of crime, growing out of its artificial state, which society (unless it should change its entire constitution for this man's unworthy sake) neither could nor ought to pardon. More safely might it pardon murder. Fauntleroy's guilt was discovered. He fled; his wife perished by the necessity of her innate nobleness, in its alliance with a being so ignoble; and betwixt her mother's death and her father's ignominy, his daughter was left worse than orphaned.

There was no pursuit after Fauntleroy. His family-connections, who had great wealth, made such arrangements with those whom he had attempted to wrong, as secured him from the retribution that would have overtaken an unfriended criminal. The wreck of his estate was divided among his creditors. His name, in a very brief space, was forgotten by the multitude who had passed it so diligently from mouth to mouth. Seldom, indeed, was it recalled, even

by his closest former intimates. Nor could it have been otherwise. The man had laid no real touch on any mortal's heart.
Being a mere image, an optical delusion, created by the
sunshine of prosperity, it was his law to vanish into the
shadow of the first intervening cloud. He seemed to leave
no vacancy; a phenomenon which, like many others that
attended his brief career, went far to prove the illusiveness
of his existence.

Not, however, that the physical substance of Fauntleroy
had literally melted into vapor. He had fled northward, to
the New England metropolis, and had taken up his abode,
under another name, in a squalid street, or court, of the
older portion of the city. There he dwelt among poverty-
stricken wretches, sinners, and forlorn, good people, Irish,
and whomsoever else were neediest. Many families were
clustered in each house together, above stairs and below, in
the little peaked garrets, and even in the dusky cellars. The
house, where Fauntleroy paid weekly rent for a chamber
and a closet, had been a stately habitation, in its day. An
old colonial Governor had built it, and lived there, long ago,
and held his levees[6] in a great room where now slept twenty
Irish bedfellows, and died in Fauntleroy's chamber, which his
embroidered and white-wigged ghost still haunted. Tattered
hangings, a marble hearth, traversed with many cracks and
fissures, a richly-carved oaken mantel-piece, partly hacked-
away for kindling-stuff, a stuccoed ceiling, defaced with great,
unsightly patches of the naked laths;—such was the chamber's
aspect, as if, with its splinters and rags of dirty splendor, it
were a kind of practical gibe at this poor, ruined man of show.

At first, and at irregular intervals, his relatives allowed
Fauntleroy a little pittance to sustain life; not from any love,
perhaps, but lest poverty should compel him, by new offences,
to add more shame to that with which he had already stained
them. But he showed no tendency to further guilt. His
character appeared to have been radically changed (as, indeed,

6. Royal receptions held on rising from bed.

from its shallowness, it well might) by his miserable fate; or, it may be, the traits now seen in him were portions of the same character, presenting itself in another phase. Instead of any longer seeking to live in the sight of the world, his impulse was to shrink into the nearest obscurity, and to be unseen of men, were it possible, even while standing before their eyes. He had no pride; it was all trodden in the dust. No ostentation; for how could it survive, when there was nothing left of Fauntleroy, save penury and shame! His very gait demonstrated that he would gladly have faded out of view, and have crept about invisibly, for the sake of sheltering himself from the irksomeness of a human glance. Hardly, it was averred, within the memory of those who knew him now, had he the hardihood to show his full front to the world. He skulked in corners, and crept about in a sort of noonday twilight, making himself gray and misty, at all hours, with his morbid intolerance of sunshine.

In his torpid despair, however, he had done an act which that condition of the spirit seems to prompt, almost as often as prosperity and hope. Fauntleroy was again married. He had taken to wife a forlorn, meek-spirited, feeble young woman, a seamstress, whom he found dwelling with her mother in a contiguous chamber of the old gubernatorial residence. This poor phantom—as the beautiful and noble companion of his former life had done—brought him a daughter. And sometimes, as from one dream into another, Fauntleroy looked forth out of his present grimy environment, into that past magnificence, and wondered whether the grandee of yesterday or the pauper of to-day were real. But, in my mind, the one and the other were alike impalpable. In truth, it was Fauntleroy's fatality to behold whatever he touched dissolve. After a few years, his second wife (dim shadow that she had always been) faded finally out of the world, and left Fauntleroy to deal as he might with their pale and nervous child. And, by this time, among his distant relatives—with whom he had grown a weary thought, linked with contagious infamy, and which they were only too willing to get rid of—he was himself supposed to be no more.

The younger child, like his elder one, might be considered as the true offspring of both parents, and as the reflection of their state. She was a tremulous little creature, shrinking involuntarily from all mankind, but in timidity, and no sour repugnance. There was a lack of human substance in her; it seemed as if, were she to stand up in a sunbeam, it would pass right through her figure, and trace out the cracked and dusty window-panes upon the naked floor. But, nevertheless, the poor child had a heart; and from her mother's gentle character, she had inherited a profound and still capacity of affection. And so her life was one of love. She bestowed it partly on her father, but, in greater part, on an idea.

For Fauntleroy, as they sat by their cheerless fireside—which was no fireside, in truth, but only a rusty stove—had often talked to the little girl about his former wealth, the noble loveliness of his first wife, and the beautiful child whom she had given him. Instead of the fairy tales, which other parents tell, he told Priscilla this. And, out of the loneliness of her sad little existence, Priscilla's love grew, and tended upward, and twined itself perseveringly around this unseen sister; as a grape-vine might strive to clamber out of a gloomy hollow among the rocks, and embrace a young tree, standing in the sunny warmth above. It was almost like worship, both in its earnestness and its humility; nor was it the less humble, though the more earnest, because Priscilla could claim human kindred with the being whom she so devoutly loved. As with worship, too, it gave her soul the refreshment of a purer atmosphere. Save for this singular, this melancholy, and yet beautiful affection, the child could hardly have lived; or, had she lived, with a heart shrunken for lack of any sentiment to fill it, she must have yielded to the barren miseries of her position, and have grown to womanhood, characterless and worthless. But, now, amid all the sombre coarseness of her father's outward life, and of her own, Priscilla had a higher and imaginative life within. Some faint gleam thereof was often visible upon her face. It was as if, in her spiritual visits to her brilliant sister, a portion of the latter's brightness had permeated our dim Priscilla, and still lingered, shedding a faint illumination through the cheerless chamber, after she came back.

As the child grew up, so pallid and so slender, and with much unaccountable nervousness, and all the weaknesses of neglected infancy still haunting her, the gross and simple neighbors whispered strange things about Priscilla. The big, red, Irish matrons, whose innumerable progeny swarmed out of the adjacent doors, used to mock at the pale Western child. They fancied—or, at least, affirmed it, between jest and earnest—that she was not so solid flesh and blood as other children, but mixed largely with a thinner element. They called her ghost-child, and said that she could indeed vanish, when she pleased, but could never, in her densest moments, make herself quite visible. The sun, at mid-day, would shine through her; in the first gray of the twilight, she lost all the distinctness of her outline; and, if you followed the dim thing into a dark corner, behold! she was not there. And it was true, that Priscilla had strange ways; strange ways, and stranger words, when she uttered any words at all. Never stirring out of the old Governor's dusky house, she sometimes talked of distant places and splendid rooms, as if she had just left them. Hidden things were visible to her, (at least, so the people inferred from obscure hints, escaping unawares out of her mouth,) and silence was audible. And, in all the world, there was nothing so difficult to be endured, by those who had any dark secret to conceal, as the glance of Priscilla's timid and melancholy eyes.

Her peculiarities were the theme of continual gossip among the other inhabitants of the gubernatorial mansion. The rumor spread thence into a wider circle. Those who knew old Moodie—as he was now called—used often to jeer him, at the very street-corners, about his daughter's gift of second-sight and prophecy. It was a period when science (though mostly through its empirical professors) was bringing forward, anew, a hoard of facts and imperfect theories, that had partially won credence, in elder times, but which modern scepticism had swept away as rubbish. These things were now tossed up again, out of the surging ocean of human thought and experience. The story of Priscilla's preternatural manifestations, therefore, attracted a kind of notice of which it would have been deemed wholly unworthy, a few years earlier. One day, a gentleman ascended the creaking staircase, and inquired which was old Moodie's chamber-door. And, several times, he came again. He was a marvellously handsome man, still youthful, too, and fashionably dressed. Except that Priscilla, in those days, had no beauty, and, in the languor of her existence, had not yet blossomed into womanhood, there would have been rich food for scandal in these visits; for the girl was unquestionably their sole object, although her father was supposed always to be present. But, it must likewise be added, there was something about Priscilla that calumny could not meddle with; and thus far was she privileged, either by the preponderance of what was spiritual, or the thin and watery blood that left her cheek so pallid.

Yet, if the busy tongues of the neighborhood spared Priscilla, in one way, they made themselves amends by renewed and wilder babble, on another score. They averred that the strange gentleman was a wizard, and that he had taken advantage of Priscilla's lack of earthly substance to subject her to himself, as his familiar spirit, through whose medium he gained cognizance of whatever happened, in regions near or remote. The boundaries of his power were defined by the verge of the pit of Tartarus, on the one hand, and the third sphere of the celestial world, on the other.[7] Again, they declared their suspicion that the wizard, with all his show of manly beauty,

7. That is, from Tartarus, the sunless abyss below Hades, to the sphere of Venus in the Ptolemaic system.

was really an aged and wizened figure, or else that his semblance of a human body was only a necromantic, or perhaps
a mechanical contrivance, in which a demon walked about.
In proof of it, however, they could merely instance a gold
band around his upper teeth, which had once been visible
to several old women, when he smiled at them from the top
of the Governor's staircase. Of course, this was all absurdity,
or mostly so. But, after every possible deduction, there remained certain very mysterious points about the stranger's
character, as well as the connection that he established with
Priscilla. Its nature, at that period, was even less understood
than now, when miracles of this kind have grown so absolutely
stale, that I would gladly, if the truth allowed, dismiss the
whole matter from my narrative.

We must now glance backward, in quest of the beautiful
daughter of Fauntleroy's prosperity. What had become of
her? Fauntleroy's only brother, a bachelor, and with no other
relative so near, had adopted the forsaken child. She grew
up in affluence, with native graces clustering luxuriantly about
her. In her triumphant progress towards womanhood, she
was adorned with every variety of feminine accomplishment.
But she lacked a mother's care. With no adequate control,
on any hand, (for a man, however stern, however wise, can
never sway and guide a female child,) her character was left
to shape itself. There was good in it, and evil. Passionate,
self-willed, and imperious, she had a warm and generous
nature; showing the richness of the soil, however, chiefly by
the weeds that flourished in it, and choked up the herbs of
grace. In her girlhood, her uncle died. As Fauntleroy was
supposed to be likewise dead, and no other heir was known
to exist, his wealth devolved on her, although, dying suddenly, the uncle left no will. After his death, there were
obscure passages in Zenobia's history. There were whispers
of an attachment, and even a secret marriage, with a fascinating and accomplished, but unprincipled young man. The

incidents and appearances, however, which led to this surmise, soon passed away and were forgotten.

Nor was her reputation seriously affected by the report.
In fact, so great was her native power and influence, and
such seemed the careless purity of her nature, that whatever
Zenobia did was generally acknowledged as right for her
to do. The world never criticised her so harshly as it does
most women who transcend its rules. It almost yielded its
assent, when it beheld her stepping out of the common path,
and asserting the more extensive privileges of her sex, both
theoretically and by her practice. The sphere of ordinary
womanhood was felt to be narrower than her development
required.

A portion of Zenobia's more recent life is told in the foregoing pages. Partly in earnest—and, I imagine, as was her
disposition, half in a proud jest, or in a kind of recklessness
that had grown upon her, out of some hidden grief—she had
given her countenance, and promised liberal pecuniary aid,
to our experiment of a better social state. And Priscilla followed her to Blithedale. The sole bliss of her life had been
a dream of this beautiful sister, who had never so much as
known of her existence. By this time, too, the poor girl was
enthralled in an intolerable bondage, from which she must
either free herself or perish. She deemed herself safest near
Zenobia, into whose large heart she hoped to nestle.

One evening, months after Priscilla's departure, when
Moodie (or shall we call him Fauntleroy?) was sitting alone
in the state-chamber of the old Governor, there came footsteps up the staircase. There was a pause on the landing-place.
A lady's musical, yet haughty accents were heard making an
inquiry from some denizen of the house, who had thrust a
head out of a contiguous chamber. There was then a knock
at Moodie's door.

"Come in!" said he.

And Zenobia entered. The details of the interview that

followed, being unknown to me—while, notwithstanding, it would be a pity quite to lose the picturesqueness of the situation—I shall attempt to sketch it, mainly from fancy, although with some general grounds of surmise in regard to the old man's feelings.

She gazed, wonderingly, at the dismal chamber. Dismal to her, who beheld it only for an instant, and how much more so to him, into whose brain each bare spot on the ceiling, every tatter of the paper-hangings, and all the splintered carvings of the mantel-piece, seen wearily through long years, had worn their several prints! Inexpressibly miserable is this familiarity with objects that have been, from the first, disgustful.

"I have received a strange message," said Zenobia, after a moment's silence, "requesting, or rather enjoining it upon me, to come hither. Rather from curiosity than any other motive—and because, though a woman, I have not all the timidity of one—I have complied. Can it be you, sir, who thus summoned me?"

"It was," answered Moodie.

"And what was your purpose?" she continued. "You require charity, perhaps? In that case, the message might have been more fitly worded. But you are old and poor; and age and poverty should be allowed their privileges. Tell me, therefore, to what extent you need my aid."

"Put up your purse," said the supposed mendicant, with an inexplicable smile. "Keep it—keep all your wealth—until I demand it all, or none! My message had no such end in view. You are beautiful, they tell me; and I desired to look at you!"

He took the one lamp that showed the discomfort and sordidness of his abode, and approaching Zenobia, held it up, so as to gain the more perfect view of her, from top to toe. So obscure was the chamber, that you could see the reflection of her diamonds thrown upon the dingy wall, and flickering with the rise and fall of Zenobia's breath. It was the splendor of those jewels on her neck, like lamps that burn before some fair temple, and the jewelled flower in her hair, more than the murky yellow light, that helped him to see her beauty. But he beheld it, and grew proud at heart; his own figure, in spite of his mean habiliments, assumed an air of state and grandeur.

"It is well!" cried old Moodie. "Keep your wealth. You are right worthy of it. Keep it, therefore, but with one condition, only!"

Zenobia thought the old man beside himself, and was moved with pity.

"Have you none to care for you?" asked she. "No daughter? —no kind-hearted neighbor?—no means of procuring the attendance which you need? Tell me, once again, can I do nothing for you?"

"Nothing," he replied. "I have beheld what I wished. Now, leave me! Linger not a moment longer; or I may be tempted to say what would bring a cloud over that queenly brow. Keep all your wealth, but with only this one condition. Be kind—be no less kind than sisters are—to my poor Priscilla!"

And, it may be, after Zenobia withdrew, Fauntleroy paced his gloomy chamber, and communed with himself, as follows: —or, at all events, it is the only solution, which I can offer, of the enigma presented in his character.

"I am unchanged—the same man as of yore!" said he. "True; my brother's wealth, he dying intestate, is legally my own. I know it; yet, of my own choice, I live a beggar, and go meanly clad, and hide myself behind a forgotten ignominy. Looks this like ostentation? Ah, but, in Zenobia, I live again! Beholding her so beautiful—so fit to be adorned with all imaginable splendor of outward state—the cursed vanity, which, half-a-lifetime since, dropt off like tatters of once gaudy apparel from my debased and ruined person, is all renewed for her sake! Were I to re-appear, my shame would go with me from darkness into daylight. Zenobia has the splendor, and not the shame. Let the world admire her, and be dazzled by her, the brilliant child of my prosperity! It is Fauntleroy that still shines through her!"

But, then, perhaps, another thought occurred to him.

"My poor Priscilla! And am I just, to her, in surrendering all to this beautiful Zenobia? Priscilla! I love her best—I love her only!—but with shame, not pride. So dim, so pallid, so shrinking—the daughter of my long calamity! Wealth were but a mockery in Priscilla's hands. What is its use, except to fling a golden radiance around those who grasp it? Yet, let Zenobia take heed! Priscilla shall have no wrong!"

But, while the man of show thus meditated—that very evening, so far as I can adjust the dates of these strange incidents—Priscilla—poor, pallid flower!—was either snatched from Zenobia's hand, or flung wilfully away!

XXIII

A VILLAGE-HALL

WELL! I betook myself away, and wandered up and down, like an exorcised spirit that had been driven from its old haunts, after a mighty struggle. It takes down the solitary pride of man, beyond most other things, to find the impracticability of flinging aside affections that have grown irksome. The bands, that were silken once, are apt to become iron fetters, when we desire to shake them off. Our souls, after all, are not our own. We convey a property in them to those with whom we associate, but to what extent can never be known, until we feel the tug, the agony, of our abortive effort to resume an exclusive sway over ourselves. Thus, in all the weeks of my absence, my thoughts continually reverted back, brooding over the by-gone months, and bringing up incidents that seemed hardly to have left a trace of themselves, in their passage. I spent painful hours in recalling these trifles, and rendering them more misty and unsubstantial than at first, by the quantity of speculative musing, thus kneaded in with them. Hollingsworth, Zenobia, Priscilla! These three had absorbed my life into themselves. Together with an inexpressible longing to know their fortunes, there was likewise a morbid resentment of my own pain, and a stubborn reluctance to come again within their sphere.

All that I learned of them, therefore, was comprised in a few brief and pungent squibs, such as the newspapers were then in the habit of bestowing on our socialist enterprise. There was one paragraph which, if I rightly guessed its purport, bore reference to Zenobia, but was too darkly hinted to convey even thus much of certainty. Hollingsworth, too, with his philanthropic project, afforded the penny-a-liners a theme for some savage and bloody-minded jokes; and, considerably to my surprise, they affected me with as much indignation as if we had still been friends.

Thus passed several weeks; time long enough for my brown and toil-hardened hands to re-accustom themselves to gloves. Old habits, such as were merely external, returned upon me with wonderful promptitude. My superficial talk, too, assumed altogether a worldly tone. Meeting former acquaintances, who showed themselves inclined to ridicule my heroic devotion to the cause of human welfare, I spoke of the recent phase of my life as indeed fair matter for a jest. But I also gave them to understand that it was, at most, only an experiment, on which I had staked no valuable amount of hope or fear; it had enabled me to pass the summer in a novel and agreeable way, had afforded me some grotesque specimens of artificial simplicity, and could not, therefore, so far as I was concerned, be reckoned a failure. In no one instance, however, did I voluntarily speak of my three friends. They dwelt in a profounder region. The more I consider myself, as I then was, the more do I recognize how deeply my connection with those three had affected all my being.

As it was already the epoch of annihilated space, I might, in the time I was away from Blithedale, have snatched a glimpse at England, and been back again. But my wanderings were confined within a very limited sphere. I hopped and fluttered, like a bird with a string about its leg, gyrating round a small circumference, and keeping up a restless activity to no purpose. Thus, it was still in our familiar Massachusetts—in one of its white country-villages—that I must next particularize an incident.

The scene was one of those Lyceum-halls, of which almost every village has now its own, dedicated to that sober and pallid, or, rather, drab-colored, mode of winter-evening entertainment, the Lecture. Of late years, this has come strangely into vogue, when the natural tendency of things would seem to be, to substitute lettered for oral methods of addressing the public. But, in halls like this, besides the winter course of lectures, there is a rich and varied series of other exhibitions.

Hither comes the ventriloquist, with all his mysterious tongues; the thaumaturgist,[8] too, with his miraculous transformations of plates, doves, and rings, his pancakes smoking in your hat, and his cellar of choice liquors, represented in one small bottle. Here, also, the itinerant professor instructs separate classes of ladies and gentlemen in physiology, and demonstrates his lessons by the aid of real skeletons, and mannikins in wax, from Paris. Here is to be heard the choir of Ethiopian melodists, and to be seen, the diorama of Moscow or Bunker Hill, or the moving panorama of the Chinese wall. Here is displayed the museum of wax figures, illustrating the wide catholicism of earthly renown by mixing up heroes and statesmen, the Pope and the Mormon Prophet,[9] kings, queens, murderers, and beautiful ladies; every sort of person, in short, except authors, of whom I never beheld even the most famous, done in wax. And here, in this many-purposed hall, (unless the selectmen of the village chance to have more than their share of the puritanism, which, however diversified with later patchwork, still gives its prevailing tint to New England character,) here the company of strolling players sets up its little stage, and claims patronage for the legitimate drama.

But, on the autumnal evening which I speak of, a number of printed handbills—stuck up in the bar-room and on the sign-post of the hotel, and on the meeting-house porch, and distributed largely through the village—had promised the inhabitants an interview with that celebrated and hitherto inexplicable phenomenon, the Veiled Lady!

The hall was fitted up with an amphitheatrical descent of seats towards a platform, on which stood a desk, two lights, a stool, and a capacious, antique chair. The audience was of a generally decent and respectable character; old farmers, in their Sunday black coats, with shrewd, hard, sun-dried faces, and a cynical humor, oftener than any other expression, in their eyes; pretty girls, in many-colored attire; pretty young

8. Magician.
9. Joseph Smith (1805–44), who founded the first Mormon church in 1830, three years after he reputedly unearthed golden tablets of sacred writing, which he translated as the Book of Mormon.

men—the schoolmaster, the lawyer, or student-at-law, the shopkeeper—all looking rather suburban than rural. In these days, there is absolutely no rusticity, except when the actual labor of the soil leaves its earth-mould on the person. There was likewise a considerable proportion of young and middle-aged women, many of them stern in feature, with marked foreheads, and a very definite line of eyebrow; a type of womanhood in which a bold intellectual development seems to be keeping pace with the progressive delicacy of the physical constitution. Of all these people I took note, at first, according to my custom. But I ceased to do so, the moment that my eyes fell on an individual who sat two or three seats below me, immoveable, apparently deep in thought, with his back, of course, towards me, and his face turned steadfastly upon the platform.

After sitting awhile, in contemplation of this person's familiar contour, I was irresistibly moved to step over the intervening benches, lay my hand on his shoulder, put my mouth close to his ear, and address him in a sepulchral, melodramatic whisper:—

"Hollingsworth! Where have you left Zenobia!"

His nerves, however, were proof against my attack. He turned half around, and looked me in the face, with great, sad eyes, in which there was neither kindness nor resentment, nor any perceptible surprise.

"Zenobia, when I last saw her," he answered, "was at Blithedale."

He said no more. But there was a great deal of talk going on, near me, among a knot of people who might be considered as representing the mysticism, or, rather, the mystic sensuality, of this singular age. The nature of the exhibition, that was about to take place, had probably given the turn to their conversation.

I heard, from a pale man in blue spectacles, some stranger stories than ever were written in a romance; told, too, with a simple, unimaginative steadfastness, which was terribly efficacious in compelling the auditor to receive them into the category of established facts. He cited instances of the miraculous power of one human being over the will and passions of another; insomuch that settled grief was but a shadow, beneath the influence of a man possessing this potency, and the strong love of years melted away like a vapor. At the bidding of one of these wizards, the maiden, with her lover's kiss still burning on her lips, would turn from him with icy indifference; the newly made widow would dig up her buried heart out of her young husband's grave, before the sods had taken root upon it; a mother, with her babe's milk in her bosom, would thrust away her child. Human character was but soft wax in his hands; and guilt, or virtue, only the forms into which he should see fit to mould it. The religious sentiment was a flame which he could blow up with his breath, or a spark that he could utterly extinguish. It is unutterable, the horror and disgust with which I listened, and saw, that, if these things were to be believed, the individual soul was virtually annihilated, and all that is sweet and pure, in our present life, debased, and that the idea of man's eternal responsibility was made ridiculous, and immortality rendered, at once, impossible, and not worth acceptance. But I would have perished on the spot, sooner than believe it.

The epoch of rapping spirits, and all the wonders that have followed in their train—such as tables, upset by invisible agencies, bells, self-tolled at funerals, and ghostly music, performed on jewsharps—had not yet arrived. Alas, my countrymen, methinks we have fallen on an evil age! If these phenomena have not humbug at the bottom, so much the worse for us. What can they indicate, in a spiritual way, except that the soul of man is descending to a lower point than it has ever before reached, while incarnate? We are pursuing a downward course, in the eternal march, and thus bring ourselves into the same range with beings whom death, in requital of their gross and evil lives, has degraded below humanity. To hold intercourse with spirits of this order, we must stoop, and grovel in some element more vile than earthly dust. These goblins, if they exist at all, are but the shadows of past mortality, outcasts, mere refuse-stuff, adjudged unworthy of the eternal world, and, on the most favorable supposition, dwindling gradually into nothingness. The less we have to say to them, the better; lest we share their fate!

The audience now began to be impatient; they signified their desire for the entertainment to commence, by thump of sticks and stamp of boot-heels. Nor was it a great while longer, before, in response to their call, there appeared a bearded personage in Oriental robes, looking like one of the enchanters of the Arabian Nights.[1] He came upon the platform from a side-door—saluted the spectators, not with a salaam, but a bow—took his station at the desk—and first blowing his nose with a white handkerchief, prepared to speak. The environment of the homely village-hall, and the absence of many ingenious contrivances of stage-effect, with which the exhibition had heretofore been set off, seemed to bring the artifice of this character more openly upon the surface. No sooner did I behold the bearded enchanter, than laying my hand again on Hollingsworth's shoulder, I whispered in his ear:—

"Do you know him?"

"I never saw the man before," he muttered, without turning his head.

But I had seen him, three times, already. Once, on occasion of my first visit to the Veiled Lady; a second time, in the wood-path at Blithedale; and, lastly, in Zenobia's drawing-room. It was Westervelt. A quick association of ideas made me shudder, from head to foot; and, again, like an evil spirit, bringing up reminiscences of a man's sins, I whispered a question in Hollingsworth's ear.

"What have you done with Priscilla?"

He gave a convulsive start, as if I had thrust a knife into

1. A series of exotic stories in Arabic (including those of Ali Baba and Aladdin) strung together by Scheherazade, who kept her sultan-husband from killing her by telling these tales for 1001 nights.

him, writhed himself round on his seat, glared fiercely into my eyes, but answered not a word.

The Professor began his discourse, explanatory of the psychological phenomena, as he termed them, which it was his purpose to exhibit to the spectators. There remains no very distinct impression of it on my memory. It was eloquent, ingenious, plausible, with a delusive show of spirituality, yet really imbued throughout with a cold and dead materialism. I shivered, as at a current of chill air, issuing out of a sepulchral vault and bringing the smell of corruption along with it. He spoke of a new era that was dawning upon the world; an era that would link soul to soul, and the present life to what we call futurity, with a closeness that should finally convert both worlds into one great, mutually conscious brotherhood. He described (in a strange, philosophical guise, with terms of art, as if it were a matter of chemical discovery) the agency by which this mighty result was to be effected; nor would it have surprised me, had he pretended to hold up a portion of his universally pervasive fluid, as he affirmed it to be, in a glass phial.

At the close of his exordium, the Professor beckoned with his hand—one, twice, thrice—and a figure came gliding upon the platform, enveloped in a long veil of silvery whiteness. It fell about her, like the texture of a summer cloud, with a kind of vagueness, so that the outline of the form, beneath it, could not be accurately discerned. But the movement of the Veiled Lady was graceful, free, and unembarrassed, like that of a person accustomed to be the spectacle of thousands. Or, possibly, a blindfold prisoner within the sphere with which this dark, earthly magician had surrounded her, she was wholly unconscious of being the central object to all those straining eyes.

Pliant to his gesture, (which had even an obsequious courtesy, but, at the same time, a remarkable decisiveness,) the figure placed itself in the great chair. Sitting there, in such visible obscurity, it was perhaps as much like the actual presence of a disembodied spirit as anything that stage-trickery could devise. The hushed breathing of the spectators proved how high-wrought were their anticipations of the wonders to be performed, through the medium of this incomprehensible creature. I, too, was in breathless suspense, but with a far different presentiment of some strange event at hand.

"You see before you the Veiled Lady," said the bearded Professor, advancing to the verge of the platform. "By the agency of which I have just spoken, she is, at this moment, in communion with the spiritual world. That silvery veil is, in one sense, an enchantment, having been dipt, as it were, and essentially imbued, through the potency of my art, with the fluid medium of spirits. Slight and ethereal as it seems, the limitations of time and space have no existence within its folds. This hall—these hundreds of faces, encompassing her within so narrow an amphitheatre—are of thinner substance, in her view, than the airiest vapor that the clouds are made of. She beholds the Absolute!"

As preliminary to other, and far more wonderful psychological experiments, the exhibitor suggested that some of his auditors should endeavor to make the Veiled Lady sensible of their presence by such methods—provided, only, no touch were laid upon her person—as they might deem best adapted to that end. Accordingly, several deep-lunged country-fellows, who looked as if they might have blown the apparition away with a breath, ascended the platform. Mutually encouraging one another, they shouted so close to her ear, that the veil stirred like a wreath of vanishing mist; they smote upon the floor with bludgeons; they perpetrated so hideous a clamor, that methought it might have reached, at least a little way, into the eternal sphere. Finally, with the assent of the Professor, they laid hold of the great chair, and were startled, apparently, to find it soar upward, as if lighter than the air through which it rose. But the Veiled Lady remained seated and motionless, with a composure that was hardly less than awful, because implying so immeasurable a distance betwixt her and these rude persecutors.

"These efforts are wholly without avail," observed the Professor, who had been looking on with an aspect of serene indifference. "The roar of a battery of cannon would be inaudible to the Veiled Lady. And yet, were I to will it, sitting in this very hall, she could hear the desert-wind sweeping over the sands, as far off as Arabia; the ice-bergs grinding one against the other, in the polar seas; the rustle of a leaf in an East Indian forest; the lowest whispered breath of the bashfullest maiden in the world, uttering the first confession of her love! Nor does there exist the moral inducement, apart from my own behest, that could persuade her to lift the silvery veil, or arise out of that chair!"

Greatly to the Professor's discomposure, however, just as he spoke these words, the Veiled Lady arose. There was a mysterious tremor that shook the magic veil. The spectators, it may be, imagined that she was about to take flight into that invisible sphere, and to the society of those purely spiritual beings, with whom they reckoned her so near akin. Hollingsworth, a moment ago, had mounted the platform, and now stood gazing at the figure, with a sad intentness that brought the whole power of his great, stern, yet tender soul, into his glance.

"Come!" said he, waving his hand towards her. "You are safe!"

She threw off the veil, and stood before that multitude of people, pale, tremulous, shrinking, as if only then had she discovered that a thousand eyes were gazing at her. Poor maiden! How strangely had she been betrayed! Blazoned abroad as a wonder of the world, and performing what were adjudged as miracles—in the faith of many, a seeress and a prophetess—in the harsher judgment of others, a mountebank —she had kept, as I religiously believe, her virgin reserve and sanctity of soul, throughout it all. Within that encircling veil, though an evil hand had flung it over her, there was as deep a seclusion as if this forsaken girl had, all the while, been sitting under the shadow of Eliot's pulpit, in the Blithedale woods, at the feet of him who now summoned her to the shelter of his arms. And the true heart-throb of a woman's affection was too powerful for the jugglery that had hitherto environed her. She uttered a shriek and fled to Hollingsworth, like one escaping from her deadliest enemy, and was safe forever!

XXIV

THE MASQUERADERS

TWO NIGHTS had passed since the foregoing occurrences, when, in a breezy September forenoon, I set forth from town, on foot, towards Blithedale.

It was the most delightful of all days for a walk, with a dash of invigorating ice-temper in the air, but a coolness that soon gave place to the brisk glow of exercise, while the vigor remained as elastic as before. The atmosphere had a spirit and sparkle in it., Each breath was like a sip of ethereal wine, tempered, as I said, with a crystal lump of ice. I had started on this expedition in an exceedingly sombre mood, as well befitted one who found himself tending towards home, but was conscious that nobody would be quite overjoyed to greet him there. My feet were hardly off the pavement, however, when this morbid sensation began to yield to the lively influences of air and motion. Nor had I gone far, with fields yet green on either side, before my step became as swift and light as if Hollingsworth were waiting to exchange a friendly hand-grip, and Zenobia's and Priscilla's open arms would welcome the wanderer's re-appearance. It has happened to me, on other occasions, as well as this, to prove how a state of physical well-being can create a kind of joy, in spite of the profoundest anxiety of mind.

The pathway of that walk still runs along, with sunny freshness, through my memory. I know not why it should be so. But my mental eye can even now discern the September grass, bordering the pleasant roadside with a brighter verdure than while the summer-heats were scorching it; the trees, too, mostly green, although, here and there, a branch or shrub has donned its vesture of crimson and gold, a week or two before its fellows. I see the tufted barberry bushes, with their small clusters of scarlet fruit; the toadstools, likewise, some spotlessly white, others yellow or red—mysterious growths, springing suddenly from no root or seed, and growing nobody can tell how or wherefore. In this respect, they resembled many of the emotions in my breast. And I still see the little rivulets, chill, clear, and bright, that murmured beneath the road, through subterranean rocks, and deepened into mossy pools where tiny fish were darting to-and-fro, and within which lurked the hermit-frog. But, no—I never can account for it—that, with a yearning interest to learn the upshot of all my story, and returning to Blithedale for that sole purpose, I should examine these things so like a peaceful-bosomed naturalist. Nor why, amid all my sympathies and fears, there shot, at times, a wild exhilaration through my frame!

Thus I pursued my way, along the line of the ancient stone-wall that Paul Dudley[2] built, and through white villages, and past orchards of ruddy apples, and fields of ripening maize, and patches of woodland, and all such sweet rural scenery as looks the fairest, a little beyond the suburbs of a town. Hollingsworth, Zenobia, Priscilla! They glided mistily before me, as I walked. Sometimes, in my solitude, I laughed with the bitterness of self-scorn, remembering how unreservedly I had given up my heart and soul to interests that were not mine. What had I ever had to do with them? And why, being now free, should I take this thraldom on me, once again? It was both sad and dangerous, I whispered to myself, to be in too close affinity with the passions, the errors, and the misfortunes, of individuals who stood within a circle of their

2. Paul Dudley (1675–1751), an important figure in the judicial system of the Massachusetts Bay Province for almost fifty years, erected numerous milestones along the roads in Norfolk County, Massachusetts.

own, into which, if I stept at all, it must be as an intruder, and at a peril that I could not estimate.

Drawing nearer to Blithedale, a sickness of the spirits kept alternating with my flights of causeless buoyancy. I indulged in a hundred odd and extravagant conjectures. Either there was no such place as Blithedale, nor ever had been, nor any brotherhood of thoughtful laborers, like what I seemed to recollect there; or else it was all changed, during my absence. It had been nothing but dream-work and enchantment. I should seek in vain for the old farm-house, and for the greensward, the potatoe-fields, the root-crops, and acres of Indian corn, and for all that configuration of the land which I had imagined. It would be another spot, and an utter strangeness.

These vagaries were of the spectral throng, so apt to steal out of an unquiet heart. They partly ceased to haunt me, on my arriving at a point whence, through the trees, I began to catch glimpses of the Blithedale farm. That, surely, was something real. There was hardly a square foot of all those acres, on which I had not trodden heavily in one or another kind of toil. The curse of Adam's posterity—and, curse or blessing be it, it gives substance to the life around us—had first come upon me there. In the sweat of my brow, I had there earned bread and eaten it, and so established my claim to be on earth, and my fellowship with all the sons of labor. I could have knelt down, and have laid my breast against that soil. The red clay, of which my frame was moulded, seemed nearer akin to those crumbling furrows than to any other portion of the world's dust. There was my home; and there might be my grave.

I felt an invincible reluctance, nevertheless, at the idea of presenting myself before my old associates, without first ascertaining the state in which they were. A nameless foreboding weighed upon me. Perhaps, should I know all the circumstances that had occurred, I might find it my wisest course to turn back, unrecognized, unseen, and never look at Blithedale more. Had it been evening, I would have stolen softly to some lighted window of the old farm-house, and peeped darkling in, to see all their well-known faces round the supper-board. Then, were there a vacant seat, I might noiselessly unclose the door, glide in, and take my place among them, without a word. My entrance might be so quiet, my aspect so familiar, that they would forget how long I had been away, and suffer me to melt into the scene, as a wreath of vapor melts into a larger cloud. I dreaded a boisterous greeting. Beholding me at table, Zenobia, as a matter of course, would send me a cup of tea, and Hollingsworth fill my plate from the great dish of pan-dowdy,[3] and Priscilla, in her quiet way, would hand the cream, and others help me to the bread and butter. Being one of them again, the knowledge of what had happened would come to me, without a shock. For, still, at every turn of my shifting fantasies, the thought stared me in the face, that some evil thing had befallen us, or was ready to befall.

Yielding to this ominous impression, I now turned aside into the woods, resolving to spy out the posture of the Community, as craftily as the wild Indian before he makes his onset. I would go wandering about the outskirts of the farm, and, perhaps catching sight of a solitary acquaintance, would approach him amid the brown shadows of the trees, (a kind of medium fit for spirits departed and revisitant, like myself,) and entreat him to tell me how all things were.

The first living creature that I met, was a partridge, which sprung up beneath my feet, and whirred away; the next was a squirrel, who chattered angrily at me, from an overhanging bough. I trod along by the dark, sluggish river, and remember pausing on the bank, above one of its blackest and most placid pools—(the very spot, with the barkless stump of a tree aslantwise over the water, is depicting itself to my fancy, at this instant)—and wondering how deep it was, and if any overladen soul had ever flung its weight of mortality in thither, and if it thus escaped the burthen, or only made it heavier. And perhaps the skeleton of the drowned wretch still lay

3. An apple pudding or deep pie.

beneath the inscrutable depth, clinging to some sunken log at the bottom with the gripe of its old despair. So slight, however, was the track of these gloomy ideas, that I soon forgot them in the contemplation of a brood of wild ducks, which were floating on the river, and anon took flight, leaving each a bright streak over the black surface. By-and-by, I came to my hermitage, in the heart of the white-pine tree, and clambering up into it, sat down to rest. The grapes, which I had watched throughout the summer, now dangled around me in abundant clusters of the deepest purple, deliciously sweet to the taste, and though wild, yet free from that un-gentle flavor which distinguishes nearly all our native and uncultivated grapes. Methought a wine might be pressed out of them, possessing a passionate zest, and endowed with a new kind of intoxicating quality, attended with such bac-chanalian ecstasies as the tamer grapes of Madeira, France, and the Rhine, are inadequate to produce. And I longed to quaff a great goblet of it, at that moment!

While devouring the grapes, I looked on all sides out of the peep-holes of my hermitage, and saw the farm-house, the fields, and almost every part of our domain, but not a single human figure in the landscape. Some of the windows of the house were open, but with no more signs of life than in a dead man's unshut eyes. The barn-door was ajar, and swing-ing in the breeze. The big, old dog—he was a relic of the former dynasty of the farm—that hardly ever stirred out of the yard, was nowhere to be seen. What, then, had become of all the fraternity and sisterhood? Curious to ascertain this point, I let myself down out of the tree, and going to the edge of the wood, was glad to perceive our herd of cows, chewing the cud, or grazing, not far off. I fancied, by their manner, that two or three of them recognized me, (as, indeed, they ought, for I had milked them, and been their chamber-lain, times without number;) but, after staring me in the face, a little while, they phlegmatically began grazing and chewing their cuds again. Then I grew foolishly angry at so cold a reception, and flung some rotten fragments of an old stump at these unsentimental cows.

Skirting farther round the pasture, I heard voices and much laughter proceeding from the interior of the wood. Voices, male and feminine; laughter, not only of fresh young throats, but the bass of grown people, as if solemn organ-pipes should pour out airs of merriment. Not a voice spoke, but I knew it better than my own; not a laugh, but its cadences were familiar. The wood, in this portion of it, seemed as full of jollity as if Comus[4] and his crew were holding their revels, in one of its usually lonesome glades. Stealing onward as far as I durst, without hazard of discovery, I saw a concourse of strange figures beneath the overshadowing branches; they appeared, and vanished, and came again, confusedly, with the streaks of sunlight glimmering down upon them.

Among them was an Indian chief, with blanket, feathers and war-paint, and uplifted tomahawk; and near him, looking fit to be his woodland-bride, the goddess Diana, with the crescent on her head, and attended by our big, lazy dog, in lack of any fleeter hound. Drawing an arrow from her quiver, she let it fly, at a venture, and hit the very tree behind which I happened to be lurking. Another group consisted of a Bavarian broom-girl, a negro of the Jim Crow order,[5] one or two foresters of the middle-ages, a Kentucky woodsman in his trimmed hunting-shirt and deerskin leggings, and a Shaker[6] elder, quaint, demure, broad-brimmed, and square-skirted. Shepherds of Arcadia, and allegoric figures from the Faerie Queen,[7] were oddly mixed up with these. Arm in arm, or otherwise huddled together, in strange discrepancy, stood grim Puritans, gay Cavaliers,[8] and Revolutionary officers, with three-cornered cocked-hats, and queues longer than their swords.

4. In John Milton's *Comus* (1634), Comus ("reveling") and a band of monsters with the heads of beasts and the bodies of humans feast, shout, and dance.
5. Such as was presented in nineteenth century minstrel shows in which white men performed in blackface.
6. A member of a religious sect which believed in the Second Coming, practiced total celibacy, and shook during worship.
7. Edmund Spenser's allegorical epic-romance, *The Faerie Queene* (1590, 1596).
8. Supporters of Charles I of England against Parliament, which was supported by the Puritans (1642–49).

A bright-complexioned, dark-haired, vivacious little gipsy, with a red shawl over her head, went from one group to another, telling fortunes by palmistry; and Moll Pitcher, the renowned old witch of Lynn,[9] broomstick in hand, showed herself prominently in the midst, as if announcing all these apparitions to be the offspring of her necromantic art. But Silas Foster, who leaned against a tree near by, in his customary blue frock, and smoking a short pipe, did more to disenchant the scene, with his look of shrewd, acrid, Yankee observation, than twenty witches and necromancers could have done, in the way of rendering it weird and fantastic.

A little further off, some old-fashioned skinkers and drawers,[1] all with portentously red noses, were spreading a banquet on the leaf-strewn earth; while a horned and long-tailed gentleman (in whom I recognized the fiendish musician, erst seen by Tam O'Shanter)[2] tuned his fiddle, and summoned the whole motley rout to a dance, before partaking of the festal cheer. So they joined hands in a circle, whirling round so swiftly, so madly, and so merrily, in time and tune with the Satanic music, that their separate incongruities were blended all together; and they became a kind of entanglement that went nigh to turn one's brain, with merely looking at it. Anon, they stopt, all of a sudden, and staring at one another's figures, set up a roar of laughter; whereat, a shower of the September leaves (which, all day long, had been hesitating whether to fall or no) were shaken off by the movement of the air, and came eddying down upon the revellers.

Then, for lack of breath, ensued a silence; at the deepest point of which, tickled by the oddity of surprising my grave associates in this masquerading trim, I could not possibly refrain from a burst of laughter, on my own separate account.

"Hush!" I heard the pretty gipsy fortuneteller say. "Who is that laughing?"

9. A famous clairvoyant (d. 1813) of Lynn, Massachusetts, whose name became a generic term for fortune-tellers in the nineteenth century.
1. Both terms mean servers of drinks.

2. In Robert Burns's long poem "Tam o'Shanter" (1791), the drunken Tam encounters the Devil in the shape of a shaggy dog playing the bagpipes.

"Some profane intruder!" said the goddess Diana. "I shall send an arrow through his heart, or change him into a stag, as I did Actaeon,[3] if he peeps from behind the trees!"

"Me take his scalp!" cried the Indian chief, brandishing his tomahawk, and cutting a great caper in the air.

"I'll root him in the earth, with a spell that I have at my tongue's end!" squeaked Moll Pitcher. "And the green moss shall grow all over him, before he gets free again!"

"The voice was Miles Coverdale's," said the fiendish fiddler, with a whisk of his tail and a toss of his horns. "My music has brought him hither. He is always ready to dance to the devil's tune!"

Thus put on the right track, they all recognized the voice at once, and set up a simultaneous shout.

"Miles! Miles! Miles Coverdale, where are you?" they cried. "Zenobia! Queen Zenobia! Here is one of your vassals lurking in the wood. Command him to approach, and pay his duty!"

The whole fantastic rabble forthwith streamed off in pursuit of me, so that I was like a mad poet hunted by chimaeras. Having fairly the start of them, however, I succeeded in making my escape, and soon left their merriment and riot at a good distance in the rear. Its fainter tones assumed a kind of mournfulness, and were finally lost in the hush and solemnity of the wood. In my haste, I stumbled over a heap of logs and sticks that had been cut for firewood, a great while ago, by some former possessor of the soil, and piled up square, in order to be carted or sledded away to the farm-house. But, being forgotten, they had lain there, perhaps fifty years, and possibly much longer; until, by the accumulation of moss, and the leaves falling over them and decaying there, from autumn to autumn, a green mound was formed, in which the softened outline of the wood-pile was still perceptible. In

---

3. In Greek mythology, the young hunter who was turned into a deer and killed by his dogs for accidentally coming upon the virgin goddess, Artemis (or Diana), bathing in a pool.

the fitful mood that then swayed my mind, I found something strangely affecting in this simple circumstance. I imagined the long-dead woodman, and his long-dead wife and children, coming out of their chill graves, and essaying to make a fire with this heap of mossy fuel!

From this spot I strayed onward, quite lost in reverie, and neither knew nor cared whither I was going, until a low, soft, well-remembered voice spoke, at a little distance.

"There is Mr. Coverdale!"

"Miles Coverdale!" said another voice—and its tones were very stern—"Let him come forward, then!"

"Yes, Mr. Coverdale," cried a woman's voice—clear and melodious, but, just then, with something unnatural in its chord—"You are welcome! But you come half-an-hour too late, and have missed a scene which you would have enjoyed!"

I looked up, and found myself nigh Eliot's pulpit, at the base of which sat Hollingsworth, with Priscilla at his feet, and Zenobia standing before them.

XXV

THE THREE TOGETHER

HOLLINGSWORTH was in his ordinary working-dress. Priscilla wore a pretty and simple gown, with a kerchief about her neck, and a calash,[4] which she had flung back from her head, leaving it suspended by the strings. But Zenobia (whose part among the masquers, as may be supposed, was no inferior one) appeared in a costume of fanciful magnificence, with her jewelled flower as the central ornament of what resembled a leafy crown, or coronet. She represented the Oriental princess, by whose name we were accustomed to know her. Her attitude was free and

---

4. A bonnet with a folded-back top.

noble, yet, if a queen's, it was not that of a queen triumphant, but dethroned, on trial for her life, or perchance condemned, already. The spirit of the conflict seemed, nevertheless, to be alive in her. Her eyes were on fire; her cheeks had each a crimson spot, so exceedingly vivid, and marked with so definite an outline, that I at first doubted whether it were not artificial. In a very brief space, however, this idea was shamed by the paleness that ensued, as the blood sank suddenly away. Zenobia now looked like marble.

One always feels the fact, in an instant, when he has intruded on those who love, or those who hate, at some acme of their passion that puts them into a sphere of their own, where no other spirit can pretend to stand on equal ground with them. I was confused—affected even with a species of terror—and wished myself away. The intentness of their feelings gave them the exclusive property of the soil and atmosphere, and left me no right to be or breathe there.

"'Hollingsworth—Zenobia—I have just returned to Blithedale," said I, "and had no thought of finding you here. We shall meet again at the house. I will retire."

"This place is free to you," answered Hollingsworth.

"As free as to ourselves," added Zenobia. "This long while past, you have been following up your game, groping for human emotions in the dark corners of the heart. Had you been here a little sooner, you might have seen them dragged into the daylight. I could even wish to have my trial over again, with you standing by, to see fair-play! Do you know, Mr. Coverdale, I have been on trial for my life?"

She laughed, while speaking thus. But, in truth, as my eyes wandered from one of the group to another, I saw in Hollingsworth all that an artist could desire for the grim portrait of a Puritan magistrate, holding inquest of life and death in a case of witchcraft;—in Zenobia, the sorceress herself, not aged, wrinkled, and decrepit, but fair enough to tempt Satan with a force reciprocal to his own;—and, in Priscilla, the pale victim, whose soul and body had been wasted by her spells. Had a pile of faggots been heaped against the rock, this hint of impending doom would have completed the suggestive picture.

"It was too hard upon me," continued Zenobia, addressing Hollingsworth, "that judge, jury, and accuser, should all be comprehended in one man! I demur, as I think the lawyers say, to the jurisdiction. But let the learned Judge Coverdale seat himself on the top of the rock, and you and me stand at its base, side by side, pleading our cause before him! There might, at least, be two criminals, instead of one."

"You forced this on me," replied Hollingsworth, looking her sternly in the face. "Did I call you hither from among the masqueraders yonder? Do I assume to be your judge? No; except so far as I have an unquestionable right of judgment, in order to settle my own line of behavior towards those, with whom the events of life bring me in contact. True; I have already judged you, but not on the world's part—neither do I pretend to pass a sentence!"

"Ah, this is very good!" said Zenobia, with a smile. "What strange beings you men are, Mr. Coverdale!—is it not so? It is the simplest thing in the world, with you, to bring a woman before your secret tribunals, and judge and condemn her, unheard, and then tell her to go free without a sentence. The misfortune is, that this same secret tribunal chances to be the only judgment-seat that a true woman stands in awe of, and that any verdict short of acquittal is equivalent to a death-sentence!"

The more I looked at them, and the more I heard, the stronger grew my impression that a crisis had just come and gone. On Hollingsworth's brow, it had left a stamp like that of irrevocable doom, of which his own will was the instrument. In Zenobia's whole person, beholding her more closely, I saw a riotous agitation; the almost delirious disquietude of a great struggle, at the close of which, the vanquished one felt her strength and courage still mighty within her, and longed to renew the contest. My sensations were as if I had come upon a battle-field, before the smoke was as yet cleared away.

And what subjects had been discussed here? All, no doubt, that, for so many months past, had kept my heart and my imagination idly feverish. Zenobia's whole character and history; the true nature of her mysterious connection with Westervelt; her later purposes towards Hollingsworth, and, reciprocally, his in reference to her; and, finally, the degree in which Zenobia had been cognizant of the plot against Priscilla, and what, at last, had been the real object of that scheme. On these points, as before, I was left to my own conjectures. One thing, only, was certain. Zenobia and Hollingsworth were friends no longer. If their heart-strings were ever intertwined, the knot had been adjudged an entanglement, and was now violently broken.

But Zenobia seemed unable to rest content with the matter, in the posture which it had assumed.

"Ah! Do we part so?" exclaimed she, seeing Hollingsworth about to retire.

"And why not?" said he, with almost rude abruptness. "What is there further to be said between us?"

"Well; perhaps nothing!" answered Zenobia, looking him in the face, and smiling. "But we have come, many times before, to this gray rock, and we have talked very softly, among the whisperings of the birch-trees. They were pleasant hours! I love to make the latest of them, though not altogether so delightful, loiter away as slowly as may be. And, besides, you have put many queries to me, at this, which you design to be our last interview; and being driven, as I must acknowledge, into a corner, I have responded with reasonable frankness. But, now, with your free consent, I desire the privilege of asking a few questions in my turn."

"I have no concealments," said Hollingsworth.

"We shall see!" answered Zenobia. "I would first inquire, whether you have supposed me to be wealthy?"

"On that point," observed Hollingsworth, "I have had the opinion which the world holds."

"And I held it, likewise," said Zenobia. "Had I not, Heaven is my witness, the knowledge should have been as free to you as me. It is only three days since I knew the strange fact that threatens to make me poor; and your own acquaintance with it, I suspect, is of at least as old a date. I fancied myself affluent. You are aware, too, of the disposition which I purposed making of the larger portion of my imaginary opulence;—nay, were it all, I had not hesitated. Let me ask you further, did I ever propose or intimate any terms of compact, on which depended this—as the world would consider it—so important sacrifice?"

"You certainly spoke of none," said Hollingsworth.

"Nor meant any," she responded. "I was willing to realize your dream, freely—generously, as some might think—but, at all events, fully—and heedless though it should prove the ruin of my fortune. If, in your own thoughts, you have imposed any conditions of this expenditure, it is you that must be held responsible for whatever is sordid and unworthy in them. And, now, one other question! Do you love this girl?"

"Oh, Zenobia!" exclaimed Priscilla, shrinking back, as if longing for the rock to topple over, and hide her.

"Do you love her?" repeated Zenobia.

"Had you asked me that question, a short time since," replied Hollingsworth, after a pause, during which, it seemed to me, even the birch-trees held their whispering breath, "I should have told you—'No!' My feelings for Priscilla differed little from those of an elder brother, watching tenderly over the gentle sister whom God has given him to protect."

"And what is your answer, now?" persisted Zenobia.

"I do love her!" said Hollingsworth, uttering the words with a deep, inward breath, instead of speaking them outright. "As well declare it thus, as in any other way. I do love her!"

"Now, God be judge between us," cried Zenobia, breaking into sudden passion, "which of us two has most mortally offended Him! At least, I am a woman—with every fault, it may be, that a woman ever had, weak, vain, unprincipled, (like most of my sex; for our virtues, when we have any, are merely impulsive and intuitive,) passionate, too, and pursuing my foolish and unattainable ends, by indirect and cunning, though absurdly chosen means, as an hereditary bond-slave must—false, moreover, to the whole circle of good, in my reckless truth to the little good I saw before me—but still a woman! A creature, whom only a little change of earthly fortune, a little kinder smile of Him who sent me hither, and one true heart to encourage and direct me, might have made all that a woman can be! But how is it with you? Are you a man? No; but a monster! A cold, heartless, self-beginning and self-ending piece of mechanism!"

"With what, then, do you charge me?" asked Hollingsworth, aghast, and greatly disturbed at this attack. "Show me one selfish end in all I ever aimed at, and you may cut it out of my bosom with a knife!"

"It is all self!" answered Zenobia, with still intenser bitterness. "Nothing else; nothing but self, self, self! The fiend, I doubt not, has made his choicest mirth of you, these seven years past, and especially in the mad summer which we have spent together. I see it now! I am awake, disenchanted, disenthralled! Self, self, self! You have embodied yourself in a project. You are a better masquerader than the witches and gipsies yonder; for your disguise is a self-deception. See whither it has brought you! First, you aimed a death-blow, and a treacherous one, at this scheme of a purer and higher life, which so many noble spirits had wrought out. Then, because Coverdale could not be quite your slave, you threw him ruthlessly away. And you took me, too, into your plan, as long as there was hope of my being available, and now fling me aside again, a broken tool! But, foremost, and blackest of your sins, you stifled down your inmost consciousness!—you did a deadly wrong to your own heart!—you were ready to sacrifice this girl, whom, if God ever visibly showed a purpose, He put into your charge, and through whom He was striving to redeem you!"

"This is a woman's view," said Hollingsworth, growing deadly pale—"a woman's, whose whole sphere of action is in the heart, and who can conceive of no higher nor wider one!"

"Be silent!" cried Zenobia, imperiously. "You know neither man nor woman! The utmost that can be said in your behalf— and because I would not be wholly despicable in my own eyes, but would fain excuse my wasted feelings, nor own it wholly a delusion, therefore I say it—is, that a great and rich heart has been ruined in your breast. Leave me, now! You have done with me, and I with you. Farewell!"

"Priscilla," said Hollingsworth, "come!"

Zenobia smiled; possibly, I did so too. Not often, in human life, has a gnawing sense of injury found a sweeter morsel of revenge, than was conveyed in the tone with which Hollingsworth spoke those two words. It was the abased and tremulous tone of a man, whose faith in himself was shaken, and who sought, at last, to lean on an affection. Yes; the strong man bowed himself, and rested on this poor Priscilla. Oh, could she have failed him, what a triumph for the lookers-on!

And, at first, I half imagined that she was about to fail him. She rose up, stood shivering, like the birch-leaves that trembled over her head, and then slowly tottered, rather than walked, towards Zenobia. Arriving at her feet, she sank down there, in the very same attitude which she had assumed on their first meeting, in the kitchen of the old farm-house. Zenobia remembered it.

"Ah, Priscilla," said she, shaking her head, "how much is changed since then! You kneel to a dethroned princess. You, the victorious one! But he is waiting for you. Say what you wish, and leave me."

"We are sisters!" gasped Priscilla.

I fancied that I understood the word and action; it meant the offering of herself, and all she had, to be at Zenobia's disposal. But the latter would not take it thus.

"True; we are sisters!" she replied; and, moved by the sweet word, she stooped down and kissed Priscilla—but not lovingly; for a sense of fatal harm, received through her, seemed to be lurking in Zenobia's heart—"We had one father! You knew it from the first; I, but a little while—else some things, that have chanced, might have been spared you. But I never wished you harm. You stood between me and an end which I desired. I wanted a clear path. No matter what I meant. It is over now. Do you forgive me?"

"Oh, Zenobia," sobbed Priscilla, "it is I that feel like the guilty one!"

"No, no, poor little thing!" said Zenobia, with a sort of contempt. "You have been my evil fate; but there never was a babe with less strength or will to do an injury. Poor child! Methinks you have but a melancholy lot before you, sitting all alone in that wide, cheerless heart, where, for aught you know—and as I, alas! believe—the fire which you have kindled may soon go out. Ah, the thought makes me shiver for you! What will you do, Priscilla, when you find no spark among the ashes?"

"Die!" she answered.

"That was well said!" responded Zenobia, with an approving smile. "There is all a woman in your little compass, my poor sister. Meanwhile, go with him, and live!"

She waved her away, with a queenly gesture, and turned her own face to the rock. I watched Priscilla, wondering what judgment she would pass, between Zenobia and Hollingsworth; how interpret his behavior, so as to reconcile it with true faith both towards her sister and herself; how compel her love for him to keep any terms whatever with her sisterly affection! But, in truth, there was no such difficulty as I imagined. Her engrossing love made it all clear. Hollingsworth could have no fault. That was the one principle at the centre of the universe. And the doubtful guilt or possible integrity of other people, appearances, self-evident facts, the testimony of her own senses—even Hollingsworth's self-accusation, had he volunteered it—would have weighed not the value of a mote of thistle-down, on the other side. So secure was she of his right, that she never thought of comparing it with another's wrong, but left the latter to itself.

Hollingsworth drew her arm within his, and soon disappeared with her among the trees. I cannot imagine how Zenobia knew when they were out of sight; she never glanced again towards them. But, retaining a proud attitude, so long as they might have thrown back a retiring look, they were no sooner departed—utterly departed—than she began slowly to sink down. It was as if a great, invisible, irresistible weight were pressing her to the earth. Settling upon her knees, she leaned her forehead against the rock, and sobbed convulsively; dry sobs, they seemed to be, such as have nothing to do with tears.

XXVI

ZENOBIA AND COVERDALE

*Z*ENOBIA had entirely forgotten me. She fancied herself alone with her great grief. And had it been only a common pity that I felt for her—the pity that her proud nature would have repelled, as the one worst wrong which the world yet held in reserve—the sacredness and awfulness of the crisis might have impelled me to steal away, silently, so that not a dry leaf should rustle under my feet. I would have left her to struggle, in that solitude, with only the eye of God upon her. But, so it happened, I never once dreamed of questioning my right to be there, now, as I had questioned it, just before, when I came so suddenly upon Hollingsworth and herself, in the passion of their recent debate. It suits me not to explain what was the analogy that I saw, or imagined, between Zenobia's situation and mine; nor, I believe, will the reader detect this one secret, hidden beneath many a revelation which perhaps concerned me less. In simple truth, however, as Zenobia leaned her forehead against the rock, shaken with that tearless agony, it seemed to me that the self-same pang, with hardly mitigated torment, leaped thrilling from her heart-strings to my own. Was it wrong, therefore, if I felt myself consecrated to the priesthood, by sympathy like this, and called upon to minister to this woman's affliction, so far as mortal could?

But, indeed, what could mortal do for her? Nothing! The attempt would be a mockery and an anguish. Time, it is true, would steal away her grief, and bury it, and the best of her heart in the same grave. But Destiny itself, methought, in its kindliest mood, could do no better for Zenobia, in the way of quick relief, than to cause the impending rock to impend a little further, and fall upon her head. So I leaned against a tree, and listened to her sobs, in unbroken silence. She was half prostrate, half kneeling, with her forehead still pressed against the rock. Her sobs were the only sound; she did not groan, nor give any other utterance to her distress. It was all involuntary.

At length, she sat up, put back her hair, and stared about her with a bewildered aspect, as if not distinctly recollecting the scene through which she had passed, nor cognizant of the situation in which it left her. Her face and brow were almost purple with the rush of blood. They whitened, however, by-and-by, and, for some time, retained this deathlike hue. She put her hand to her forehead, with a gesture that made me forcibly conscious of an intense and living pain there.

Her glance, wandering wildly to-and-fro, passed over me, several times, without appearing to inform her of my presence. But, finally, a look of recognition gleamed from her eyes into mine.

"Is it you, Miles Coverdale?" said she, smiling. "Ah, I perceive what you are about! You are turning this whole affair into a ballad. Pray let me hear as many stanzas as you happen to have ready!"

"Oh, hush, Zenobia!" I answered. "Heaven knows what an ache is in my soul!"

"It is genuine tragedy, is it not?" rejoined Zenobia, with a sharp, light laugh. "And you are willing to allow, perhaps, that I have had hard measure. But it is a woman's doom, and I have deserved it like a woman; so let there be no pity, as, on my part, there shall be no complaint. It is all right now, or will shortly be so. But, Mr. Coverdale, by all means, write this ballad, and put your soul's ache into it, and turn your sympathy to good account, as other poets do, and as poets must, unless they choose to give us glittering icicles instead of lines of fire. As for the moral, it shall be distilled into the final stanza, in a drop of bitter honey."

"What shall it be, Zenobia?" I inquired, endeavoring to fall in with her mood.

"Oh, a very old one will serve the purpose," she replied. "There are no new truths, much as we have prided ourselves on finding some. A moral? Why, this:—that, in the battle-field of life, the downright stroke, that would fall only on a man's steel head-piece, is sure to light on a woman's heart, over which she wears no breastplate, and whose wisdom it is, therefore, to keep out of the conflict. Or this:—that the whole universe, her own sex and yours, and Providence, or Destiny, to boot, make common cause against the woman who swerves one hair's breadth out of the beaten track. Yes; and add, (for I may as well own it, now,) that, with that one hair's breadth, she goes all astray, and never sees the world in its true aspect, afterwards!"

"This last is too stern a moral," I observed. "Cannot we soften it a little?"

"Do it, if you like, at your own peril, not on my responsibility," she answered; then, with a sudden change of subject, she went on:—"After all, he has flung away what would have served him better than the poor, pale flower he kept. What can Priscilla do for him? Put passionate warmth into his heart, when it shall be chilled with frozen hopes? Strengthen his hands, when they are weary with much doing and no performance? No; but only tend towards him with a blind, instinctive love, and hang her little, puny weakness for a clog upon his arm! She cannot even give him such sympathy as is worth the name. For will he never, in many an hour of darkness, need that proud, intellectual sympathy which he might have had from me?—the sympathy that would flash light along his course, and guide as well as cheer him? Poor Hollingsworth! Where will he find it now?"

"Hollingsworth has a heart of ice!" said I, bitterly. "He is a wretch!"

"Do him no wrong!" interrupted Zenobia, turning haughtily upon me. "Presume not to estimate a man like Hollingsworth! It was my fault, all along, and none of his. I see it now! He never sought me. Why should he seek me? What had I to offer him? A miserable, bruised, and battered heart, spoilt long before he met me! A life, too, hopelessly entangled with a villain's! He did well to cast me off. God be praised, he did it! And yet, had he trusted me, and borne with me a little longer, I would have saved him all this trouble."

She was silent, for a time, and stood with her eyes fixed on the ground. Again raising them, her look was more mild and calm.

"Miles Coverdale!" said she.

"Well, Zenobia!" I responded. "Can I do you any service?"

"Very little," she replied. "But it is my purpose, as you may well imagine, to remove from Blithedale; and, most likely, I may not see Hollingsworth again. A woman in my position, you understand, feels scarcely at her ease among former friends. New faces—unaccustomed looks—those only can she tolerate. She would pine, among familiar scenes; she would be apt to blush, too, under the eyes that knew her secret; her heart might throb uncomfortably; she would mortify herself, I suppose, with foolish notions of having sacrificed the honor of her sex, at the foot of proud, contumacious man. Poor womanhood, with its rights and wrongs! Here will be new matter for my course of lectures, at the idea of which you smiled, Mr. Coverdale, a month or two ago. But, as you have really a heart and sympathies, as far as they go, and as I shall depart without seeing Hollingsworth, I must entreat you to be a messenger between him and me."

"Willingly," said I, wondering at the strange way in which her mind seemed to vibrate from the deepest earnest to mere levity. "What is the message?"

"True;—what is it?" exclaimed Zenobia. "After all, I hardly know. On better consideration, I have no message. Tell him—tell him something pretty and pathetic, that will come nicely and sweetly into your ballad—anything you please, so it be tender and submissive enough. Tell him he has murdered me! Tell him that I'll haunt him!"—she spoke these words with the wildest energy—"And give him—no, give Priscilla—this!"

Thus saying, she took the jewelled flower out of her hair; and it struck me as the act of a queen, when worsted in a combat, discrowning herself, as if she found a sort of relief in abasing all her pride.

"Bid her wear this for Zenobia's sake," she continued. "She is a pretty little creature, and will make as soft and gentle a wife as the veriest Bluebeard[5] could desire. Pity that she must fade so soon! These delicate and puny maidens always do. Ten years hence, let Hollingsworth look at my face and Priscilla's, and then choose betwixt them. Or, if he pleases, let him do it now!"

How magnificently Zenobia looked, as she said this! The effect of her beauty was even heightened by the over-consciousness and self-recognition of it, into which, I sup-

5. The central character in Charles Per-   and killed six wives (1697).
rault's folk tale of a man who married

pose, Hollingsworth's scorn had driven her. She understood the look of admiration in my face; and—Zenobia to the last—it gave her pleasure.

"It is an endless pity," said she, "that I had not bethought myself of winning your heart, Mr. Coverdale, instead of Hollingsworth's. I think I should have succeeded; and many women would have deemed you the worthier conquest of the two. You are certainly much the handsomest man. But there is a fate in these things. And beauty, in a man, has been of little account with me, since my earliest girlhood, when, for once, it turned my head. Now, farewell!"

"Zenobia, whither are you going?" I asked.

"No matter where," said she. "But I am weary of this place, and sick to death of playing at philanthropy and progress. Of all varieties of mock-life, we have surely blundered into the very emptiest mockery, in our effort to establish the one true system. I have done with it; and Blithedale must find another woman to superintend the laundry, and you, Mr. Coverdale, another nurse to make your gruel, the next time you fall ill. It was, indeed, a foolish dream! Yet it gave us some pleasant summer days, and bright hopes, while they lasted. It can do no more; nor will it avail us to shed tears over a broken bubble. Here is my hand! Adieu!"

She gave me her hand, with the same free, whole-souled gesture as on the first afternoon of our acquaintance; and being greatly moved, I bethought me of no better method of expressing my deep sympathy than to carry it to my lips. In so doing, I perceived that this white hand—so hospitably warm when I first touched it, five months since—was now cold as a veritable piece of snow.

"How very cold!" I exclaimed, holding it between both my own, with the vain idea of warming it. "What can be the reason? It is really deathlike!"

"The extremities die first, they say," answered Zenobia, laughing. "And so you kiss this poor, despised, rejected hand!

Well, my dear friend, I thank you! You have reserved your homage for the fallen. Lip of man will never touch my hand again. I intend to become a Catholic, for the sake of going into a nunnery. When you next hear of Zenobia, her face will be behind the black-veil; so look your last at it now— for all is over! Once more, farewell!"

She withdrew her hand, yet left a lingering pressure, which I felt long afterwards. So intimately connected, as I had been, with perhaps the only man in whom she was ever truly interested, Zenobia looked on me as the representative of all the past, and was conscious that, in bidding me adieu, she likewise took final leave of Hollingsworth, and of this whole epoch of her life. Never did her beauty shine out more lustrously, than in the last glimpse that I had of her. She departed, and was soon hidden among the trees.

But, whether it was the strong impression of the foregoing scene, or whatever else the cause, I was affected with a fantasy that Zenobia had not actually gone, but was still hovering about the spot, and haunting it. I seemed to feel her eyes upon me. It was as if the vivid coloring of her character had left a brilliant stain upon the air. By degrees, however, the impression grew less distinct. I flung myself upon the fallen leaves, at the base of Eliot's pulpit. The sunshine withdrew up the tree-trunks, and flickered on the topmost boughs; gray twilight made the wood obscure; the stars brightened out; the pendent boughs became wet with chill autumnal dews. But I was listless, worn-out with emotion on my own behalf, and sympathy for others, and had no heart to leave my comfortless lair, beneath the rock.

I must have fallen asleep, and had a dream, all the circumstances of which utterly vanished at the moment when they converged to some tragical catastrophe, and thus grew too powerful for the thin sphere of slumber that enveloped them. Starting from the ground, I found the risen moon shining upon the rugged face of the rock, and myself all in a tremble.

XXVII

MIDNIGHT

I T COULD not have been far from midnight, when I came beneath Hollingsworth's window, and finding it open, flung in a tuft of grass, with earth at the roots, and heard it fall upon the floor. He was either awake, or sleeping very lightly; for scarcely a moment had gone by, before he looked out and discerned me standing in the moonlight.

"Is it you, Coverdale?" he asked. "What is the matter?"

"Come down to me, Hollingsworth!" I answered. "I am anxious to speak with you."

The strange tone of my own voice startled me, and him, probably, no less. He lost no time, and soon issued from the house-door, with his dress half-arranged.

"Again, what is the matter?" he asked, impatiently.

"Have you seen Zenobia," said I, "since you parted from her, at Eliot's pulpit?"

"No," answered Hollingsworth; "nor did I expect it."

His voice was deep, but had a tremor in it. Hardly had he spoken, when Silas Foster thrust his head, done up in a cotton handkerchief, out of another window, and took what he called—as it literally was—a squint at us.

"Well, folks, what are ye about here?" he demanded. "Aha, are you there, Miles Coverdale? You have been turning night into day, since you left us, I reckon; and so you find it quite natural to come prowling about the house, at this time o' night, frightening my old woman out of her wits, and making her disturb a tired man out of his best nap. In with you, you vagabond, and to bed!"

"Dress yourself quietly, Foster," said I. "We want your assistance."

I could not, for the life of me, keep that strange tone out of my voice. Silas Foster, obtuse as were his sensibilities, seemed to feel the ghastly earnestness that was conveyed in it, as well as Hollingsworth did. He immediately withdrew his head, and I heard him yawning, muttering to his wife, and again yawning heavily, while he hurried on his clothes. Meanwhile, I showed Hollingsworth a delicate handkerchief, marked with a well-known cypher, and told where I had found it, and other circumstances which had filled me with a suspicion so terrible, that I left him, if he dared, to shape it out for himself. By the time my brief explanation was finished, we were joined by Silas Foster, in his blue woollen frock.

"Well, boys," cried he, peevishly, "what is to pay now?"

"Tell him, Hollingsworth!" said I.

Hollingsworth shivered, perceptibly, and drew in a hard breath betwixt his teeth. He steadied himself, however, and looking the matter more firmly in the face than I had done, explained to Foster my suspicions and the grounds of them, with a distinctness from which, in spite of my utmost efforts, my words had swerved aside. The tough-nerved yeoman, in his comment, put a finish on the business, and brought out the hideous idea in its full terror, as if he were removing the napkin from the face of a corpse.

"And so you think she's drowned herself!" he cried.

I turned away my face.

"What on earth should the young woman do that for?" exclaimed Silas, his eyes half out of his head with mere surprise. "Why, she has more means than she can use or waste, and lacks nothing to make her comfortable, but a husband—and that's an article she could have, any day! There's some mistake about this, I tell you!"

"Come," said I, shuddering. "Let us go and ascertain the truth."

"Well, well," answered Silas Foster, "just as you say. We'll take the long pole, with the hook at the end, that serves to get the bucket out of the draw-well, when the rope is broken. With that, and a couple of long-handled hay-rakes, I'll answer for finding her, if she's anywhere to be found. Strange enough! Zenobia drown herself! No, no, I don't believe it.

She had too much sense, and too much means, and enjoyed life a great deal too well."

When our few preparations were completed, we hastened, by a shorter than the customary route, through fields and pastures, and across a portion of the meadow, to the particular spot, on the river-bank, which I had paused to contemplate, in the course of my afternoon's ramble. A nameless presentiment had again drawn me thither, after leaving Eliot's pulpit. I showed my companions where I had found the handkerchief, and pointed to two or three footsteps, impressed into the clayey margin, and tending towards the water. Beneath its shallow verge, among the water-weeds, there were further traces, as yet unobliterated by the sluggish current, which was there almost at a stand-still. Silas Foster thrust his face down close to these footsteps, and picked up a shoe, that had escaped my observation, being half imbedded in the mud.

"There's a kid-shoe that never was made on a Yankee last," observed he. "I know enough of shoemaker's craft to tell that. French manufacture; and see what a high instep!— and how evenly she trod in it! There never was a woman that stept handsomer in her shoes than Zenobia did. Here," he added, addressing Hollingsworth, "would you like to keep the shoe?"

Hollingsworth started back.

"Give it to me, Foster," said I.

I dabbled it in the water, to rinse off the mud, and have kept it ever since. Not far from this spot, lay an old, leaky punt, drawn up on the oozy river-side, and generally half-full of water. It served the angler to go in quest of pickerel, or the sportsman to pick up his wild-ducks. Setting this crazy barque afloat, I seated myself in the stern, with the paddle, while Hollingsworth sat in the bows, with the hooked pole, and Silas Foster amidships, with a hay-rake.

"It puts me in mind of my young days," remarked Silas, "when I used to steal out of bed to go bobbing for horn-pouts[6] and eels. Heigh-ho!—well!—life and death together make sad

6. Catfish.

work for us all. Then, I was a boy, bobbing for fish; and now I am getting to be an old fellow, and here I be, groping for a dead body! I tell you what, lads, if I thought anything had really happened to Zenobia, I should feel kind o' sorrowful."

"I wish, at least, you would hold your tongue!" muttered I.

The moon, that night, though past the full, was still large and oval, and having risen between eight and nine o'clock, now shone aslantwise over the river, throwing the high, opposite bank, with its woods, into deep shadow, but lighting up the hither shore pretty effectually. Not a ray appeared to fall on the river itself. It lapsed imperceptibly away, a broad, black, inscrutable depth, keeping its own secrets from the eye of man, as impenetrably as mid-ocean could.

"Well, Miles Coverdale," said Foster, "you are the helmsman. How do you mean to manage this business?"

"I shall let the boat drift, broadside foremost, past that stump," I replied. "I know the bottom, having sounded it in fishing. The shore, on this side, after the first step or two, goes off very abruptly; and there is a pool, just by the stump, twelve or fifteen feet deep. The current could not have force enough to sweep any sunken object—even if partially buoyant —out of that hollow."

"Come, then," said Silas. "But I doubt whether I can touch bottom with this hay-rake, if it's as deep as you say. Mr. Hollingsworth, I think you'll be the lucky man, to-night, such luck as it is!"

We floated past the stump. Silas Foster plied his rake manfully, poking it as far as he could into the water, and immersing the whole length of his arm besides. Hollingsworth at first sat motionless, with the hooked-pole elevated in the air. But, by-and-by, with a nervous and jerky movement, he began to plunge it into the blackness that upbore us, setting his teeth, and making precisely such thrusts, methought, as if he were stabbing at a deadly enemy. I bent over the side of the boat. So obscure, however, so awfully mysterious, was that dark stream, that—and the thought made me shiver like a leaf—I might as well have tried to look into the enigma of the eternal world, to discover what had become of Zenobia's soul, as into the river's depths, to find her body. And there, perhaps, she lay, with her face upward, while the shadow of the boat, and my own pale face peering downward, passed slowly betwixt her and the sky.

Once, twice, thrice, I paddled the boat up stream, and again suffered it to glide, with the river's slow, funereal motion, downward. Silas Foster had raked up a large mass of stuff, which, as it came towards the surface, looked somewhat like a flowing garment, but proved to be a monstrous tuft of water-weeds. Hollingsworth, with a gigantic effort, upheaved a sunken log. When once free of the bottom, it rose partly out of water—all weedy and slimy, a devilish-looking object, which the moon had not shone upon for half a hundred years —then plunged again, and sullenly returned to its old resting-place, for the remnant of the century.

"That looked ugly!" quoth Silas. "I half thought it was the Evil One on the same errand as ourselves—searching for Zenobia!"

"He shall never get her!" said I, giving the boat a strong impulse.

"That's not for you to say, my boy!" retorted the yeoman. "Pray God he never has, and never may! Slow work this, however! I should really be glad to find something. Pshaw! What a notion that is, when the only good-luck would be, to paddle, and drift and poke, and grope, hereabouts, till morning, and have our labor for our pains! For my part, I shouldn't wonder if the creature had only lost her shoe in the mud, and saved her soul alive, after all. My stars, how she will laugh at us, tomorrow morning!"

It is indescribable what an image of Zenobia—at the breakfast-table, full of warm and mirthful life—this surmise of Silas Foster's brought before my mind. The terrible phantasm of her death was thrown by it into the remotest and dimmest back-ground, where it seemed to grow as improbable as a myth.

"Yes, Silas; it may be as you say!" cried I.

The drift of the stream had again borne us a little below the stump, when I felt—yes, felt, for it was as if the iron hook had smote my breast—felt Hollingsworth's pole strike some object at the bottom of the river. He started up, and almost overset the boat.

"Hold on!" cried Foster. "You have her!"

Putting a fury of strength into the effort, Hollingsworth heaved amain, and up came a white swash to the surface of the river. It was the flow of a woman's garments. A little higher, and we saw her dark hair, streaming down the current. Black River of Death, thou hadst yielded up thy victim Zenobia was found!

Silas Foster laid hold of the body—Hollingsworth, likewise, grappled with it—and I steered towards the bank, gazing, all the while, at Zenobia, whose limbs were swaying in the current, close at the boat's side. Arriving near the shore, we all three stept into the water, bore her out, and laid her on the ground, beneath a tree.

"Poor child!" said Foster—and his dry old heart, I verily believe, vouchsafed a tear—"I'm sorry for her!"

Were I to describe the perfect horror of the spectacle, the reader might justly reckon it to me for a sin and shame. For more than twelve long years I have borne it in my memory, and could now reproduce it as freshly as if it were still before my eyes. Of all modes of death, methinks it is the ugliest. Her wet garments swathed limbs of terrible inflexibility. She was the marble image of a death-agony. Her arms had grown rigid in the act of struggling, and were bent before her, with clenched hands; her knees, too, were bent, and—thank God for it!—in the attitude of prayer. Ah, that rigidity! It is impossible to bear the terror of it. It seemed—I must needs impart so much of my own miserable idea—it seemed as if her body must keep the same position in the coffin, and that her skeleton would keep it in the grave, and that when Zenobia rose, at the Day of Judgment, it would be in just the same attitude as now!

One hope I had; and that, too, was mingled half with fear. She knelt, as if in prayer. With the last, choking consciousness, her soul, bubbling out through her lips, it may be, had given itself up to the Father, reconciled and penitent. But her arms! They were bent before her, as if she struggled against Providence in never-ending hostility. Her hands! They were clenched in immitigable defiance. Away with the hideous thought! The flitting moment, after Zenobia sank into the dark pool—when her breath was gone, and her soul at her lips—was as long, in its capacity of God's infinite forgiveness, as the lifetime of the world.

Foster bent over the body, and carefully examined it.

"You have wounded the poor thing's breast," said he to Hollingsworth. "Close by her heart, too!"

"Ha!" cried Hollingsworth, with a start.

And so he had, indeed, both before and after death.

"See!" said Foster. "That's the place where the iron struck her. It looks cruelly, but she never felt it!"

He endeavored to arrange the arms of the corpse decently by its side. His utmost strength, however, scarcely sufficed to bring them down; and rising again, the next instant, they bade him defiance, exactly as before. He made another effort, with the same result.

"In God's name, Silas Foster," cried I, with bitter indignation, "let that dead woman alone!"

"Why, man, it's not decent!" answered he, staring at me in amazement. "I can't bear to see her looking so! Well, well," added he, after a third effort, "'tis of no use, sure enough; and we must leave the women to do their best with her, after we get to the house. The sooner that's done, the better."

We took two rails from a neighboring fence, and formed a bier by laying across some boards from the bottom of the boat. And thus we bore Zenobia homeward. Six hours before, how beautiful! At midnight, what a horror! A reflection occurs to me, that will show ludicrously, I doubt not, on my page, but must come in, for its sterling truth. Being the woman that she was, could Zenobia have foreseen all these ugly circumstances of death, how ill it would become her, the altogether unseemly aspect which she must put on, and, especially, old Silas Foster's efforts to improve the matter, she would no more have committed the dreadful act, than have exhibited herself to a public assembly in a badly-fitting garment! Zenobia, I have often thought, was not quite simple in her death. She had seen pictures, I suppose, of drowned persons, in lithe and graceful attitudes. And she deemed it well and decorous to die as so many village-maidens have, wronged in their first-love, and seeking peace in the bosom of the old, familiar stream—so familiar that they could not dread it—where, in childhood, they used to bathe their little feet, wading mid-leg deep, unmindful of wet skirts. But, in Zenobia's case, there was some tint of the Arcadian affectation that had been visible enough in all our lives, for a few months past.

This, however, to my conception, takes nothing from the tragedy. For, has not the world come to an awfully sophisticated pass, when, after a certain degree of acquaintance with it, we cannot even put ourselves to death in whole-hearted simplicity?

Slowly, slowly, with many a dreary pause—resting the bier often on some rock, or balancing it across a mossy log, to take fresh hold—we bore our burthen onward, through the moonlight, and, at last, laid Zenobia on the floor of the old farm-house. By-and-by, came three or four withered women, and stood whispering around the corpse, peering at it through their spectacles, holding up their skinny hands, shaking their night-capt heads, and taking counsel of one another's experience what was to be done.

With those tire-women,[7] we left Zenobia!

XXVIII

BLITHEDALE-PASTURE

BLITHEDALE, thus far in its progress, had never found the necessity of a burial-ground. There was some consultation among us, in what spot Zenobia might most fitly be laid. It was my own wish, that she should sleep at the base of Eliot's pulpit, and that, on the rugged front of the rock, the name by which we familiarly knew her— ZENOBIA—and not another word, should be deeply cut, and left for the moss and lichens to fill up, at their long leisure. But Hollingsworth (to whose ideas, on this point, great deference was due) made it his request that her grave might be dug on the gently sloping hill-side, in the wide pasture, where, as we once supposed, Zenobia and he had planned to build their cottage. And thus it was done, accordingly.

She was buried very much as other people have been, for hundreds of years gone by. In anticipation of a death, we Blithedale colonists had sometimes set our fancies at work to arrange a funereal ceremony, which should be the proper symbolic expression of our spiritual faith and eternal hopes; and this we meant to substitute for those customary rites, which were moulded originally out of the Gothic gloom, and, by long use, like an old velvet-pall, have so much more than their first death-smell in them. But, when the occasion came, we found it the simplest and truest thing, after all, to content ourselves with the old fashion, taking away what we could,

---

7. Dressing assistants (*tire* meaning apparel); those who will dress the body for burial.

but interpolating no novelties, and particularly avoiding all frippery of flowers and cheerful emblems. The procession moved from the farm-house. Nearest the dead walked an old man in deep mourning, his face mostly concealed in a white handkerchief, and with Priscilla leaning on his arm. Hollingsworth and myself came next. We all stood around the narrow niche in the cold earth; all saw the coffin lowered in; all heard the rattle of the crumbly soil upon its lid—that final sound, which mortality awakens on the utmost verge of sense, as if in the vain hope of bringing an echo from the spiritual world.

I noticed a stranger—a stranger to most of those present, though known to me—who, after the coffin had descended, took up a handful of earth, and flung it first into the grave. I had given up Hollingsworth's arm, and now found myself near this man.

"It was an idle thing—a foolish thing—for Zenobia to do!" said he. "She was the last woman in the world to whom death could have been necessary. It was too absurd! I have no patience with her."

"Why so?" I inquired, smothering my horror at his cold comment in my eager curiosity to discover some tangible truth, as to his relation with Zenobia. "If any crisis could justify the sad wrong she offered to herself, it was surely that in which she stood. Everything had failed her—prosperity, in the world's sense, for her opulence was gone—the heart's prosperity, in love. And there was a secret burthen on her, the nature of which is best known to you. Young as she was, she had tried life fully, had no more to hope, and something, perhaps, to fear. Had Providence taken her away in its own holy hand, I should have thought it the kindest dispensation that could be awarded to one so wrecked."

"You mistake the matter completely," rejoined Westervelt.

"What, then, is your own view of it?" I asked.

"Her mind was active, and various in its powers," said he; "her heart had a manifold adaptation; her constitution an infinite buoyancy, which (had she possessed only a little patience to await the reflux of her troubles) would have borne her upward, triumphantly, for twenty years to come. Her beauty would not have waned—or scarcely so, and surely not beyond the reach of art to restore it—in all that time. She had life's summer all before her, and a hundred varieties of brilliant success. What an actress Zenobia might have been! It was one of her least valuable capabilities. How forcibly she might have wrought upon the world, either directly in her own person, or by her influence upon some man, or a series of men, of controlling genius! Every prize that could be worth a woman's having—and many prizes which other women are too timid to desire—lay within Zenobia's reach."

"In all this," I observed, "there would have been nothing to satisfy her heart."

"Her heart!" answered Westervelt, contemptuously. "That troublesome organ (as she had hitherto found it) would have been kept in its due place and degree, and have had all the gratification it could fairly claim. She would soon have established a control over it. Love had failed her, you say! Had it never failed her before? Yet she survived it, and loved again—possibly, not once alone, nor twice either. And now to drown herself for yonder dreamy philanthropist!"

"Who are you," I exclaimed, indignantly, "that dare to speak thus of the dead? You seem to intend a eulogy, yet leave out whatever was noblest in her, and blacken, while you mean to praise. I have long considered you as Zenobia's evil fate. Your sentiments confirm me in the idea, but leave me still ignorant as to the mode in which you have influenced her life. The connection may have been indissoluble, except by death. Then, indeed—always in the hope of God's infinite mercy—I cannot deem it a misfortune that she sleeps in yonder grave!"

"No matter what I was to her," he answered, gloomily, yet without actual emotion. "She is now beyond my reach. Had she lived, and hearkened to my counsels, we might have served each other well. But there Zenobia lies, in yonder pit, with the dull earth over her. Twenty years of a brilliant lifetime thrown away for a mere woman's whim!"

Heaven deal with Westervelt according to his nature and deserts!—that is to say, annihilate him. He was altogether earthy, worldly, made for time and its gross objects, and incapable—except by a sort of dim reflection, caught from other minds—of so much as one spiritual idea. Whatever stain Zenobia had, was caught from him; nor does it seldom happen that a character of admirable qualities loses its better life, because the atmosphere, that should sustain it, is rendered poisonous by such breath as this man mingled with Zenobia's. Yet his reflections possessed their share of truth. It was a woful thought, that a woman of Zenobia's diversified capacity should have fancied herself irretrievably defeated on the broad battle-field of life, and with no refuge, save to fall on her own sword, merely because Love had gone against her. It is nonsense, and a miserable wrong—the result, like so many others, of masculine egotism—that the success or failure of woman's existence should be made to depend wholly on the affections, and on one species of affection; while man has such a multitude of other chances, that this seems but an incident. For its own sake, if it will do no more, the world should throw open all its avenues to the passport of a woman's bleeding heart.

As we stood around the grave, I looked often towards Priscilla, dreading to see her wholly overcome with grief. And deeply grieved, in truth, she was. But a character, so simply constituted as hers, has room only for a single predominant affection. No other feeling can touch the heart's inmost core, nor do it any deadly mischief. Thus, while we see that such a being responds to every breeze, with tremulous vibration, and imagine that she must be shattered by the first rude blast, we find her retaining her equilibrium amid shocks that might have overthrown many a sturdier frame. So with Priscilla! Her one possible misfortune was Hollingsworth's unkindness; and that was destined never to befall her—never yet, at least—for Priscilla has not died.

But, Hollingsworth! After all the evil that he did, are we to leave him thus, blest with the entire devotion of this one true heart, and with wealth at his disposal, to execute the long contemplated project that had led him so far astray? What retribution is there here? My mind being vexed with precisely this query, I made a journey, some years since, for the sole purpose of catching a last glimpse at Hollingsworth, and judging for myself whether he were a happy man or no. I learned that he inhabited a small cottage, that his way of life was exceedingly retired, and that my only chance of encountering him or Priscilla was, to meet them in a secluded lane, where, in the latter part of the afternoon, they were accustomed to walk. I did meet them, accordingly. As they approached me, I observed in Hollingsworth's face a depressed and melancholy look, that seemed habitual; the powerfully built man showed a self-distrustful weakness, and a childlike, or childish, tendency to press close, and closer still, to the side of the slender woman whose arm was within his. In Priscilla's manner, there was a protective and watchful quality, as if she felt herself the guardian of her companion, but, likewise, a deep, submissive, unquestioning reverence, and also a veiled happiness in her fair and quiet countenance.

Drawing nearer, Priscilla recognized me, and gave me a kind and friendly smile, but with a slight gesture which I could not help interpreting as an entreaty not to make myself known to Hollingsworth. Nevertheless, an impulse took possession of me, and compelled me to address him.

"I have come, Hollingsworth," said I, "to view your grand edifice for the reformation of criminals. Is it finished yet?"

"No—nor begun!" answered he, without raising his eyes. "A very small one answers all my purposes."

Priscilla threw me an upbraiding glance. But I spoke again, with a bitter and revengeful emotion, as if flinging a poisoned arrow at Hollingsworth's heart.

"Up to this moment," I inquired, "how many criminals have you reformed?"

"Not one!" said Hollingsworth, with his eyes still fixed on the ground. "Ever since we parted, I have been busy with a single murderer!"

Then the tears gushed into my eyes, and I forgave him. For I remembered the wild energy, the passionate shriek, with which Zenobia had spoken those words—'Tell him he has murdered me! Tell him that I'll haunt him!'—and I knew what murderer he meant, and whose vindictive shadow dogged the side where Priscilla was not.

The moral which presents itself to my reflections, as drawn from Hollingsworth's character and errors, is simply this:—that, admitting what is called Philanthropy, when adopted as a profession, to be often useful by its energetic impulse to society at large, it is perilous to the individual, whose ruling passion, in one exclusive channel, it thus becomes. It ruins, or is fearfully apt to ruin, the heart; the rich juices of which God never meant should be pressed violently out, and distilled into alcoholic liquor, by an unnatural process; but should render life sweet, bland, and gently beneficent, and insensibly influence other hearts and other lives to the same blessed end. I see in Hollingsworth an exemplification of the most awful truth in Bunyan's book[8] of such;—from the very gate of Heaven, there is a by-way to the pit!

But, all this while, we have been standing by Zenobia's grave. I have never since beheld it, but make no question that the grass grew all the better, on that little parallelogram of pasture-land, for the decay of the beautiful woman who slept beneath. How much Nature seems to love us! And how readily, nevertheless, without a sigh or a complaint, she converts us to a meaner purpose, when her highest one—that of conscious, intellectual life, and sensibility—has been untimely baulked! While Zenobia lived, Nature was proud of

8. John Bunyan's *The Pilgrim's Progress* (1678), a Puritan allegory of the soul's search for salvation.

her, and directed all eyes upon that radiant presence, as her fairest handiwork. Zenobia perished. Will not Nature shed a tear? Ah, no! She adopts the calamity at once into her system, and is just as well pleased, for aught we can see, with the tuft of ranker vegetation that grew out of Zenobia's heart, as with all the beauty which has bequeathed us no earthly representative, except in this crop of weeds. It is because the spirit is inestimable, that the lifeless body is so little valued.

XXIX

MILES COVERDALE'S CONFESSION[9]

I T REMAINS only to say a few words about myself. Not improbably, the reader might be willing to spare me the trouble; for I have made but a poor and dim figure in my own narrative, establishing no separate interest, and suffering my colorless life to take its hue from other lives. But one still retains some little consideration for one's self; so I keep these last two or three pages for my individual and sole behoof.

But what, after all, have I to tell? Nothing, nothing, nothing! I left Blithedale within the week after Zenobia's death, and went back thither no more. The whole soil of our farm, for a long time afterwards, seemed but the sodded earth over her grave. I could not toil there, nor live upon its products. Often, however, in these years that are darkening around me, I remember our beautiful scheme of a noble and unselfish life, and how fair, in that first summer, appeared the prospect that it might endure for generations, and be perfected, as the ages rolled away, into the system of a

9. Hawthorne added this chapter to the novel some time between April 30, 1852, when he completed the rest of the manuscript, and May 14, when he received first proof. The manuscript was sent to Edwin P. Whipple, an American critic (see note, p. 277) on May 2, and the chapter may have been added at Whipple's suggestion. Certainly the chapter was added before the manuscript was sent to the publisher. The title "Hollingsworth" on the manuscript title page has been changed to "The Blithedale Romance"; and it could be argued that this change in title is consistent with the addition of the chapter.

people, and a world. Were my former associates now there—
were there only three or four of those true-hearted men, still
laboring in the sun—I sometimes fancy that I should direct
my world-weary footsteps thitherward, and entreat them to
receive me, for old friendship's sake. More and more, I feel
that we had struck upon what ought to be a truth. Posterity
may dig it up, and profit by it. The experiment, so far as its
original projectors were concerned, proved long ago a failure,
first lapsing into Fourierism, and dying, as it well deserved,
for this infidelity to its own higher spirit. Where once we
toiled with our whole hopeful hearts, the town-paupers, aged,
nerveless, and disconsolate, creep sluggishly afield. Alas,
what faith is requisite to bear up against such results of
generous effort!

My subsequent life has passed—I was going to say, happily
—but, at all events, tolerably enough. I am now at middle-
age—well, well, a step or two beyond the midmost point, and
I care not a fig who knows it!—a bachelor, with no very
decided purpose of ever being otherwise. I have been twice
to Europe, and spent a year or two, rather agreeably, at each
visit. Being well to do in the world, and having nobody but
myself to care for, I live very much at my ease, and fare
sumptuously every day. As for poetry, I have given it
up, notwithstanding that Doctor Griswold[1]—as the reader, of
course, knows—has placed me at a fair elevation among our
minor minstrelsy, on the strength of my pretty little volume,
published ten years ago. As regards human progress, (in spite
of my irrepressible yearnings over the Blithedale reminiscences,) let them believe in it who can, and aid in it who
choose! If I could earnestly do either, it might be all the
better for my comfort. As Hollingsworth once told me, I lack
a purpose. How strange! He was ruined, morally, by an
overplus of the very same ingredient, the want of which, I
occasionally suspect, has rendered my own life all an emptiness. I by no means wish to die. Yet, were there any cause,

1. Rufus Wilmot Griswold (1815–57),   *America* (1842).
the compiler of *The Poets and Poetry of*

in this whole chaos of human struggle, worth a sane man's
dying for, and which my death would benefit, then—provided,
however, the effort did not involve an unreasonable amount
of trouble—methinks I might be bold to offer up my life. If
Kossuth,[2] for example, would pitch the battle-field of Hungarian rights within an easy ride of my abode, and choose a
mild, sunny morning, after breakfast, for the conflict, Miles
Coverdale would gladly be his man, for one brave rush upon
the levelled bayonets. Farther than that, I should be loth to
pledge myself.

I exaggerate my own defects. The reader must not take
my own word for it, nor believe me altogether changed from
the young man, who once hoped strenuously, and struggled,
not so much amiss. Frostier heads than mine have gained
honor in the world; frostier hearts have imbibed new warmth,
and been newly happy. Life, however, it must be owned,
has come to rather an idle pass with me. Would my friends
like to know what brought it thither? There is one secret—I
have concealed it all along, and never meant to let the least
whisper of it escape—one foolish little secret, which possibly
may have had something to do with these inactive years of
meridian manhood, with my bachelorship, with the unsatis-
fied retrospect that I fling back on life, and my listless glance
towards the future. Shall I reveal it? It is an absurd thing
for a man in his afternoon—a man of the world, moreover,
with these three white hairs in his brown moustache, and that
deepening track of a crow's foot on each temple—an absurd
thing ever to have happened, and quite the absurdest for an
old bachelor, like me, to talk about. But it rises in my throat;
so let it come.

I perceive, moreover, that the confession, brief as it shall
be, will throw a gleam of light over my behavior throughout
the foregoing incidents, and is, indeed, essential to the full
understanding of my story. The reader, therefore, since I
have disclosed so much, is entitled to this one word more. As

2. Lajos Kossuth (1802–94), leading figure in the Hungarian revolution for independence from Austria (March, 1848)
and, for three months in 1849, the president of the newly proclaimed republic.

I write it, he will charitably suppose me to blush, and turn away my face:—[3]

I—I myself—was in love—with—PRISCILLA!

THE END.

3. This paragraph does not appear in the manuscript in the Pierpont Morgan Library but does appear in the first edition, published by Ticknor, Reed, and Fields. Apparently Hawthorne added this paragraph to the proof.

Backgrounds and Sources

Hawthorne's Life at Brook Farm

NATHANIEL HAWTHORNE

From His Letters and Journals†

Oak Hill, April 13, 1841

Ownest love,

Here is thy poor husband in a polar Paradise! I know not how to interpret this aspect of Nature—whether it be of good or evil omen to our enterprise. But I reflect that the Plymouth pilgrims arrived in the midst of storm and stept ashore upon mountain snow-drifts;[1] and nevertheless they prospered, and became a great people—and doubtless it will be the same with us. I laud my stars, however, that thou wilt not have thy first impressions of our future home from such a day as this. Thou wouldst shiver all thy life afterwards, and never realize that there could be bright skies, and green hills and meadows, and trees heavy with foliage, when now the whole scene is a great snow-bank, and the sky full of snow likewise. Through faith, I persist in believing that spring and summer will come in their due season; but the unregenerated[2] man shivers within me, and suggests a doubt whether I may not have wandered within the precincts of the Arctic circle, and chosen my heritage among everlasting snows. Dearest, provide thyself with a good stock of furs;

† The letters in this section (except for those to David Mack, William B. Pike, and George W. Curtis) are to Sophia Peabody, Hawthorne's fiancée. Although Hawthorne calls himself "husband" and Sophia "wife," they were not married until July 9, 1842, about eight months after Hawthorne left Brook Farm.

The letters to Sophia Peabody are from *Love Letters of Nathaniel Hawthorne* (Chicago: Dofobs Society, 1907). Hawthorne's journal entries are from *The American Notebooks* (Columbus: Ohio State University Press). His letter to David Mack was first published by Manning Hawthorne in "Hawthorne and Utopian Socialism," *New England Quarterly*, 12 (1939), 727–28.

The letter to William Pike is from Rose Hawthorne Lathrop, *Memories of Hawthorne* (Boston & New York: 1897), p. 152. The letter to George Curtis is quoted by Roy Harvey Pearce in the Introduction to the Centenary Edition of *The Blithedale Romance* (Columbus: Ohio State University Press, 1964), p. xxiii.

A convenient compilation of documents relating to Brook Farm is Henry W. Sams, ed., *Autobiography of Brook Farm* (Englewood Cliffs, N.J.: Prentice-Hall, 1958). Accounts of the relationship of Brook Farm to Hawthorne's life and *Blithedale* are Arlin Turner, "Autobiographical Elements in Hawthorne's *The Blithedale Romance*," *Texas Studies in English*, 15 (1935), 39–62; and Joseph T. Gordon, "Hawthorne and Brook Farm," *Emerson Society Quarterly*, 33, 4th Quarter (1963), 51–61.

1. In *Of Plymouth Plantation* (written 1630–50), William Bradford writes of the Pilgrims' landing: "And for the season it was winter, and they that know the winters of that country know them to be sharp and violent, and subject to cruel and fierce storms, dangerous to * * * search an unknown coast."

2. Hawthorne uses the word which the Pilgrims would have used to designate one who has not undergone a conversion to the faith.

and if thou canst obtain the skin of a polar bear, thou wilt find it a very suitable summer dress for this region. Thou must not hope ever to walk abroad, except upon snow-shoes, nor to find any warmth, save in thy husband's heart.

Belovedest, I have not yet taken my first lesson in agriculture, as thou mayest well suppose—except that I went to see our cows foddered, yesterday afternoon. We have eight of our own; and the number is now increased by a transcendental heifer, belonging to Miss Margaret Fuller.[3] She is very fractious, I believe, and apt to kick over the milk pail. Thou knowest best, whether, in these traits of character, she resembles her mistress. Thy husband intends to convert himself into a milk-maid, this evening; but I pray heaven that Mr. Ripley[4] may be moved to assign him the kindliest cow in the herd—otherwise he will perform his duty with fear and trembling.

Ownest wife, I like my brethren in affliction very well; and couldst thou see us sitting round our table, at meal-times, before the great kitchen-fire, thou wouldst call it a cheerful sight. Mrs. Barker[5] is a most comfortable woman to behold; she looks as if her ample person were stuffed full of tenderness—indeed, as if she were all one great, kind heart. Wert thou but here, I should ask for nothing more—not even for sunshine and summer weather; for thou wouldst be both, to thy husband. * * *

Thy husband has the best chamber in the house, I believe; and though not quite so good as the apartment I have left, it will do very well. I have hung up thy two pictures; and they give me a glimpse of summer and of thee. The vase I intended to have brought in my arms; but could not very conveniently do it yesterday; so that it still remains at Mrs. Hillards,[6] together with my carpet. I shall bring them the next opportunity. * * *

April 14, 10 A.M. Sweetest, I did not milk the cows last night, because Mr. Ripley was afraid to trust them to my hands, or me to

3. Margaret Ossoli Fuller (1810–50), one of the more important Transcendentalists, was a frequent visitor at Brook Farm, the principles of which rather than the actuality appealed to her. She was famous for her "conversations" (a series of discussion groups from 1839 to 1844), some of which were held at Brook Farm. Her most famous work is *Woman in the Nineteenth Century* (1845), the most complete study of feminism in nineteenth-century America. That she was the prototype for Zenobia has been a matter of critial debate since the novel first appeared. See, for example, Oscar Cargill, "Nemesis and Nathaniel Hawthorne," *PMLA*, 52 (1937), 848–62; William Peirce Randel, "Hawthorne, Channing, and Margaret Fuller," *American Literature*, 10

(1939), 472–76; Austin Warren, "Hawthorne, Margaret Fuller, and 'Nemesis,'" *PMLA*, 54 (1939), 615–18.
4. George Ripley (1802–80) was the chief organizer of Brook Farm and one of its directors.
5. Ellen Barker was not a member of the community; she was hired to help get the place in order for the members who began arriving in early April, 1841.
6. The wife of George Hillard (1808–79), a lawyer with literary interests, in whose house Hawthorne took up lodgings late in 1839. In 1846, Hillard handled Hawthorne's suit against the Brook Farm Association for money he felt was owed him. Although the court awarded Hawthorne $585, the money was probably never paid.

their horns—I know not which. But this morning, I have done wonders.[7] Before breakfast, I went out to the barn, and began to chop hay for the cattle; and with such "righteous vehemence" (as Mr. Ripley says) did I labor, that, in the space of ten minutes, I broke the machine. Then I brought wood and replenished the fires; and finally sat down to breakfast and ate up a huge mound of buckwheat cakes. After breakfast, Mr. Ripley put a four-pronged instrument into my hands, which he gave me to understand was called a pitch-fork; and he and Mr. Farley[8] being armed with similar weapons, we all three commenced a gallant attack upon a heap of manure. This affair being concluded, and thy husband having purified himself, he sits down to finish this letter to his most beloved wife. Dearest, I will never consent that thou come within a half a mile of me, after such an encounter as that of this morning. Pray Heaven that this letter retain none of the fragrance with which the writer was imbued. As for thy husband himself, he is peculiarly partial to the odor; but that whimsical little nose of thine might chance to quarrel with it.

Belovedest, Miss Fuller's cow hooks the other cows, and has made herself ruler of the herd, and behaves in a very tyrannical manner. Sweetest, I know not when I shall see thee; but I trust it will not be longer than till the end of next week. I love thee! I love thee! I would thou wert with me; for then would my labor be joyful—and even now, it is not sorrowful. Dearest, I shall make an excellent husbandman. I feel the original Adam reviving within me.[9]

Brook Farm, April 28, 1841

* * *

Belovedest, thy husband was caught by a cold, during his visit to Boston. It has not affected his whole frame, but took entire possession of his head, as being the weakest and most vulnerable part. Never didst thou hear anybody sneeze with such vehemence and frequency; and his poor brain has been in a thick fog—or rather, it

7. In a letter to John Sullivan Dwight on May 6, 1841, Mrs. George Ripley writes: "Hawthorne is one to reverence, to admire with that deep admiration so refreshing to the soul. He is our prince—prince in everything—yet despising no labour and very athletic and able-bodied in the barnyard and field" (Zoltan Hraszti, *The Idyll of Brook Farm* [Boston: Boston Public Library, 1937], p. 18.)
8. Frank Farley, a thirty-year-old farmer from the West, was an enormously popular member of the community, both for his practical knowledge and for his wit

and culture. In July his health broke down and he had to leave Brook Farm.
9. Reflections of this letter to be found in *The Blithedale Romance* include: the snowstorm (pp. 10–11, 18); the Pilgrims (pp. 13, 108); cow kicking over pail (p. 60); kitchen fire (pp. 9, 12–13, 22); Mrs. Barker/Foster (p. 13); the apartment (p. 37). Hawthorne's references to unceasing manual labor in this letter and in others quoted in this section are but summarily treated in Coverdale's account of his life at Blithedale(pp. 60–61, 75–76, 190, 192).

seemed as if his head were stuffed with coarse wool. I know not when I have been so pestered before; and sometimes I wanted to wrench off my head, and give it a great kick, like a foot-ball. This annoyance has made me endure the bad weather with even less than ordinary patience; and my faith was so far exhausted, that, when they told me yesterday that the sun was setting clear, I would not even turn my eyes towards the west. But, this morning, I am made all over anew; and have no greater remnant of my cold, than will serve as an excuse for doing no work to-day.[1]

Brook Farm, June 1, 1841

Very dearest,

I have been too busy to write thee a long letter by this opportunity; for I think this present life of mine gives me an antipathy to pen and ink, even more than my Custom-House experience did.[2] I could not live without the idea of thee, nor without spiritual communion with thee; but, in the midst of toil, or after a hard day's work in the gold mine,[3] my soul obstinately refuses to be poured out on paper. That abominable gold mine! Thank God, we anticipate getting rid of its treasures, in the course of two or three days. Of all hateful places, that is the worst; and I shall never comfort myself for having spent so many days of blessed sunshine there. It is my opinion, dearest, that a man's soul may be buried and perish under a dung-heap or in a furrow of the field, just as well as under a pile of money.[4]

Boston, July 18, 1841

To David Mack, Esq.[5]

My Dear Sir:—

Your letter has this moment been put in my hands. I truly thank you for it and wish to lose no time in correcting some misapprehensions which have been caused by your judging of my feelings through the medium of third persons—and partly from my brief and imperfect communications to you last Sunday.

I have never felt that I was called upon by Mr. Ripley to devote so much of my time to manual labor, as has been done, since my residence at Brook Farm; nor do I believe that others have felt constrained of that kind from him personally. We have never looked upon him as a master, or an employer, but as a fellow laborer on

1. Hawthorne's cold is reflected in the novel on pp. 36–38 and his feeling of being made anew on pp. 56–57.
2. Hawthorne was a measurer of salt and coal in the Boston Custom House for several years before going to Brook Farm.
3. Manure pile.
4. The idea of labor's deadening effect in this letter and that of August 12, 1841, is reflected in the novel on pp. 37–38, 61.
5. David Mack (1804–78), a lawyer, teacher, and devotee of liberal causes, considered joining Brook Farm, which he visited in 1841. Hawthorne had discussed the matter with him a few days before he wrote him.

the same terms with ourselves, with no more right to bid us perform any one act of labor than we have to bid him. Our constraint has been entirely that of circumstances which were as much beyond his control as our own; and as there is no way of escaping this constraint except by leaving the farm at once—and that step none of us were prepared to take because (though attributing less importance to the success of this immediate enterprise than Mr. Ripley does) we still felt that its failure would be very inauspicious to the prospects of this community. For my own part there are private and personal motives which, without the influence of those shared by us all, would still make me wish to bear all the drudgery of this one summer's labor were it much more onerous than I have found it. It is true that I do not infrequently regret that the summer is passing with so little enjoyment of nature and my own thoughts and with the sacrifice of some objects that I had hoped to accomplish. Such were the regrets to which I alluded last Sunday, but Mr. Ripley cannot be held responsible for the disagreeable circumstances which cause them.

I recollect speaking very despondently, perhaps despairingly, of the prospects of the situation. My views in this respect vary somewhat with the state of my spirits but I confess that of late my hopes are never very sanguine. I form my judgment, however, not from anything that has passed within the precincts of Brook Farm but from external circumstances—from the improbability that adequate funds will be raised or that any feasible plan can be suggested for proceeding without a very considerable capital. I likewise perceive that there would be some very knotty points to be discussed, even had we capital enough to buy an estate. These considerations have somewhat lessened the heartiness and cheerfulness with which I formerly went forth to the fields and perhaps have interposed a medium of misunderstanding between Mr. Ripley and us all. His zeal will not permit him to doubt of eventual success; and he perceives, or imagines, a more intimate connection between our present farming operations and our ultimate enterprise than is visible to my perceptions. But as I said before the two things are sufficiently connected to make me desirous of giving my best efforts to the promotion of the former.

You will see, I think, from what I have now stated, that there was no pressing necessity for me, or my fellow laborers, to dishearten Mr. Ripley by expressing dissatisfaction with our present mode of life. It is our wish to give his experiment a full and fair trial; and if his many hopes are to be frustrated we should be loth to give him reason to attribute the failure to lack of energy and perseverance in his associates. Nevertheless, we did, several days since, (he and

myself, I mean) have a conversation on this subject; and he is now
fully possessed of my feelings in respect to personal labor. * * *

Brook Farm, August 12, 1841

* * *

Belovedest, I am very well, and not at all weary; for yesterday's
rain gave us a holyday; and moreover the labors of the farm are not
so pressing as they have been. And—joyful thought!—in a little
more than a fortnight, thy husband will be free from his bondage—
free to think of his Dove—free to enjoy Nature—free to think and
feel![6] I do think that a greater weight will then be removed from
me, than when Christian's burthen fell off at the foot of the cross.[7]
Even my Custom House experience was not such a thraldom and
weariness; my mind and heart were freer. Oh, belovedest, labor is
the curse of this world, and nobody can meddle with it, without
becoming proportionably brutified. Dost thou think it a praise-
worthy matter, that I spent five golden months in providing food for
cows and horses? Dearest, it is not so. Thank God, my soul is not
utterly buried under a dungheap. I shall yet rescue it, somewhat
defiled, to be sure, but not utterly unsusceptible of purification.

Brook Farm, August 22, 1841

* * *

Dearest wife, it is extremely doubtful whether Mr. Ripley will
succeed in locating his community on this farm. He can bring Mr.
Ellis[8] to no terms; and the more they talk about the matter, the
farther they appear to be from a settlement. Thou and I must form
other plans for ourselves; for I can see few or no signs that Providence purposes to give us a home here. I am weary, weary, thrice
weary of waiting so many ages. Yet what can be done? Whatever
may be thy husband's gifts, he has not hitherto shown a single one
that may avail to gather gold. I confess that I have strong hopes of
good from this arrangement with Munroe;[9] but when I look at the
scanty avails of my past literary efforts, I do not feel authorized to
expect much from the future. Well; we shall see. Other persons have
bought large estates and built splendid mansions with such little
books as I mean to write; so perhaps it is not unreasonable to hope
that mine may enable me to build a little cottage—or, at least, to

6. Here Hawthorne is anticipating his
forthcoming visit to Salem; his sojourn
lasted from September 1 to September 22.
The sentiments expressed here (except for
the love element) are similar to those of
Coverdale when he contemplates going to
Boston, pp. 127–30.
7. A reference to one of Hawthorne's
favorite books, John Bunyan's *The Pil-*
grim's Progress (1678).
8. The owner of the property on which
Brook Farm was established.
9. James Munroe, a publisher, expected
to reprint Hawthorne's *Grandfather's*
Chair series, but Hawthorne became dissatisfied with the arrangements and nothing came of the plan. It was issued
instead by Tappan and Dennet in 1842.

buy or hire one. But I am becoming more and more convinced, that we must not lean upon the community. Whatever is to be done, must be done by thy husband's own individual strength. Most beloved, I shall not remain here through the winter, unless with an absolute certainty that there will be a home ready for us in the spring. Otherwise I shall return to Boston,—still, however, considering myself an associate of the community; so that we may take advantage of any more favorable aspect of affairs. Dearest, how much depends on those little books!

Salem, September 3, 1841

* * *

Dearest, I have been out only once, in the day time, since my arrival. How immediately and irrecoverably (if thou didst not keep me out of the abyss) should I relapse into the way of life in which I spent my youth! If it were not for my Dove, this present world would see no more of me forever. The sunshine would never fall on me, no more than on a ghost. Once in a while, people might discern my figure gliding stealthily through the dim evening—that would be all. I should be only a shadow of the night; it is thou that givest me reality, and makest all things real for me. If, in the interval since I quitted this lonely old chamber, I had found no woman (and thou wast the only possible one) to impart reality and significance to life, I should have come back hither ere now, with the feeling that all was a dream and a mockery. Dost thou rejoice that thou hast saved me from such a fate? Yes; it is a miracle worthy even of thee, to have converted a life of shadows into the deepest truth, by thy magic touch. * * *

Sweetest, it seems very long already since I saw thee; but thou hast been all the time in my thoughts; so that my being has been continuous. Therefore, in one sense, it does not seem as if we had been parted at all. But really I should judge it to be twenty years since I left Brook Farm; and I take this to be one proof that my life there was an unnatural and unsuitable, and therefore an unreal one. It already looks like a dream behind me.[1] The real Me was never an associate of the community; there has been a spectral Appearance there, sounding the horn at day-break, and milking the cows, and hoeing potatoes, and raking hay, toiling and sweating in the sun, and doing me the honor to assume my name. But be not thou deceived, Dove of my heart. This Spectre was not thy husband. Nevertheless, it is somewhat remarkable that thy husband's hands have, during this past summer, grown very brown and rough; insomuch that many people persist in believing that he, after all, was the

---

1. Hawthorne's sense of the unreality of Brook Farm is echoed in Coverdale's rumination on p. 135.

238 · *Nathaniel Hawthorne*

aforesaid spectral horn-sounder, cow-milker, potato-hoer, and hay raker. But such a people do not know a reality from a shadow.

Brook Farm, September 22, 1841

Dearest love, here is thy husband again, slowly adapting himself to the life of this queer community, whence he seems to have been absent half a life time—so utterly has he grown apart from the spirit and manners of the place. Thou knowest not how much I wanted thee, to give me a home-feeling in the spot—to keep a feeling of coldness and strangeness from creeping into my heart and making me shiver. Nevertheless, I was most kindly received; and the fields and woods looked very pleasant, in the bright sunshine of the day before yesterday. I had a friendlier disposition towards the farm, now that I am no longer obliged to toil in its stubborn furrows.[2] Yesterday and to-day, however, the weather has been intolerable—cold, chill, sullen, so that it is impossible to be on kindly terms with mother Nature. Would I were with thee, mine own warmest and truest-hearted wife! * * *

Belovedest, I doubt whether I shall succeed in writing another volume of Grandfather's Library,[3] while I remain at the farm. I have not the sense of perfect seclusion, which has always been essential to my power of producing anything. It is true, nobody intrudes into my room; but still I cannot be quiet. Nothing here is settled—everything is but beginning to arrange itself—and though thy husband would seem to have little to do with aught beside his own thoughts, still he cannot but partake of the ferment around him. My mind will not be abstracted. I must observe, and think, and feel, and content myself with catching glimpses of things which may be wrought out hereafter. Perhaps it will be quite as well that I find myself unable to set seriously about literary occupation for the present. It will be good to have a longer interval between my labor of the body and that of the mind. I shall work to the better purpose, after the beginning of November. Meantime, I shall see these people and their enterprise under a new point of view, and perhaps be able to determine whether thou and I have any call to cast in our lot among them. * * *

September 23— * * *

Belovedest, I do wish the weather would put off this sulky mood. Had it not been for the warmth and brightness of Monday, when I arrived here, I should have supposed that all sunshine had left Brook Farm forever. I have no disposition to take long walks, in

2. Upon his return, Hawthorne was a "boarder" rather than a workingman.
3. This refers to a series of children's history books which Hawthorne planned to write as a source of income. Three were written and published: *Grandfather's Chair* (December 1840), *Famous Old People* (January 1841), *Liberty Tree* (March 1841).

such a state of the sky; nor have I any buoyancy of spirit. Thy husband is a very dull person, just at this time. I suspect he wants thee. It is his purpose, I believe, either to walk or ride to Boston, about the end of next week, and give thee a kiss—after which he will return quietly and contentedly to the farm. Oh what joy, when he will see thee every day!

We had some tableaux last night.[4] They were * * * very stupid, (as, indeed, was the case with all I have ever seen) but do not thou tell Mrs. Ripley so. She is a good woman, and I like her better than I did—her husband keeps his old place in my judgment. Farewell, thou gentlest Dove—thou perfectest woman—thou desirablest wife.

Brook Farm, October 21, 1841

Ownest beloved, * * * What atrocious weather! In all this month, we have not had a single truly October day; it has been a real November month, and of the most disagreeable kind. I came to this place in one snowstorm, and shall probably leave it in another; so that my reminiscences of Brook Farm are likely to be the coldest and dreariest imaginable.

[JOURNAL ENTRY APRIL 8, 1843]

We talked of Brook Farm, and the singular moral aspects which it presents, and the great desirability that its progress and developments should be observed, and its history written.[5]

[JOURNAL ENTRY JULY 27, 1844]

* * * here is a whole colony of little ant-hills, a real village of them; they are small, round hillocks, formed of minute particles of gravel, with an entrance in the centre; and through some of them blades of grass or small shrubs have sprouted up, producing an effect not unlike that of trees overshadowing a homestead. Here is a type of domestic industry—perhaps, too, something of municipal institutions—perhaps, likewise (who knows) the very model of a community, which Fourierites[6] and others are stumbling in pursuit of.

4. Coverdale mentions *tableaux vivants* on p. 98.
5. "We" means Hawthorne and Emerson. For Emerson's view of Brook Farm and its relationship to the intellectual history of its time and place, see his "Historic Notes of Life and Letters in New England," partially reprinted below. An interesting study of Emerson's and Hawthorne's parallel views of communitarian reform is Gustaaf Van Cromphout's "Emerson, Hawthorne, and *The Blithedale Romance, Georgia Review,* 25 (1971), 471–80.
6. When Hawthorne was at Brook Farm, the community was a simple, private cooperative established by Ripley and formed as a stock company under the name Brook Farm Institute of Agriculture and Education. By 1844 the community had become part of the Associationist Movement which was sweeping the country and—amidst much argument—was attempting to embody Charles Fourier's principles for the reorganization of society. Popularized in America by Albert Brisbane (1809–90), Fourier's plan called for the creation of phalanxes, that is, self-sufficient social units of 1,600 to 2,000 men, women, and children (a figure which

Possibly, the student of such philosophies should go to the ant, and find that nature has given him his lesson there. Meantime, like a malevolent genius, I drop a few grains of sand into the entrance of one of these dwellings, and thus quite obliterate it. And, behold, here comes one of the inhabitants, who has been abroad upon some public or private business, or perhaps to enjoy a fantastic walk—and cannot any longer find his own door. What surprise, what hurry, what confusion of mind, are expressed in all his movements! How inexplicable to him must be the agency that has effected this mischief. The incident will probably be long remembered in the annals of the ant-colony, and be talked of in the winter days, when they are making merry over their hoarded provisions. But come, it is time to move. The sun has shifted his position, and has found a vacant space through the branches, by means of which he levels his rays full upon my head. Yet now, as I arise, a cloud has come across him, and makes everything gently sombre in an instant. Many clouds, voluminous and heavy, are scattered about the sky, like the shattered ruins of a dreamer's Utopia; but we will not send our thoughts thitherward now, nor take one of them into our present observations. The clouds of any one day, are material enough, alone, for the observation either of an idle man or a philosopher.

[FROM A LETTER TO WILLIAM B. PIKE, JULY 24, 1851]

When I write another romance, I shall take the Community for a subject, and shall give some of my experiences and observations at Brook Farm.[7]

[JOURNAL ENTRY JULY 31, 1851]

Before supper, Mrs. Tappan came in, with two or three volumes of Fourier's works, which I wished to borrow, with a view to my next Romance.[8]

Fourier claimed to have discovered scientifically and which represented all possible variations of the also scientifically discovered twelve fundamental passions of man). By following only the inclinations of their individual natures (preferably an individual should have some thirty inclinations), the group would develop their own natures to the fullest and create perfect (because complementary) social "Harmony." Brook Farm eventually became the American center of Fourierism and the place of publication of *The Phalanx* (later *The Harbinger*), a journal devoted to the propagation of Fourierism. Although Hawthorne was connected only with the earlier stage of Brook Farm—

when it was a simple, private retreat for well-meaning Transcendentalists—he retained his interest in the community and watched it develop its later public role in the cause of Fourierism.

7. One of Hawthorne's closest friends, Pike (1811–76) was an associate of Hawthorne's in both the Boston (1839–41) and Salem (1846–49) Custom Houses. According to Hawthorne's son Julian, Pike "probably knew Hawthorne more intimately than any other man did."

8. Caroline Sturgis Tappan was one of Hawthorne's acquaintances from Brook Farm days. In 1850–51 the Hawthorne's rented the Red Cottage in Lenox from the Tappans.

[FROM A LETTER TO GEORGE W. CURTIS, JULY 14, 1852]

Do not read [*The Blithedale Romance*] as if it had anything to do with Brook Farm (which essentially it has not) but merely for its own story and characters.[9]

RALPH WALDO EMERSON

From His Journals†

Hawthorne boasts that he lived at Brook Farm during its heroic age: then all were intimate and each knew well the other's work: priest and cook conversed at night of the day's work. Now they complain that they are separated and such intimacy can not be; there are a hundred souls.

9. Curtis (1824–92) came from Providence in 1842 to be prepared for college at the Brook Farm Institute of Education; he left with George P. Bradford two years later when the community became Fourieristic. His "The Duty of the American Scholar to Politics and the Times" (1856) marked the beginning of a distinguished career as lecturer, editor, and writer in the service of such social issues as the antislavery movement, women's rights, and Civil Service reform.

† *Emerson's Journals*, ed. Edward Waldo Emerson (Cambridge, Mass.: Riverside Press, 1911), VI, pp. 441–42. The entry is undated; Emerson entered it into his journal some time between August 25 and September 3, 1843.

Hawthorne's Attitude
Toward Mesmerism

NATHANIEL HAWTHORNE

From His Letters

Brook Farm, October 18, 1841

Most dear wife, I received thy letter and note, last night, and was much gladdened by them; for never has my soul so yearned for thee as now. But, belovedest, my spirit is moved to talk to thee to day about these magnetic miracles,[1] and to beseech thee to take no part in them. I am unwilling that a power should be exercised on thee, of which we know neither the origin nor the consequence, and the phenomena of which seem rather calculated to bewilder us, than to teach us any truths about the present or future state of being. If I possessed such a power over thee, I should not dare to exercise it; nor can I consent to its being exercised by another. Supposing that this power arises from the transfusion of one spirit into another, it seems to me that the sacredness of an individual is violated by it;[2] there would be an intrusion into thy holy of holies—and the intruder would not be thy husband! Canst thou think, without a shrinking of thy soul, of any human being coming into closer communion with thee than I may?—than either nature or my own sense of right would permit me? *I* cannot. And, dearest, thou must remember, too, that thou art now a part of me, and that, by surrendering thyself to the influence of this magnetic lady, thou surrenderest more than thine own moral and spiritual being— allowing that the influence *is* a moral and spiritual one. And,

† The letters in this section are from *Love Letters of Nathaniel Hawthorne* (Chicago: The Dofobs Society, 1907). They were written to Hawthorne's fiancée, Sophia Peabody.
1. Hawthorne's awareness of contemporary interest in mesmerism ("magnetic miracles") is reflected throughout *The Blithedale Romance*, especially pp. 5–6, 100–108, 171–74, 181–88; his personal fear of mesmerism (evidenced in these letters) is echoed by Coverdale on pp. 182–85, 187–88. An excellent study of mesmerism in America during the 1830s and 1840s and of Hawthorne's handling of the subject is to be found in Taylor

Stoehr, "Hawthorne and Mesmerism," *Huntington Library Quarterly*, 33 (1969), 33–60.
2. Compare: "A moral philosopher to buy a slave, or otherwise get possession of a human being, and to use him for the sake of experiment, by trying the operation of a certain vice on him" (*American Notebooks*, 1841). "The Unpardonable Sin might consist in a want of love and reverence for the Human Soul; in consequence of which, the investigtator pried into its dark depths, not with a hope or purpose of making it better, but from a cold philosophical curosity [*sic*] * * *" (*American Notebooks*, 1844).

sweetest, I really do not like the idea of being brought, through thy medium, into such an intimate relation with Mrs. Park![3]

Now, ownest wife, I have no faith whatever that people are raised to the seventh heaven, or to any heaven at all, or that they gain any insight into the mysteries of life beyond death, by means of this strange science. Without distrusting that the phenomena which thou tellest me of, and others as remarkable, have really occurred, I think that they are to be accounted for as the result of a physical and material, not of a spiritual, influence. *Opium* has produced many a brighter vision of heaven (and just as susceptible of proof) than those which thou recountest. They are dreams, my love—and such dreams as thy sweetest fancy, either waking or sleeping, could vastly improve upon. And what delusion can be more lamentable and mischievous, than to mistake the physical and material for the spiritual? What so miserable as to lose the soul's true, though hidden, knowledge and consciousness of heaven, in the mist of an earth-born vision? Thou shalt not do this. If thou wouldst know what heaven is, before thou comest thither hand in hand with thy husband, then retire into the depths of thine own spirit, and thou wilt find it there among holy thoughts and feelings; but do not degrade high Heaven and its inhabitants into any such symbols and forms as those which Miss Larned[4] describes—do not let an earthly effluence from Mrs. Park's corporeal system bewilder thee, and perhaps contaminate something spiritual and sacred. I should as soon think of seeking revelations of the future state in the rottenness of the grave—where so many do seek it.

Belovedest wife, I am sensible that these arguments of mine may appear to have little real weight; indeed, what I write does no sort of justice to what I think. But I care the less for this, because I know that my deep and earnest feeling upon the subject will weigh more with thee than all the arguments in the world. And thou wilt know that the view which I take of this matter is caused by no want of faith in mysteries, but from a deep reverence of the soul, and of the mysteries which it knows within itself, but never transmits to the earthly eye or ear. Keep thy imagination sane—that is one of the truest conditions of communion with Heaven.

Dearest, after these grave considerations, it seems hardly worth while to submit a merely external one; but as it occurs to me, I will write it. I cannot think, without invincible repugnance, of thy holy name being bruited abroad in connection with these magnetic phenomena. Some (horrible thought!) would pronounce my Dove an impostor; the great majority would deem thee crazed; and even the

---

3. Cornelia Park, an old friend, became Sophia's mesmerist when the Peabodys moved to Boston.

4. A somnambulist, or medium, with whom Mrs. Park experimented.

few believers would feel a sort of interest in thee, which it would be anything but pleasant to excite. And what adequate motive can there be for exposing thyself to all this misconception? Thou wilt say, perhaps, that thy visions and experiences would never be known. But Miss Larned's are known to all who choose to listen.

Brook Farm, June 30, 1842

* * *

Belovedest, didst thou sleep well, last night? My pillow was haunted with ghastly dreams, the details whereof have flitted away like vapors, but a strong impression remains about thy being magnetised. God save me from any more such! I awoke in an absolute quake. Dearest, I cannot oppose thy submitting to so much of this influence as will relieve thy headache; but, as thou lovest me, do not suffer thyself to be put to sleep. My feeling on this point is so strong, that it would be wronging us both to conceal it from thee.

Hawthorne's Use of
The American Notebooks in
The Blithedale Romance

NATHANIEL HAWTHORNE

From His Journals†

[Old Moodie]

[JOURNAL ENTRY MAY 7, 1850]

Walking the side-walk, in front of this grog-shop of Parkers,[1] (or, sometimes, in cold or rainy days, taking his station inside) there is generally to be observed an elderly ragamuffin, in a dingy and battered hat, an old surtout, and a more than shabby general aspect; a thin face and red-nose, a patch over one eye, and the other half-drowned in moisture; he leans in a slightly stooping posture on a stick, forlorn and silent, addressing nobody, but fixing his one moist eye on you with a certain intentness. He is a man who has been in decent circumstances at some former period of life, but, falling into decay, (perhaps by dint of too frequent visits at Parker's bar) he now haunts about the place, (as a ghost haunts the spot where he was murdered) to "collect his rents", as Parker says—that is, to catch an occasional ninepence from some charitable acquaintance, or a glass of liquor at the bar. The word "ragamuffin," which I have used above, does not accurately express the man; because there is a sort of shadow or delusion of respectability about him; and a sobriety, too, and kind of decency, in his groggy and red-nosed destitution.[2]

[Priscilla]

[JOURNAL ENTRY OCTOBER 9, 1841]

Still dismal weather. Our household, being composed in great measure of children and young people, is generally a cheerful one

---

† Hawthorne's journal entries are from *The American Notebooks*, ed. Claude M. Simpson (Columbus: Ohio State University Press, 1972).

1. A saloon-restaurant which Hawthorne frequented in Boston.
2. For the use Hawthorne made of this passage, see pp. 5–6, 76–77, 161–67.

enough, even in gloomy weather. For a week past, we have been especially gladdened with a little sempstress from Boston, about seventeen years old, but of such a petite figure that, at first view, one would take her to be hardly in her teens. She is very vivacious and smart, laughing, singing, and talking, all the time—talking sensibly, but still taking the view of matters that a city girl naturally would. If she were larger than she is, and of less pleasing aspect, I think she might be intolerable; but being so small, and with a white skin, healthy as a wild flower, she is really very agreeable; and to look at her face is like being shone upon by a ray of the sun. She never walks, but bounds and dances along; and this motion, in her small person, does not give the idea of violence. It is like a bird, hopping from twig to twig, and chirping merrily all the time. Sometimes she is a little vulgar; but even that works well enough into her character, and accords with it. On continued observation and acquaintance, you discover that she is not a little girl, but really a little woman, with all the prerogatives and liabilities of a woman. This gives a new aspect to her character; while her girlish impression still continues, and is strangely combined with the sense that this frolicsome little maiden has the material for that sober character, a wife. She romps with the boys, runs races with them in the yard, and up and down the stairs, and is heard scolding laughingly at their rough play. She asks William Allen[3] to put her "on top of that horse;" whereupon he puts his large brown hands about her waist, and, swinging her to-and-fro, places her on horseback. By the bye, William threatened to rivet two horse shoes round her neck, for having clambered, with the other girls and boys, upon a load of hay; whereby the said load lost its balance, and slided off the cart. She strings the seed-berries of roses together, making a scarlet necklace of them, which she wears about her neck. She gathers everlasting flowers, to wear in her hair or bonnet, arranging them with the skill of a dress-maker. In the evening, she sits singing by the hour together, with the musical part of the establishment—often breaking into laughter, whereto she is incited by the tricks of the boys. The last thing you hear of her, she is tripping up stairs, to bed, talking lightsomely or singing; and you meet her in the morning, the very image of lightsome morn itself, smiling briskly at you, so that one takes her for a promise of cheerfulness through the day. Be it said, among all the rest, there is a perfect maiden modesty in her deportment; though I doubt whether the boys, in their rompings with her, do not feel that she has past out of her childhood.[4]

3. William Brockway Allen owned three shares in Brook Farm and managed the agricultural operations until he found the farm too unprofitable and left before

June, 1842.
4. For the use Hawthorne made of this passage, see pp. 26, 31, 55–56, 67–70.

[*Coverdale's Hermitage*]

[JOURNAL ENTRY SEPTEMBER 26, 1841]

Within the verge of the meadow, mostly near the firm shore of pasture ground, I found several grape vines, hung with abundance of large purple grapes. The vines had caught hold of maples and alders, and climbed to the top, curling round about and interwreathing their twisted folds in so intimate a manner, that it was not easy to tell the parasite from the supporting tree or shrub. Sometimes the same vine had enveloped several shrubs, and caused a strange tangled confusion, converting all these poor plants to the purposes of its own support, and hindering them growing to their own benefit and convenience. The broad vine-leaves, some of them yellow or yellowish-tinged, were seen apparently growing on the same stems with the silver maple leaves, and those of the other shrubs, thus married against their will by this conjugal twine; and the purple clusters of grapes hung down from above and in the midst, so that a man might gather grapes, if not of thorns, yet of as alien bushes. One vine had ascended almost to the tip-top of a large white pine tree, spreading its leaves and hanging its purple clusters among all its boughs—still climbing and clambering, as if it would not be content till it crowned the very summit of the tree with a wreath of its own foliage and a cluster of grapes. I mounted high into the tree, and ate grapes there, while the vine wreathed still higher into the depths of the tree, above my head. The grapes were sour, being not yet fully ripe; some of them, however, were sweet and pleasant. The vine embraces the trees like a serpent.[5]

[*The Farewell to the Swine*]

[JOURNAL ENTRY OCTOBER 1, 1841]

I have been looking at our four swine, not of the last lot, but those in process of fatting. They lie among the clean rye straw in their stye, nestling close together; for they seem to be a sensitive beast to the cold; and this is a clear, bright, chrystal, north-west windy, cool morning. So there lie these four black swine, as deep among the straw as they can burrow, the very symbols of slothful ease and sensual comfort. They seem to be actually oppressed and overburthened with comfort. They are quick to notice any one's approach to the stye, and utter a low grunt—not drawing a breath for that particular purpose, but grunting with their ordinary breath

5. For the use Hawthorne made of this passage, see pp. 91–92.

—at the same time turning an observant, though dull and sluggish eye upon the visitor. They seem to be involved and buried in their own corporeal substance, and to look dimly forth at the outer world. They breathe not easily, and yet not with difficulty or discomfort; for the very unreadiness and oppression with which their breath comes, appears to make them sensible of the deep sensual satisfaction which they feel. Swill, the remnant of their last meal, remains in their trough, denoting that their food is more abundant than even a hog can demand. Anon, they fall asleep, drawing short and heavy breaths, which heave their huge sides up and down; but at the slightest noise, they sluggishly unclose their eyes, and give another gentle grunt. They also grunt among themselves, apparently without any external cause, but merely to express their swinish sympathy. I suppose it is the knowledge that these four grunters are doomed to die within two or three weeks, that gives them a sort of awfulness in my conception; it makes me contrast their present gross substance of fleshly life with the nothingness speedily to come.[6]

[*Views from Coverdale's Window*]

[JOURNAL ENTRY MAY 7, 1850]

I take an interest in all the nooks and crannies and every development of cities; so here I try to make a description of the view from the back windows of a house in the centre of Boston, at which I glance in the intervals of writing.[7] The view is bounded, at perhaps thirty yards distance (or perhaps not so much,) by a row of opposite brick dwellings, standing, I think, on Temple-place; houses of the better order, with tokens of genteel families visible in all the rooms betwixt the basements and the attic windows in the roof; plate-glass in the rear drawing-rooms, flower-pots in some of the windows of the upper stories; occasionally, a lady's figure, either seated, or appearing with a flitting grace, or dimly manifest farther within the obscurity of the room. A balcony with a wrought iron fence running along under the row of drawing-room windows above the

6. For the use Hawthorne made of this passage, see pp. 133–34. Hawthorne was clearly fascinated by pigs: "If my wife's permission can be obtained, I have serious thoughts of inducting a new incumbent into this part of the parsonage. It is our duty to support a pig, even if we have no design of feasting upon his flesh; and for my own part, I have a great sympathy and interest for the whole race of porkers, and should have much amusement in studying the character of a pig. Perhaps I might try to bring out 'his moral and intellectual nature, and cultivate his affections" (*American Note-*

books, August 9, 1842). See also *Love Letters*, II, p. 201, and *American Notebooks*, pp. 3–4, 137, and 148–49.
7. "The greater picturesqueness and reality of back-yards, and everything appertaining to the rear of a house; as compared with the front, which is fitted up for the public eye. There is much to be learnt, always, by getting a glimpse at rears. When the direction of a road has been altered, so as to pass the rear of farm-houses, instead of the front, a very noticeable aspect is presented" (*American Notebooks*, between June 1, 1842, and July 27, 1844).

basement. In the space betwixt this opposite row of dwellings, and that in which I am situated, are the low out-houses of the above described dwellings, with flat-roofs; or solid brick walls, with walks on them, and high railings, for the convenience of the washer-women in hanging out their clothes. In the intervals betwixt these ranges of out houses or walks, are grass-plots, already green, because so sheltered; and fruit-trees, now beginning to put forth their leaves, and one of them, a cherry tree, almost in full blossom. Birds flutter and sing among these trees. I should judge it a good site for the growth of delicate fruit; for quite enclosed on all sides by houses; the blighting winds cannot molest the trees; they have sunshine on them a good part of the day, though the shadow must come early; and I suppose there is a rich soil about their roots. I see grape vines clambering against one wall, and also peeping over another, where the main body of the vine is invisible to me. In another place, a frame is erected for a grape vine, and probably it will produce as rich clusters as the vines of Madeira, here in the heart of the city, in this little spot of fructifying earth, while the thunder of wheels rolls about it on every side. The trees are not all fruit-trees; one pretty well-grown buttonwood tree aspires upward above the roofs of the houses. In the full verdure of summer, there will be quite a mass or curtain of foliage, between the hither and the thither row of houses.[8]

[JOURNAL ENTRY MAY 14, 1850]

In the back ground of the house; a cat occasionally stealing along on the roofs of the low outhouses; descending the flight of wooden steps into the brick area, investigating the shed, and entering all dark and secret places; cautious, circumspect, as if in search of something; noiseless; attentive to every noise. Moss grows on spots of the roof; there are little boxes of earth, here and there, with plants in them. The grass-plots appertaining to each of the houses whose rears are opposite ours (standing in Temple-place) are perhaps ten or twelve feet broad, and three times as long. Here and there is a large, painted garden-pot, half buried in earth; besides the large trees in blossom, there are little ones,—probably of last years setting out. Early in the day, chamber-maids are seen hanging the bed-clothes out of the upper-windows; at the window of the basement of the same house, I see a woman ironing. Were I a solitary prisoner, I should not doubt to find occupation of deep interest for my whole day, in watching only one of these houses. One of the houses seems to be quite shut up; all the blinds in the three windows

8. For the use Hawthorne made of this passage, see pp. 137–38, 140–41.

of each of the four stories being closed; although, in the roof-windows of the attic-story, the curtains are hung carelessly upward, instead of being drawn. I think the house is empty—perhaps for the summer. The visible side of the whole row of houses is now in the shade—they looking, in this direction, towards, I should say, the southwest. Later in the day, they are wholly covered with sunshine, and continue so through the afternoon; and at evening, the sunshine slowly withdraws upward, gleams aslant upon the windows, perches on the chimneys, and so disappears. The upper part of the spire, and the weather-cock, of the Park-street church, appears over one of the houses, looking as if it were close behind; it shows the wind to be east. At one of the windows of the third story, sits a woman in a colored dress, diligently sewing on something white; she sews not like a lady, but with an occupational air. Her dress, I observe, on closer observation, is a kind of loose morning sack, with, I think, a silky gloss on it; and she seems to have a silver-comb in her hair—no, this latter item is a mistake.

Sheltered as the space is between the two rows of houses, a puff of the east-wind finds its ways in, and shakes off some of the withering blossoms from the cherry-trees.

Quiet as this prospect is, there is a continual and near thunder of wheels, proceeding from Washington-street. In a building not far off, there is a hall for exhibitions; and, sometimes, in the evenings, loud music is heard from it; or, if a diorama be exhibiting (that of Bunker Hill, for-instance, or the burning of Moscow) an immense racket of imitative cannon and musketry.[9]

[JOURNAL ENTRY MAY 16, 1850]

It has been an easterly rain yesterday and to-day, with occasional lightenings up; and then a heavy downfal of the gloom again. Scene out of the rear windows; the glistening roofs of the opposite houses; the chimneys, now and then, choked with their own smoke, which a blast drives down their throats. The church-spire has a mist about it. Once, this morning, a solitary dove came and lit on the peak of an attic-window, and looked down into the areas; remaining in this position a considerable time. Now, he has taken a flight and alighted on the roof of this house, directly over the window at which I sit, so that I can look up and see his head and beak, and the tips of his claws. The roofs of the low out-houses are black with moisture; the gutters are full of water; and there is a little puddle where there is place for it in the hollow of a board. On the grass-plots are strewn the fallen blossoms of the cherry-trees; and over the

9. For the use Hawthorne made of this passage, see pp. 136–38, 140–41, 143.

scene broods a parallelogram of sombre sky. Thus it will be all day, as it was yesterday; and, in the evening, one window after another will be lit up; in the drawing-rooms, through the white curtains, may be seen the gleam of an astral lamp, like a fixed star; in the basement-rooms, the work of the kitchen going forward; in the upper chambers, here and there, a light where perchance some lovely damsel is disrobing herself for bed.[1]

[*A Boston Saloon*]

[JOURNAL ENTRY MAY 7, 1850]

I did not go out yesterday afternoon, but after tea I went to Parker's. The drinking and smoking shop is no bad place to see one kind of life. The front apartment is for drinking. The door opens into Court Square, and is denoted, usually, by some choice specimens of dainties exhibited in the windows, or hanging beside the door-post; as, for instance, a pair of canvas-back ducks, distinguishable by their delicately mottled feathers; an admirable cut of raw beefsteak; a ham, ready boiled, and with curious figures traced in spices on its outward fat; a half, or perchance the whole, of a large salmon, when in season; a bunch of partridges, &c, &c. A screen stands directly before the door, so as to conceal the interior from an outside barbarian. At the counter stand, at almost all hours,— certainly at all hours when I have chanced to observe,—tipplers, either taking a solitary glass, or treating all round, veteran topers, flashy young men, visitors from the country, the various petty officers connected with the law, whom the vicinity of the Court-House brings hither. Chiefly, they drink plain liquors, gin, brandy, or whiskey, sometimes a Tom and Jerry, a gin cocktail (which the bartender makes artistically, tossing it in a large parabola from one tumbler to another, until fit for drinking), a brandy-smash, and numerous other concoctions. All this toping goes forward with little or no apparent exhilaration of spirits; nor does this seem to be the object sought,—it being either, I imagine, to create a titillation of the coats of the stomach and a general sense of invigoration, without affecting the brain. Very seldom does a man grow wild and unruly.

The inner room is hung round with pictures and engravings of various kinds,—a painting of a premium ox, a lithograph of a Turk and of a Turkish lady, and various showily engraved tailors' advertisements, and other shop bills; among them all, a small painting of a drunken toper, sleeping on a bench beside the grog-shop,—a

1. For the use Hawthorne made of this passage, see pp. 137–38, 137, 148–49.

ragged, half-hatless, bloated, red-nosed, jolly, miserable-looking devil, very well done, and strangely suitable to the room in which it hangs. Round the walls are placed some half a dozen marble-topped tables, and a centre-table in the midst; most of them strewn with theatrical and other show-bills; and the large theatre bills, with their type of gigantic solidity and blackness, hung against the walls.[2]

[JOURNAL ENTRY MAY 16, 1850]

In a bar-room, a large oval basin let into the counter, with a brass tube rising from the centre, out of which gushes continually a miniature fountain, and descends in a soft, gentle, never ceasing rain into the basin, where swim a company of gold fishes. Some of them gleam brightly in their golden armor; others have a dull white aspect, going through some process of transmutation. One would think that the atmosphere, continually filled with tobacco-smoke, might impregnate the water unpleasantly for the scaly people; but then it is continually flowing away, and being renewed. And what if some toper should be seized with the freak of emptying his glass of gin or brandy into the basin? Would the fishes die, or merely get jolly?[3]

[*The Masqueraders*]

[JOURNAL ENTRY SEPTEMBER 28, 1841]

A picnic party in the woods, yesterday, in honor of Frank Dana's birth-day, he being six years old.[4] I strolled into the woods, after dinner, with Mr. Bradford;[5] and in a lonesome glade, we met the apparition of an Indian chief, dressed in appropriate costume of blanket, feathers, and paint, and armed with a musket. Almost at the same time a young gipsey fortune teller came from among the trees, and proposed to tell my fortune; which while she was doing, the goddess Diana (known on earth as Miss Ellen Slade)[6] let fly an arrow and hit me smartly in the hand. This fortune teller and goddess were a fine contrast, Diana being a blonde, fair, quiet, with a moderate composure; and the gipsey (Ora Gannet)[7] a bright,

2. For the use Hawthorne made of this passage, see pp. 160–64.
3. For the use Hawthorne made of this passage, see p. 164.
4. A nephew of Sophia Dana Ripley; the boy died two years later.
5. George P. Bradford (1807–90) Hawthorne admired for his ability to combine physical labor and literary interests; he became Brook Farm's Director of Belles Lettres but left in 1843 because of the ar-

guments over Fourierism.
6. A very attractive sixteen-year-old member of Brook Farm.
7. Deborah "Ora" Gannett (Hawthorne misspelled her name) left Brook Farm in 1844 when the Community's reputation was declining because of rumors of free love and cabalism; in 1890 she published "A Girl of Sixteen at Brook Farm" in the *Atlantic Monthly*.

vivacious, dark-haired, rich-complexioned damsel—both of them very pretty; at least, pretty enough to make fifteen years enchanting. Accompanied by these denizens of the wild wood, we went onward, and came to a company of fantastic figures, arranged in a ring for a dance or game. There was a Swiss girl, an Indian squaw, a negro of the Jim Crow order, one or two foresters; and several people in Christian attire; besides children of all ages. Then followed childish games, in which the grown people took part with mirth enough— while I, whose nature it is to be a mere spectator both of sport and serious business, lay under the trees and looked on. Meanwhile, Mr. Emerson[8] and Miss Fuller,[9] who had arrived an hour or two before, came forth into the little glade where we were assembled. Here followed much talk.

The ceremonies of the day concluded with a cold collation of cakes and fruit. All was pleasant enough; "an excellent piece of work;—would 'twere done!" It has left a fantastic impression on my memory, this intermingling of wild and fabulous characters with real and homely ones, in the secluded nook of the woods. I remember them with the sunlight breaking through overshadowing branches, and they appearing and disappearing confusedly— perhaps starting out of the earth; as if the every day laws of Nature were suspended for this particular occasion. There are the children, too, laughing and sporting about, as if they were at home among such strange shapes—and anon bursting into loud uproar of lamentation, when the rude gambols of the merry-makers chance to overturn them. And, apart, with a shrewd Yankee observation of the scene, stands our friend Orange,[1] a thickset, sturdy figure, in his blue frock, enjoying the fun well enough, yet rather laughing with a perception of its nonsensicallness, than at all entering into the spirit of the thing.[2]

[*Zenobia's Drowning*]

[JOURNAL ENTRY JULY 1845]

On the night of July 9th, a search for the dead body of a drowned girl. She was a Miss Hunt, about nineteen years old; a girl of education and refinement, but depressed and miserable for want of sympathy—her family being an affectionate one, but uncultivated, and incapable of responding to her demands. She was of a melancholic temperament, accustomed to solitary walks in the woods. At this time, she had the superintendence of one of the

8. See note, p. 258.
9. See note 3, p. 232.
1. T. J. Orange, a farmer from the neighborhood; his stance parallels that of Silas

Foster in "The Masqueraders" (p. 194).
2. For the use Hawthorne made of this passage, see pp. 193–95.

district-schools, comprising sixty scholars, particularly difficult of management. Well; Ellery Channing[3] knocked at the door, between 9 and 10 in the evening, in order to get my boat, to go in search of this girl's drowned body. He took the oars, and I the paddle, and we went rapidly down the river, until, a good distance below the bridge, we saw lights on the bank, and the dim figures of a number of people waiting for us. Her bonnet and shoes had already been found on this spot, and her handkerchief, I believe, on the edge of the water; so that the body was probably at no great distance, unless the current (which is gentle, and almost imperceptible) had swept her down.

We took in General Buttrick,[4] and a young man in a blue frock, and commenced the search; the general and the other man having long poles, with hooks at the end, and Ellery a hay-rake, while I steered the boat. It was a very eligible place to drown one's self. On the verge of the river, there were water-weeds; but after a few steps, the bank goes off very abruptly, and the water speedily becomes fifteen or twenty feet deep. It must be one of the deepest spots in the whole river; and, holding a lantern over it, it was black as midnight, smooth, impenetrable, and keeping its secrets from the eye as perfectly as mid-ocean could. We caused the boat to float once or twice past the spot where the bonnet &c had been found; carefully searching the bottom at different distances from the shore—but, for a considerable time without success. Once or twice the poles or the rake caught in bunches of water-weed, which, in the star-light, looked like garments; and once Ellery and the General struck some substance at the bottom, which they at first mistook for the body; but it was probably a sod that had rolled in from the bank. All this time, the persons on the bank were anxiously waiting, and sometimes giving us their advice to search higher or lower, or at such and such a point. I now paddled the boat again past the point where she was supposed to have entered the river, and then turned it, so as to let it float broadside downwards, about midway from bank to bank. The young fellow in the blue frock sat on the next seat to me, plying his long pole.

We had drifted a little distance below the group of men on the bank, when this fellow gave a sudden start—"What's this?" cried he. I felt in a moment what it was; and I suppose the same electric shock went through everybody in the boat. "Yes; I've got her!" said he; and heaving up his pole with difficulty, there was an appearance of light garments on the surface of the water; he made a strong

3. William Ellery Channing (1817–1901) married Margaret Fuller's sister and lived in Concord, where he wrote poetry and was associated with various Transcendentalists—especially Thoreau, who quotes his poetry in *Walden*.
4. Probably Joshua Buttrick, who owned a farm near the Concord River; Thoreau complimented him as "a farmer who is a man of sentiment."

effort, and brought so much of the body above the surface, that there could be no doubt about it. He drew her towards the boat, grasped her arm or hand; and I steered the boat to the bank, all the while looking at this dead girl, whose limbs were swaying in the water, close at the boat's side. The fellow evidently had the same sort of feeling in his success as if he had caught a particularly fine fish; though mingled, no doubt, with horror. For my own part, I felt my voice tremble a little, when I spoke, at the first shock of the discovery; and at seeing the body come to the surface, dimly in the starlight. When close to the bank, some of the men stepped into the water and drew out the body; and then, by their lanterns, I could see how rigid it was. There was nothing flexible about it; she did not droop over the arms of those who supported her, with her hair hanging down, as a painter would have represented her; but was all as stiff as marble. And it was evident that her wet garments covered limbs perfectly inflexible. They took her out of the water, and deposited her under an oak-tree; and by the time we had got ashore, they were examining her by the light of two or three lanterns.

I never saw nor imagined a spectacle of such perfect horror. The rigidity, above spoken of, was dreadful to behold. Her arms had stiffened in the act of struggling; and were bent before her, with the hands clenched. She was the very image of a death-agony; and when the men tried to compose her figure, her arms would still return to that same position; indeed it was almost impossible to force them out of it for an instant. One of the men put his foot upon her arm, for the purpose of reducing it by her side; but, in a moment, it rose again. The lower part of the body had stiffened into a more quiet attitude; the legs were slightly bent, and the feet close together. But that rigidity!—it is impossible to express the effect of it; it seemed as if she would keep the same posture in the grave, and that her skeleton would keep it too, and that when she rose at the day of Judgment, it would be in the same attitude.

As soon as she was taken out of the water, the blood began to stream from her nose. Something seemed to have injured her eye, too; perhaps it was the pole, when it first struck the body. The complexion was a dark red, almost purple; the hands were white, with the same rigidity in their clench as in all the rest of the body. Two of the men got water, and began to wash away the blood from her face; but it flowed and flowed, and continued to flow; and an old carpenter, who seemed to be skilful in such matters, said that this was always the case, and that she would continue to "purge," as he called it, in this manner, until her burial, I believe. He said, too, that the body would swell, by morning, so that nobody would know her. Let it take what change it might, it could scarcely look more horrible than it did now, in its rigidity; certainly, she did not look as if she had gotten grace in the world whither she had precipitated herself; but rather, her stiffened death-agony was an emblem of inflexible judgment pronounced upon her. If she could have foreseen, while she stood, at 5 o'clock that morning, on the bank of the river, how her maiden corpse would have looked, eighteen hours afterwards, and how coarse men would strive with hand and foot to reduce it to a decent aspect, and all in vain—it would surely have saved her from this deed. So horribly did she look, that a middle-aged man, David Buttrick,[5] absolutely fainted away, and was found lying on the grass, at a little distance, perfectly insensible. It required much rubbing of hands and limbs to restore him.

Meantime, General Buttrick had gone to give notice to the family that the body was found; and others had gone in search of rails, to make a bier. Another boat now arrived, and added two or three more horror-struck spectators. There was a dog with them, who looked at the body, as it seemed to me, with pretty much the same feelings as the rest of us—horror and curiosity. A young brother of the deceased, apparently about twelve or fourteen years old, had been on the spot from the beginning. He seemed not much moved, externally, but answered questions about his sister, and the number of the brothers and sisters, (ten in all,) with composure. No doubt, however, he was stunned and bewildered with the scene—to see his sister lying there, in such terrific guise, at midnight, under an oak, on the verge of the black river, with strangers clustering about her, holding their lanterns over her face; and that old carpenter washing the blood away, which still flowed forth, though from a frozen fountain. Never was there a wilder scene. All the while, we were talking about the circumstances, and about an inquest, and whether or no it was necessary, and of how many it should consist; and the old carpenter was talking of dead people, and how he would as lief handle them as living ones.

By this time, two rails had been procured, across which were laid some boards or broken oars from the bottom of a boat; and the body, being wrapt in an old quilt, was laid upon this rude bier. All of us took part in bearing the corpse, or in steadying it. From the bank of the river to her father's house, there was nearly half a mile of pasture-ground, on the ascent of the hill; and our burthen grew very heavy, before we reached the door. What a midnight procession it was! How strange and fearful it would have seemed, if it could have been foretold, a day beforehand, that I should help carry a dead body along that track! At last, we reached the door, where appeared an old gray-haired man, holding a light; he said nothing, seemed calm, and after the body was laid upon a large table, in

5. David Buttrick (b. 1801) lived on a farm north of Concord; his relationship   to General Buttrick is not known.

what seemed to be the kitchen, the old man disappeared. This was the grandfather. Good Mrs. Pratt[6] was in the room, having been sent for to assist in laying out the body; but she seemed wholly at a loss how to proceed; and no wonder—for it was an absurd idea to think of composing that rigidly distorted figure into the decent quiet of the coffin. A Mrs. Lee had likewise been summoned, and shortly appeared, a withered, skin-and-bone looking woman; but she, too, though a woman of skill, was in despair at the job, and confessed her ignorance how to set about it. Whether the poor girl did finally get laid out, I know not, but can scarcely think it possible. I have since been told that, on stripping the body, they found a strong cord wound round the waist, and drawn tight—for what purpose is impossible to guess.

"Ah, poor child!"—that was the exclamation of an elderly man, as he helped draw her out of the water. I suppose one friend would have saved her; but she died for want of sympathy—a severe penalty for having cultivated and refined herself out of the sphere of her natural connections.

She is said to have gone down to the river at 5 in the morning, and to have been seen walking to and fro on the bank, so late as 7—there being all that space of final struggle with her misery. She left a diary, which is said to exhibit (as her whole life did) many high and remarkable traits. The idea of suicide was not a new one with her; she had before attempted, walking up to her chin into the water, but coming out again, in compassion to the agony of a sister, who stood on the bank. She appears to have been religious, and of a high morality.

The reason, probably, that the body remained so near the spot where she drowned herself, was, that it had sunk to the bottom of perhaps the deepest spot in the river, and so was out of the action of the current.[7]

6. The Minot Pratts, two of the original Brook farmers, left the Community in April 1845 and moved to Concord.

7. For the use Hawthorne made of this passage, see pp. 211–19.

Emerson's Views on Reform, Romantic Idealism, and Brook Farm

RALPH WALDO EMERSON

Historic Notes of Life and Letters in New England†

* * *

There are always two parties, the party of the Past and the party of the Future; the Establishment and the Movement. At times the resistance is reanimated, the schism runs under the world and appears in Literature, Philosophy, Church, State, and social customs. It is not easy to date these eras of activity with any precision, but in this region one made itself remarked, say in 1820 and the twenty years following. * * * The former generations acted under the belief that a shining social prosperity was the beatitude of man, and sacrificed uniformly the citizen to the State. The modern mind believed that the nation existed for the individual, for the guardianship and education of every man. This idea, roughly written in revolutions and national movements, in the mind of the philosopher had far more precision; the individual is the world.

This perception is a sword such as was never drawn before. It divides and detaches bone and marrow, soul and body, yea, almost the man from himself. It is the age of severance, of dissociation, of freedom, of analysis, of detachment. Every man for himself. * * *

† From "Historic Notes of Life and Letters in New England," in *Lectures and Biographical Sketches* (vol. X of *Emerson's Works*), ed. J. E. Cabot (Boston and New York: Houghton, Mifflin, 1883). The essay was written in 1865 and published in 1883.

Since Emerson (1803–82) was the central figure in the Transcendentalist movement, it was to be expected that George Ripley would make a concerted effort to convince him to become a part of Brook Farm. In the late 1840s, by talk and letter, Ripley tried, but without success. Although Emerson was hospitable to new experiments in living and considered the "design" of Brook Farm to be "noble and humane" (if not always practical),

he was too much committed to "private reform" to ever allow himself to become a part of any communitarian scheme. To "join this body," he wrote in his journal the day after a visit from Ripley, "would be to traverse all my long trumpeted theory, and the instinct which spoke from it, that one man is a counterpoise to a city—that a man is stronger than a city, that his solitude is more prevalent and beneficient than the concert of crowds." He did, however, make frequent visits to the Farm, which he enjoyed, and came to see that, despite its relatively brief history, Brook Farm was an important event in the lives of those that lived there and a significant moment in the history of the New England intellect.

The social sentiments are weak; the sentiment of patriotism is weak; veneration is low; the natural affections feebler than they were. People grow philosophical about native land and parents and relations. There is an universal resistance to ties and ligaments once supposed essential to civil society. The new race is stiff, heady and rebellious; they are fanatics in freedom; they hate tolls, taxes, turnpikes, banks, hierarchies, governors, yea, almost laws. They have a neck of unspeakable tenderness; it winces at a hair. They rebel against theological as against political dogmas; against mediation, or saints, or any nobility in the unseen.

* * * Instead of the social existence which all shared, was now separation. Every one for himself; driven to find all his resources, hopes, rewards, society and deity within himself.

The young men were born with knives in their brain, a tendency to introversion, self-dissection, anatomizing of motives. * * *

Whether from [the upsurge of romantic idealism in philosophy, religion, and literature][1] or whether by a reaction of the general mind against the too formal science, religion and social life of the earlier period,—there was, in the first quarter of our nineteenth century, a certain sharpness of criticism, an eagerness for reform, which showed itself in every quarter. It appeared in the popularity of Lavater's Physiognomy,[2] now almost forgotten. Gall and Spurzheim's Phrenology[3] laid a rough hand on the mysteries of animal and spiritual nature, dragging down every sacred secret to a street show. The attempt was coarse and odious to scientific men, but had a certain truth in it; it felt connection where the professors denied it, and was a leading to a truth which had not yet been announced. On the heels of this intruder came Mesmerism, which broke into the inmost shrines, attempted the explanation of miracle and prophecy, as well as of creation. What could be more revolting to the contemplative philosopher! But a certain success attended it, against all expectation. It was human, it was genial, it affirmed unity and connection between remote points, and as such was excellent criticism on the narrow and dead classification of what passed for science; and the joy with which it was greeted was an instinct of the people which no true philosopher would fail to profit by. * * *

Dr. Channing[4] took counsel in 1840 with George Ripley, to the

1. Words in brackets added by the editors of this Norton Critical Edition.
2. Johann Kaspar Lavater's *Physiognomy* (1775–78) was a popular, pseudoscientific treatise on the method of discovering the qualities of the mind from the lineaments of the body.
3. Franz Joseph Gall (1758–1828) and Johann Kaspar Spurzheim (1776–1832) wrote extensively on phrenology, a system for ascertaining precisely the talents and dispositions of men from the exter-

nal appearance of their skulls.
4. William Ellery Channing (1780–1842), a Boston minister whose break (in 1819) with orthodox Calvinism made him known as the "apostle" of Unitarianism. His liberal religious and social ideas helped to prepare the way for Transcendentalism and other idealistic cultural movements. In an omitted section of the essay, Emerson calls him "the star of the American Church."

point whether it were possible to bring cultivated, thoughtful people together, and make society that deserved the name. * * *

Some time afterwards * * * Mr. and Mrs. Ripley * * * invited a limited party of ladies and gentlemen. I had the honor to be present. Though I recall the fact, I do not retain any instant consequence of this attempt, or any connection between it and the new zeal of the friends who at that time began to be drawn together by sympathy of studies and of aspiration. Margaret Fuller, George Ripley, Dr. Convers Francis, Theodore Parker, Dr. Hedge, Mr. Brownson, James Freeman Clarke, William H. Channing,[5] and many others, gradually drew together and from time to time spent an afternoon at each other's houses in a serious conversation. * * *

I think there prevailed at that time a general belief in Boston that there was some concert of *doctrinaires* to establish certain opinions and inaugurate some movement in literature, philosophy, and religion, of which design the supposed conspirators were quite innocent; for there was no concert, and only here and there two or three men or women who read and wrote, each alone, with unusual vivacity. Perhaps they only agreed in having fallen upon Coleridge and Wordsworth and Goethe, then on Carlyle, with pleasure and sympathy.[6] Otherwise, their education and reading were not marked, but had the American superficialness, and their studies were solitary. I suppose all of them were surprised at this rumor of a school or sect, and certainly at the name of Transcendentalism, given nobody knows by whom, or when it was first applied. As these persons became in the common chances of society acquainted with each other, there resulted certainly strong friendships, which of course were exclusive in proportion to their heat: and perhaps those persons who were mutually the best friends were the most private and had no ambition of publishing their letters, diaries, or conversation.

5. For Fuller, see note 3, p. 232; for Ripley, see note 3, p. 3; for Brownson, see note †, p. 271; for Parker, see note 3, p. 3. Convers Francis (1795–1863) was a Harvard Divinity School Professor whose specialty was German idealistic philosophy. Frederick Henry Hedge (1805–90) was a colleague of Francis in the Harvard Divinity Schools, also specializing in German idealistic philosophy, about which he wrote extensively; the Transcendental Club, which Emerson describes above, was sometimes referred to as the Hedge Club. James Freeman Clarke (1810–88), a liberal Unitarian minister, wrote extensively on religious subjects and collaborated with Emerson and William H. Channing on *Memoirs of Margaret Fuller Ossoli* (1852). William Henry Channing (1810–

84), a Unitarian minister and Christian Socialist, was associated with Brook Farm throughout its six-year history; he lived there for a while, preached often, and contributed to the *Harbinger*; converted to the principles of Fourierism, he became secretary of the American Union of Associationists (1847), which included such Brook Farmers as George Ripley, Charles Dana, and John Dwight; he was the nephew of William Ellery Channing.
6. Samuel Taylor Coleridge (1772–1834), English poet and critic; William Wordsworth (1770–1850), English poet; Johann Wolfgang von Goethe (1749–1832), German poet, dramatist, critic, and novelist; Thomas Carlyle (1795–1881), English historian, biographer, and social critic. All important figures in the Romantic Movement.

From that time meetings were held for conversation, with very little form, from house to house, of people engaged in studies, fond of books, and watchful of all the intellectual light from whatever quarter it flowed. Nothing could be less formal, yet the intelligence and character and varied ability of the company gave it some notoriety and perhaps waked curiosity as to its aims and results.

Nothing more serious came of it than the modest quarterly journal called "The Dial"[7] which, under the editorship of Margaret Fuller, and later of some other,[8] enjoyed its obscurity for four years. All its papers were unpaid contributions, and it was rather a work of friendship among the narrow circle of students than the organ of any party. Perhaps its writers were its chief readers: yet it contained some noble papers by Margaret Fuller, and some numbers had an instant exhausting sale, because of papers by Theodore Parker. * * *

These reformers were a new class. Instead of the fiery souls of the Puritans, bent on hanging the Quaker,[9] burning the witch and banishing the Romanist,[1] these were gentle souls, with peaceful and even with genial dispositions, casting sheep's-eyes even on Fourier and his houris.[2] It was a time when the air was full of reform. * * *

And truly I honor the generous ideas of the Socialists, the magnificence of their theories, and the enthusiasm with which they have been urged. They appeared the inspired men of their time. Mr. Owen[3] preached his doctrine of labor and reward, with the fidelity and devotion of a saint, to the slow ears of his generation. Fourier, almost as wonderful an example of the mathematical mind of France as La Place[4] or Napoleon, turned a truly vast arithmetic to the question of social misery, and has put men under the obligation which a generous mind always confers, of conceiving magnificent hopes and making great demands as the right of man. He took his measure of that which all should and might enjoy, from no soup-society or charity-concert, but from the refinements of palaces, the wealth of universities, and the triumphs of artists. He thought

7. Published quarterly from July 1840 to April 1844, *The Dial* was the organ of the New England Transcendentalist movement, publishing articles on literature, philosophy, and religion.
8. Emerson himself.
9. The Quakers, also known as the Society of Friends, originated in England under George Fox (1624–91) and began immigrating to America in the 1650s. Emphasizing a personal religion without formal ceremony, they were persecuted by the Puritans both because of their opposition to theocracy and because of the highly emotional characteristics of their religious experience.
1. A Roman Catholic. The Puritan hatred of hierarchical forms of church government and ceremonial vestments and rituals led to their attacks on Catholics in all of the English colonies except Maryland, Rhode Island, and Pennsylvania.
2. Dark-eyed virgins who lived with the blessed in the Muslim Paradise.
3. Robert Owen (1771–1858), known as "the father of English socialism," came to America in 1824 to test his theory that socialized agricultural communities of 1,200 persons were the ideal conditions for effecting economic, moral and educational reform. In 1826, he began such a community, New Harmony, in Indiana; but it lasted only two years.
4. Pierre Simon de La Place (1749–1827) was a French astronomer and mathematician.

nobly. A man is entitled to pure air, and to the air of good conversation in his bringing up, and not, as we or so many of us, to the
poor-smell and musty chambers, cats and fools. Fourier carried a
whole French Revolution in his head, and much more. Here was
arithmetic on a huge scale. His ciphering goes where ciphering
never went before, namely, into stars, atmospheres, and animals, and
men and women, and classes of every character. It was the most
entertaining of French romances, and could not but suggest vast
possibilities of reform to the coldest and least sanguine. * * *

Certainly we listened with great pleasure to such gay and magnificent pictures. The ability and earnestness of the advocate and his
friends, the comprehensiveness of their theory, its apparent directness of proceeding to the end they would secure, the indignation
they felt and uttered in the presence of so much social misery,
commanded our attention and respect. It contained so much truth,
and promised in the attempts that shall be made to realize it so
much valuable instruction, that we are engaged to observe every
step of its progress. Yet in spite of the assurances of its friends that
it was new and widely discriminated from all other plans for the
regeneration of society, we could not exempt it from the criticism
which we apply to so many projects for reform with which the brain
of the age teems. Our feeling was that Fourier had skipped no fact
but one, namely Life. He treats man as a plastic thing, something
that may be put up or down, ripened or retarded, moulded, polished, made into solid or fluid or gas, at the will of the leader; or
perhaps as a vegetable, from which, though now a poor crab, a very
good peach can by manure and exposure be in time produced,—but
skips the faculty of life, which spawns and scorns system and
system-makers; which eludes all conditions; which makes or sup-
plants a thousand phalanxes and New Harmonies with each pulsa-
tion. There is an order in which in a sound mind the faculties
always appear, and which, according to the strength of the individual, they seek to realize in the surrounding world. The value of
Fourier's system is that it is a statement of such an order externized,
or carried outward into its correspondence in facts. The mistake is
that this particular order and series is to be imposed, by force or
preaching and votes, on all men, and carried into rigid execution. * * *

Yet, in a day of small, sour and fierce schemes, one is admon-
ished and cheered by a project of such friendly aims and of such
bold and generous proportion; there is an intellectual courage and
strength in it which is superior and commanding; it certifies the
presence of so much truth in the theory, and in so far is destined to
be fact.

It argued singular courage, the adoption of Fourier's system, to even a limited extent, with his books lying before the world only defended by the thin veil of the French language. The Stoic said, Forbear, Fourier said, Indulge. * * * Fourier was very French indeed. He labored under a misapprehension of the nature of women. The Fourier marriage was a calculation how to secure the greatest amount of kissing that the infirmity of human constitution admitted. It was false and prurient, full of absurd French superstitions about women; ignorant how serious and how moral their nature always is; how chaste is their organization; how lawful a class.

It is the worst of community that it must inevitably transform into charlatans the leaders, by the endeavor continually to meet the expectation and admiration of this eager crowd of men and women seeking they know not what. Unless he have a Cossack[5] roughness of clearing himself of what belongs not, charlatan he must be.

It was easy to see what must be the fate of this fine system in any serious and comprehensive attempt to set it on foot in this country. As soon as our people got wind of the doctrine of Marriage held by this master,[6] it would fall at once into the hands of a lawless crew who would flock in troops to so fair a game, and, like the dreams of poetic people on the first outbreak of the old French Revolution, so theirs would disappear in a slime of mire and blood. * * *

Brook Farm

The West Roxbury association was formed in 1841, by a society of members, men and women, who bought a farm in West Roxbury, of about two hundred acres, and took possession of the place in April. * * *

It was a noble and generous movement in the projectors, to try an experiment of better living. They had the feeling that our ways of living were too conventional and expensive, not allowing each to do what he had a talent for, and not permitting men to combine cultivation of mind and heart with a reasonable amount of daily labor. At the same time, it was an attempt to lift others with themselves, and to share the advantages they should attain, with others now deprived of them.

There was no doubt great variety of character and purpose in the members of the community. It consisted in the main of young people,—few of middle age, and none old. Those who inspired and organized it were of course persons impatient of the routine, the uniformity, perhaps they would say the squalid contentment of society around them, which was so timid and skeptical of any

5. An adjective suggesting the qualities of the Cossacks, a people of the southern Soviet Union and adjacent parts of Asia who were noted as cavalrymen and ruth-less adventurers.

6. Fourier advocated the abolition of marriage but not of sexual relationships.

progress. One would say then that impulse was the rule in the society, without centripetal balance; perhaps it would not be severe to say, intellectual sans-culottism,[7] an impatience of the formal, routinary character of our educational, religious, social and economical life in Massachusetts. Yet there was immense hope in these young people. There was nobleness; there were self-sacrificing victims who compensated for the levity and rashness of their companions. The young people lived a great deal in a short time, and came forth some of them perhaps with shattered constitutions. And a few grave sanitary influences of character were happily there, which, I was assured, were always felt. * * *

The Founders of Brook Farm should have this praise, that they made what all people try to make, an agreeable place to live in. All comers, even the most fastidious, found it the pleasantest of residences. It is certain that freedom from household routine, variety of character and talent, variety of work, variety of means of thought and instruction, art, music, poetry, reading, masquerade, did not permit sluggishness or despondency; broke up routine. There is agreement in the testimony that it was, to most of the associates, education; to many, the most important period of their life, the birth of valued friendships, their first acquaintance with the riches of conversation, their training in behavior. * * *

It was a curious experience of the patrons and leaders of this noted community, in which the agreement with many parties was that they should give so many hours of instruction in mathematics, in music, in moral and intellectual philosophy, and so forth,—that in every instance the new comers showed themselves keenly alive to the advantages of the society, and were sure to avail themselves of every means of instruction; their knowledge was increased, their manners refined,—but they became in that proportion averse to labor, and were charged by the heads of the departments with a certain indolence and selfishness. * * *

Of course every visitor found that there was a comic side to this Paradise of shepherds and shepherdesses. There was a stove in every chamber, and every one might burn as much wood as he or she would saw. The ladies took cold on washing-day; so it was ordained that the gentlemen-shepherds should wring and hang out clothes; which they punctually did. And it would sometimes occur that when they danced in the evening, clothespins dropped plentifully from their pockets. The country members naturally were surprised to observe that one man ploughed all day and one looked out of the window all day, and perhaps drew his picture, and both received at night the same wages. * * *

7. Extreme radicalism.

In Brook Farm was this peculiarity, that there was no head. In every family is the father; in every factory, a foreman; in a shop, a master; in a boat, the skipper; but in this Farm, no authority; each was master or mistress of his or her actions; happy, hapless anarchists. They expressed, after much perilous experience, the conviction that plain dealing was the best defence of manners and moral between the sexes. People cannot live together in any but necessary ways. The only candidates who will present themselves will be those who have tried the experiment of independence and ambition, and have failed; and none others will barter for the most comfortable equality the chance of superiority. Then all communities have quarrelled. Few people can live together on their merits. There must be kindred, or mutual economy, or a common interest in their business, or other external tie.

The society at Brook Farm existed, I think, about six or seven years, and then broke up, the Farm was sold, and I believe all the partners came out with pecuniary loss. Some of them had spent on it the accumulations of years. I suppose they all, at the moment, regarded it as a failure. I do not think they can so regard it now, but probably as an important chapter in their experience which has been of lifelong value. What knowledge of themselves and of each other, what various practical wisdom, what personal power, what studies of character, what accumulated culture many of the members owed to it! What mutual measure they took of each other! It was a close union, like that in a ship's cabin, of clergymen, young collegians, merchants, mechanics, farmers' sons and daughters, with men and women of rare opportunities and delicate culture, yet assembled there by a sentiment which all shared, some of them hotly shared, of the honesty of a life of labor and of the beauty of a life of humanity. The yeoman saw refined manners in persons who were his friends; and the lady or the romantic scholar saw the continuous strength and faculty in people who would have disgusted them but that these powers were now spent in the direction of their own theory of life.

Criticism

Contemporary Reviews

From the *Christian Examiner* (September 1852)†

[A *Misleading* "*History*" *of Brook Farm*]

The preface to this captivating volume is by no means the least important part of it. And yet we would advise all readers who wish to peruse the work under an illusion which will add an intense interest to its pages, to postpone the preface till they have gone through the book. Certainly one has reason to believe that Mr. Hawthorne is presenting in these pages a story, which, however it may depend for its decorative and fanciful details upon his rich imagination, is essentially a delineation of life and character as presented at "Brook Farm." It is well known that he was a member of that community of amiable men and women, who undertook there to realize their ideas of a better system of social relations. He fixes there the scene of his story, with frequent reference to the localities around, keeping up a close connection with the neighboring city of Boston; and the volume owes very much of its lifelike fidelity of representation to the reader's supposition that the characters are as real as the theory and the institution in which they have their parts. Yet in the preface Mr. Hawthorne, with a charming frankness which neutralizes much of the charm of his story, repudiates altogether the matter-of-fact view so far as regards his associates at "Brook Farm," and pleads necessity as his reason for confounding fact and fiction.

We cannot but regard the license which Mr. Hawthorne allows himself in this respect as open to grave objection. Seeing that many readers obtain all their knowledge of historical facts from the incidental implications of history which are involved in a well-drawn romance, we maintain that a novelist has no right to tamper with actual verities. His obligation to adhere strictly to historic truth is all the more to be exacted whenever the character and good repute of any real pesron are involved. Now Mr. Hawthorne is a daring offender in this respect. It is the only drawback upon our high admiration of him. We trust he will take no offence at this our free expression of opinion, when, while offering to him a respectful and grateful homage for all the spiritual glow and all the human wisdom which we find on his pages, we venture to question his right to misrepresent the facts and characters of assured history. If he

† From an unsigned review in the *Christian Examiner*, 55 (September 1852), 292–94.

shaded and clouded his incidents somewhat more obscurely, if he removed them farther back or farther off from the region of our actual sight and knowledge, he would be safer in using the privileges of the romancer. But he gives us such distinct and sharp boundary lines, and deals so boldly with matters and persons, the truth of whose prose life repels the poetry of his fiction, that we are induced to confide in him as a chronicler, rather than to indulge him as a romancer. Thus in his "Scarlet Letter" he assures us in his preface that he has historical papers which authenticate the story that follows. That story involves the gross and slanderous imputation that the colleague pastor of the First Church in Boston, who preached the Election Sermon the year after the death of Governor Winthrop, was a mean and hypocritical adulterer, and went from the pulpit to the pillory to confess to that character in presence of those who had just been hanging reverently upon his lips. How would this outrageous fiction, which is utterly without foundation, deceive a reader who had no exact knowledge of our history! * * * In his "Blithedale Romance," Mr. Hawthorne ventures upon a similar freedom, though by no means so gross a one, in confounding fact and fiction. So vividly does he present to us the scheme at Brook Farm, to which some of our acquaintance were parties, so sharply and accurately does he portray some of the incidents of life there, that we are irresistibly impelled to fix the real names of men and women to the characters of his book.[1] We cannot help doing this. We pay a tribute to Mr. Hawthorne's power when we confess that we cannot believe that he is drawing upon his imagination. We ask, Whom does he mean to describe as Zenobia? Is it Mrs. ——, or Miss ——? Then, as we know that no one of the excellent women who formed the community at "Brook Farm" was driven to suicide by disappointed love, we find ourselves constructing the whole character from a combination of some half a dozen of the women whose talents or peculiarities have made them prominent in this neighborhood. We can gather up in this way all the elements of his Zenobia, except the comparatively unimportant one of queenly beauty which he ascribes to her. We leave to the help-meet of the author to settle with him the issue that may arise from his description of himself as a bachelor.

* * *

1. Maurice A. Crane's unpublished dissertation, "A Textual and Critical Edition of Hawthorne's *Blithedale Romance*" (University of Illinois, 1953) lists numerous such examples, pp. lxxvi–lxxvii: for Zenobia, Margaret Fuller, Caroline Sturgis, Mrs. George Ripley, Mrs. Almira Barlow, and Fanny Kemble; for Hollingsworth, Bronson Alcott, Albert Brisbane, Orestes Brownson, Elihu Burritt, William Henry Channing, Charles A. Dana, Ralph Waldo Emerson, Horace Mann, Theodore Parker, and William Pike.

From the *Westminster Review* (October 1852)†

[*Imagination as Truer Than History*]

* * *

We are cautioned, in the preface, against the notion (otherwise very liable to be entertained) that this is a history of Brook Farm under a fictitious disguise. * * * Imaginary as the characters are, however, the supposition that Zenobia is an apograph[1] of Margaret Fuller, may not be so far wrong. That extraordinary woman could not have been absent from the mind of the novelist—nay, must have inspired his pencil, whilst sketching "the high-spirited woman bruising herself against the narrow limitations of her sex." And, in so far as it is the embodiment of this sentiment or relation, we may have in the career of Zenobia (not in its details, but in its essential features), a missing chapter in Margaret Fuller's life—unwritten hitherto, because never sufficiently palpable to come under the cognizance of the biographer, and only capable of being unveiled by the novelist, whose function it is to discern the intents of the heart, and to describe things that are not as though they were. We may, at least, venture to say that the study of Zenobia will form an excellent introduction to the study of her supposed prototype. There are problems both in biography and in history which imagination only can solve; and in this respect, "Blithedale," as a whole, may tell a truer tale with its fictions than Brook Farm with its facts. Hence it is that our author, while expressing an earnest wish that the world may have the benefit of the latter, felt that it belonged to him to furnish it with the former. * * *

From *Brownson's Quarterly Review* (October 1852)†

[*The Spirit, Not the Actuality, of Brook Farm*]

* * *

The Blithedale Romance we have read with a good deal of interest, for much in it is connected with some of our personal friends.

† From an unsigned essay, "Contemporary Literature of America," *Westminster Review*, 58 (October 1852), 592–98. The essay has been attributed to George Eliot by James D. Rust, "George Eliot on *The Blithedale Romance*," *Boston Public Library Quarterly*, 7 (1955), 207–15.
1. A copy.
† From an unsigned review in *Brownson's Quarterly Review*, n.s., 6 (October 1852), 561–64. The author, Orestes Brownson, was an important force in the inception of Brook Farm (1841) because of his influence on George Ripley, the founder. Although he sent his son to Brook Farm School, made frequent visits, and admired some of the participants, by 1843 he had come to consider such communities as "humbug."

* * * Mr. Hawthorne was for a brief period one of the communitarians, attracted more, we apprehend, by the romance of the thing, than by any real belief in the principles of the establishment, or deep sympathy with its objects.[1] Under the name of Miles Coverdale he sketches in this little volume his experiences during his brief residence at Brook Farm as one of the regenerators of society, mingled with various romantic instances which did, and many more which did not happen, but which might have happened. He has treated the institution and the characters of his associates with great delicacy and tenderness. He enjoys a quiet laugh and indulges in a little gentle satire, now and then, and upon the whole makes the experiment appear, as it in reality was, a folly born of honest intentions and fervent zeal in behalf of society. But he brings none of the real actors in the comedy, or farce, or tragedy, whichever it may have been, upon the stage. We can recognize in the personages of his Romance individual traits of several real characters who were there, but no one has his or her whole counterpart in one who was actually a member of the community. There was no actual Zenobia, Hollingsworth, or Priscilla there, and no such catastrophe as described ever occurred there; yet none of these characters are purely imaginary. Hollingsworth, in relation to his one fixed purpose, had his counterpart there, and the author has given us in Miles Coverdale much that we dare affirm to have been true of himself. Still, there has been no encroachment on the sanctity of private character, and pain has been given, we presume, to no private feeling. The reader may collect from the Romance the general tone, sentiment, hopes, fears, and character of the establishment, but very little of the actual persons engaged in it, or of the actual goings-on at Brook Farm.

* * *

1. Hawthorne's love letters to Sophia Peabody indicate that he was concerned primarily with finding a practical basis for his marriage; however, the excitement about Brook Farm which enveloped Elizabeth Peabody's book shop in Boston and all of the young, reform-minded intellectuals who frequented it undoubtedly affected both her sister Sophia and Hawthorne. Elizabeth Peabody's "Plan of the West Roxbury Community," published in *The Dial*, II (January, 1842), pp. 361–72, is one of the most enthusiastic tributes to this communal attempt "to live a religious and moral life."

From the *Athenaeum* (July 1852) †

[An *Eminently American Book*]

* * *

This "Blithedale Romance" is eminently an American book;—not, however, a book showing the America of *Sam Slick* and *Leather-Stocking*,[1]—the home of the money-making droll rich in mother-wit, or of the dweller in the wilderness rich in mother-poetry.—Mr. Hawthorne's America is a vast new country, the inhabitants of which have neither materially nor intellectually as yet found their boundaries,—a land heaving with restless impatience, on the part of some among its best spirits, to exemplify new ideas in new forms of civilized life. But Mr. Hawthorne knows that in America, as well as in worlds worn more threadbare, poets, philosophers and philanthropists however vehemently seized on by such fever of vain-longing, are forced to break themselves against the barriers of Mortality and Time—to allow for inevitable exceptions—to abide unforeseen checks,—in short, to re-commence their dream and their work with each fresh generation, in a manner tantalizing to enthusiasts who would grasp perfection for themselves and mankind, and that instantaneously.—The author's sermon is none the less a sermon because he did not mean it as such.[2] He must be fully believed when he tells us that, while placing the scene of his third tale in a Socialist community he had no intention of pronouncing upon Socialism, either in principle or in practice. Mr. Hawthorne's preface assures us that he conjured up his version of Brook Farm, Roxbury, merely as a befitting scene for the action of certain beings of his mind, without thought of lesson or decision on a question so grave and complex. This, however, makes him all the more valuable as a witness. The thoughtful reader will hardly fail to draw some morals for himself from a tale which, though made up of exceptional personages, is yet true to human characteristics and

† From an unsigned review in the London *Athenaeum* (July 10, 1852), 741–43. The author is Henry F. Chorley, Hawthorne's greatest admirer among the English reviewers.
1. Sam Slick is the main character in a series of books by the Canadian humorist Thomas Chandler Haliburton (1796–1865); Leather-Stocking is one of the nicknames of Natty Bumppo, the central figure in James Fenimore Cooper's five-novel saga of the early American frontier (1823–41).
2. The *Westminster Review* (October 1852), however, accused Hawthorne of being "sadly deficient in moral depth and earnestness. * * * So many morals—one a-piece for Coverdale and Hollingsworth, and two and a-half for Zenobia—are symptomatic of weak moral power, arising from feebleness of moral purpose."

human feelings, and pregnant with universal emotion as well as with deep special meaning.

* * *

From the *Westminster Review* (October 1852)†

[*Socialism as Mere Scaffolding*]

* * * Everybody will naturally regard this story, whether fact or fiction, as a socialistic drama, and will expect its chief interest as such to be of a moral kind. "Blithedale," whatever may be its relation to Brook Farm, is itself a socialistic settlement, with its corresponding phases of life, and therefore involves points both of moral and material interest, the practical operation of which should have been exhibited so as to bring out the good and evil of the system. But this task Hawthorne declines, and does not "put forward the slightest pretensions to illustrate a theory, or elicit a conclusion favourable or otherwise to Socialism." He confines himself to the delineation of its picturesque phases, as a "thing of beauty," and either has no particular convictions respecting its deeper relations, or hesitates to express them. It was not necessary for him to pass judgment upon the theories of Fourier or Robert Owen.[1] He had nothing to do with it as a theory; but as a phase of life it demanded appropriate colouring. Would he paint an ideal slave-plantation merely for the beauty of the thing, without pretending to "elicit a conclusion favourable or otherwise" to slavery? Could he forget the moral relations of this system, or drop them out of his picture, "merely to establish a theatre a little removed from the highway of ordinary travel, where the creatures of his brain may play their phantasmagorical antics without exposing them to too close a comparison with the actual events of real life?" In respect of involving moral relations, the two cases are analogous, and the one may be rendered morally colourless with no more propriety than the other. "Blithedale," then, as a socialistic community, is merely used here as a scaffolding—a very huge one—in the construction of an edifice considerably smaller than itself! And then, the artist leaves the scaffolding standing! Socialism, in this romance, is prominent enough to fill the book, but it has so little business in it, that it does not even grow into an organic part of the story, and contributes nothing whatever toward the final catastrophe. It is a theatre—and, as such, it should have a neutral tint; but it should also be made of neutral stuff; and its erection, moreover, should not be contem-

† From an unsigned essay, "Contemporary Literature of America," *Westminster Review*, 58 (October 1852), 592–98.
1. Charles Fourier (1772–1837), French socialist author and social reformer. See note 9, p. 49. Robert Owen (1771–1858), originator of English socialism. See note 3, p. 261.

poraneous with the performance of the play. But the incongruity becomes more apparent when we consider the kind of play acted in it. Take the moral of Zenobia's history, and you will find that Socialism is apparently made responsible for consequences which it utterly condemned, and tried, at least, to remedy. We say, apparently, for it is really not made responsible for anything, good, bad, or indifferent. It forms a circumference of circumstances, which neither mould the characters, nor influence the destinies, of the individuals so equivocally situated,—forms, in short, not an essential part of the picture, but an enormous fancy border, not very suitable for the purpose for which it was designed. Zenobia's life would have been exhibited with more propriety, and its moral brought home with more effect, in the "theatre" of the world, out of which it really grew, and of which it would have formed a vital and harmonious part. Zenobia and Socialism should have been acted in the ready-made theatre of ordinary humanity, to see how it would fare with them there. Having occupied the ground, Hawthorne owed it to truth, and to a fit opportunity, so to dramatize his experience and observation of Communistic life, as to make them of practical value for the world at large.

From the *Spectator* (July 1852)†

[*The Dangers of Social Innovation*]

* * *

The framework of *The Blithedale Romance* is founded on a Communist attempt of some enthusiasts at Blithedale farm, rather after the fashion of Godwin[1] and other admirers of the principles of the first French Revolution than after modern Socialist schemes. At the head of this party, though hardly belonging to it, is Hollingsworth, a quondam blacksmith, of great heart and natural powers, whose whole soul is embarked in a project for reforming criminals. A woman called Zenobia, of full rich beauty, independent spirit, and high intellectual power, is also a principal; and represents the advocate of the "rights of women," chafing at the control which convention and the real or assumed superiority of man enforce upon the sex. There is also another conspicuous female, Priscilla, who exhibits the clinging, devoted, feminine character, seeing nothing but the person she loves. The real story turns upon the passion of Zenobia for Hollingsworth, his preference for Priscilla, and the suicide of the proud, passionate, ill-regulated, queenly Zenobia. * * *

† From an unsigned review in the *Spectator*, 25 (July 3, 1852), 637–38.
1. William Godwin (1756–1836), English radical writer, believed that proper education would make reason rather than law the mainstay of society, thus eliminating the need for any form of government.

One lesson impressed by the book is the danger of a woman, no matter what her gifts, deviating ever so little from the received usages of society;[2] though this lesson is by no means new, and it had been done as conclusively already. Another, a newer and a more important moral, is the danger of earnest philanthropy swallowing up every other feeling, till your genuine philanthropist becomes as hard, as selfish, and as indifferent to the individual results of his conduct, if it forward his end, as the most adamantine conqueror or statesman. This feeling, the more extreme and engrossing in proportion to the comprehension of the philanthropist's nature and consciousness, without any sort of regard to the feasibility or importance of its project, is not perhaps so much illustrated by the catastrophe as noted by passing occurrences. It is a moral, however, that cannot be too strongly impressed; for it actuates classes as well as individuals, and with a less sense of responsibility. * * *

Mr. Hawthorne is not a disciple of that school of human perfectibility which has given rise to plans of pantisocracy and similar Arcadias.

From the *North British Review* (November 1853)†

[A *Satire on Social Reformation*]

* * *

Mr. Hawthorne's *chef-d'œuvre*[1] is, however, his last work, "The Blithedale Romance." In this tale, the writer, with an irony of withering calmness, exposes the vanity and selfishness which underlie the seemingly worthy and benevolent purposes of the various *dramatis personæ*, who engage themselves in one of the many schemes of politico-moral reformation which moderns have invented as substitutes for the reformation of themselves.[2] * * * Miles Coverdale, who tells the story, is a poetaster, *à la* Goethe,[3] who prides himself on his perceptive powers, and thinks that he is doing his work in overlooking the active world, and, as the gust inspires him, setting what he sees to second-rate verse. He engages with the rest in a Socialist scheme, not because he has faith in it, or in anything else, but because he is sick of his old mode of doing nothing, and yearns for a new one.

---

2. The *Southern Quarterly Review* (October 1852) suggested that Hawthorne, instead of having Zenobia commit suicide, "should have converted her, by marriage —the best remedy for such a case—from the errors of her ways, and left her, a mother, with good prospects of numerous progeny."

† From an unsigned essay, "American Novels," *North British Review*, 20 (November 1853), 57–64.

1. Masterpiece.

2. The *North American Review* (January 1853), p. 237, put it more harshly: "They are all abnormal; and where else should we be so likely to find an assemblage of abnormals as under the auspices of Socialistic reform?"

3. In Johann Wolfgang von Goethe's *Faust*, the Poet in the "Prelude on the Stage" stuffily rejects the gusto of everyday experience, believing that only in "some peaceful heavenly nook" can real poetry be written.

Zenobia is the pseudonym of a lady who is a sort of Yankee George Sand.[4] It is clear that her "antecedents" have been question-able. She has been no stranger, from her girlhood upwards, to what the French call Love, and we are permitted to infer that she takes part in the scheme with the presentiment that something may turn up in the way of a good novelesque amour, and she is not altogether mistaken. This character, like all the rest, is powerfully given, and in the true way; that is, by glimpses, as we see characters in nature, and not by the way of elaborate portraiture. * * *

Silas Foster, who evidently has no care for or real apprehension of what the Communist scheme means, and takes part in it only because he finds his vocation wherever there are pigs to keep and cows to drive, is the one point of reality in all the phantasmagoria of conceit, and its concomitant passions and imbecilities. * * *

It is in the exquisite perception of moral and social phenomena * * * that Mr. Hawthorne excels every other modern writer we are acquainted with. We have seen the remorseless anatomy with which the subtle hypocricies of the Rev. Mr. Dimmesdale[5] were exposed to laughter and pity. False societies impose upon our author no more than false persons; witness the last paragraph of the foregoing extract, and the following passage, in which the vanity and selfish-ness which form the basis of at least ninety-nine hundredths of our modern schemes of social reformation stand skinned alive. * * *

From *Graham's Magazine* (September 1852)†

[*The Narrator as Interpreter*]

* * *

The scene of the story is laid in Blithedale, an imaginary com-munity on the model of the celebrated Brook Farm, of Roxbury, of which Hawthorne himself was a member. The practical difficulties in the way of combining intellectual and manual labor on socialist principles constitute the humor of the book; but the interest centres in three characters, Hollingsworth, Zenobia, and Priscilla. These are represented as they appear through the medium of an imagined mind, that of Miles Coverdale, the narrator of the story, a person indolent of will, but of an apprehensive, penetrating, and inquisitive intellect. This discerner of spirits only tells us his own discoveries;

4. Pseudonym of Aurore Dupin (1804–76), French novelist whose name in the mid-nineteenth cenutry became synony-mous with the liberated woman, especially in matters of sex.
5. The adulterous minister in Hawthorne's *The Scarlet Letter* (1850).
† From an unsigned review in *Graham's Magazine*, 41 (September 1852), 333–34.

The author, Edwin Percy Whipple, was a critic Hawthorne very much admired. Hawthorne sent Whipple the manuscript of *Blithedale* for his judgment before sending it to the publisher; Whipple's re-actions may have influenced the choice of title as well as several changes in the text.

and there is a wonderful originality and power displayed in thus representing the characters. What is lost by this mode, on definite views, is more than made up in the stimulus given both to our acuteness and curiosity, and its manifold suggestiveness. We are joint watchers with Miles himself, and sometimes find ourselves disagreeing with him in his interpretation of an act or expression of the persons he is observing. The events are purely mental, the changes and crises of moods of mind. Three persons of essentially different characters and purposes, are placed together; the law of spiritual influence, the magnetism of soul on soul begins to operate; and the processes of thought and emotion are then presented in perfect logical order to their inevitable catastrophe. These characters are Hollingsworth, a reformer, whose whole nature becomes ruthless under the dominion of one absorbing idea—Zenobia, a beautiful, imperious, impassioned, self-willed woman, superbly endowed in person and intellect, but with something provokingly equivocal in her character—and Priscilla, an embodiment of feminine affection in its simplest type. Westervelt, an elegant piece of earthliness, "not so much born as damned into the world," plays a Mephistophelian[1] part in this mental drama; and is so skilfully represented that the reader joins at the end, with the author, in praying that Heaven may annihilate him.

* * *

[Organic Unity]
* * *

"The Blithedale Romance," * * * seems to us the most perfect in execution of any of Hawthorne's works, and as a work of art, hardly equalled by anything else which the country has produced. It is a real organism of the mind, with the strict unity of one of Nature's own creations. It seems to have grown up in the author's nature, as a tree or plant grows from the earth, in obedience to the law of its germ. This unity cannot be made clear by analysis; it is felt in the oneness of impression it makes on the reader's imagination. The author's hold on the central principle is never relaxed; it never slips from his grasp; and yet every thing is developed with a victorious ease which adds a new charm to the interest of the materials. The romance, also, has more thought in it than either of its predecessors; it is literally crammed with the results of most delicate and searching observation of life, manners and character, and of the most piercing imaginative analysis of motives and tendencies; yet nothing seems labored, but the profoundest reflections glide unobtrusively into the free flow of the narration and descrip-

1. Characteristic of the devil in the Faust legend to whom Faust sold his soul.

tion, equally valuable from their felicitous relation to the events and
persons of the story, and for their detached depth and power. The
work is not without a certain morbid tint in the general coloring of
the mood whence it proceeds; but this peculiarity is fainter than is
usual with Hawthorne.

* * *

From the *Atlantic Monthly* (May 1860)†

[*Imaginative Wholeness*]
* * *

"The Blithedale Romance" * * * illustrates the operation, indicates the quality, and expresses the power, of the author's genius.
His great books appear not so much created by him as through him.
They have the character of revelations,—he, the instrument, being
often troubled with the burden they impose on his mind. His profoundest glances into individual souls are like the marvels of clair-
voyance. It would seem, that, in the production of such a work as
"The Blithedale Romance," his mind had hit accidentally, as it
were, on an idea or fact mysteriously related to some morbid sentiment in the inmost core of his nature, and connecting itself with
numerous scattered observations of human life, lying unrelated in
his imagination. In a sort of meditative dream, his intellect drifts in
the direction to which the subject points, broods patiently over it,
looks at it, looks into it, and at last looks through it to the law by
which it is governed. Gradually, individual beings, definite in spiritual quality, but shadowy in substantial form, group themselves
around this central conception, and by degrees assume an outward
body and expression corresponding to their internal nature. On the
depth and intensity of the mental mood, the force of the fascination
it exerts over him, and the length of time it holds him captive,
depend the solidity and substance of the individual characterizations. In this way Miles Coverdale, Hollingsworth, Westervelt,
Zenobia, and Priscilla become real persons to the mind which has
called them into being. He knows every secret and watches every
motion of their souls, yet is, in a measure, independent of them, and
pretends to no authority by which he can alter the destiny which
consigns them to misery or happiness. They drift to their doom by
the same law by which they drifted across the path of his vision.
Individually, he abhors Hollingsworth, and would like to annihilate
Westervelt, yet he allows the superb Zenobia to be their victim; and
if his readers object that the effect of the whole representation is

† From an unsigned essay, "Nathaniel   1860), 614–22. The author was Edwin
Hawthorne," *Atlantic Monthly*, 5 (May   Percy Whipple.

painful, he would doubtless agree with them, but profess his incapacity honestly to alter a sentence. He professes to tell the story as it was revealed to him; and the license in which a romancer might indulge is denied to a biographer of spirits. Show him a fallacy in his logic of passion and character, point out a false or defective step in his analysis, and he will gladly alter the whole to your satisfaction; but four human souls, such as he has described, being given, their mutual attractions and repulsions will end, he feels assured, in just such a catastrophe as he has stated.

* * *

From the *New Monthly Magazine* (June 1853)†

[*Effective Artistry*]
* * *

"The Blithedale Romance" we esteem, in *spite* of its coming last, the highest and best of Mr. Hawthorne's works. The tale is narrated with more ingenuity and ease; the characters are at least equal to their predecessors, and the style is at once richer and more robust— more mellowed, and yet more pointed and distinct. A true artist has planned and has filled up the plot, ordering each conjunction of incidents, and interweaving the cross-threads of design and destiny with masterly tact; skilled in the by-play of suggestion, hint, and pregnant passing intimation—in the harmonious development of once scattered and seemingly unrelated forces. His humor is fresher in quality, and his tragic power is exercised with almost oppressive effect—at times making the boldest, oldest romance-reader

> Hold his breath
> For a while;

at others, making all *but* him lose the dimmed line in blinding tears. There are scenes that rivet themselves on the memory—such as Coverdale's interview with Westervelt in the woodland solitude, followed by his observation of another rencontre from his leafy hermitage in the vine-entangled pine-tree; and the dramatic recital of Zenobia's Legend; and the rendezvous at Eliot's Pulpit; and above all, the dreadful errand by midnight in quest of the Dead—intensified in its grim horror by the contrasted temperaments of the three searchers, especially Silas Foster's rude matter-of-fact hardness, probing with coarse unconscious finger the wounds of a proud and sensitive soul. There are touches of exquisite pathos in the evolution of the tale of sorrow, mingled with shrewd "interludes" of irony and humor which only deepen the distress. * * *

† From an unsigned essay, "American Authorship," *New Monthly Magazine*, 98 (June 1853), 202–12.

From the *Westminster Review* (October 1852)†

[*Analytical Characterization and Structural Disunity*]

* * * Hawthorne's *forte* is the analysis of character, and not the dramatic arrangement of events. "To live in other lives, and to endeavour—by generous sympathies, by delicate intuitions, by taking note of things too slight for record, and by bringing his spirit into manifold acquaintance with the companions whom God assigned him—to learn the secret which was hidden even from themselves,"—this, which is the estimate formed of Miles Coverdale, has its original in the author himself. The adoption of the autobiographical form (now so common in fictions) is, perhaps, the most suitable for the exercise of such peculiar powers. Not more than six or seven characters are introduced, and only four of them are prominent figures. They have, therefore, ample room for displaying their individuality, and establishing each an independent interest in the reader's regards. But this is not without disadvantages, which become more apparent towards the close. The analysis of the characters is so minute, that they are too thoroughly individualized for dramatic co-operation, or for that graduated subordination to each other which tends to give a harmonious swell to the narrative, unity to the plot, and concentrated force to the issue. They are simply contemporaries, obliged, somehow, to be on familiar terms with each other, and, even when coming into the closest relationship, seeming rather driven thereto by destiny, than drawn by sympathy. It is well that the *dramatis personæ* are so few. They are a manageable number, and are always upon the stage; but had there been more of them, they would only have presented themselves there in turns, which, with Hawthorne's slow movement, would have been fatal to their united action and combined effect. Even with a consecutive narrative, and a concentration of interest, the current flows with an eddying motion, which tends to keep them apart, unless, as happens once or twice, it dash over a precipice, and then it both makes up for lost time, and brings matters to a point rather abruptly. But the main tendency is toward isolation—for the ruling faculty is analytic. It is ever hunting out the anomalous; it discovers more points of repulsion than of attraction; and the creatures of its fancy are all morbid beings—all "wandering stars," plunging, orbitless, into the abyss of despair—confluent but not commingling streams, winding along to the ocean of disaster and death; for all have a

† From an unsigned essay, "Contemporary Literature of America," *Westminster Review*, 58 (October 1852), 592–98.

wretched end—Zenobia and Priscilla, Hollingsworth and Coverdale
—the whole go to wreck.

* * *

From the *American Whig Review* (November 1852)†

[A Morbid and Suspicious Nature]

* * *

When an author sits down to make a book, he should not alone
consult the inclinations of his own genius regarding its purpose or
its construction. If he should happen to be imbued with strange,
saturnine doctrines, or be haunted by a morbid suspicion of human
nature, in God's name let him not write one word.[1] Better that all
the beautiful, wild thoughts with which his brain is teeming should
moulder for ever in neglect and darkness, than that one soul was
overshadowed by stern, uncongenial dogmas, which should have
died with their Puritan fathers. It is not alone necessary to produce
a work of art. The soul of beauty is Truth, and Truth is ever
progressive. The true artist therefore endeavors to make the world
better. He does not look behind him, and dig out of the graves of
past centuries skeletons to serve as models for his pictures; but
looks onward for more perfect shapes, and though sometimes
obliged to design from the defective forms around him, he infuses,
as it were, some of the divine spirit of the future into them, and lo!
we love them with all their faults. But Mr. Hawthorne discards all
idea of successful human progress. All his characters seem so
weighed down with their own evilness of nature, that they can
scarcely keep their balance, much less take their places in the universal march. * * * It is a pity that Mr. Hawthorne should not have
been originally imbued with more universal tenderness. It is a pity
that he displays nature to us so shrouded and secluded, and that he
should be afflicted with such a melancholy craving for human curi-
osities. His men are either vicious, crazed, or misanthropical, and
his women are either unwomanly, unearthly, or unhappy. His books
have no sunny side to them. They are unripe to the very core. * * *

A thought crosses us, whether Mr. Hawthorne would paint a
wedding as well as a death; whether he could conjure as distinctly

† From an unsigned review in the *American Whig Review*, 16 (November 1852),
417–24.
1. William B. Pike, on the contrary, in a
letter to Hawthorne (July 18, 1852),
praises Hawthorne's ability to penetrate
the morbid and inexplicable in human nature: "In this book, as in 'The Scarlet
Letter,' you probe deeply,—you go down
among the moody silences of the heart, and those depths whence come motives that give complexion to actions, and
make in men what are called states of
mind; being conditions of mind which
cannot be removed either by our own reasoning or by the reasonings of others"
(Julian Hawthorne, *Hawthorne and His
Wife*, I [Boston: James R. Osgood, 1884],
p. 444).

before our vision the bridal flowers, as he has done the black, damp weeds that waved around the grave of Zenobia. We fear not. His genius has a church-yard beauty about it, and revels amid graves, and executions, and all the sad leavings of mortality.

From the *American Whig Review* (November 1852)†

[*Excessive Imperfection in Characters*]

* * *

Let us review his characters, and see if we can find anything genial among them. Hollingsworth in importance comes first. A rude fragment of a great man. Unyielding as granite in any matters on which he has decided, yet possessing a latent tenderness of nature that, if he had been the creature of other hands than Mr. Hawthorne's, would have been his redemption. But our author is deeply read in human imperfection, and lets no opportunity slip of thrusting it before his readers. * * *

Readers will perchance say that Mr. Hawthorne has a right to deal with his characters according to his pleasure, and that we are not authorized to quarrel with the length of their noses, or the angularities of their natures. No doubt. But, on the other hand, Mr. Hawthorne has no right to blacken and defame humanity, by animating his shadowy people with worse passions and more imperfect souls than we meet with in the world.

Miles Coverdale, the narrator of the tale, is to us a most repulsive being. A poet, but yet no poetry in his deeds. A sneering, suspicious, inquisitive, and disappointed man, who rejects Hollingsworth's advances because he fears that a connection between them may lead to some ulterior peril; who allows Zenobia to dominate over his nature, because she launches at him a few wild words, and who forsakes the rough, healthy life of Blithedale, because he pines for Turkey carpets and a sea-coal fire. Such is the man upon whose dictum Mr. Hawthorne would endeavor covertly to show the futility of the enterprise in whose favor he was once enlisted. * * *

The Zenobia of our author does not command our interest. Her character, though poetically colored, is not sufficiently powerful for a woman that has so far outstridden the even pace of society. She has a certain amount of courage and passion, but no philosophy. Her impulses start off in the wrong direction, nor does she seem to possess the earnestness necessary to induce a woman to defy public opinion. She is a mere fierce, wild wind, blowing hither and thither, with no fixity of purpose, and making us shrink closer every moment from the contact.[1]

In truth, with the exception of Priscilla, who is faint and shadowy, the dramatis personæ at Blithedale are not to our taste. There is a bad purpose in every one of them—a purpose, too, which is neither finally redeemed nor condemned.

* * *

From *Blackwood's Magazine* (May 1855)†

[*Unnatural Characters*]

* * *

In the *Blythedale* [sic] *Romance* we have still less of natural character, and more of a diseased and morbid conventional life. American patriots ought to have no quarrel with our saucy tourists and wandering notabilities, in comparison with the due and just quarrel they have with writers of their own. What extraordinary specimens of womankind are Zenobia and Priscilla, the heroines of this tale! What a meddling, curious, impertinent rogue, a psychological Paul Pry,[1] is Miles Coverdale, the teller of the story! How thoroughly worn out and *blasé* must that young world be, which gets up excitements in its languid life, only by means of veiled ladies, mysterious clairvoyants, rapping spirits, or, in a milder fashion, by sherry-cobbler and something cocktails for the men, and lectures on the rights of women for the ladies. We enter this strange existence with a sort of wondering inquiry whether any *events* ever take place there, or if, instead, there is nothing to be done but for everybody to observe everybody else, and for all society to act on the universal impulse of getting up a tragedy somewhere, for the pleasure of looking at it; or if that may not be, of setting up supernatural intercourse one way or another, and warming up with occult and forbidden influences the cold and waveless tide of life. We do not believe in Zenobia drowning herself. It is a piece of sham entirely, and never impresses us with the slightest idea of reality. Nor are we moved with any single emotion throughout the entire course of the tale. There is nothing touching in the mystery of old Moodie; nothing attractive in the pale clairvoyant Priscilla—the victim, as we are led to suppose, of Mesmerism and its handsome diabolical professor. We are equally indifferent to the imperious and

---

1. George S. Hillard, in a letter to Hawthorne (July 27, 1852), took another view: "Zenobia is a splendid creature, and I wish there were more such rich and ripe women about" (Julian Hawthorne, *Hawthorne and His Wife*, I [Boston:

James R. Osgood, 1884], p. 448).
† From an unsigned essay, "Modern Novelists—Great and Small," *Blackwood's Magazine*, 77 (May 1855), 562–66.
1. An inquisitive, meddlesome fellow, from John Poole's farce, *Paul Pry* (1825).

splendid Zenobia, and to the weak sketchy outline of Hollingsworth, whose "stern" features are washed in with the faintest water-colours, and who does not seem capable of anything but of making these two women fall in love with him. The sole thing that looks true, and seems to have blood in its veins, is Silas Foster, the farmer and manager of practical matters for the Utopian community, which proposes to reform the world by making ploughmen of themselves. Could they have done it honestly, we cannot fancy any better plan for the visionary inhabitants of the farm and the romance of Blythedale. Honest work might do a great deal for these languid philosophers; and Mr Hawthorne himself, we should suppose, could scarcely be in great condition for dissecting his neighbours and their "inner nature" after a day's ploughing or reaping; but mystery, Mesmerism, love, and jealousy, are too many for the placid angel of agriculture, and young America by no means makes a success in its experiment, either by reforming others or itself.

After all, we are not ethereal people. We are neither fairies nor angels. Even to make our conversation—and, still more, to make our life—we want more than thoughts and fancies—we want *things.* You may sneer at the commonplace necessity, yet it *is* one; and it is precisely your Zenobias and Hollingsworths, your middle-aged people, who have broken loose from family and kindred, and have no *events* in their life, who do all the mischief, and make all the sentimentalisms and false philosophies in the world. * * *

Mr Hawthorne, we are afraid, is one of those writers who aim at an intellectual audience, and address themselves mainly to such. We are greatly of opinion that this is a mistake and a delusion, and that nothing good comes of it. The novelist's true audience is the common people—the people of ordinary comprehension and everyday sympathies, whatever their rank may be.

* * *

From the *New Monthly Magazine* (June 1853)†

[*Vivid and Accurate Characters*]

* * *

Upon the bearing of the romance on Socialism we need not descant, the author explicitly disclaiming all intent of pronouncing *pro* or *con* on the theories in question. As to the characters, too, he as explicitly repudiates the idea, which in the teeth of such disclaimer, and of internal evidence also, has been attributed to him, of portraying in the Blithedale actors the actual companions of his

† From an unsigned essay, "American Authorship," *New Monthly Magazine*, 98   (June 1853), 202–12.

Brook Farm career—or other American celebrities (as though Margaret Fuller were Zenobia, because both living on "Rights of Woman" excitement, and both dying by drowning!) The characters are few; but each forms a study. The gorgeous Zenobia—from out whose imposing nature was felt to breathe an influence "such as we might suppose to come from Eve, when she was just made, and her Creator brought her to Adam, saying 'Behold! here is a woman!' " —not an influence merely fraught with especial gentleness, grace, modesty, and shyness, but a "certain warm and rich characteristic, which seems, for the most part, to have been refined away out of the feminine system." Hollingsworth—by nature deeply and warmly benevolent, but restricting his benevolence exclusively to one channel, and having nothing to spare for other great manifestations of love to man, nor scarcely for the nutriment of individual attachments, unless they minister in some way to the terrible egotism which he mistakes for an angel of God:—with something of the woman moulded into his great stalwart frame, and a spirit of prayer abiding and working in his heart;—but himself grown to be the bond-slave of his philanthropic theory, which has become to him in effect a cold spectral monster of his own conjuring; persuading himself that the importance of his public ends renders it allowable to throw aside his private conscience; embodying himself in a project, which the disenchanted Zenobia reprobates with hissing defiance as "self, self, self!" Priscilla, again: a weakly bud that blossoms into health and hope under the fostering clime of Blithedale, where she seems a butterfly at play in a flickering bit of sunshine, and mistaking it for a broad and eternal summer—though her gayety reveals at times how delicate an instrument she is, and what fragile harp-strings are her nerves—a being of slender and shadowy grace, whose mysterious qualities make her seem diaphanous with spiritual light. Silas Foster, too: "lank, stalwart, uncouth, and grisly-bearded;" the prose element, and very dense prose, too, in the poetry of the Communists; with his palm of sole-leather and his joints of rusty iron, and his brain (as Zenobia pronounces it) of Savoy cabbage. And old Moodie, or Fauntleroy —that finished picture of a skulking outcast—shy and serpentine— with a queer appearance of hiding himself behind the patch on his left eye—a deplorable gray shadow—mysterious, but not mad; his mind only needing to be screwed up, like an instrument long out of tune, the strings of which have ceased to vibrate smartly and sharply—"a subdued, undemonstrative old man, who would doubtless drink a glass of liquor, now and then, and probably more than was good for him; not, however, with a purpose of undue exhilaration, but in the hope of bringing his spirits up to the ordinary level of the world's cheerfulness." Miles Coverdale himself is no lay figure in the group of actors. His character is replete with interest, whether as a partial presentment of the author's own person, or as a type of no uncommon individuality in this age of "yeast." We have in him a strange but most true "coincidence" of warm feeling and freezing reflection, of the kind deep heart and the vexed and vacillating brain, of a natural tendency to faith and a constitutional taint of scepticism, of the sensuous, indolent epicurean and the habitual cynic, of the idealist—all hope, and the realist—all disappointment. It is this fusion of opposite, not contradictory qualities, which gives so much piquancy and flavor to Coverdale's character, and his author's writings in general.

* * *

Modern Essays in Criticism

IRVING HOWE

Hawthorne: Pastoral and Politics†

No portrait of Hawthorne, wrote Henry James, "is at all exact which fails to insist upon the constant struggle which must have gone on between his shyness and his desire to know something of life; between what may be called his evasive and inquisitive tendencies." This remark provides a clue not merely to Hawthorne but to a good many other American writers, including James himself, for it focuses on the dualities of moral attitude and literary approach that cut through so much of our literature. In the work of Hawthorne, and especially in *The Blithedale Romance*, they are particularly severe: his outer moral conventionality (the "blue-eyed Nathaniel") as against his suppressed recalcitrance, which sometimes breaks out as an extreme boldness of moral speech; the frequent Augustan[1] deadness of his prose as against its occasional release into pure and passionate lucidity; the mild and almost somnolent surface of his mind, so utterly unimpressive in its own right, as against the vital emotional strength beneath.

Throughout his life Hawthorne was caught up in what we would now call a crisis of religious belief. His acute moral sense had been largely detached from the traditional context of orthodox faith, but it had found little else in which to thrive, certainly no buoying social vision—which may explain why he turned so often to allegory, the one literary mode in which it might be possible to represent the moral sense as an independent force. Estranged from the dominant progressivist thought of his time, Hawthorne could summon no large enthusiasms nor pledge himself to any social movement; his prevalent temper was skeptical, though a powerful impulse within him worked to assault and deride his skepticism. But what is so curiously "modern" about Hawthorne's crisis of belief is that he seems to have been drawn less to belief itself—he was quite free from the mania for certainty—than to the enlargements of feeling that might come with belief, the passions it might release and regulate. In its assumptions this attitude toward religious belief

---

† "Hawthorne: Pastoral and Politics," from Irving Howe, *Politics and the 'Novel* (New York: Horizon Press, 1957), pp. 163–75.

1. An adjective derived from Augustus, Emperor of Rome (27 B.C.–A.D. 14), and suggesting a learned, self-consciously polished style. [*Editors.*]

might almost be called "pragmatic," odd as that word seems in relation to Hawthorne.

As a 19th century American he could not acquiesce in Puritan dogma, but as a man who had neither the enthusiasm nor the fatuousness of Transcendental optimism he could not break free from the Puritan mode of vision. He did not see *what* the Puritans had seen, he saw *as* they had seen. He felt that no matter how questionable the notion of "original sin" might be as doctrine or how distasteful if allowed to become the substance of a practical morality, it nonetheless touched upon a fundamental truth concerning human beings. This truth he reduced from a dogma to an insight, defending it on empirical grounds rather than as revelation.

Similar problems of belief troubled him, though far less acutely, in politics. A democrat by hesitation rather than conviction, he disliked reformers, distrusted the Abolitionists, and sympathized with that wing of the Democratic Party, a mediocre small-souled wing, which hoped to patch up a truce of expediency with the slave-owning South. In an age blazing with certainty, he had to make his way on doubt. The breakdown of faith in God, human capacity and social progress that would later shake the world, was foreshadowed in his life, and though he seldom made these opinions explicit, they form the buried foundations of his visible work.

Yet one cannot read his novels without seeing that in addition to the skeptic there is a man so eager for experiment in personal life that at times the "inquisitive tendency" becomes sheer hunger. This Hawthorne finds himself drawn, against his will and sometimes without his conscious knowledge, to moral outlaws who dare what he himself never even desired to dare. This Hawthorne yearns for some great liberating transformation which will bring him, for the first time, into full vibrant life. His mind was sluggish, mild, rationalistic; his creative self was passionate, warmly receptive, sometimes even sensual. It would be oversimplifying to see these two strands as always in opposition, for that would have made his life unendurable; but the two strands are there.

The quiet of Hawthorne's life was interrupted by a few adventures, a few raids on experience, of which the most interesting was perhaps his brief participation in Brook Farm, the utopian community of the 1840's. Most of Hawthorne's biographers, refusing to reach beneath the surface of his reminiscence, have assumed that since he did not agree with the ideas of the reformers he entered the Brook Farm community simply to find a way of supporting his future wife. But that hardly seems a sufficient reason, for it is unlikely that so hard-headed a man as Hawthorne would have thought Brook Farm a good financial investment, or would have thought of it primarily as a good investment. More plausible, though admittedly speculative, is the assumption that Hawthorne, apart from motives of convenience and perhaps without fully realizing it himself, was seeking in Brook Farm another kind of investment, an investment in shared life. What may have tempted him was not the ideas of the reformers, but their large enthusiasm, their animating idealism, their implicit faith in the possibility of human communication.

And despite its antipathy to the reformers, despite the tone of aggressive mockery it generally takes toward them, *The Blithedale Romance* makes it abundantly clear that Brook Farm had struck deeply and forever into Hawthorne's consciousness. In his own secretive way he had come up against many of the problems that would dominate the 20th century novel: the relation between ideology and utopia, the meeting between politics and sex.

The dualism that controls almost everything in *The Blithedale Romance* is that between subject and object, narrator and event. At the special points where the novel breaks down, the trouble is not merely one of literary structure, it also involves a radical uncertainty as to the possibilities of knowledge. Everything is seen through the eyes of Coverdale, a timid "minor poet" recalling his stay at Blithedale, the utopian community modelled after Brook Farm; and so methodical is the evasiveness and mystification with which he presents the action that one begins to suspect the book is hampered less by literary clumsiness than by some psychological block of which he is merely the symptom.

Coverdale is a self-portrait of Hawthorne, but a highly distorted and mocking self-portrait, as if Hawthorne were trying to isolate and thereby exorcise everything within him that impedes full participation in life. The tendency to withdrawal that is so noticeable in Coverdale represents not merely a New Englander's fear of involvement in the dangers of society; it is also a moony narcissism by means of which an habitual observer, unable to validate his sense of the external world, tries magically to deny its reality. This symbolic annihilation of whatever resists control of the will reaches its climax when Hawthorne destroys, physically and psychologically, the two main characters who threaten Coverdale, though nothing in the logic of the plot requires so violent or extreme a conclusion.

As against the ineffectual Coverdale—who, by the way, lacks neither intelligence nor shrewdness—Hawthorne sets up several centers of anxiety. Blithedale itself, a place of idealism and effort; Zenobia, a sexually magnificent and intellectually daring woman who is shown as the central figure of the community; Hollingsworth, a reformer who has come to Blithedale to "bore from within" in behalf of a monomaniacal scheme for salvaging convicts; and finally Priscilla, a sweet priss of a girl who represents the feminine principle in its most conservative aspect (that which makes the family go round)—all these challenge Coverdale, for all tempt him to break out of the circle of selfhood. His problem then becomes, how can he drain off some of their energy and power without himself taking the risks of commitment? Emotional parasitism is an obvious course, but with obvious limitations; in the end Hawthorne simply "rescues" Coverdale by suppressing the conflicts that threaten to liberate him—and thereby, it might be added, destroying the novel.

Coverdale's relation to the utopian community is one of the first but still among the best treatments in American writing of what happens when a hesitant intellectual attaches himself to a political enterprise. Looking back from his withered bachelorhood Coverdale is proud that at least once in his life he dared to plunge: "Whatever else I repent of, let it be reckoned neither among my sins nor my follies that I once had force and faith enough to form generous hopes of the world's destiny. . . ." And throughout the book Hawthorne retains a qualified affection for that side of New England utopianism which would later prompt Parrington to speak of Brook Farm as "a social poem fashioned out of Yankee homespun."

When Coverdale finally leaves Blithedale, he does so from a feeling—it will reappear in many American novels—that he is inadequate to public life, incapable of the monolithic enthusiasms a utopian politics demands. ("The greatest obstacle to being heroic," he shrewdly notes, "is the doubt whether one may not be going to prove one's self a fool.") Partly, too, he "sees through" the utopian impulse, discovering what would hardly surprise or shock a more realistic and experienced man: that behind its ideal claims it often shelters personal inadequacy and ideological fanaticism. And finally he grows weary of that constant depreciation of the present in the name of an ideal future which seems so necessary to utopian radicalism: "I was beginning to lose the sense of what kind of world it was, among innumerable schemes of what it might or ought to be."

Yet all of this, though pointed enough, is not very far from the usual criticism of utopian politics or, for that matter, from the usual attack upon 19th century ideas of progress; and what really distinguishes *The Blithedale Romance* is another kind of criticism doubleedged, subtle and generally unnoticed. Hawthorne saw that, motives apart, the formation of isolated utopian communities is seldom a threat to society; he understood that no matter how pure its inner moral aspirations might be, the utopian community could not avoid functioning as part of the materialistic world it detested.

I very soon became sensible [says Coverdale] that, as regarded society at large, we stood in a position of new hostility, rather than new brotherhood . . . Constituting so pitiful a minority as now, we were inevitably estranged from the rest of mankind in pretty fair proportion with the strictness of our mutual bond among ourselves.

And at another point:

The peril of our new way of life was not lest we should fail to become practical agriculturists, but that we should probably cease to be anything else.

It is interesting, and a little amusing, to note how closely these caustic observations approach the Marxist criticism of utopian communities. For if Hawthorne's sentences are transposed into economic terms, what he is saying is that by virtue of being subject to the demands and pressures of the market, the utopian community becomes a competitive unit in a competitive society ("we stood in a position of new hostility") and must therefore be infected with its mores. The utopian who would cut himself off from the ugly world must, to preserve his utopia, become a "practical agriculturist"—which means to model his utopia upon the society he rejects.

This criticism,[2] which strikes so hard a blow at the political fancies of many 19th century American intellectuals, is advanced by Hawthorne with a cruel and almost joyous insistence, but that does not make it any the less true. Hawthorne, of course, was as far from the Marxist imagination as anyone could be, but almost any criticism of utopian politics from a point of view committed to struggle within the world would have to render a similar judgment.

If Hawthorne criticizes the utopian impulse on the ground that it does not really succeed in avoiding the evil of the great world, he also implies that another trouble with utopianism is that it does not bring its followers into a sufficiently close relation with the evil of the great world. And in the context of the novel these two ideas are not as incompatible as they might seem.

For the whole utopian venture at Blithedale, with its effort to transform the impulse of political idealism into a pastoral retreat, bears a thoroughly innocent air. It is an innocence peculiar to many 19th century American intellectuals, who believed that politics, when it was not simply a vulgarity to be avoided, could be engaged in by proclaiming a series of moral precepts. (Though Emerson shied away from the utopian communities, they were actually founded on his principle that individual regeneration must precede

2. Nor was Hawthorne alone in making it. His sister-in-law Elizabeth Peabody wrote in the 1840's that Brook Farm proved little beyond the fact that "gentlemen, if they will work as many hours as boors, will succeed even better in culti- vating a farm." And Emerson, who understood very well the precarious relation between intellectuals and society, wrote in his journal that he refused to join Brook Farm because to do so would be "to hide my impotency in the thick of a crowd."

social politics—the only difference being that in the utopian communities a number of individuals came together to seek their regeneration in common.) This innocence—or perhaps one should speak
of a willed search for innocence—was of course related to the
hopelessly crude and corrupt nature of our "ordinary" national
politics, and it showed itself in no more endearing form than its
assumption that "ordinary" politics could be gotten away from, or
supplanted, by the politics of pastoral retreat. America itself having
in some sense gone astray, utopianism would remake it in the small.

The characters in *The Blithedale Romance*, even those who are
meant as figures of worldliness, also share in this New England
innocence. For while Zenobia and Hollingsworth, the one a radical
in behavior and the other a radical in ideology, are treated as figures
of enviable passion and experience, there is a tacit recognition
throughout the book that it is only by Coverdale's standards that
they can seem so rich in passion and experience. Hollingsworth,
writes Hawthorne, "ought to have commenced his investigation of
[the reform of criminals] by perpetrating some huge sin in his
proper person, and examining the conditions of his conscience
afterwards." To be sure, this trenchant observation is put into the
mouth of Coverdale, who is frequently envious of Hollingsworth's
political passion; but there is surely nothing unfamiliar, or at odds
with our sense of psychological realism, in Coverdale's need to
depreciate that which he most admires. It is as if Hawthorne, soon
to punish Zenobia and Hollingsworth for their putative boldness,
can accept his desire to punish them only through a half-suppressed
feeling that, in reality, they are not bold enough.

The uneasy mixture of skepticism and yearning that complicates
Hawthorne's treatment of the utopian community can also be seen
in his approach to Zenobia and Hollingsworth as individuals.
Zenobia rules the book. "Passionate, luxurious, lacking simplicity,
not deeply refined," she is the frankest embodiment of sensuality in
Hawthorne's work. Except for Hollingsworth, whose appetite runs
to political notions rather than human flesh, everyone in the book is
drawn to her. For she alone is really alive, she alone is open in her
sexuality. As if to cover up the freedom of his characterization,
Hawthorne also endows her with a somewhat operatic manner, but
this does not seriously detract from Zenobia's power and when one
remembers how difficult and damaging the role of feminine reformer must have been in 19th century New England it even has a
certain appropriateness. Throughout the book Zenobia is celebrated
in rhapsodic outbursts:

> Zenobia had a rich, though varying color. It was, most of the
> while, a flame, and anon a sudden paleness. Her eyes glowed. . . .
> Her gestures were free, and strikingly impressive. The whole

woman was alive with a passionate intensity, which I now perceived to be the phase in which her beauty culminated. Any passion would have become her well; and passionate love, perhaps,
the best of all.

In her opulent, inaccessible sexuality Zenobia becomes a kind of
New England earth goddess—though, given Hawthorne's estimate
of New England women, a very intellectual goddess too. Both ways,
she is the name of his desire.

Hawthorne quickly penetrates to the source and nature of Zenobia's sexuality; he relates it, both in its power and its limitations, to
her political boldness. He understands that in her person is realized
the threat to traditional modes of life which the others merely talk
about. And he sees how, in turn, her political boldness contributes
to and sanctions her personal freedom:

> She made no scruple of over-setting all human institutions, and
> scattering them as with a breeze from her fan. A female reformer,
> in her attacks upon society, has an instinctive sense of where the
> life lies, and is inclined to aim directly at that spot. Especially the
> relation between the sexes is naturally among the earliest to attract
> her attention.

This powerful insight Hawthorne puts to two uses, making
Zenobia into a vibrant woman who challenges established social
norms but also showing how this very challenge twists and depletes
her life. For as Zenobia ruefully admits, "the whole universe, her
own sex and yours, and Providence, and Destiny, to boot, make
common cause against the woman who swerves one hair's-breadth
out of the beaten track."

But if Zenobia's intellectual and political audacity makes possible
a new kind of personal freedom, it also involves the danger of a
confusion of sexual roles. Zenobia's unconventionality as a woman
allows her a certain masculine energy and arrogance, and while this
brings her public satisfactions it also prevents her from winning
Hollingsworth's love; for he is one of those reformers who prefers
that his own wife be tame and submissive. In a brilliant little passage Hawthorne hints at the tragi-comic difficulties of Zenobia's
position. Asked at the beginning of the book whether she knows
Hollingsworth, Zenobia replies, "No, only as an auditor—auditress,
I mean—of some of his lectures."

Can Zenobia, however, be both the personification of forbidden
sexuality and a woman capable of so revealing a slip as the one I
have just quoted? Is Hawthorne "cheating" when he portrays
Zenobia as a richly feminine figure yet particularly open to the
dangers of subverting the feminine role?

Whatever the difficulty may be with Zenobia, it is not in Hawthorne's initial conception of her, which is marvellously deep and subtle; in fact, it is one of his major intuitive strokes that he notices how the political atmosphere which encourages a freer sexuality also threatens the feminine role. The trouble lies in Hawthorne's presentation, his unwillingness or incapacity to live up to the promise of his opening pages. For, like everything else in the book, Zenobia comes through only in flickers; we do not see her in a developed action that would call upon the intelligence she undoubtedly has; the speculative insights into the relation between her public and private selves appear mainly as occasional remarks that do not affect the bulk of the novel. Either because he draws back from his subject, fearful of his own boldness, or because he would not work up an action by which to sustain his subject, Hawthorne does not show us Zenobia in the motions and gestures of life. And that, of course, is one reason he can imply that she is not so thoroughly a figure of passion and experience as Coverdale supposes. The more she is to be shown as a temptress, the more must her temptations be called into question.

What is true for Zenobia as a projection of desire is truer still for Hollingsworth as a warning against the dangers of ideology. A number of recent critics have praised Hawthorne's presentation of Hollingsworth as a prophetic anticipation of the reformer who is cold to everything but his own scheme. Were Hollingsworth "there," were he endowed with a certain contingency and thickness and color of presentation, this point might well be true. For it is clearly Hawthorne's intention to show in Hollingsworth the utopian impulse as it has hardened into an inhumane ideology. But in the novel as Hawthorne wrote it, Hollingsworth is a dismal failure. He never *does* anything, he seldom displays any emotional fluidity or complexity, he is rarely given one of those saving human touches which, by their very presence, would make more credible his essential inhumanity.

There are, of course, a few passages in which Hawthorne breathes a little life into him—as when Hollingsworth, with that single-minded sincerity which is a form of blindness, asks Coverdale, "How can you be my life-long friend, except you strive with me toward the great object of my life?" or when Zenobia bursts out that Hollingsworth's political dedication "is all self! . . . Nothing else; nothing but self, self, self!"

Such passages, however, do little but suggest how great was Hawthorne's opportunity and how seldom he seized it, for Hollingsworth conforms so neatly to Hawthorne's skepticism concerning reformers that he cannot have much reality of his own. Nothing is granted any scope in the book that would allow Hollingsworth to resist or complicate the point he is meant to illustrate. Presumably a warning against the terrible consequences of a fanatic ideology, he is seldom allowed any vitality as a character because Hawthorne's sense of him is itself so thoroughly ideological. What Hawthorne had wished to warn against in his portrait of Hollingsworth becomes a crucial deficiency of the portrait itself.

Any critic who cares enough to write about *The Blithedale Romance* runs the risk of suggesting that it is a better book than it actually is, for its themes would appear so close to our current preoccupations that they need merely be stated in order to arouse interest. And with a novel so abundant in potentiality and so limited in realization there is the further danger of writing about the book it might have been—a very good book, indeed!—rather than the one it is. Yet by any serious reckoning *The Blithedale Romance* must be called a remarkable failure by a very remarkable writer.

One way of testing this judgment is to consider how difficult it is to specify the novel's controlling significance. It is possible to trace the assumptions behind Hawthorne's treatment of utopian radicalism; to observe the partial success with which he has drawn figures appropriate to the utopian community and has noticed the relationship between politics and sex, ideology and utopia as they take shape in such an environment. But none of this is yet to see the book as a coherent work of art, a disciplined whole that is informed by a serious moral interest—and that, I think, is precisely what cannot be done.

One can, to be sure, offer a number of generalized thematic statements. But it is not possible closely to relate Hawthorne's serious thematic intentions with most of the happenings in the book, which consist of mistaken identities belatedly discovered, secret marriages long repented of, spiritual exercises and hypnotic experiments, melodramatic suicides and Gothic flim-flam.[3] Between the serious matter, confined mostly to the first fifty pages, and a tedious gimcrack plot there is seldom any vital relation.

How then are we to account for this radical incoherence?

In a recent essay on Hawthorne, Philip Rahv has written that "the emotional economy" of *The Blithedale Romance* "is throughout one of displacement . . . the only genuine relationship is that of Coverdale to Zenobia: the rest is mystification. But the whole point of Coverdale's behavior is to avoid involvement." The remark is keen, though I would qualify it by adding that there does seem to be one other relationship which for Coverdale has elements of risk and involvement: his aborted discipleship to Hollingsworth. He draws back from Zenobia's personal freedom, he draws back from Hollingsworth's political commitment, and in both cases he finds rea-

3. Gothic nonsense; that is, an excessive emphasis on the irrational, grotesque, and mysterious. [*Editors.*]

sons, often good enough in their own right, with which to rationalize his timidity. Zenobia and Hollingsworth together stand for "the world," the dangerous beckoning world of experience and liberation. To cheat Coverdale of these temptations, Hawthorne must end the novel by drowning Zenobia and breaking Hollingsworth's spirit.

And yet . . . one feels drawn to the book, to its sudden sparks of perception, its underground passions. Henry James saw enough possibilities in its subject to base one of his major novels upon it: *The Bostonians*, in many ways, is the masterpiece that Hawthorne's book might have been.[4] But even James did not exhaust its possibilities, and if ever a novel is written that dives beneath the surface of political life in 20th century America its author may find a storehouse of hidden reserves in Hawthorne's great failure *The Blithedale Romance*.

ROY R. MALE

The Pastoral Wasteland: *The Blithedale Romance*†

In *The Blithedale Romance* (1852) Hawthorne arrived at his definitive criticism of the recurring American efforts at transformation without tragedy. While his ever optimistic contemporaries were busy converting trees into lumber, whales into oil, and water into power, Hawthorne adhered to his "one idea": that moral conversion, which is the only kind that really matters, cannot be achieved through intellectual schemes, incessant industry, or technological progress. A spiritual sea change must be *suffered*; this is unfortunate, but there is no other way. "There is no instance in all history," he wrote in his life of Pierce,[1] "of the human will and intellect having perfected any great moral reform by methods which it adapted to that end."

With this central idea in mind, Hawthorne composed *The Blithedale Romance* by selecting and manipulating his observations and experiences of a decade: the gruesome suicide of a woman in the prime of life; the contemporary delusion of mesmerism; the Brook Farm experiment; the quiet, determined drinkers at Parker's grog-

---

4. The influence of *The Blithedale Romance* on James's novel has been discussed by Marius Bewley, *The Complex Fate* (London: Chatto and Windus, 1952), pp. 11–30, and in two essays by Robert Emmet Long: "The Society and the Masks: *The Blithedale Romance* and *The Bostonians*," *Nineteenth-Century Fiction*, 19 (1964), 105–22; and "Transformations: *The Blithedale Romance* to

Howells and James," *American Literature*, 47 (1976), 552–71. [*Editors*.]
† From Roy R. Male, *Hawthorne's Tragic Vision* (Austin: University of Texas Press, 1957), 139–56.
1. Hawthorne published a campaign biography of his college friend Franklin Pierce (president of the United States, 1853–57) in 1852. [*Editors*.]

shop; the gulf between the intellectual and the yeoman; his interest
in the dangerously sterile but fascinating role of the withdrawn
observer. In 1842 he set down one hint of the story to come when
he wrote in his notebook: "To allegorize life with a masquerade,
and represent mankind generally as masquers. Here and there a
natural face may appear." The vision of life that emerged ten years
later, though it lacks the tense conflict of The Scarlet Letter, is far
richer than one usually realizes upon first reading. The book seems
to me to be perfectly achieved and just as relevant in the age of
extrasensory perception and atomic conversion as it was in the era
of mesmerism. Until recently, criticism of The Blithedale Romance
so often dwelled upon such peripheral matters as whether or not
Zenobia resembled Margaret Fuller that it remains one of the most
underrated works in American fiction.

Now that the demands for a prosaic realism in fiction have re-
ceded, it is unnecessary to labor the point that The Blithedale
Romance is not an ineffectual effort at a documentary of Brook
Farm, nor is it merely Hawthorne's satirical comment on philanthropists and reform movements. As he stated in the preface and in
a letter to G. W. Curtis,[2] the real subject of the book is neither
Brook Farm nor socialism. His work presents, as Henry James
would say, "experience liberated, so to speak; experience disen-
gaged, disembroiled, disencumbered, exempt from the conditions
which usually attach to it,"[3] so that its deepest implications may be
explored. The implications in this instance are not pleasant to contemplate, but to a generation educated by D. H. Lawrence, T. S.
Eliot, Thomas Mann, and Robert Penn Warren[4] they probably
seem more real than they did in 1852. The Blithedale community
stands as the type of all those efforts in the Western world to ignore
Solomon's wisdom about the seasons,[5] to purify by escaping from
time into space, to achieve rebirth by putting on a mask. The comic
masquerade, as Hawthorne viewed it, is the mode of changing our
minds, and as such it is vitally necessary. The mischief comes when
we expect it to change our hearts.

Blithedale, then, turns out to be an ironic name, thinly veiling

2. George William Curtis (1824–92), American writer, journalist, editor, and lyceum lecturer. See note 9, p. 241, and excerpt, p. 241. [Editors.]
3. Twenty-five years after publishing The American (1877), James wrote a Preface for the work, in which he classifies it as a Romance and defines the "only general attribute of projected romance" as the kind of experience described above. [Editors.]
4. David Herbert Lawrence (1885–1930), English novelist and poet; Thomas Stearns Eliot (1888–1965), American-

born British poet, critic, and playwright; Thomas Mann (1875–1955), German novelist, short-story writer, and critic; Robert Penn Warren (1905–   ), American novelist and critic. [Editors.]
5. Noted for his wealth and wisdom, Solomon was king of Israel in the tenth century B.C. In Ecclesiastes III, he urges man to rely on God's providence since "All things have their season" and, essentially, man "cannot add any thing, nor take away from those things which God hath made." [Editors.]

what ultimately emerges as a pastoral wasteland. The inhabitants of the community debate over a name for their utopia; some favor calling it "The Oasis," but "others insisted on a proviso for reconsidering the matter at a twelve-month's end, when a final decision might be had, whether to name it 'The Oasis,' or 'Sahara'." By the end of the book it is obvious that Blithedale, far from being "the one green spot in the moral sand-waste of the world," has instead simply revealed its own barrenness. What the inhabitants hope will be a May Day—a warm, "hearty" purification—turns out to be a winter's tale told in retrospect by a frosty bachelor.

Hawthorne deliberately wrote, I suspect, toward the "big scene" that he felt to be securely within his grasp—the midnight discovery of Zenobia's suicide. Soon after the story opens, to cite but one instance, Zenobia prophesies her fate with "the entrance of the sable knight Hollingsworth and this shadowy snow-maiden, who, precisely at the stroke of midnight, shall melt away at my feet in a pool of ice-cold water and give me my death with a pair of wet slippers." Coverdale's dream, in which he foresees "a dim shadow" of the catastrophe, thus provides an explicit comment on Hawthorne's method of subtly anticipating later events.

The Blithedale experiment is, first, an attempt to avoid the embrace of time. Coverdale and his friends ride "far beyond the strike of city clocks" into pure, snow-covered space. Theirs is an effort to blur the distinction between seasons, to overcome the desolation of winter by the warmth of their reforming zeal. "We can never call ourselves regenerated men," says one of Coverdale's companions, "till a February northeaster shall be as grateful to us as the softest breeze of June." They declare May Day a "movable festival," and it is only the ineffectual Coverdale who gradually senses the blank unreality of their "spick-and-span novelty." By the time he decides to leave the community, he has finally attained a wisdom that, though commonplace elsewhere, seems downright orphic after life at Blithedale: "Times change, and people change," he tells Priscilla; "and if our hearts do not change as readily, so much the worse for us."

Acting as a measure of the community's failure, therefore, is the temporal structure of the book. Narrated by one who has withdrawn from life, the story unfolds against the background of the seasons.[6] Viewed against the fundamental rhythms of nature, the various human efforts at rebirth without roots become even more frustrating. Recalling the firelight, which at the beginning of the Blithedale experiment had made the men look "full of youth, warm

---

6. Richard Harter Fogle has pointed out that the seasons are an important element in the structure. *Hawthorne's Fiction:* *The Light and the Dark* (Norman: University of Oklahoma Press, 1952), 141–42.

blood, and hope," Coverdale ruefully remarks that its genial glow has now dwindled to the "phosphoric glimmer . . . which exudes . . . from the damp fragments of decayed trees." He explicitly proclaims his own rebirth in May: having passed through a kind of death, he is "quite another man," "clothed anew." And later he finds a "hermitage" in the weeds that suggests the perfect shelter of the womb. It is "a hollow chamber of rare seclusion" in which his individuality is "inviolate." Sitting there, Coverdale prophesies a rebirth in October: "I . . . fore-reckoned the abundance of my vintage. It gladdened me to anticipate the surprise of the Community when, like an allegorical figure of rich October, I should make my appearance, with shoulders bent beneath the burden of ripe grapes and some of the crushed ones crimsoning my brows with a blood-stain." But this fruitful October never comes for him, and in the end he is forced to acknowledge that his life has been "all an emptiness."

There are other futile attempts at regeneration. The drinkers in the saloon achieve "renewed youth and vigor, the brisk, cheerful sense of things present and to come"—a feeling that lasts "for about a quarter of an hour." The fate of these people is typified in the picture of a drunkard that hangs on the wall. "The death-in-life was too well portrayed. . . . Your only comfort lay in the forced reflection, that real as he looked, the poor caitiff was but imaginary—a bit of painted canvas." The mesmerist, Westervelt, also offers a new life. He speaks of "a new era that was dawning upon the world; an era that would link soul to soul with a closeness that should finally convert both worlds into one great, mutually conscious brotherhood." The "cold and dead materialism" of this brotherhood is matched by the mechanical method of conversion advocated by Fourier. Drain the salt from the sea, as he had proposed, transform the water to lemonade, and all the savor is gone.[7] *The Blithedale Romance* is thus a kind of *Walden*[8] in reverse. (Zenobia, coincidentally, anticipates Thoreau's exact words when she says of her experience in the community: "It was good; but there are other lives as good or better.") The story begins in the spring and ends with the fall; the whole progression is condensed in the exhilaration of the brisk September day that makes Coverdale buoyant at first but later only emphasizes his "sickness of the spirits."

The effort to reform the spirit externally, then, leads to disintegration. Sharply contrasted to the dynamic wholeness of nature are the images of rigidity, mutilation, and decay that lead inexorably to the

7. For Hawthorne's reference to this theory, see p. 49. [*Editors.*]
8. *Walden* (1854) is a narrative essay in which Henry David Thoreau (1817–62) describes his efforts to live "a life of simplicity, independence, magnanimity, and trust" in a hut on the shore of Walden Pond, near Concord. Thoreau's experiment is an attempt to reform the spirit internally, withdrawn from society or community; his emphasis is on individualism. [*Editors.*]

discovery of Zenobia's horribly rigid and mutilated corpse. It is "the marble image of a death-agony," the catastrophe that Coverdale dimly foresaw when he awakened from his dream after the first evening in Blithedale and saw the moon shining on the snowy landscape, which looked "like a lifeless copy of the world in marble." Zenobia is cast aside like "a broken tool" by the inflexible Hollingsworth; and Coverdale's cool analysis of Hollingsworth is, as he himself admits, a kind of dissection. "If we take the freedom to put a friend under our microscope," he says, "we inevitably tear him into bits." The Blithedale group is "gentility in tatters," while the visitors from town, the ratlike Moodie and the infamous Westervelt, embody a decadent materialism. The mesmerist's discourse is like "a current of chill air issuing out of a sepulchral vault, and bringing the smell of corruption along with it."

The second major pattern of images is one of withdrawal and concealment. As Frank Davidson has pointed out,[9] everyone in the book except Silas Foster and his pigs is veiled in one form or another. Priscilla, the Veiled Lady, is "insulated" from time and space; the pseudonym of Zenobia is a "sort of mask in which she comes from the world, retaining all the privileges of privacy—a contrivance, in short, like the white drapery of the Veiled Lady." Old Moodie hides behind his alias and his patch; Westervelt's gold teeth reveal him to Coverdale as a humbug whose "face, for aught I knew, might be removable like a mask." Hollingsworth's mask is his philanthropic project: "You are a better masquerader than the witches and gypsies yonder," Zenobia tells him, "for your disguise is a self-deception." The whole community has, of course, withdrawn from life into a kind of masquerade, but Coverdale finds it necessary to retreat even further into the hermitage. His typical stance finds him "a little withdrawn from the window."

The failure of Blithedale may be summed up as a misplaced faith in the comic vision of life as a mode of emotional conversion. The essence of the comic vision, as Hawthorne considered it, lay in the breaking of bonds—links with the past, ties with social classes. As Melville's mentor Solomon said, there is "a time to embrace, and a time to refrain from embracing," and the communitarians have confused the tragic usefulness of the one with the comic purpose of the other.

* * *

9. "Toward a Re-evaluation of *The Blithedale Romance*," *New England Quarterly*, 25 (1952), 374–83.

A. N. KAUL

[Community and Society]†

In *The Scarlet Letter* Hawthorne had noted the utopian aspect of the Puritan migration to New England. In *The Blithedale Romance* he presents the utopian experiment of Brook Farm as an extension of the Puritan tradition. The backward glance of comparison runs like a rich thread through the pattern of the latter novel, making explicit the significance which the American romancer saw in this otherwise quixotic enterprise.

The day on which the visionaries assemble at Blithedale—to begin "the life of Paradise anew"—is bleaker and less encouraging than the day of the Pilgrims' landing as described by William Bradford.[1] How conscious Hawthorne's narrator is of the suggested parallel we notice when, seated by the blazing hearth of the farmhouse at the end of the tempestuous journey, he reflects that "the old Pilgrims might have swung their kettle over precisely such a fire as this" and that, though Blithedale was hardly a day's walk from the old city, "we had transported ourselves a world-wide distance from the system of society that shackled us at breakfast-time." The Blithedalers are careful to distinguish the moral idealism of their motivation from the guiding principles of other contemporary communitarians. When Miles Coverdale reads the works of Fourier during his convalescence, he concludes that the world was mistaken in equating Blithedale with Fourierism "inasmuch as the two theories differed, as widely as the zenith from the nadir, in their main principles." Hollingsworth, to whom Coverdale puts the case, dismisses the Frenchman in an impassioned speech which is a curious amalgam of Hawthorne and the elder James.[2] Fourier, Hollingsworth declares, "has committed the unpardonable sin; for what more monstrous iniquity could the Devil himself contrive than to choose the selfish principle,—the principle of all human wrong, the very blackness of man's heart, the portion of ourselves which we shudder at, and which it is the whole aim of spiritual discipline to eradicate,—to choose it as the master-workman of his system? To seize upon and foster whatever vile, petty, sordid, filthy, bestial, and

† From A. N. Kaul, *The American Vision: Actual and Ideal Society in Nineteenth-Century Fiction* (New Haven: Yale University Press, 1963), pp. 196–213. Notes are by the editors of this Norton Critical Edition.
1. Bradford describes that day (November 11, 1620) in his *Of Plymouth Plantation* (written 1630–50): "Being thus arrived in good harbor, and brought safe to land, they fell upon their knees and blessed the God of Heaven who had brought them over the vast and furious ocean, and delivered them from all the perils and miseries thereof."
2. Henry James, Sr. (1811–82), the father of Henry James, the novelist, and William James, the psychologist and philosopher, was a religiously oriented critic of society who stressed "the immanence of God in the unity of mankind."

abominable corruptions have cankered into our nature, to be the
efficient instruments of his infernal regeneration!" Since "the selfish
principle" at the base of organized society is also the chief reason
for the Blithedalers' withdrawal from it, in denouncing Fourier,
Hollingsworth is stating by implication their own different purpose.
The irony here, however, lies in the fact—which will be noted more
fully later—that this criticism of Fourier remains the ultimate comment on Hollingsworth himself. The true importance of the Blithedale experiment, as Hawthorne presents it, is that it embodies the
visionary hope for mankind which was coeval with the American
settlement itself. Miles Coverdale puts the claim for it explicitly
when he opens a later chapter, "Eliot's Pulpit," by saying: "Our
Sundays at Blithedale were not ordinarily kept with such rigid observance as might have befitted the descendants of the Pilgrims,
whose high enterprise, as we sometimes flattered ourselves, we had
taken up, and were carrying it onward and aloft, to a point which
they never dreamed of attaining."

In many ways Hawthorne was, as Mrs. Q. D. Leavis says, the
unwilling heir of the Puritans. But this is far from being true with
regard to the tradition of idealism which was a part of his inheritance. On the contrary, he affirmed it in the only serious way in
which an artist can affirm tradition: by becoming its critic. It must
be said in passing that as far as the actual experiment of Brook
Farm is concerned, Hawthorne's motives in joining it were as mixed
as those of his ancestors in coming to America. On the one hand,
there was the practical expectation of a comfortable livelihood for
himself and Sophia. On the other, there was a good deal of simple
faith in the theory behind the venture—enough faith, at any rate, to
induce him to stake a thousand dollars from his meager resources
on its success. Brook Farm, as he says in the preface to the novel,
was "essentially a day-dream, and yet a fact," and indeed, in the
curious episode of his association with it, one finds it difficult to
separate the hard-headed Yankee from the wild-eyed dreamer. Perhaps, like Coverdale, he hoped that in the long run "between theory
and practice, a true and available mode of life might be struck
out."

However, be his personal motivation what it may, the important
thing to realize is that Brook Farm presented Hawthorne with an
appropriate subject for his theme. In "Earth's Holocaust," the fantasy which describes an attempted regeneration, he had observed
that it mattered little whether the attempt was made in the time past
or time to come. The contours of the action were indeed hidden in
the whole history of America. *The Scarlet Letter* had dealt with it at
its very source in the seventeenth century. In *Blithedale* Hawthorne
brought the action up to date. Here again was an embodiment of
the archetypal American experience: withdrawal from a corrupt

society to form a regenerate community. The basis for regeneration had of course shifted from theological to economic theory; social morality was no longer embedded in metaphysics. In this sense Hawthorne was marking realistically enough the shift in tradition that had occurred over the centuries. * * * although in America, unlike Europe, the communitarian tradition developed in unbroken continuity from its chiliastic source in the seventeenth century, the experimenters of the nineteenth century were communitarians first and sectarians only in the second place—or not at all. Moreover, it was no longer confined to alien groups. Ripley's community[3] was both native in composition and secular in purpose.

It is to emphasize the action of withdrawal and to underline the exercise of that radical choice which America was supposed to have made permanently available to mankind that the novel opens in society, with Coverdale about to take the plunge which he later compares to the Pilgrims' world-wide leap across the Atlantic. In the temporary movement of the story back to society, which occurs in the middle of the novel, we get some richly evoked scenes of Boston life. This is the most detailed body of social description in Hawthorne, and it comes very close to the best manner of European fiction. Hawthorne is not, however, a "social" novelist, and this presentation is the background rather than the milieu of the action, which explores not a social problem but the possibility of repudiating organized society in its entirety. The subject is not Boston life but rather the drama of Boston and Blithedale, or the American dialectic between actual society and ideal community. The theme is not reform but social regeneration.

While the Blithedalean visionaries acknowledge their kinship with the American Puritans of the seventeenth century, their own enterprise arises primarily from a repugnance to the principle of economic individualism, from the fact that society has come to be organized exclusively on the basis of the force which had caused the failure of Bradford's communitarian experiment but which Bradford had accepted as an inevitable factor of God's dispensation for the New World. Of course the Blithedale community has other avowed objectives, like the belief in agriculture as the true foundation of the good life. This, however, constitutes the ridiculous part of their venture, and is treated uniformly as such by Hawthorne. It is indeed the chief target of the mild but persistent comedy in which Silas Foster, together with the pigs and the manure dump, serves to point out the reality behind the masquerade, while Miles Coverdale, like Shakespeare's Touchstone,[4] performs the function of more

3. Brook Farm.
4. The court jester in Shakespeare's *As You Like It* (1600), whose realistic wit deflates the sentimental pretensions of the pastoral view of life.

articulate comic exposure. Hawthorne, as much as Melville, faced but overcame the nineteenth-century temptation toward the Arcadian relapse.[5] It is true that outdoor life helps both Priscilla and Coverdale to add sunburn to their cheeks. But, as Coverdale observes:

> The peril of our new way of life was not lest we should fail in becoming practical agriculturists, but that we should probably cease to be anything else. . . . The clods of earth, which we so constantly belabored and turned over and over, were never etherealized into thought. Our thoughts, on the contrary, were fast becoming cloddish. Our labor symbolized nothing, and left us mentally sluggish in the dusk of the evening. Intellectual activity is incompatible with any large amount of bodily exercise. The yeoman and the scholar—the yeoman and the man of finest moral culture, though not the man of sturdiest sense and integrity—are two distinct individuals, and can never be melted or welded into one substance.

Hawthorne is exposing here again the fallacy of the virgin scene: the assumption that a new and regenerated life demands the total repudiation of man's accumulated moral and material achievement, and that, as soon as the heritage of the past is abandoned, regeneration begins of its own accord. In a later chapter, while describing the exciting bustle of city life, Coverdale goes on to say how all this "was just as valuable, in its way, as the sighing of the breeze among the birch-trees that overshadowed Eliot's pulpit." When in the same chapter he observes a scene of simple domestic affection, being fresh from the discords he has witnessed at Blithedale, he reflects that he had not "seen a prettier bit of nature" during his summer in the country than the actors in that scene had shown him here "in a rather stylish boarding-house."

One should be careful, however, not to divert the ridicule that Hawthorne reserves for the Arcadia to other aspects of the community idea. As a matter of fact, though he presents Blithedale in its single corporate image, he clearly distinguishes between the different values involved in its broad spectrum. For instance, he does not debunk the issue of the equality of the sexes as he does the cult of agriculture. His attitude toward it is ambiguous in the sense that he accords to it the dignity of a serious though not one-sided argument. It is true that even the ardent feminist Zenobia gives in to Hollingsworth's view that should women ever dream of straying from their natural subservience to man, the male sex must "use its physical force, that unmistakable evidence of sovereignty, to scourge them back within their proper bounds!" But as Coverdale

5. The assumption that the closer a society is to nature the more morally beneficient and humanly satisfying it will be. Herman Melville's *Typee* (1846)—which Hawthorne reviewed—a novel set on a Marquesan island, explores the decisive limitations as well as the idyllic aspects of a primitive existence.

reflects a moment later, is such submission to male egotism a token of woman's true nature or is it "the result of ages of compelled degradation?" Together with this goes the further reflection that "women, however intellectually superior, so seldom disquiet themselves about the rights or wrongs of their sex, unless their own individual affections chance to lie in idleness, or to be ill at ease." Thus, while Zenobia's side of the case is presented as unquestionably superior to Hollingsworth's Nietzschean[6] bombast, the whole issue of feminist reform is seen as a secondary question—an unfortunate consequence of the general distortion of human relations in society. With regard to the primary cause of such dislocations— which is indeed the cause of the Blithedalean withdrawal— Hawthorne leaves us in no doubt. Early in the novel, while commenting on the first day's assembly at Blithedale, Coverdale observes:

> If ever men might lawfully dream awake, and give utterance to their wildest visions without dread of laughter or scorn on the part of the audience,—yes, and speak of earthly happiness, for themselves and mankind, as an object to be hopefully striven for, and probably attained,—we who made that little semicircle round the blazing fire were those very men. We had left the rusty iron framework of society behind us; we had broken through many hindrances that are powerful enough to keep most people on the weary tread-mill of the established system, even while they feel its irksomeness almost as intolerable as we did. We had stepped down from the pulpit; we had flung aside the pen; we had shut up the ledger . . . It was our purpose . . . [to show] mankind the example of a life governed by other than the false and cruel principles on which human society has all along been based.
>
> And, first of all, we had divorced ourselves from pride, and were striving to supply its place with familiar love. . . . We sought our profit by mutual aid, instead of wresting it by the strong hand from an enemy, or filching it craftily from those less shrewd than ourselves (if, indeed, there were any such in New England), or winning it by selfish competition with a neighbor; in one or another of which fashions every son of woman both perpetrates and suffers his share of the common evil, whether he chooses it or no.

Whatever one may say of Blithedale and its members as things eventually turn out, there is no question about the force with which the vision of an ideal community is presented here. Nor is there any ambiguity about the distribution of sympathies as between the values avowed by Coverdale and those which govern the "iron framework of society." The visionaries stand—in theory at least—

6. Friedrich Nietzsche (1844–1900), German philosopher, argued that the emancipation of women can lead only to her enfeeblement and to the loss of her charming nature.

upon the principle of human brotherhood as against the predatory competitiveness of the established system. Blithedale itself, as we shall see, is finally judged in terms of its own professed values and not by the standards and norms of society. It is only when, and insofar as, the visionaries themselves turn out to be men of iron masquerading in Arcadian costume, that Blithedale is dismissed as a humbug—as false as society but more hypocritical. But this process of criticism—of exposing the same basic drives twice over and of showing the corrupted rebel as more reprehensible than the original villain—does not lead to a reversal of values involved in the challenge. It makes for a more clear-sighted affirmation. Nor does the novelist, as distinct from the characters who are all more or less ironically presented, abandon his position with regard to "the common evil" of exploitative individualism which every person in society either suffers from or perpetrates. Hawthorne's attitude, it must be said, does not involve the repudiation of individual freedom and choice. On the contrary, like the elder James, he insists on the primacy of the moral person in all social arrangements. But the individualism he champions is not incompatible with, but rather tends toward and finds its richest fulfillment in, the human community.

Since the story is mainly concerned with the fortunes of the Blithedale community, the image of the surrounding society occupies of necessity a marginal position. Yet this is strictly true only in a physical sense. In reality, the main characters of the story, who are all communitarians, carry with themselves, more or less visibly, the outwardly repudiated social values and attitudes—like old earth clinging to tufts of transplanted grass. It is this fact which makes *Blithedale* an exploration of the dialectical rather than simply the oppositional relation between actual society and the aspiration toward a better community life. But, apart from this, one of the most remarkable feats of the novel is the manner in which the two peripheral characters—old Moodie and Westervelt—are made to suggest concretely certain sinister forces working in the depths of the social world. Although one would at first sight suppose them to belong wholly to the machinery of romance, even their connection with the central theme of *Blithedale* is close enough for one to conclude that Hawthorne's apologia in the preface with regard to the introduction of the communitarian experiment into the romance should be treated in the same light as Mark Twain's celebrated warning against finding a moral in *Huckleberry Finn*.[7] Where Hawthorne maintains cautiously that the whole treatment of Brook

---

7. Twain prefaced his novel (1884) with a tongue-in-cheek "Notice" that "Persons attempting to find a motive in this narrative will be prosecuted; persons attempting to find a moral in it will be banished; persons attempting to find a plot in it will be shot."

Farm is "altogether incidental to the main purpose of the romance," one feels the whole romance is in reality a characteristically modulated projection of the main society-community theme.

In *The Seven Gables* Hawthorne had observed that in nineteenth-century America, "amid the fluctuating waves of our social life, somebody is always at the drowning-point." This process and the consequent sense of insecurity are exemplified in *Blithedale*—more starkly and less sentimentally than in the case of Hepzibah Pyncheon[8]—by old Moodie: the grandee of yesterday become the pauper of today; Fauntleroy turned into "a gray kennel-rat." This is a motif which recurs in a good deal of later American fiction, the career of George Hurstwood in *Sister Carrie*[9] being a case which readily comes to mind. Hawthorne's method, however, is one of poetic, or "romantic," evocation rather than the "realistic" accumulation of minute detail, and his purpose is not so much to show the impassable gulf between classes as to point out the morally untenable nature of those distinctions which separate man from man in society. It is only in this sense that the fact of the relation between Zenobia and Priscilla becomes more meaningful than a mere contrivance of romantic plotting, for the sisterhood that is avowed at Blithedale but denied in society is not a playful masquerade as Zenobia seems to think; it is a reflection of the true nature of things.

In Westervelt, who is also connected with Zenobia and Priscilla, the projected force is one of secret power. The relation between him and the poor seamstress Priscilla is not unlike that between Ethan Brand and Esther[1] and mesmerism is to that extent presented as a peculiarly sinister variation of exploitative science. It makes "a delusive show of spirituality" but is "really imbued throughout with a cold and dead materialism." Westervelt represents in this sense the final degradation of the Puritan tradition. However, just as Hawthorne had explored the social implications of Puritan theology, he uses here the new psychic phenomenon to embody a sociological insight. These subtle transferences and suggested correlations are characteristic of Hawthorne's complex fictional method. Westervelt is in many ways the polished gentleman, a representative of the social type in which Coverdale sees a partial reflection of his own pre-Blithedale existence. But he is also a wizard the gold band around whose false teeth reveals him somehow as a "moral and physical humbug." Yet his power, though exerted invisibly, is real

8. The pathetic old maid of reduced circumstances in Hawthorne's *The House of the Seven Gables* (1851).
9. In Theodore Dreiser's novel (1900), George Hurstwood, an intelligent and successful businessman, through a series of mischances, sinks down the social scale, ending up a beggar and finally a suicide.
1. In Hawthorne's "Ethan Brand" (1850), Brand, through some kind of unspecified intellectual power, annihilates the soul of an innocent girl named Esther.

enough. In its remote control it suggests the exploitative power which technology was putting into the hands of men: the power to bring individuals into total bondage while leaving them outwardly free and untouched. Westervelt's human shape is thus "a necromantic, or perhaps a mechanical contrivance, in which a demon walked about." He, too, affirms faith in a golden future and speaks publicly of the dawning era "that would link soul to soul" in "mutually conscious brotherhood," but he speaks of it "as if it were a matter of chemical discovery." As against the brotherhood of voluntary love, which is based upon the magnetic chain of human sympathy, Westervelt's mesmeric union is enforced bondage, destructive of true individuality as well as true community.

The brotherhood of love and mutual sympathy, which is lacking or perverted in an individualist social system, is precisely what the Blithedale community has taken for the foundation of its life. It is likewise the basis of Hawthorne's criticism of Blithedale itself. What the novel finally calls in doubt is not the values avowed by the visionaries but their means, materials, and ultimately the depth and sincerity of their professions. Zenobia is a dilettante who, until she meets Hollingsworth, expects from Blithedale nothing worse than a naughty frolic and hardly anything better than a pleasant interlude in rusticity. She takes the experiment as a stage set for an unaccustomed personal role, and a curious theatricality accompanies her doings at Blithedale right up to the manner of her suicide. Coverdale is at heart a well-meaning sybarite who has joined the community out of boredom with an aimless life, although the sense of direction and purpose he develops while there is a different matter. He and Zenobia share between themselves the accusation that the Veiled Lady levels at Theodore in Zenobia's own legend: "Dost thou come hither, not in holy faith, nor with a pure and generous purpose, but in scornful scepticism and idle curiosity?" For his detachment and lack of faith Coverdale indeed suffers the same fate as Theodore does for not saving from her bondage the girl he eventually loves: he relapses into a purposeless life haunted by his lost dream. Zenobia pays for her scorn and impure motives by a gruesome death.

The one person at Blithedale who lacks neither faith nor energy is Hollingsworth. But his faith is not the faith in a regenerate community, and his energy, like that of the Puritan magistrates with whom he is explicitly compared, drives him into a moral blindness of unique opacity. Unlike the dilettantish triflers, he is in deadly earnest, and he is a true builder rather than a dreamer of schemes. What he seeks to build, however, is not a regenerate community but an enduring edifice for the treatment of criminals. His monomaniacal preoccupation with crime is the nineteenth-century equivalent of

the Puritan absorption with sin. If Coverdale testifies to the ineffectuality of nineteenth-century American idealism, Hollingsworth
remains a permanently frightening symbol of what happens to a
visionary scheme when it is geared to an individual's ruthless egotism and overwhelming energy. As Hawthorne insists in several
places, Hollingsworth's plan of criminal reform was motivated by
an initially noble impulse. But he has fallen into the reformer's
occupational disease of monomania—a danger which Emerson
noted in "New England Reformers": "Do not be so vain of your
one objection. Do you think there is only one? Alas! my good
friend, there is no part of society or of life better than any other
part." Hawthorne, a true visionary of the hopeful American years,
had the same objection to reformist zeal; and Hollingsworth's
scheme becomes truly criminal when, in pursuit of its success, he
subverts the nobler purpose of total regeneration embodied in the
Blithedale community, destroying in the process also the faith and
happiness of its other members. The key chapter for understanding
the developments which lead eventually to the failure of the community, is the one appropriately entitled "A Crisis." It is here that
Hollingsworth repudiates the communitarian idea, and we realize
how he has used the experiment as a covert base for his own
operations. He has made arrangements with Zenobia, on morally
dubious grounds, for the financial support of his reformist enterprise. Nor is he prepared to accept Coverdale's suggestion that he
reveal his design to the other members of the community. On the
contrary, he invites Coverdale, too, to become his collaborator and
join in the subversion of the Blithedale experiment. "And have you
no regrets," Coverdale inquires, "in overthrowing this fair system of
our new life, which has been planned so deeply, and is now beginning to flourish so hopefully around us? How beautiful it is, and, so
far as we can yet see, how practicable! The ages have waited for us,
and here we are, the very first that have essayed to carry on our
mortal existence in love and mutual help! Hollingsworth, I would be
loath to take the ruin of this enterprise upon my conscience." To
which the indomitable man replies: "Then let it rest wholly upon
mine!" When Coverdale refuses to join him finally, rather than
tolerate a friend who does not share his own fanatical purpose,
Hollingsworth repudiates the bond of personal friendship too.

This man of iron thus possesses all those attributes that Hawthorne had enumerated in *The Seven Gables* as constituting the
essential moral continuity between the Puritan of the seventeenth
century and his descendant of the nineteenth. Like the members of
that persistent clan, he is brutal in personal relations and dishonest
in public ones, "laying his purposes deep, and following them out
with an inveteracy of pursuit that knew neither rest nor conscience;

trampling on the weak, and, when essential to his ends, doing his
utmost to beat down the strong." His altruistic professions notwithstanding, Hollingsworth reveals in himself finally the same egotism,
selfish principle, or ruthless individualism which the Blithedalean
visionaries identified as the "common evil" of the established system. In *The Seven Gables* Hawthorne had said that the truth about
a public man is often best discovered in a woman's view of him, and
in *Blithedale* it is indeed a disillusioned Zenobia who gives utterance
to the moral obliquity of Hollingsworth's character. "It is all self!"
she declares in one of the climaxial scenes of the novel. "Nothing
else; nothing but self, self, self! The fiend, I doubt not, has made his
choicest mirth of you these seven years past, and especially in the
mad summer which we have spent together. I see it now! I am
awake, disenchanted, disenthralled! Self, self, self!"

Thus at Blithedale, too, instead of brotherhood there is selfhood,
instead of faith there is skepticism, and instead of love there is fresh
antagonism. It is not that, as Coverdale puts it, the Blithedaleans
stand in a position of "new hostility, rather than new brotherhood"
with regard to the society at large; because, as Coverdale himself
adds, this could not fail to be the case so long as they were in "so
pitiful a minority." Their estrangement from society is inevitable in
"proportion with the strictness of our mutual bond among ourselves." The criticism of the Blithedale community therefore lies not
in its hostile relation to the surrounding social system but rather in
the absence of the promised bond within itself and in the divergence
between its theory of mutual sympathy on the one hand and its
reality of fresh antagonisms and mutual suspicions on the other.

* * *

LEO B. LEVY

The Blithedale Romance: Hawthorne's "Voyage Through Chaos"†

The historical consciousness that determines the vision of past,
present, and future in *The Scarlet Letter* and *The House of the
Seven Gables* takes a sociological form in Hawthorne's third romance: the focus is now upon the uncertain and shifting character
of contemporary society. In the account of the performance of the
Veiled Lady with which *The Blithedale Romance* begins, Hawthorne
identifies the contending social forces that have brought his fictional
utopia into being: first, the picturesque, associated with a dying

† From *Studies in Romanticism*, 8 (1968), 1–15.

agrarian order; and second, the utilitarian character of science, foreshadowing the appearance of an urban and technological age. The characters and themes of the work may be understood as the sum of the conflicts generated by these forces.

As the story opens, Coverdale is preparing to leave for Blithedale the next day. Old Moodie has stopped him in the street as he returns to his apartments, but he is preoccupied with contrasting the "wonderful exhibition" of hypnotism that he has just witnessed with the style of such demonstrations in an earlier period. Musing over the question of whether he has been confronted with "the birth of a new science, or the revival of an old humbug," he observes that "the exhibitor affects the simplicity and openness of scientific experiment," whereas formerly the mesmerist's aim was to cultivate "the strongest attitude of opposition to ordinary facts." His intention was to meet the requirements of "picturesque disposition," defined as the use of "all the arts of mysterious arrangement . . . and artistically contrasted light and shade." But now the picturesque has become obsolescent. In following the new fashion, the mesmerist, "even if he profess to tread a step or two across the boundaries of the spiritual world, yet carries with him the laws of our actual life, and extends them over his preternatural conquests." A style based upon the model of empirical investigation has replaced the picturesque, which, according to Coverdale, began its gradual decline "twelve or fifteen years ago."

The scientific innovations upon which the hypnotist draws are only a partial expression of continuing changes that affect the whole population. The character of the audience, "all looking rather suburban than rural," noted at the second appearance of the Veiled Lady, leads Coverdale to remark that "in these days there is absolutely no rusticity, except when the actual labor of the soil leaves its earth-mould on the person." The extinction of predominantly rural America at the moment of its proposed revival at Blithedale threatens all traditional ties and institutions. Coverdale is appalled by the state of affairs, prophesied by a man in blue spectacles, that may prevail in the new age:

> At the bidding of one of these wizards, the maiden, with her lover's kiss still burning on her lips, would turn from him with icy indifference; the newly-made widow would dig up her buried heart out of her young husband's grave before the sods had taken root upon it; a mother, with her babe's milk in her bosom, would thrust away her child. Human character was but soft wax in his hands; and guilt, or virtue, only the forms into which he should see fit to mould it. The religious sentiment was a flame which he could blow up with his breath, or a spark that he could utterly extinguish. It is unutterable, the horror and disgust with which I lis-

tened, and saw that, if these things were to be believed, the individual soul was virtually annihilated, and all that is sweet and pure in our present life debased. . . . But I would have perished on the spot, sooner than believe it.

The wizard, representative of the dehumanizing force of a mechanized society, resembles Coverdale himself, whose pious tribute to the "sweet and pure" and whose protested disbelief do not conceal the fact that he is part of the process from which he shrinks. Analytic and manipulative, Coverdale stands mid way between the old and the new, impersonally examining the souls of his friends, ready to judge by conventional standards but acutely conscious of the changes of which he is himself a symptom.

In the hotel room to which he retreats after leaving Blithedale, Coverdale puts the utopian venture in the context of rapid and sweeping change: "True," he says, "if you look at it in one way, it had been only a summer in the country. But, considered in a profounder relation, it was part of another age, a different state of society, a segment of an existence peculiar in its aims and methods, a leaf of some mysterious volume interpolated into the current history which time was writing off." The historical processes that have shaped his destiny and that of the community are here recognized as steps in a continuing sequence, suggesting that Hawthorne, often criticized for not having produced a transcription of the life he knew at Brook Farm, was keenly aware of the forces that shaped the utopian movement. If *The Blithedale Romance* is not a documentary novel, it is a transparency through which the making of Brook Farm may be seen. It reflects a profound grasp of the central motivation of that enterprise—a desire to escape an encroaching technological and urban revolution and to preserve the agrarian ideal of an earlier America. It is more than a rejection of the utopian vision: its theme—that the human heart cannot know itself well enough to enter the kingdom of heaven on earth—applies with equal force in Hawthorne's other writings to the general condition of man. With this in mind, one can without difficulty recognize the utopian community of the novel as a microcosm of the society in which Hawthorne lived and wrote.

The romance builds upon the paradox of a future based upon the restoration of a simpler mode of life, derived from the values of an earlier period. The country corresponds to the past, the city to the present and the future. Eliot's pulpit, the scene of the terrible break between Hollingsworth and Zenobia, remains the uncultivated tract where the Apostle Eliot preached to the Indians two centuries before. The sternness of the Puritan age, mitigated by after-growths that soften the wilderness, persists in Hollingsworth's zeal and Coverdale's fantasy of condemning to the stake those who have failed to confide in him. Reading the radical prophets of his day, Coverdale imagines their voices mingling with those coming out of the ruins of the past. He half seriously proposes to Hollingsworth that they set about creating the legend and myth that will lend historical dignity to their project; he yearns for the new, but also for a society grown old, in which creeping plants will cover the cottages, moss gather on the walls, and trees cover them with shadow.

This double awareness appears again as he weighs the claims of country and town: he thinks of himself as "a traveller, long sojourning in remote regions, and at length sitting down amid customs once familiar." These "customs" flood in upon him in the sounds from the hotel and from the pavement below. He hears the music of a military band, the ringing of fire bells, and the applause of spectators at a nearby exhibition of a mechanical diorama, all of which he finds as welcome "as the sighing of the breeze among the birch-trees that over-shadowed Eliot's pulpit." He submits to "the entangled life of many men together, sordid as it was, and empty of the beautiful" —a prospect that competes with his "taste for solitude and natural scenery." Under pressure of these alternatives, his sensations resolve themselves into a state in which "there was a newness and an oldness oddly combining themselves into one impression."

His involvement in the old is seen in the pleasure he takes in the practice of picturesque painters and tourists who try to gain access to nature by taking her off guard. As .he works in the fields, he discerns "a richer picturesqueness in the visible scene of earth and sky. There was, at such moments, a novelty, an unwonted aspect, on the face of Nature, as if she had been taken by surprise and seen at unawares, with no opportunity to put off her real look, and assume the mask with which she mysteriously hides herself from mortals." But this point of view is little more than one of Coverdale's amusements: it is framed by the labor he detests, as becomes evident when he cites the romantic stereotype of which the picturesque exercise is a part: "Each stroke of the hoe was to uncover some aromatic root of wisdom." He then expresses Hawthorne's own complaint that intellectual activity is incompatible with manual labor—a direct contravention of the commonly voiced creed of the Brook Farmers.

As he enters the visual world of Old Moodie, the grandee turned pauper, Coverdale resorts to the commonplace that the picturesque is all but inaccessible to the confirmed city dweller. He supposes that Moodie sees through a blackened glass that deprives the landscape of life, and he recreates the beautiful scene that the old man cannot see—the circling Charles river, capes and headlands against a level meadow, a woodland penetrated by showers of light and rising heat-vapor—a perfect picturesque painting. Imagery of this kind also invests the utopian experiment with foreboding at the first gathering of the members. The wood-fire in the parlor of the farmhouse is described as a "genial glow" reduced to "the merest phosphoric glimmer, like that which exudes, rather than shines, from damp fragments of decayed trees, deluding the benighted wanderer through a forest." Thus "Paradise anew" begins in the setting of a "chill mockery of fire."

Hawthorne is unique among American practitioners of picturesque art in this inversion of the values which for others—Cooper, Bryant, Emerson, and Thoreau among them[1]—were entirely honorific. But he resembles these writers in his alignment of spatial values: the city is visualized in claustrophobic images, as in the oppression of closed rooms and neighboring tenements associated with Priscilla. The limitless space and endless sky at Blithedale terrify her. Coverdale also moves uneasily against the countryside, converting open space into the protection and concealment of his tree-top hermitage, which he declares is the symbol of his individuality. Hawthorne implies that the boundlessness of the country is the visual counterpart of the openness and self-surrender demanded by the utopian community—a demand which Coverdale, and the others, cannot meet. The masses of foliage and the secluded chamber formed by the decay of pine-branches help him keep himself intact. This vantage point, a "perfect nest for Robinson Crusoe or King Charles," suggests the two extremes of individualism, one adventurously triumphant and the other pathetically destroyed, which urge themselves upon Coverdale. His precarious identity is a consequence of a style of life that only a metropolitan environment could sustain.

Part of the dream of the Brook Farmers was that the advantages of urban culture could be united with those of the country; Coverdale is the refutation of this hope. Minor poet, bachelor, dilettante, he is free, but also discontented. He can choose among many persons, but he lacks close ties. He can advance himself as a man of letters, but his achievements as a poet do not bulk large. He is intellectual but without an allegiance that releases him from the triviality of his existence. He is a new kind of individual, lacking the security and the relation to Europe that Cooper described in such works as *Home As Found*—a man alone in Boston in a time when flight across the ocean seemed less meaningful than flight into the countryside.

1. James Fenimore Cooper (1789–1851), author of such novels as *The Deerslayer* (1851) and *The Last of the Mohicans* (1826); William Cullen Bryant (1794–1878), romantic poet, author of, for example, "Thanatopsis" (1817); Ralph Waldo Emerson (1803–82), essayist and sage of American Transcendentalism, author of *Nature* (1836) and "Self-Reliance" (1841); Henry David Thoreau (1817–62), in his own words, "a mystic, a transcendentalist, and a natural philosopher," author of *Walden* (1854). [*Editors.*]

He is the displaced person whom Richard Poirier has identified as "an example of the particular kind of sensibility that was to find fuller expression in those crucial years 1890–1914 when modern literature had its birth."[2] In noting that *The Blithedale Romance* reflects a "conscious confusion of Emersonian images with conflicting images and tones of social dandyism" (p. 116), Poirier implies that the social dislocations behind the book place rural and urban America in conflict. "Dandyism" is perhaps too specialized a term to describe Coverdale his aestheticism resembles the early romantic pattern, he is not hostile to middle-class values, and his alienation has not produced in him the aristocratic mannerisms of the dandy. There is no doubt, however, that he is a focal point of currents in American life that had not previously found fictional expression.

In turning the values of the pastoral into an instrument for the exposure of the folly and pretenses of the colonists, Hawthorne combines the picturesque as a synonym of the natural with the pastoralism that reaches him through Spenser, Shakespeare, Milton, and Goldsmith[3]—to mention only those writers upon whom he obviously draws. Through these conventions he projects the chief difficulty that confronts Coverdale and his other characters—their confusion of the natural and the artificial, and of the spontaneous and the premeditated. The ruling metaphor of the masque—of deception, concealment, of play-acting as a dissimulation of selfishness, egotism, and passion—derives from the self-consciousness of citydwellers assuming a literary attitude toward the country. This perspective had its roots in actuality: conditions at Brook Farm as Hawthorne observed them coincided with the requirements of romance, "offering an available foothold between fiction and reality" and providing the "atmosphere of strange enchantment" which the romancer in America would otherwise have to invent. The truth of this peculiar circumstance is confirmed in the memoirs of the participants: the theatricals, charades, and tableaux of the romance had their counterparts at Roxbury.[4]

2. *A World Elsewhere: The Place of Style in American Literature* (New York, 1966), p. 115.
3. Using shepherds or country folk as characters and an idyllic rural life as setting, these authors presented sophisticated comments on society and the condition of man: Edmund Spenser (1552–99), English poet in, for example, *The Shephearde's Calendar* (1579); William Shakespeare (1564–1616), English dramatist and poet, in *As You Like It* (c. 1600); John Milton (1608–74), English poet and pamphleteer, in *Lycidas* (1637); Oliver Goldsmith (c. 1730–74), English dramatist, novelist, poet, and essayist, in *The Deserted Village* (1769) and *The Vicar of Wakefield* (1766). [*Editors.*]

4. George W. Curtis, to whom Hawthorne pays tribute in his preface, appeared on one occasion as Fanny Ellsler "in a low-necked, short-sleeved, book-muslin dress and a tiny ruffled apron, making courtesies and pirouetting down the path." At a fancy-dress ball in the parlor of the Pilgrim House in midwinter, "the Shaws and the Russels . . . came attired as priests and dervishes. The beautiful Anna Shaw was superb as a portly Turk. . . . George W. Curtis as Hamlet, led the quadrille with Carrie Shaw as a Greek girl" (*Early Letters of George William Curtis to John S. Dwight*, ed. George Willis Cooke [New York and London, 1898], p. 17). Cooke is quoting from Mrs. Georgiana Bruce Kirby's

When Zenobia is imagined in "the garb of Eden," Coverdale and Westervelt meet in the forest of Arden, or tired laborers strike the attitude of "Goldsmith's old folks under the village thorn-tree," Hawthorne is in effect quoting from the literature of the pastoral just as Eliot or Pound cite literary fragments in order to pose an incongruity of past and present.[5] Three modes of dress symbolize a progression from the opulence of the seventeenth-century masque to picturesque raggedness and thence to the genre realism of the authentic American farmer: in the absence of "beribboned doublets, silk breeches and stockings, and slippers fastened with artificial roses," the members of the community resemble "a gang of beggars, or banditti," until this attire is replaced by "honest home-spun and linsey-woolsey." This modulation from playfulness to earnestness suggests, however faintly, the possibility of success at Blithedale. Recovering from his illness, Coverdale declares that he has nothing to do in life, "that I know of, unless to make pretty verses, and play a part, with Zenobia and the rest of the amateurs, in our pastoral"; but later when he returns from Boston on a beautiful fall day he thinks of the farm as the home where he might be buried. Grown-up men and women "making a play-day of the years that were given us to live in" become competent yeomen, and poetical Arcadians are transformed into a "little army of saints and martyrs." These alternatives, however are unequal; it cannot be said that Coverdale's desire for "a true and available mode of life" balances the pleasure he takes in turning the spectacle he watches into the stage of his private theater.

The make-believe of pastoralism as a deliberately chosen simplification is entirely of the surface. Its dangers appear as the jollity of Comus and his crew in the woods is succeeded by the ominous tableau of Hollingsworth as Puritan magistrate, Zenobia as sorceress, and Priscilla her pale victim in an "inquest of life and death in a case of witch-craft." Zenobia's suicide, the sequel to this episode, is partly the result of her acquiescence in the image of the wronged village girl upon which she seizes in order to dramatize her rejection by Hollingsworth. She yields to the idea of a pathetic and romantic end in response to the pictures she has seen "of drowned persons in lithe and graceful attitudes." Sensitive to the absurdity of the masquerades in which she has played a part, she is nevertheless drawn to the pathos of the ruined girl who dies for love. There is

---

Years of Experience. Similar episodes in the daily life of the farm are described by Marianne Dwight in *Letters from Brook Farm 1844–1847*, ed. Amy L. Reed (Poughkeepsie, N.Y., 1928).

5. Ezra Pound (1885–1972), American poet and critic, author of the *Cantos*, an intricate tapestry of allusions and quotations from hundreds of literary works; Thomas Stearns Eliot (1888–1965), American-born British poet and essayist, author of *The Waste Land* (1922), a complex mosaic of allusions and quotations. [*Editors.*]

point in Westervelt's bitterness over this waste, for Zenobia was neither the betrayed maiden nor the accomplished lady, but a victim of the conflict between urban and rural possibilities, neither of which permitted her to know or to judge correctly her own feelings. In her grotesque death, every miscalculation of this woman of the future is measured; her visions of the revised status of her sex in a new society, expressed in her boldness and personal freedom, are savagely defeated.

Philip Rahv has found something vindictive in the destruction of this passionate woman, and Irving Howe has explored the connection between her sexuality and the political implications of *The Blithedale Romance*, observing that in her Hawthorne recognizes "the threat to traditional modes of life which the others merely talk about."[6] But this romance is less a defense of traditional society than an account of its collapse; the power of Zenobia's love is so great that it tears apart the fabric of pretension that holds the community together. Hawthorne's well-known hostility to the feminist cause is less significant than the natural force that he attributes to her. The celebrated flower that she wears is the exotic emblem of her sexual vitality. In one scene she casts the wilting flower to the floor, "as unconcernedly as a village girl would throw away a faded violet." In this context the rural image defines the genuine simplicity of which she is capable; its import is expanded in the observation that "it would still more have befitted the bounteous nature of this beautiful woman to scatter fresh flowers from her hand, and to revive faded ones by her touch." Her intimacy with nature contains the hint of mythological or magical powers greater than those worshipped by the Blithedale farmers in their devotion to the soil. In this sense, Zenobia's potentialities cannot be assimilated to the demands of either the old or the new order, and she remains the victim of both.

If we read Hawthorne's first three romances in sequence, the impression is unmistakable that in *The Blithedale Romance* he has discovered a new territory. The gloomy moralizing and manipulation of Gothic effects of earlier work have given way to a lightness of tone and an analytic detachment that suggest a new mode of fictional discourse—a mode evolved in order to come to terms with the quality of contemporary life. From this point of view, Hollingsworth is an anachronism, a continuation of the practice of tracing a cycle of moral development or disintegration in abstract terms that border on the allegorical. Hawthorne declines to present in human terms what he calls "the process by which godlike benevolence has been debased into all-devouring egotism." His analysis of the "overruling purpose" that guides such persons puts the problem outside

6. *Politics and the Novel* (New York, 1957), p. 171.

the limit within which the novelist can assign causes and effects: "it does not so much impel them from without, nor even operate as a motive power within, but grows incorporate with all that they think and feel, and finally converts them into little else save that one principle." This view suggests a universal moral disorder, beyond psychological or sociological analysis, as if Hollingsworth were unaffected by the competing forces at work in Coverdale, Zenobia, and (as we shall see) Priscilla. But certain inferences, which Hawthorne does not draw, seem inescapable: one critic finds that Hollingsworth has "the moral attributes of a civilization founded on iron and steel,"[7] noting that he is described as "a steel engine" and suggesting that his occupation of blacksmith reinforces this identity. It is unlikely, however, that his trade is intended to identify him with industrial rather than agrarian values; more fundamental are the ideas to which he falls prey, which reach him from the intellectual centers of a civilization in turmoil. It is not his benevolence that is fraudulent, but "philanthropy" as a specifically modern remedy for the ills of that civilization.

Thus Hollingsworth sacrifices Zenobia, Priscilla, and his friendship with Coverdale to his grand obsession, his project for the reformation of criminals. Like Zenobia and Priscilla, he is undermined by the confusion of the roles thrust upon him: in addition to the kindly man and the obsessed schemer, he is "the great shaggy, swarthy man" whom Zenobia loves. Ironically, the great force of a mutual attraction cannot survive their divergent reforming ideologies. He is first seen in "his shaggy great-coat all covered with snow, so that he looked quite as much like a polar bear as a modern philanthropist." The absence of "external polish, or mere courtesy of manner"—the urbane accomplishments of Coverdale—prompts Hawthorne to liken him to "a tolerably educated bear." His masculinity, with its connotations of uncouthness and ruggedness, becomes progressively intimidating. He glares "from the thick shrubbery of his meditations like a tiger out of a jungle," and he is pictured as the dragon before whom the people have exposed Priscilla. The ferocity of the bear, the tiger, and the dragon has devoured the tenderness that was once part of his manhood.

Perhaps the most important of his roles is that of the false messiah: he is the "holy and benevolent blacksmith" whom Westervelt characterizes as "a man of iron in more senses than one." He belongs in the familiar Hawthornian tradition of the man of religious vocation betrayed by self-righteousness and zeal. As a member of "our apostolic society, whose mission was to bless mankind," he alone inaugurates the venture with a prayer. He has something of the appearance of an Old Testament prophet, "decidedly marked

---

7. Charles L. Sanford, *The Quest for Paradise* (Urbana, Ill., 1961), p. 183.

out by a light of transfiguration." Coverdale informs him that it is his vocation to be a priest, and that his tenderness is "the reflection of God's own love." His readiness for martyrdom is pronounced. If Westervelt is the prophet of the emerging science of a secular age, Hollingsworth represents the infection of the religious impulses by the persuasive force of the idea of progress.

Priscilla is the most complex expression in religious terms of the crisis to which the utopian movement was a response. Conventionally, she has been regarded as "the symbol of faith, which pierces intuitively to spiritual truth,"[8] but this is at best a partial view. Zenobia tells Hollingsworth that God was striving to redeem him through Priscilla, but he marries Priscilla cynically, for her money, and since her love for him is not accompanied by an understanding of his sins, she cannot become the instrument of his redemption. She is a guardian, not a religious guide. Hawthorne is explicit on this point: "protective" and "watchful," displaying toward her ward "a deep, submissive, unquestioning reverence," Priscilla believes that Hollingsworth is without a fault. The most dreadful irony of the story is that Hollingsworth—weak, self-distrustful, childishly dependent, in need of help if he is to find expiation—has for a life-long companion a woman who offers him only blind adoration. Like all of Hawthorne's spirit-maidens, she is clinging, frail, beyond reproach. She may be "the pure heart" and the "moral touchstone"[9] of the book, but she is unable to articulate these values, either verbally or through her presence.

She is a Cinderella figure, living in abject poverty and nourishing the vision of a glamorous world symbolized by a beautiful sister whom she has never seen. Her intense desire to enter vicariously into this world is apparently conducive to the development of her sibylline attributes—she sees hidden things and hears voices in the silence; she talks "of distant places, and splendid rooms, as if she had just left them." She lives in the midst of an uncomprehending generation of immigrants among the ruins of the past: twenty Irishmen now sleep in the great reception room of the mansion of an old colonial governor. This once magnificent structure is a shambles of tattered hangings, a cracked marble hearth, a mantelpiece despoiled of its rich carving, and a stuccoed ceiling marred by ugly laths. The dignified past and the Boston slums intermingle; the swarming progeny of Irish matrons represent the squalor that has overtaken the older part of the city and its wretched inhabitants. A "pale, western child," Priscilla is mocked by the Irish women; she is the strange "ghost-child" who they believe can make herself invisible at will. Her gift of second-sight and prophecy is despised, Hawthorne

8. Richard H. Fogle, *Hawthorne's Fiction: The Light and the Dark*, revised ed. (Norman, Okla., 1964), p. 188.
9. Fogle, p. 188.

explains, because "modern scepticism" has destroyed the possibility of faith, and science, through its "empirical professors," has claimed the supernatural for its own. The new age exploits this modern-day sibyl; Westervelt, learning of Priscilla's talents, calls at her dingy dwelling to take advantage of her "lack of earthly substance to subject her to himself, as his familiar spirit."

Hawthorne remains ambiguous about the precise nature of her enslavement, though he declares that she "was enthralled in an intolerable bondage, from which she must either free herself or perish." Her actual performance as the Veiled Lady demonstrates only an immunity to deafening noise, and her powers of levitation depend upon wires attached to her chair. We know only that her danger derives from Westervelt's "cold and dead materialism." Since he is also a spokesman "of a new era that was dawning upon the world," in which the present and the future will become "one great, mutually conscious brotherhood," it is impossible to separate his sinister activities from the idealism of the Blithedale group. Priscilla is the medium through which he transmits the quintessential concept of the idealist—the Absolute, which he has cheapened and corrupted; in a larger sense she is also the medium of the equally suspect motives of Hollingsworth and Zenobia, and of the cold curiosity of Coverdale. Her submissiveness to these influences has a symbolic as well as a psychological interest, as if she were in some sense the church, or the spiritual potentiality of the church, when it becomes the captive institution of a technological age. It is possible, as two recent critics have argued, that Hawthorne may have "originally intended her to represent a fallen or exploited innocence which would eventually be redeemed through the utopian therapeutics of the Blithedale experiment,"[1] though this intention seems to have been finally reversed.

A Priscilla damaged or soiled by her urban origins, whose spiritual gifts have been rendered inoperative by a sordid environment, has led to the proposal that "her strangely cloistered past was spent in the practice of sexual activities of less than a pristine or conventionally wholesome nature."[2] But this conception, and the "discovery" of sexual activity in Priscilla's visit to Coverdale's room, is simply not within Hawthorne's frame of reference. The silk purses that she knits have been a temptation few critics have resisted: Coverdale wonders if the purse she presents to him "were not a symbol of Priscilla's own mystery." Commenting on its delicacy and beauty, he notes the "peculiar excellence . . . in the almost impossibility that any uninitiated person should discover the aperture."

1. Barbara F. Lefcowitz and Allan B. Lefcowitz, "Some Rents in the Veil: New Light on Priscilla and Zenobia in *The* *Blithedale Romance*," *Nineteenth-Century Fiction*, XXI (December, 1966), 268.

2. Lefcowitz, p. 267.

322 · Leo B. Levy

The explicitness of this is bound to startle the reader committed to a
literal understanding of such analogies. What is defined here is her
inaccessibility, which derives from the enigma of an impenetrable
identity. Her being is the collective total of whatever transmits itself
through her. In calling her "the little psychic prostitute," D. H.
Lawrence puts the emphasis where it belongs: her trances cor-
respond to the working of consciousness "without a soul in it."[3] She
is the medium of those who are dead to the soul.

Coverdale first perceives her as an alienated, exiled spirit, "some
desolate kind of creature, doomed to wander about in snowstorms."
At Blithedale, however, she undergoes a metamorphosis which,
though soon arrested, is obviously intended to describe the evolution
of a city girl transported to the country. This change is represented
in flower and plant imagery: in Boston, she is "like a flower-shrub
that had done its best to blossom in too scanty light"; she is remi-
niscent "of plants that one sometimes observes doing their best to
vegetate among the bricks of an enclosed court, where there is
scanty soil, and never any sunshine." Her assimilation to the natural
and the picturesque is rapid; she becomes exuberant, happy, and
wild. Zenobia finds it ridiculous that "she thinks it such a paradise
here, and all of us . . . such angels!" In this benign interlude,
Coverdale observes that she "kept budding and blossoming, and
daily putting on some new charm . . . it seemed as if we could see
Nature shaping out a woman before our very eyes." The prostitute
becomes "perfectly modest, delicate, and virgin-like." Something of
Hawthorne's genuine faith in the curative powers of a natural setting appears in his allegorical portrait of Priscilla as "the very picture of the New England spring."

It is a severely circumscribed faith, however. This development is
abruptly terminated in the drawing room of the Boston boarding
house where Priscilla has been brought with the aid of Zenobia,
who wishes to dispose of her rival for Hollingsworth's affections.
No longer the slum girl or the blossoming country maiden, she
appears in the dazzling radiance of a pure white dress, her innocence now embellished in the fashionable mode of the town. Her
situation is a mockery of the rags-to-riches motif: what appears as a
progression from urban shabbiness and rural naturalness to an entirely new splendor, corresponding to the dreams of her childhood,
conceals a return to servitude. We can only wonder, as Coverdale
does, about Zenobia's motives in "evolving so much loveliness out
of this poor girl." In the unexpected complementary beauty of the
two women their identities seem to converge, as if they were to
exchange places, as indeed they do in their relation to Hollingsworth and to their father's estate. Priscilla's "rescue" by Hollings-

3. *Studies in Classic American Literature* (New York, 1953), pp. 118, 119.

worth deepens her tragedy, and when Coverdale finally declares that *he* is in love with her, we can scarcely believe him, or believe that it matters. In her very different way, Priscilla is no less a scapegoat figure than Billy Budd:[4] both are sacrificial victims to an impossible ideal, and both are incorporated into a *status quo* in which brotherhood and justice remain out of reach of the societies that have used them.

The Blithedale experience turns into what Hawthorne variously describes as a crisis, a vortex, an upheaval, and most tellingly in Zenobia's phrase, "a voyage through chaos." We can be sure that Hawthorne was deeply concerned about the disruptions that turned thousands of people toward such experiments. To the extent that Coverdale is an autobiographical character, he is the measure of Hawthorne's reservations; he is in any case the seismograph upon which every psychological tremor registers, and it is this sensitivity that constitutes his resemblance to the later characters of Henry James. In divining character and motive through the reading of subliminal cues, James's predecessor was not far behind him. In *The Blithedale Romance*, the characters silently and deeply fathom one another; in the drawing room, for example, Coverdale interprets the appearance of the two women as an unverbalized expression of the drastically altered situation he is attempting to understand. His colloquy with Zenobia consists of piecing together fragments of information and of guessing at the unseen from the seen. The smallest change in tone or manners is laden with desperate import, and the scene turns into a struggle for ascendancy between himself and Zenobia. When he fails to reconstruct what has happened, he retires from the field with the consolation of still more intricate speculations ahead.

Hawthorne not only identifies the sensibility upon which James was to build; he traces its origin to the breakdown of familiar modes of life. *The Blithedale Romance* is not a tract on the evils of the factory system or an essay on the decline of a rural society; it proceeds by way of modest observations of large inferential value, as in the notation of Coverdale's view from his hotel room of the people below, "cut out on one identical pattern, like little wooden toy-people of German manufacture." From his window, the roofs of all the buildings appear as one. Perplexed and annoyed, he regrets that he cannot "resolve this combination of human interests into well-defined elements." A sociology of the city, of which Coverdale here perceives the need, awaited *The Bostonians*, but *The Blithedale*

---

4. The title character in a novelette by Herman Melville (1819–91). Billy Budd, though essentially innocent and sympathized with by the captain of his ship and all its crew, is condemned and executed for killing a petty officer on his ship, only to become a legend among the sailors who "instinctively felt that Billy was a sort of man as incapable of mutiny as of wilful murder." [*Editors.*]

Romance is a step in this direction. For such a purpose, Hawthorne saw the value of an internal narrator whose integrity could be doubted precisely because he was as damaged by the conditions he describes as any of the other characters. The whole tone of the romance derives from an abnormal pitch of awareness that is almost Poe-esque, though without Poe's macabre quality.[5] Coverdale's voyeurism is the pathological expression of his acknowledged emptiness and his need to enter into the lives of others through an act of sympathy. His empathic gifts are in inverse ratio to his sense of exclusion. The quickened rhythms of the prose that conveys the quality of his consciousness, the swift transitions from keen perceptions to defensive or malicious reactions, the alternations of genuine involvement and frightened withdrawal, and the conscious triviality of his own emotions—all these shape the recollections of a man who has tried with his friends to cross the bridge from an America they find lacking to a land of dreams. The utopian vision is universal, but in the United States, as this romance demonstrates, it found itself compromised by the difficulty of adapting the values of agrarian life to an advancing industrial order whose outlines Hawthorne perceived with remarkable prescience.

HANS-JOACHIM LANG

The Blithedale Romance: A History of Ideas Approach†
* * *

II

In 1841, Hawthorne joined the Brook Farmers "with hope—a transcendental hope."[1] We need not take seriously the strictly economic interpretation in the standard biography. It is self-contradictory, since Hawthorne had to believe in the idea of Brook Farm in the first place, before he could think his share in the farm to be a good investment. Even worse, we have to reckon with a considerable amount of evasion and distortian, before we can hope to get at the

---

5. Edgar Allan Poe (1809–49) defined his concept of poetic unity as one of mood or emotion, with special emphasis on the beauty of melancholy. In his fiction, his absorption in atmosphere, his personal involvement with the narrator or protagonist, and his breathless evocations often complemented his macabre tendencies, which used old castles, clanking irons, and ghost ships to suggest the horrors of death and decay and to demonstrate that terror was "not of Germany, but of the soul." [Editors.]

† From Literatur und Sprache der Vereinigten Staaten, Hans Helmcke, Klaus Lubbers, and Renate Schmidt-von Bardeleben, eds. (Heidelberg, Germany: Carl Winter, 1969), pp. 88–106. Certain of the author's citations of published material have been expanded by the editors of this Norton Critical Edition; his notes have been renumbered and some have been omitted.
1. B. R. McElderry, "The Transcendental Hawthorne," Midwest Quarterly, 2 (1961), 308–9.

facts. Julian Hawthorne, in his father's biography, devoted only one page out of 950 to Brook Farm, justifying this extraordinary procedure as follows:

> The subject of this community has been so exhaustively and exhaustingly canvassed of late, and it seems to be intrinsically so barren of interest and edification, save only for the eminent names that were at first connected with it, that the present writer has pleasure in passing over it without further remark.[2]

The story of Hawthorne's defeat by the "gold mine" (the dunghill) of Brook Farm is too well known for repetition. We need not assume that he was particularly proud of his defeat. Before we regard Miles Coverdale as a self-portrait of Hawthorne, we should rather interpret it as a sort of self-punishment. For, as Lawrence Hall pointed out,

> it is quite foolish to presume, as critics have, either that Hawthorne felt a negligible interest in the West Roxbury Community as a social trial, or that he remained singularly untouched by the motivation and spirit that vitalized it.[3]

But Hawthorne was proud to have belonged to the community in its first, in, as he called it, its heroic phase, and he regretted its later Fourieristic development as a lapse from grace. Hawthorne gave to reform movements a full measure of his sympathy and a full measure of his sanity. He was not alone in his attempts to strike a balance. In "Montaigne; or, The Skeptic"[4] Emerson wrote:

> The superior mind will find itself equally at odds with the evils of society, and with the projects that are offered to relieve them. The wise skeptic is a bad citizen; no conservative; he sees the selfishness of property, and the drowsiness of institutions. But neither is he fit to work with any democratic party that ever was constituted.... It stands in his mind, that our life in this world is not of quite so easy interpretation as churches and school-books say. He does not wish to take ground against these benevolences, to play the part of the devil's attorney, and blazon every doubt and sneer that darkens the sun from him. But he says, There are doubts.

Hawthorne's friend E. P. Whipple may even have provided the novelist with his central symbol when he wrote on "Stupid Conservatism and Malignant Reform."[5]

2. Julian Hawthorne, *Nathaniel Hawthorne and His Wife*, I (Boston and New York: Houghton Mifflin, 1896), p. 200.
3. Lawrence S. Hall, *Hawthorne: Critic of Society* (New Haven: Yale University Press, 1944), p. 26.
4. Michel Eyquem de Montaigne (1533–93), French philosopher and essayist, whose *Essays* are brilliant examples of the skeptical mind. [*Editors.*]
5. Published in 1849. [*Editors.*]

326 · Hans-Joachim Lang

Intemperance in the advocacy of temperance, illiberality in the advocacy of liberalism, intolerance in sustaining toleration, are now the chief signs of that strange masquerade of the passions which passes with some, who are not by instinct philanthropists, under the name of philanthropy.

Whipple claimed "that the severest trial of philanthropy is to war with selfishness without catching the disease," and found that

> it is curious that a man should claim to be a philanthropist on the ground that he has renounced the first principle of philanthropy, and considers moral power as too valuable a thing to be wasted on the rogues he would still convert.[6]

This is a nearly complete rationale of Hollingsworth. It is only an apparent digression if we speculate why Hawthorne should have chosen the names Holgrave and Hollingsworth for his two radicals, because it will lead us to the investigation of British radicalism at the turn of the century. It is well known that Hawthorne as a novelist aimed at authenticity of names. The arch radical of that time had been Thomas Holcroft, a self-made man and Jack-of-all-Trades, also the author of a "novel of purpose" that must be claimed as a predecessor or even an early specimen of the so-called Newgate Novel.[7] *Memoirs of Bryan Perdue: A Novel* was written against capital punishment for forgery and related crimes, and its hero ejaculates:

> The sacrifice of human victims is not the way to remove offense from the earth, but to create it. . . . [In prison] I was not exposed to the vulgar and odious ribaldry of extreme ignorance, educated in extreme wretchedness! I was surrounded by the enlightened, who gave me instruction, and the humane who stretched out the arm to save me; for mortal was the danger in which I stood! Oh, that criminals might ever more have these advantages! . . . Oh, that the guilty might be sent, like patients afflicted with dangerous disease, to hospitable mansions, that might be humanely constructed for their reception, and their reform![8]

This, of course, is Hollingsworth's master-plan. Whether Hawthorne was familiar with *Memoirs of Bryan Perdue* does not seem to be known, but we are on no uncertain ground with *Things As They Are; or, The Adventures of Caleb Williams* by Holcroft's friend William Godwin. This is one of the great seminal novels of the eighteenth century, with ramifications extending, in America alone.

6. E. P. Whipple, "Stupid Conservatism and Malignant Reform," *Literature and Life* (Boston and New York: Houghton Mifflin, 1888), pp. 323, 332, 334.
7. Keith Hollingsworth, *The Newgate Novel, 1830–1847* (Detroit: Wayne State University Press, 1963), p. 13.

8. *Memoirs of Bryan Perdue* (London, 1805), III, pp. 126–127. Cf. II, pp. 189–190: "The grand plan . . . must be the work of some individual . . . There are heads enough to conceive and perfect the plan, but where is the heart?"

to Hawthorne, Poe, and Melville.[9] It is a story of linked destinies, of the disastrous entanglement caused by the ruling passions of two men who were born to love and revere each other, but were destined to hate and persecution. In pursuit of his ruling passion for "fair fame", Squire Falkland becomes a criminal; unable to withstand his curiosity, his secretary Williams becomes a sharer of the horrible secret, which turns out to be the bane of his life as well. The persecuted Williams fights back and brings Falkland before a court of justice, but the novel ends with a famous *volte face:* Williams reproaches himself with inhumanity:

> Why should my reflections perpetually centre upon myself?— self, an overweening regard to which has been the source of my errors! Falkland, I will think only of thee . . . A nobler spirit lived not among the sons of men. Thy intellectual powers were truly sublime, and thy bosom burned with a godlike ambition. But of what use are talents and sentiments in the corrupt wilderness of human society? It is a rank and rotten soil, from which every finer shrub draws poison as it grows.[1]

The anarchistic philosopher's point is clear: without society and its false ideals (of fair fame) Falkland and Williams would have loved each other. The point begs the question, since Godwin cannot produce his ideal society.[2]

We cannot see the import of Godwin's point for *The Blithedale Romance* unless we regard the novel as resuming the argument of *The Scarlet Letter.* In the place of a highly righteous and repressive society, such as the utopian colony founded by the Massachusetts

9. Burton R. Pollin, *Godwin Criticism: A Synoptic Bibliography* (Toronto: University of Toronto Press, 1967).

1. William Godwin, *Caleb Williams* (London, 1831), p. 451.

2. Hawthorne seems to have taken the idea seriously, for the reflection at the end of *The Scarlet Letter* which scandalized a few reviewers bears at least a family resemblance: "It is a curious subject of observation and inquiry, whether hatred and love be not the same thing at bottom. Each, in its utmost development, supposes a high degree of intimacy and heart-knowledge; each renders one individual dependent for the food of his affections and spiritual life upon another; each leaves the passionate lover, or the no less passionate hater, forlorn and desolate by the withdrawal of his object. Philosophically considered, therefore, the two passions seem essentially the same, except that one happens to be seen in a celestial radiance, and the other in a dusky and lurid glow." American Fourierists harked back to Godwin in their clear-cut distinction between evil society and good humanity; e.g., J. S. Dwight on "Association in its Connection with Education," lecture before the New England Fourier Society, in Boston, February 29, 1844: "The heart tends to Love; which is the enjoyment of Unity. Ignorance is only another name for the mental confusion of losing one's place in the Universal Order. Selfishness and Sin, in the same manner, are only involuntary discord, unwelcome isolation; every one tries to love, tries to work his way somehow, even by his selfishness, to the central heart of things, that he may feel and return its warmth. Yet the blind earnestness of this very effort brings him into conflict with his neighbor. Striving to love him and draw near to him, he finds himself in competition with him; one succeeds by the other's failing. All these individual wills, or natures, born for harmony, and seeking it, but seeking it by private paths that lead to private ends, have only multiplied strife by all their earnestness . . ." Quoted from H. W. Sams, ed., *Autobiography of Brook Farm* (Englewood Cliffs, N.J.: Prentice-Hall, 1958), p. 105.

Bay Puritans, we have a society as permissive as is compatible with verisimilitude. It was at this important juncture that F. O. Matthiessen went astray in *American Renaissance,* censuring as Hawthorne's failure his very intention, namely to keep the community a mere stage, if an appropriate one, for the movements of his four main figures. He did not want "to project individuals against a fully developed society"; he did not want to "bridge the gap between foreground and background." He wanted his characters to react on each other in a—so to speak—chemically pure state.

When *The Scarlet Letter* was published, a reviewer had asked: "Is the French era actually begun in our literature?" Charles Hale, on the other hand, suspected that Hawthorne must be a German at heart.[3] So we had better investigate the German sources of Hawthorne's immoralism. It is not suggested that Hawthorne had actually read the most infamous German novel up to that date, Goethe's *The Elective Affinities,* but he could not possibly have helped to become intimately acquainted with the concept of "elective affinities." Margaret Fuller had courageously defended the novel in *The Dial;* George William Curtis and John Sullivan Dwight knew it; Hawthorne's friend George P. Bradford translated three chapters of it for F. H. Hedge's *The Prose Writers of Germany* (1847).[4] When Bradford reminisced of life on Brook Farm nearly forty years later, he found

> one great charm of the life at first, and indeed long after, . . . in the free and natural intercourse for which it gave opportunity, and in the working of the elective affinities which here had a fuller play; so that although there was a kindly feeling running through the family generally, little groups of friends drawn together into closer relations by taste and sympathy soon declared themselves.[5]

Sophia Ripley, the founder's patient wife, tired of the "intense moods" of undisciplined girls around her, is reported to have said, "I'm sick of the word 'affinity'!" Nobody could possibly have es-

3. A. C. Coxe, "The Writings of Hawthorne," *The Church Review,* 3 (January, 1851), 506. Attacking the "consecration of its own" idea found by Hester in her adultery, the reviewer continued: "We suppose this sort of sentiment must be charged to the doctrines enforced at 'Brook-farm,' although 'Brook-farm' itself could never have been Mr. Hawthorne's home, had not other influences prepared him for such a Bedlam." 510. Charles Hale, "Nathaniel Hawthorne," *To-Day: A Boston Literary Journal,* 2 (September 18, 1852), 177.
4. M. Fuller, "Goethe," *The Dial* (July 1841), 31–34; *Letters of George William Curtis to John Sullivan Dwight,* ed.

G. W. Cooke (New York and London, 1898), p. 249; J. S. Dwight, "Goethe's Autobiography", *The Harbinger* II, 127. On Bradford's translation, cf. Henry A. Pochmann, *German Culture in America. Philosophical and Literary Influences, 1600–1900* (Madison: University of Wisconsin Press, 1957), p. 448: ". . . significant as the only sampling of Goethe's novel available to English readers before Boylan's version of 1854."
5. G. P. Bradford, "Reminiscences of Brook Farm," *Century,* 45 (November, 1892), 142–243. Cf. *The Journals of Ralph Waldo Emerson,* ed. E. W. Emerson and W. E. Forbes (Boston 1909–14), VI, p. 391.

caped it, and Hawthorne himself used it in the story "The Birth-mark," soon after leaving Brook Farm.

Before more evidence piles up, it may be useful to suggest what the concept of "elective affinities" is likely to add to our understanding of Hawthorne's novel. It is in the tragic vein, as is *The Elective Affinities*. The plots work out quite differently, because Coverdale's sins are sins of omission. Whereas in Goethe's novel the affinities among four people have had their full sway, in Hawthorne's plot Coverdale is not bold enough. He imagines Zenobia naked and commits the sin of wicked interpretation of her status as a woman, but he shrinks from the smell of pine smoke in her gruel. Since he fails to become either Priscilla's protector or Zenobia's lover, the two women gravitate towards the strong man Hollingsworth, leaving Coverdale outside and to his meditation that

> it was both sad and dangerous, I whispered to myself, to be in too close affinity with the passions, the errors, and the misfortunes, of individuals who stood within a circle of their own, into which, if I stept at all, it must be as an intruder, and at a peril that I could not estimate.

Much too late Coverdale discovers his love for Priscilla, but the reader, meditating for himself on "elective affinities" and ideal matings of the four main characters, is free to match the two virtual couples in such a way that a "weak" and a "strong" character are brought together—Coverdale and Zenobia, Hollingsworth and Priscilla! The characterizations in the Preface—"the self-concentrated Philanthropist; the high-spirited Woman . . . ; the weakly Maiden . . . ; the Minor Poet . . ."—leave little doubt that Hawthorne very carefully matched his four figures. * * * When Hawthorne had sent his novel to his friend Pike, a Swedenborgian, the latter wrote him on July 17, 1852:

> Almost all the novel-writers I have read, although truthful to nature, go through only some of the strata; but you are the only one who breaks through the hard-pan . . . Love is undoubtedly the deepest, profoundest, of the deep things of man, having its origin in the depths of depths,—the inmost of all the emotions that ever manifest themselves on the surface. . . . In "Blithedale," as in "The Scarlet Letter," you show how such things take place, and open the silent, unseen, internal elements which first set the machinery in motion, which works out results so strange to those who penetrate only to a certain depth in the soul.[6]

It was not just by chance that a Swedenborgian was able to recognize *The Blithedale Romance* as a novel about the passions and about selfhood. Hawthorne brought Goethe and Swedenborg next

6. Julian Hawthorne, I, pp. 444, 445.

to each other in "The Hall of Fantasy."[7] But there is still another name to be mentioned in this connection. Hawthorne studied Charles Fourier when the Brook Farmers had become converts, and once again when he wrote his novel.[8] Here is another area of radical thought to explore, indispensable for an historical understanding of *The Blithedale Romance*.

III

Nobody in our century is likely to connect Goethe, Swedenborg, and Fourier, but for the Brook Farmers they were indeed closely related. John Sullivan Dwight in an article on "Goethe's Autobiography," published in Brook Farm's periodical *The Harbinger*, gave status to the German writer by connecting him with the French seer:

> Unity in Variety was the sentiment at the bottom of all his speculations, all his works of art. This he ever celebrated. In his studies of nature, in his botanical, mineralogical, optical and other investigations, his methods were so much like Fourier's, that one must needs regret that those two great minds, antipodes of each other as they were in some things, did not meet and compare notes. Glimmerings, too, of something like an idea of human Association, of social groupings, in his mystical visions of education, and of a passional philosophy in his "Elective Affinities," flicker across his works. You feel that he had got glimpses of secrets, which he never fully read, or deemed it seasonable to unfold.

Fourier, on the contrary, withheld little of his visions of a better world. As Emerson recalled in "Montaigne; or, The Skeptic,"

> Charles Fourier announced that "the attractions of man are proportioned to his destinies;" in other words, that every desire predicts its own satisfaction. Yet, all experience exhibits the reverse of this. . . .

In Godwin's anarchistic philosophy, individuals living under ideal conditions would order their relations on strictly reasonable and utilitarian grounds—and on duty. Personal affection, at least in the first and more radical version of *Political Justice*,[9] was frowned at. Fourier's happy disclosure opened vistas of harmony unheard of

---

7. " 'Were ever two men of transcendent imagination more unlike?' " Cf. J. S. Dwight "In religion we have Swedenborg; in social economy Fourier; in music Beethoven;" and C. A. Dana: "The chief characteristic of this epoch is, its tendency, everywhere apparent, to unity in universality; and the men in whom this tendency is most fully expressed are Swedenborg, Fourier and Goethe." Both quoted in J. H. Noyes, *History of American Socialisms* (repr. New York, 1961), pp. 546, 548.

8. R. Stewart, ed., *The American Notebooks by Nathaniel Hawthorne* (New Haven: Yale University Press, 1932), pp. 219, 226, 328 n. 556.

9. *An Enquiry Concerning the Principles of Political Justice and Its Influence on General Virtue and Happiness* (1793), by William Godwin (1756–1836), offers a clear anarchic social philosophy for morality and government. [*Editors.*]

and unseen before. In a riot of pre-Darwinian argument from design, he envisioned the reindeer in the cold North as joyfully attracted to the North, destined by God to be so joyfully attracted.

The gospel according to Fourier had two major sides: one dealing with "attractive industry," the other dealing with "passional attractions." American Fourierists protested that they were merely interested in the Frenchman's industrial ideas and that Fourier was their teacher, not their master. The public remained suspicious, and the apostles were not completely ingenuous.[1] Henry James, Jr. said of Brook Farm that

> the relations of the sexes were neither more nor less than what they usually are in American life, excellent; and in such particulars the scheme was thoroughly conservative and irreproachable.[2]

Sexual relations may have been excellent from any point of view, but not quite from that of conventional society, or "civilization," as it was contemptuously called by the Farmers. There is at least one piece of incontrovertible evidence. Marianne Dwight, to whom we owe many of the most revealing letters from Brook Farm, then in her late twenties, wrote to her dear friend Anna Parsons:

> I don't know how I feel about Fred and Mary,—glad and happy when I think of them, and yet not wholly confident. There is al-

1. For broad popular consumption, the doctrine was made to appear particularly conservative: *A Concise Exposition of the Doctrine of Association* . . . By Albert Brisbane (New York, 1843), pp. 9–10. G. Ripley in *The Harbinger* (January 3, 1846): "We trust the public will one day understand, that as advocates of Association, Fourier is not our Master, but our Teacher. . . . With the speculations of Fourier, which are admitted to be of the boldest character, we have no practical concern whatever. They are independent of his views concerning a reform in the relations of commerce and industry; and in no respect, do we hold ourselves responsible for their character," 61. Henry James, Sr. was bolder in his explanations: "No man . . . is justified in proposing an increased liberty in love, unless he at the same time furnish us with a superior social order, or an order which is not based upon the family institution. If like Fourier he can eliminate a social order which is founded upon a harmony of all the primitive sentiments of man, or an entire harmony of the passions, then *with reference to that social condition*, he is not only justified in demanding liberty of love, but he is actually bound to do so. For in an harmonic state of society, every normal passion of the human breast claims a free ultimation, that is, an equal respect with every other

passion. It would accordingly save a vast deal of virtuous vituperation towards Fourier, if men would be willing to observe that he never predicates liberty in love of our present social disorder, but altogether of a divinely, or, what is the same thing, a scientifically organized society, in respect to which he cannot choose but predicate it." *The Harbinger*, VII, 197. James had translated Victor Hennequin's *Love in the Phalanstery*; later on he took part in a three-cornered debate with Stephen Pearl Andrews and Horace Greeley, eventually published by the former as *Love, Marriage, and Divorce, and the Sovereignty of the Individual. A Discussion* . . . (Boston, 1889). In his autobiography, Brisbane admitted to have kept "intuitions and visions" of Fourier to himself when he advocated Association as a practical measure: "I aimed to keep in unity with the state of public feeling, and I carefully avoided launching into those universal conceptions which I knew would pass for visionary if not for positive insanity. . . . I said nothing about marriage . . . Yet, notwithstanding all this precaution, the press and many of the clergy sniffed the danger. . . ." Redelia Brisbane, *Albert Brisbane. A Mental Biography* . . . (Boston, 1893), p. 210.
2. Henry James, *Hawthorne*, Tony Tanner, ed. (London: Aurora, 1967), p. 85.

332 · *Hans-Joachim Lang*

ways in the future so much less of happiness, than is anticipated
by these ecstatic lovers. I cannot think of Fred as married,—and
belonging to any *one*. I don't like to think of myself in the matter
at all, and I ought not, but this is human weakness—and I can't
help fearing, that, for a while at least he must belong less to *me*
than he has done. . . . Why do people foolishly want to marry? I
am getting to think that Fourier is right, and in full harmony
there will be no marriage—at least marriage will be a very different
thing from what it now is.[3]

Fourier and Free Love were connected in public opinion. The
fact that so many sons and daughters of the Puritans assembled
under his solemn brow is in itself a tragicomedy of New England
intellectual history. Hawthorne's mother-in-law was so scandalized
by Fourier that she wrote, "The French have been and are still
corrupt, and have lost all true ideas relative to woman." Her daughter Sophia could explain why:

> Fourier wrote just after the Revolution; and this may account
> somewhat for the monstrous system he proposes, because then the
> people worshipped a naked woman as the Goddess of Reason. . . .
> It is very plain . . . that he had entirely lost his moral sense.[4]

Hawthorne himself was more tolerant, or he would not have reviewed *Typee* the way he did. But Melville himself, when he came
to lecture on "The South Seas" as a grumpy older gentleman, related his meeting with "a pale young man with poetic look, dulcet
voice, and Armenian beard—a disciple of Fourier," asking for information as to the prospects of a community on a South Sea
island, preferably in Typee Valley. The young man is probably
apocryphal, but Melville's answer is to the effect that the Typees
were rather conservative and would be likely to eat an expedition of
people with new-fangled notions.[5]

We need not doubt Hawthorne's whole-hearted contempt for
Fourierism, not because of its advocacy of changes in "the world's
artificial system," but because it went so much against the grain of
his own spirituality. The limits of the real and the ideal had become
somewhat unsettled among the Transcendentalists, and Hawthorne
even had to admonish his bride, when she was tempted to avail
herself of the help of a mesmerist against her persistent headaches:

> I have no faith whatever that people are raised to the seventh
> heaven, or to any heaven at all, or that they gain any insight into
> the mysteries of life beyond death, by means of this strange sci-
> ence. Without distrusting that the phenomena which thou tellest
> me of, and others as remarkable, have realy occurred, I think that

3. Amy L. Reed, ed., *Letters from Brook Farm, 1844–1847, by Marianne Dwight* (Poughkeepsie, N.Y., 1928), pp. 86–87.
4. Julian Hawthorne, I, pp. 267–269.

5. M. M. Sealts, *Melville as Lecturer* (Cambridge, Mass.: Harvard University Press, 1957), p. 171.

they are to be accounted for as the result of a physical and material, not of a spiritual, influence. . . . They are dreams, my love. . . . And what delusion can be more lamentable and mischievous, than to mistake the physical and material for the spiritual? What so miserable as to lose the soul's true, though hidden, knowledge and consciousness of heaven, in the mist of an earth-born vision? . . . Keep thy imagination sane—that is one of the truest conditions of communion with Heaven. . . . Love is the true magnetism. . . .[6]

These persuasions account for Holgrave's winning of Phoebe in *The House of the Seven Gables* and for the figure of Westervelt. They do not account for the whole action, because in *The Blithedale Romance* Hawthorne dealt with all four of what Fourier called the "Affective Passions": Friendship, Love, Ambition, Paternity. All four are frustrated.

The following quotations from Fourier's American disciples prove that Hawthorne was not exaggerating and "Gothicizing" when he introduced "the Veiled Lady-Fauntleroy-Westervelt business" into his novel. When Fourier's birthday was celebrated at Brook Farm, April 7, 1845, according to the report in *The Harbinger*, "the bust of FOURIER in plaster lately received from Paris; his brow wreathed with myrtle," stood at one end of the hall.

At the opposite end of the room hung the banner of Association, composed of the primary colors, and bordered with white, the emblem of Unity. Over the banner a plain tablet of azure was placed, on which the words UNIVERSAL UNITY, were emblazoned in letters of silvery white. The Lyre, intertwined with flowers, as an emblem of harmony, the frame of which was white, and the strings of the seven prismatic colors, corresponding to the scale of the seven spiritual passions, occupied a conspicuous place on one side of the room; and opposite to it an inscription from the New Testament, containing the promise of the blessed Comforter as confirming the hopes which swell with rapture the breasts of those who have faith that Association will fulfil the glorious prophecies of inspiration, and bring down upon earth the kingdom of Heaven. Another tablet was inscribed with the fundamental law of Fourier, *Les Attractions sont proportionelle aux Destinees.* [sic] The tables offered a simple and elegant repast.[7]

Even after the failure of Brook Farm, John Sullivan Dwight continued prophesying on Fourier's Birthday, as in 1849, when he brought the following toast:

"To Joy! to Liberty! to Childhood's Mirth! to Youth's Enthusiasm! to the warm life-thrill of Attraction felt through every fibre of existence! The times are coming—the Harmonic Times of

6. *Love Letters of Nathaniel Hawthorne, 1839–41 and 1841–63* (Chicago, 1907), pp. 63–65.

7. Henry W. Sams, *Autobiography of Brook Farm* (Englewood Cliffs, N.J., 1958), p. 135.

Unity and Love—when the Passions in their purity shall prove themselves divine; when Liberty shall not be license, nor amusement folly; when every faculty, the humblest as the highest, shall find supreme delight in Uses. . . .[8]

And here is Marianne Dwight reporting on the preaching of William Henry Channing. The topic was "devotedness to the cause; the necessity of entire self-surrender."

He compared our work with . . . that of the crusaders. . . . He compared us too with the Quakers, who see God only in the inner light, . . . with the Methodists, who seek to be in a state of rapture in their sacred meetings, whereas we should maintain in daily life, in every deed, on all occasions, a feeling of religious fervor; with the perfectionists, who are, he says, the only sane religious people, as they believe in perfection, and their aim is one with ours. Why should we, how dare we tolerate ourselves or one another in sin?[9]

It was the leader of the perfectionist Oneida community, John Humphrey Noyes, who, in his *History of American Socialisms* (1870), wrote a spiritual history of Brook Farm in a series of quasi-biblical "begats":

"The simple truth is that Brook Farm and the *Harbinger* meant to propagate Fourierism, but succeeded only in propagating Swedenborgianism. . . . Swedenborgianism went deeper into the hearts of the people than the Socialism that introduced it, because it was a *religion*." . . . The entire historical sequence which seems to be established by the facts now before us, may be stated thus: Unitarianism produced Transcendentalism; Transcendentalism produced Brook Farm; Brook Farm married and propagated Fourierism; Fourierism had Swedenborgianism for its religion; and Swedenborgianism led the way to Modern Spiritualism.[1]

This historical sequence can be illustrated by the biographies of leading communitarians turned spiritualists. Albert Brisbane, foremost of American Fourierists, is a case in point. After the attempt to bring down heaven on earth had failed, the temptation to lift the veil and get a glimpse of heaven proved overwhelming. While the Brockton Community of the early 1850's merely experimented with Free Love and "affinities," the Mountain Cove Community had even been founded by rapping spirits. The Mountain Cove Circular predicted:

And he will destroy in this mountain the face of the covering cast over all people, and the veil that is spread over all nations. He will swallow up death in victory.[2]

8. G. W. Cooke, *John Sullivan Dwight. Brook-Farmer, Editor, and Critic of Music* (Boston, 1898), p. 140.
9. *Letters from Brook Farm*, pp. 144–145.

1. *History of American Socialisms*, pp. 538, 550.
2. Ibid., pp. 570–1.

Westervelt, with his prediction of

> a new era that was dawning upon the world; an era that would link
> soul to soul, and the present life to what we call futurity, with a
> closeness that should finally convert both worlds into one great,
> mutually conscious brotherhood.

—Westervelt was no imaginative extravagance on Hawthorne's part,
but a rather muted specimen of the spirit of the times.

It will not do to object that such excrescences had nothing to do
with either Brook Farm or Fourierism. Georgiana Bruce (who had
left Brook Farm in 1845) reported that when she became hypo-
chondriacal and feared she had tuberculosis,

> the fair, slender Maria E. . . . magnetized by Miss Russell, became
> clairvoyante, and one day, when I fancied that I was sliding down,
> going from bad to worse, and my recovery and hold on this world
> becoming precarious, . . .

kindly obliged with a diagnosis and came out with the verdict:

> "You wish for death . . . it is futile. You have much work yet to
> do. You imagine that your lungs are diseased; on the contrary; they
> are remarkably sound. I have examined the tissues minutely. They
> are fitted to withstand much trial. The sensation which disturbs
> you is caused by a slight constriction of the upper part of the
> oesophagus.[3]

Another clairvoyante, Marianne Dwight's friend Anna Parsons,
"read" the character of Fourier by holding a piece of his handwrit-
ing against her forehead. Both Brisbane and Channing were very
pleased with the results. As Marianne wrote her brother Frank,

> Anna says she had many impressions impossible to express in
> language. Of the visible presence of Fourier in the room at the
> time (and he staid some time) she cannot in language give an
> idea,— but says it was real, and her communion with him, by
> question and answer, as real as any communion she has with any
> living person. I doubt not the truth of this. . . .[4]

Fourier himself had been no materialist, as Brisbane described him:

> He accepted the great intuitions of humanity, and among them
> that of immortality, though his conceptions on this subject were
> very different from those generally entertained. . . . He believed
> that around every globe there exists an atmosphere of forces. . . .
> He calls these forces "Aromas." Now, around our globe is an
> aromal world, and when the physical body dies, the soul with its
> nervous body—its aromal body—passes into this aromal region,
> and there lives a life of a much higher order as regards power and

3. Georgiana B. Kirby, *Years of Experi-*   179–80.
ence (New York and London, 1887), pp.   4. *Letters from Brook Farm*, p. 108.

spiritual capacity in all directions. . . . One of the arguments which Fourier offers in support of his theory on the immortality of the soul is that, "Attractions are proportional to Destinies." . . . The attraction of immortality . . . was a fundamental indication to him of the truth of the intuition. Every attraction in man that is normal and original is an indication of his social function and destiny. . . . "The sun is inhabited like the planets, but it is a world of a far superior order. Here the soul enters upon a still higher career; where all the faculties with which it is endowed are called into full play. Then, having gained all the experience and development that is possible in the center of its own system, it is promoted to the rank of Citizen of the Universe, with the privilege of passing from sun to sun and visiting the infinite variety of worlds which the telescope reveals to us."[5]

Can we blame Brisbane that he went out from Fourier's presence

> so deeply impressed with his magnificent vision, that life on earth seemed to me utterly empty. For days after I was possessed with the strongest desire to get away from this world and to be able by some means to participate in that grand, Cosmic life.[6]

IV

With the development of radical thought in mind, one can hardly fail to discover the controlling themes of *The Blithedale Romance*. In Albert Brisbane's *Social Destiny of Man* (1840) we find that

> the Active passional principle in man is also a *full and indivisible Harmony*; capable of vast developments, associations and combinations, commencing with sympathies between individuals, and extending to an association of the entire race on the globe.[7]

Hawthorne, indeed, did commence with relations between individuals in his novel, but he did not arrive at a specious unity of souls flowing into souls. Fourier's "Four Affective Passions" (Friendship, Love, Ambition, Paternity) did not lead to "Passional Harmonies" and to "Unityism," because some of the "Nine Permanent Scourges of Civilization" were still active in Blithedale. "Universal Selfishness" and "Duplicity of Social Action" were easier to eliminate on Brisbane's "Analytical and Synthetical Table of the Passional System" than among the characters of Blithedale, each with his or her own past.[8] Hawthorne set sister against sister, friend against friend. Stressing individual responsibility, he went out of his way to deal out poetic justice, though contemporary critics often found him wanting on this point. Or we may call it dramatic

5. Berthold Brisbane, *Albert Brisbane. A Mental Biography* (Boston, 1893), pp. 187–189. The last quotation is from Fourier, verbatim.
6. Ibid., p. 190.

7. Albert Brisbane, *Social Destiny of Man: or, Association and Reorganization of Industry* (Philadelphia, 1840), p. 208.
8. Ibid., pp. 82, 160.

irony: Coverdale, who had drawn back from Old Moodie when first approached by him, deservedly fails to win the prize, Priscilla. Priscilla, the gentle parasite, ends up with having to support the strong man she merely wanted to cling to. Hollingsworth, who wanted to reform criminals, becomes a sort of criminal himself. A notebook entry of Hawthorne's perhaps not yet connected with the novel reads: "to point out the moral slavery of one who deems himself a freeman."[9] This certainly fits Zenobia's case. She is free to campaign for women's rights, but not free not to fall in love with the shaggy authoritarian monster Hollingsworth. The sexual passion of the "strong" woman and the intellectual passion of the "strong" man, combined with the passivity of the two "weak" characters, make sad havoc of all four lives. Even without a highly repressive society, life is a battle-field.

With the basic themes understood, the development of the action is consistent, swift and powerful; it is not difficult to distinguish, apart from a prologue and an epilogue, five acts of the dramatic movement. Hawthorne advised George William Curtis not to read the novel "as if it had anything to do with Brook Farm (which essentially it has not) but merely for its own story and characters"[1] *The Blithedale Romance* has indeed a much wider frame of reference, but a more intimate knowledge of Brook Farm, especially in its later Fourieristic phase, is helpful. The present occasion was one for revealing the more ludicrous side of these pre-Civil War aspirations; it is only just to add that they had a very noble side as well. That Hawthorne in his time should have equally offended progressives and conservatives was probably inescapable. But it was a pity that Henry James, Jr., the son of a Fourierist and Swedenborgian father, should have had a mind too fine to be violated by an idea, or that he should have set the tone for modern criticism of *The Blithedale Romance*.

PHILIP RAHV

The Dark Lady of Salem†

* * *

[Hawthorne's][1] tales and romances * * * bring to life * * * possibly the most resplendent and erotically forceful woman in American fiction. She dominates all the other characters because she alone

9. *American Notebooks*, p. 97.
1. Quoted in the Introduction to the Centenary Edition of *The Blithedale Romance*, Roy Harvey Pearce, ed. (Columbus: Ohio State University Press, 1964),
p. xxiii.
† From *Partisan Review*, 8 (1941), 362–81.
1. Word in brackets added by the editors of this Norton Critical Edition.

personifies the contrary values that her author attached to experience. Drawn on a scale larger than reality, she is essentially a mythic being, the incarnation of hidden longings and desires, as beautiful, we are repeatedly told, as she is "inexpressibly terrible," a temptress offering the ascetic sons of the puritans the "treasure-trove of a great sin."

We come to know this dark lady under four different names—as Beatrice in the story *Rappaccini's Daughter*, Hester in *The Scarlet Letter*, Zenobia in *The Blithedale Romance*, and Miriam in *The Marble Faun*. Her unity as a character is established by the fact that in each of her four appearances she exhibits the same physical and mental qualities and plays substantially the same role. Hawthorne's description of her is wonderfully expressive in the fullness of its sensual imaginings. He is ingenious in devising occasions for celebrating her beauty, and conversely, for denigrating, albeit in equivocal language, her blonde rival—the dove-like, virginal, snow-white maiden of New England. But the two women stand to each other in the relation of the damned to the saved, so that inevitably the dark lady comes to a bad end while the blonde is awarded all the prizes—husband, love, and absolute exemption from moral guilt.

* * *

Zenobia and Miriam wholly exemplify Hawthorne's bias against the dark lady, a bias which, instead of being supported and objectified by a credible presentation of her misdeeds, is limited in its expression to atmospheric effects, insinuations, and rumors. He wants to destroy the dark lady at the same time that he wants to glorify her; hence his indictment of her is never really driven home. This divided intention cannot but impair the dramatic structures of *The Blithedale Romance* and *The Marble Faun*, and these two narratives are in fact much inferior to *The Scarlet Letter*.

But the *Romance*, with its marvelous sense of place and weather and with its contrasted tableaux of town and country, has a unique appeal of its own. Both James and Lawrence have testified to its attraction. The former speaks of it as "leaving in the memory an impression analogous to that of an April day—an alternation of brightness and shadow, of broken sun-patches and sprinkling clouds." James also thought that in Zenobia Hawthorne made his nearest approach to the complete creation of a character. But this vivid brunette is treated with much less sympathy than Hester—and perhaps the reason is that since she exerts greater sexual power she must needs be subjected to firmer measures of control. At any rate, his attitude to her is markedly more subjective, and this note of subjectivity is one of the charms of the *Romance*, the unfailing charm of the confessional tone and of the personal modulation. The story is told through a narrator by the name of Miles Coverdale, a minor Boston poet in whom one easily discerns many features of the author.

No sooner does Coverdale come upon Zenobia in Blithedale—a Utopian colony inhabited by a "little army of saints and martyrs"— than her beauty moves him to rhapsodic appreciation; he is in a fever of susceptibility, and the very next day a fit of sickness lays him low. His illness and exhaustion render him even more sensitive —morbidly so—to what he calls "Zenobia's sphere." (What a master stroke, this episode of Coverdale's illness, with its suggestions of a rite of passage from one mode of life to another!) Obviously infatuated with her, he is not the man to submit to such a feeling. But what is plainly a psychological detour—analysts would see in it an example of protective displacement—he persuades himself that his real attachment is to Zenobia's half-sister, the mediumistic, shadowy snow-maiden who is the Prissy of the tale. This convenient self-deception permits him to covet Zenobia and to pry into her affairs without in any way committing himself to her—for how could he, a paleface poet with overcharged scruples, make up to a woman who is "passionate, luxurious, lacking simplicity, not deeply refined, incapable of pure and perfect taste"? Moreover, as if to spare him further trouble, both females fall in love not with him but with the fanatical reformer Hollingsworth, who is a mere stick of a character, a travesty as a reformer and even a worse travesty as a lover. The emotional economy of this story is throughout one of displacement. It is evident on every page that the only genuine relationship is that of Coverdale to Zenobia; the rest is mystification. But the whole point of Coverdale's behavior is to avoid involvement. As Zenobia tells him in one of the final bang-up scenes, his real game is "to grope for human emotions in the dark corners of the heart"—strictly in the hearts of other people, to be sure. He plays perfectly the role of the ideal Paul Pry that Hawthorne envisaged for himself in the earlier passages of his journals.

Though vowing that he adores the ethereal Priscilla, Coverdale is nevertheless quite adept at belittling her by means of invidious comparisons that strike home despite their seemingly general reference. Some finicky people, he reflects after his first encounter with Zenobia, might consider her wanting in softness and delicacy, but the truth is that "we find enough of these attributes everywhere; preferable . . . was Zenobia's bloom, health, and vigor, which she possessed in such overflow that a man might well have fallen in love with her for their sake only." And again: "We seldom meet with women nowadays, and in this country, who impress us as being women at all;—their sex fades away and goes for nothing . . . a certain warm and rich characteristic seems to have been refined away out of the feminine system." Finally, in view of these frequent digs at Prissy, there can be no doubt that Westervelt, the villain of the piece, is really speaking for Coverdale when he describes her as "one of those "delicate, young creatures, not uncommon in New England, and whom I suppose to have become what we find them by the gradual refining away of the physical system among your women. Some philosophers choose to glorify this habit of body by terming it spiritual; but in my opinion, it is rather the effect of unwholesome food, bad air, lack of outdoor exercise, and neglect of bathing, on the part of these damsels and their female progenitors, all resulting in a kind of hereditary dyspepsia. Zenobia, with her uncomfortable surplus of vitality, is far the better model of womanhood."

But this "better model of womanhood" commits suicide for want of love, while the obstreperous Hollingsowrth is collared by Prissy and dragged to the altar. The puritan morality of predestination takes its toll as the story closes. Humanity is divided into the damned and the saved, irretrievably so, and never the twain shall meet. Yet the *Romance*, despite its mechanically enforced moral lessons, stands out among Hawthorne's works for its outspokenness and for its bold and free characterization of Coverdale and Zenobia. In its painful doubleness, in its feeling of combined attraction and repulsion, the relationship between these two characters is one of the most meaningful and seminal in American literature. It is intrinsically the relationship between New England and the world, and again the connection with James comes to mind. Zenobia can be understood as an earlier and cruder version of Madame de Vionnet (of *The Ambassadors*), whose worldly motives and passionate nature Lambert Strether finally comes to understand and to accept; and Coverdale, too, is reproduced in James, and not in one type alone. One recognizes his kinship with Strether, who has overcome the obsession with sin and is priming himself to enter forbidden territory, no less than with such a curious figure as the spying, eavesdropping protagonist of *The Sacred Fount*, whose neurotic fear and envy of life find an outlet in a mania of snooping and prying into the lives of his neighbors. In this nameless Jamesian snooper the "peephole" motif reaches its culmination: it has become his medium of existence and his intellectual rationale besides.[2]

2. Two earlier studies of Zenobia as one of Hawthorne's "dark women" are to be found in D. H. Lawrence, *Studies in Classic American Literature* (New York: Thomas Seltzer, 1923), pp. 156–62, and Frederic I. Carpenter, "Puritans Preferred Blondes: The Heroines of Melville and Hawthorne," *New England Quarterly*, 9 (1936), 262–4. [*Editors.*]

BARBARA F. LEFCOWITZ and ALLAN B. LEFCOWITZ

Some Rents in the Veil: New Light on Priscilla and Zenobia†

* * *

I

Critics have almost unanimously accepted Priscilla as a paradigm of innocence and goodness, a personification of pure spirit or of the "blonde principle of purity."[1] Though some, notably Robert Stanton and Virginia Birdsall,[2] have recognized her unconvincing and ambiguous qualities, such deficiencies have generally been attributed to Hawthorne's growing doubts about the possibility of spiritual goodness manifesting itself in a world increasingly marked by skepticism and materialism. From this point of view, it is the exploitative and spiritually bankrupt nature of the moral environment that renders Priscilla inadequate and corruptible, not any *a priori* hesitancy or ambivalence about her intrinsic plausibility.

Contrary to these earlier theories, it is the thesis of this study that Priscilla's ambiguity is not so much an effect as a cause: that is, the novel's suggestion of a pernicious moral climate develops from Hawthorne's ambivalent conceptualization of Priscilla's ontological status as the personification of an unalloyed spiritual good. Despite, or indeed because of, his Puritanical leanings, the delineation of a clear-cut dichotomy between the "white" characterizations of pure good and their antitheses in the dark, seductive, guilty, and eventually defeated heroines like Hester, Beatrice Rappaccini, Zenobia, and Miriam was for Hawthorne an artistic burden fraught with doubts and inconsistencies. How else explain, for instance, his obvious fascination and involvement with the psychological profundities of the dark ladies—that is, prior to the point where he is compelled to reject them—and the superficial, even stereotyped treatment of their virginal counterparts, who become increasingly abstract and

† From *Nineteenth-Century Fiction*, 21 (1966), 263–75. Certain of the authors' references to published material have been expanded by the editors of this Norton Critical Edition; the author's notes have been renumbered and some have been omitted.
1. The phrase was originated, in a somewhat different context, by Frederic I. Carpenter, "Puritans Prefer Blondes: The Heroines of Melville and Hawthorne," *NEQ*, IX (June, 1936), 262. For the monolithic view of Priscilla as a spiritual paradigm, see among others: Harry Levin, *The Power of Blackness* (Cambridge, 1958), pp. 88–89; Morton Cronin, "Hawthorne on Romantic Love and the Status of Women," *PMLA*, LXIX (March, 1954), 89–98; Hyatt Waggoner, *Hawthorne: a Critical Study* (Cambridge, 1955), p. 188.

2. Robert Stanton, "The Trial of Nature: An Analysis of *The Blithedale Romance*," *PMLA*, LXXVI (Dec., 1961), 528–538; Virginia Ogden Birdsall, "Hawthorne's Fair-Haired Maidens: The Fading Light," *PMLA*, LXXV (June, 1960), 250–256.

unreal on the precarious journey from Phoebe through Priscilla to Hilda?[3] In his inability to cope with his white heroines as human characters, subject to the pains and flaws of sensuous existence, it seems that Hawthorne could only assert their anachronistic values by transmuting them from their original material-symbolic context into analogues of pure intellectual theory.

Shift of the white heroine from ambiguous character to monolithic abstraction occurs most dramatically about midway in *The Blithedale Romance*, simultaneously with the growing denigration and eventual rejection of the book's counterheroine, Zenobia—who is herself subjected to a process of abstraction in the opposite direction, though with only limited success. Before we can assess that breakdown, however, we must undertake a full and hitherto unattempted analysis of Priscilla's ontological ambivalence, in terms of both action and symbol, particularly in conjunction with the more overt ambivalence that accompanies Hawthorne's presentation of Zenobia.

Priscilla's most obvious symbolic analogue consists of her elaborately contrived silk purses. As small, closed objects with both aesthetic and utilitarian connotations, the purses encompass at least two symbolic possibilities: covert sexuality and concealed guilt. Indeed, a salient and frequently iterated characteristic of Priscilla is her association with the narrow, the clandestine, and the limited— an association that lies in sharp contrast with Zenobia's open, "outdoor" qualities. Zenobia herself is one of the first to recognize the syndrome:

> Oh, we women judge one another by tokens that escape the obtuseness of masculine perception! . . . Poor thing! She has been stifled with the heat of a salamander stove, in a small, close room.

Coverdale, not exactly a man of the wild, open vision himself, makes a similar observation:

> She had been bred up, no doubt, in some close nook, some inauspiciously sheltered court of the city, where the uttermost rage of a tempest, though it might scatter down the slates of the roof into the bricked area, could not shake the casement of her little room. The sense of vast, undefined space, pressing from the outside against the black panes of our uncurtained windows, was fearful to the poor girl, heretofore accustomed to the narrowness of human limits. . . . A little parallelogram of sky was all that she had hitherto known of nature.

Even her eyes appear as partially closed, though "through [their] narrowed apertures" she can gaze most penetratingly into the eyes

---

3. See Philip Rahv's "The Dark Lady of Salem," page 337 of this book. [*Editors.*]

of others; at other points, she is likened to a bud which hides its mystery behind folded petals, or a heart which is "deep but of small compass." Elsewhere we see her clutching a sealed letter against her bosom "with both hands clasped over it, in a way that had probably grown habitual to her"—a gesture of concealed guilt which, as Roy Male has noted, suggests an interesting comparison with the scarlet letter openly displayed on the bosom of Hester Prynne, who in many respects prefigures the "open" Zenobia as a literary character.[4]

The primary emblematic clue to the nature of the closed, curtained room that constituted Priscilla's pre-Blithedale experience can be found, through analogy, in Coverdale's revealing description of her ubiquitous purses: produced by some mysterious wooden instruments, the purses contain a "peculiar excellence," which "besides the great delicacy and beauty of their manufacture, lay in the almost impossibility that any uninitiated person should discover the aperture; although, to a practised touch, they would open as wide as charity or prodigality might wish. *I wondered if it were not a symbol of Priscilla's own mystery*" (italics added).

Even one who is rightfully cautious about considering literary symbols as if they were the objects of a Freudian treasure hunt cannot help but notice the sexual implications of the purse motif, and while precise delineation of the erotic mysteries concealed by the silk purse is not possible in terms of a one-to-one allegorical proof, certainly there is sufficient evidence in the opening chapters to suggest to the reader that at least part of Priscilla's strangely cloistered past was spent in the practice of sexual activities of less than a pristine or conventionally wholesome nature. These sexual implications are not, however, fully developed in the course of the novel;[5] thus, to state baldly and unequivocally that Priscilla was a prostitute would, of course, be a gross oversimplification of her final ontology. Yet there are a number of hints that Hawthorne either originally intended her to represent a fallen or exploited innocence which would eventually be redeemed through the utopian therapeutics of the Blithedale experiment, or that either consciously or unconsciously he wished to perceive beneath the chaste surface of

4. Roy R. Male, *Hawthorne's Tragic Vision* (Austin, 1957), p. 150.

5. Other critics to recognize the importance of *Blithedale*'s sexual motifs are Robert Emmet Long and Rudolph von Abele. Long, however, interprets them only in the context of a counterforce to the novel's concern with utopianism: "In *The Blithedale Romance*, sexual compulsion is one of the chief countermovements to the aspiration of selflessness and philanthropy; the collapse of Blithedale represents, in part, the deeper place it has in desires than moral earnestness" ("The Society and The Masks: *The Blithedale Romance* and *The Bostonians*," *NCF*, XIX [Sept., 1964], 120). Von Abele notes the symbolic connection between Priscilla's purses and her covert sexuality, but does not explore further implications except to link her concealed passions with Puritanical-Victorian conventionality *(The Death of the Artist* [The Hague, 1955], p. 80).

the fair New England heroine a propensity toward sensual involvement that differed only in appearance and perhaps degree from that of her dark-haired sisters—perhaps in order to rationalize his fascination with the latter, or to underscore the "lurid intermixture" of good and evil that he found elsewhere to mark all that is complex and real in a morally ambiguous universe.

Certainly there is much to suggest a background of prostitution, and likewise to suggest that the whole mesmerism-clairvoyance-veiled lady trope may have been merely a safe Puritanical cover (or veil) for the sinister facts of Priscilla's true past identity. Consider, for example, especially in the light of the purses' sexual implications, that the sly and unsavory Mr. Moodie, Priscilla's putative father, used to sell a "good many" of them, and that like Priscilla he is associated with hidden mysteries and closed spaces. We are told, moreover, that behind the partial mask of his black eye patch he has been seen "lurking in corners or getting behind a door, whenever practicable, and holding out his hand, with some little article in it which he wishes you to buy," a portrait of sinister mercantilism suggestive of more than simply the ravages of an emerging industrialism—suggestive, in fact, of some of its most extreme social concomitants. Furthermore, what of Coverdale's admission that, indeed, he himself was the possessor of one of those bartered purses; that he has, at the start of the novel, just returned from a "wonderful exhibition" of the veiled lady's skills, and that her "sisterhood" has "grown too numerous to attract much individual notice"?

Even more suggestive evidence of Coverdale's possible liaison at some point with a less than innocent Priscilla is intimated in the highly connotative scene where she visits his sick chamber at Blithedale. First Priscilla hands him "an exquisitely wrought night-cap," which in terms of symbolic connotation is analogous with the elaborately embroidered silk purses; her presentation is accompanied by the added comment that the cap is for Coverdale's "use, not beauty," a normally innocent statement made meaningful in the context of the tableau. Later in the same episode Priscilla reluctantly yields to Coverdale the sealed letter which she holds against her bosom, and in the process reminds him of Margaret Fuller—an identification usually associated with the passionate Zenobia, and not with the phlegmatic Priscilla, unless we are to assume that this identification is an adumbration of Zenobia's and Priscilla's role as the dual components of a split character.

Finally, the possibility that Priscilla's past involved some kind of *sub rosa*[6] sexual activities is corroborated by several other pieces of evidence: the frequent allusions to the unhappy—even terrifying—

6. Secret. [*Editors.*]

nature of her past experience;[7] the interesting fact that it is Hollingsworth, the reformer, who brings her to Blithedale (Coverdale wonders whether it is "possible that he might have brought one of his guilty patients, to be wrought upon and restored to spiritual health"); Zenobia's ironic and double-edged comment that Priscilla "is the type of womanhood, such as man has spent centuries in making it"; contemporary associations between the seamstress profession and that of the prostitute or fallen woman;[8] links between mesmerism and sexual exploitation;[9] parallels between the description of Zenobia's boarding house drawing-room and typical parlor houses, or high class bordellos, of the day.[1] Coverdale, one might

7. In "Mythopoesis in *The Blithedale Romance,*" *PMLA,* LXXV (Dec. 1960), 591–596, Peter Murray notes that Priscilla's past involved a state of "captivity in the household of a king of the underworld," p. 594); his analysis tends, however, to over-mythicize—and over-romanticize—what is in reality a social captivity.

8. According to a statistical survey conducted in the 1850's, women in the needle trades (including seamstresses, tailoresses, dressmakers, embroiderers, fur-sewers, etc.) were second only to domestic servants in entering the ranks of prostitution; see William W. Sanger, *History of Prostitution: Its Extent, Causes, and Effects Throughout the World* (New York, 1858), p. 524. Some of the reasons for the high correlation between the two professions can be gauged from Dr. Sanger's comments on the social background of the seamstress at the time: "What is the position of the needle-woman? Far worse than that of the servant. The latter has a home and food in addition to her wages; the former must lodge and keep herself out of earnings which do not much exceed in amount the servant's pay. The labor by which this miserable pittance is earned, so truthfully depicted in the universally known 'Song of the Shirt,' is distressing and enervating to a degree. Working from early dawn to late at night, with trembling fingers, aching head, and very often an empty stomach, the poor seamstress ruins her health to obtain a spare and insufficient living. . . ." (p. 527). Sewing and shop girls also were useful, because of their contact with the fashionable class, as intermediaries in abetting the secret liaisons that took place in clandestine "houses of assignation" (Sanger, pp. 568, 572).

9. Another trope in the novel, Zenobia's acquiescence to Westervelt's use of Priscilla, is a kind of mesmeric prostitution. But only in Chapter 23 does mesmerism directly appear in the action, and then not without sexual overtones:

He cited instances of the miraculous power of one human being over the will and passions of another. . . . At the bidding of one of these wizards, the maiden, with her lover's kiss still burning on her lips, would turn from him with icy indifference; the newly-made widow would dig up her buried heart out of her young husband's grave before the sods had taken root upon it; a mother, with her babe's milk in her bosom, would thrust away her child.

Coverdale seems to recognize the implications of prostitution when he feels constrained to assert that Priscilla "had kept, as I religiously believe, her virgin reserve and sanctity of soul throughout it all."

We might further note that Hawthorne's attitude toward mesmeric phenomena is ambivalent. While he was writing *Blithedale,* more scientific and favorable works about animal magnetism were appearing; see J. W[are], "Animal Magnetism," *Christian Examiner,* LI (Nov., 1851), 395–435. In fact, Hawthorne may be expressing his impatience with the entire problem as well as his plot device when he has Coverdale exclaim after discussing the rumors about Westervelt's necromantic power: "Its nature at that period was even less undersood than now, when miracles of this kind have grown so absolutely stale, that I would gladly, if the truth allowed, dismiss the whole matter from my narrative."

1. Cf. the description of Zenobia's drawing-room and iron-balustraded boarding house with Sanger's description of the typical upper-class "parlor houses" of the 1850's: "The houses in which this class of courtesans reside are furnished with a lavish display of luxury, scarcely in accordance with the dictates of good taste however, and mostly exhibiting a quantity of magnificent furniture crowded together without taste or judgment for the sake of ostentation. The most costly cabinet and upholstery work is freely employed in their decoration, particularly in the rooms used as reception parlors. Large mirrors adorn the walls, which are frequently handsome frescoes and gilt. Paintings and

say Hawthorne, appears to recognize the implications in Priscilla's past when in his hurried and belated summary of her history he finds it necessary to affirm (after she has been etherealized and idealized):

> Except that Priscilla, in those days had no beauty, and, in the languor of her existence, had not yet blossomed into womanhood, there would have been rich food for scandal in these visits. . . . But it must likewise be added, there was something about Priscilla that calumny could not meddle with.

Though Hawthorne did not write an *ur-Sister Carrie*,[2] possibly because of the bowdlerian times and a wife of delicate sensibilities, the suggestions and implications concerning Priscilla are sufficient to open the whole question of her innocence, purity, and status as an analogue of the supposedly immaculate white heroine. Moreover, we must reconsider in the light of Priscilla's latent potentialities the larger problem of Hawthorne's ambivalent attitude toward one of his favorite artistic devices: the juxtaposition of two heroines—one dark, passionate, alien, and mysterious and the other light, virginal, native New England, and, as it turns out, even more mysterious. Did he really believe in the values suggested by the white heroines— the Phoebes, Alice Pyncheons, and Hildas—or was he compelled by certain repressive forces of his psyche to employ these figures, who are, after all, rather conventional variations on a common romantic trope? May they be simply means of assuaging his guilt, or signs that he was unable to break away from the prevailing aesthetic norms of his day? Are they capable of standing as autonomous figures, or are they parts of a split composite character, comprehensible only when reunited with their dark, unrepressed foils?[3]

II

If Priscilla has her Pandora's box, it is Zenobia, however, who is the ostensible Pandora of the story, "fresh from Vulcan's workshop, and full of the celestial warmth by dint of which he had tempered and moulded her." Though on the surface she is completely in apposition with Priscilla—Zenobia is identified with openness and

---

engravings in rich frames, vases and statuettes, add their charms. Carpets of luxurious softness cover the floors, while sofas, ottomans, and easy chairs abound. . . . By means of a small aperture in the front door, covered by a wrought-iron lattice-work, the candidates for admission can be examined before entrance is given. . . ."

2. *Ur*, from the Greek, is a prefix meaning "original"; that is, in *Blithedale* Hawthorne did not write the first story of a "fallen" woman who succeeds despite her questionable past. *Sister Carrie* (1900), by Theodore Dreiser, is the story of a

working girl who becomes the mistress first of a worldly, vulgar salesman and later of a more intelligent and cultured businessman, and whose character and life disintegrate as she rises to success as an actress. [*Editors.*]

3. Murray briefly suggests the possibility that Zenobia and Priscilla are parts of a composite character, but does not carry out the idea beyond identifying them respectively as the Aphrodite and Persephone "aspects of the feminine personality" ("Mythopoesis in *The Blithedale Romance* . . ." p. 593).

availability, overt passion and the outdoors as contrasted with Priscilla's covert, hermetic qualities—in actuality, they seem to be related to one another as the major and minor key of the same melody, or the manifest and latent content of the same dream. For example, though Zenobia's outstanding symbolic prop is the exotic tropical flower she wears in her hair, Priscilla also has her small panoply of flower associations—consisting of pallid blossoms, frail anemones, and—at one point—weeds. Likewise Zenobia has her share of Priscilla-like masks, hidden mysteries, and sealing allusions. Indeed, it is the common attribute of "veiledness" and deception, rather awkwardly corroborated by the fact that they share the same enigmatic family past, which constitutes the "singular anomaly of likeness coexisting with perfect dissimilitude" that Coverdale notes in the sick-chamber scene.

The "dissimilitude" that separates the two women can most readily be discerned in the symbolic apposition of open flower to closed purse. Yet, when it comes to the difficult problem of assessing Hawthorne's value judgment of his characters, the difference appears as one of degree rather than kind—especially when we consider the second, only slightly less apparent means of contrast between Priscilla and Zenobia, the antinomy of tropical flower in full bloom vs. frail, wilted blossoms. If it was Hawthorne's intention or compulsion, spurred by either external or internal moral demands, to set up Zenobia as the dark embodiment of seduction which must be rejected in the end, certainly both her character as it finally appears and her symbolic properties belie any such rigid possibilities. Like Beatrice in "Rappaccini's Daughter," of whom she is in many respects an elaboration, she is deliberately mysterious and enigmatic; if her flower is a *fleur du mal*[4] with magical powers of seduction, a phony trinket, or a "relic" of her guilty past, it is at the same time a token of her natural vitality and passion. Indeed as with the analysis of the manifest content of a dream as opposed to its repressed latent content, Hawthorne seems to be more conscious of Zenobia's paradoxical attributes, considerably more so than he is of the "latent" Priscilla. Obviously Zenobia attracts his sympathies, and at times approaches the status of a true tragic heroine; even if he may have originally desired to restrict her within relatively self-contained allegorical limits, she emerges not as a bloodless caricature of either moral evil or unbridled passion, but like Hester and Miriam contains an ambiguous blend of Transcendentalist self-will and powerful eroticism which causes her always to be poised at the edge of the whirlpool.

As the book progresses, one feels that the entire network of overlapping associations between the heroines is constantly under

4. Flower of evil. [*Editors.*]

threat of dissolution, as if Hawthorne could not make up his mind whether to value the Zenobia perplex of his (ultimately) idealized version of Priscilla, and is at the same time incapable of taking that crucial step further to embrace both possibilities simultaneously, along with their corresponding ambiguities. When the strain finally does cause the whole vision to break down into near-allegory, it is this same inability to maintain the ambivalent frame of reference that not only widens the schism between Priscilla and Zenobia, but weakens both the aesthetic unity and psychological verity of the novel. The break occurs most overtly in that section of the book where the action returns to the city from the pastoral dream world of Blithedale. Beginning with Zenobia's symbolic act of dropping "a white linen curtain between the festoons" of the crimson drapes that grace the windows of the boardinghouse ("It fell like the drop-curtain of a theatre, in the interval between the acts"), Priscilla becomes increasingly ethereal, pallid, and passive, more the flimsy paradigm of some vague principle of floating good, so that we can almost hear the virginal Hilda's doves flying in the distance. At the same time as Priscilla becomes "a leaf floating on the dark current of events" lacking both substance and free will, Hawthorne attempts to contain the character of Zenobia through a similar process of abstraction: "I malevolently beheld the true character of the woman, passionate, luxurious, lacking simplicity, not deeply refined, incapable of pure and perfect taste." However, such efforts to restrict Zenobia to some kind of definite allegorical limits are doomed to fail. Struggling against his attraction to the Byronic titaness.[5] Coverdale notes:

> But, the next instant, she was too powerful for all my opposing struggle. I saw how fit it was that she should make herself as gorgeous as she pleased, and should do a thousand things that would have been ridiculous in the poor, thin, weakly characters of other women. To this day, however, I hardly knew whether I then beheld Zenobia in her truest attitude, or whether that were the truer one in which she had presented herself at Blithedale. In both there was something like the illusion which a great actress flings around her.

While Zenobia may defy attempts at abstraction and allegorization,[6] Priscilla obviously lacks the necessary proteanism—or per-

---

5. The Byronic hero such as appeared in George Gordon, Lord Byron's *Childe Harold's Pilgrimage* (1812–18), a man of loneliness and mystery, disappointed and disillusioned by the world, yet defiantly and passionately heroic. [*Editors.*]
6. Even in death, Zenobia resists attempts at formal containment: if she is finally forced by death into the familiar Haw-

thornian form of a "marble image," the resultant "statue" or aesthetic stasis embodies only the gestures of a violent struggle against that very containment. As Coverdale notes in retrospect: "Were I to describe the perfect horror of the spectacle, the reader might justly reckon it to me for a sin and shame. For more than twelve long years I have borne it in my haps, on a philosophical plane, her gossamer existence can only be sustained if she is transmuted from character to theory, from idiosyncratic individual to idealized allegorical type. With Priscilla etherealized as frail heroine, dressed in pure white and blown about by the tempests of external evil, any hints of a sinister past or latent propensities toward passion and sin (that is, toward full involvement in the human condition) give way to Hawthorne's need to abstract from her a spotless paradigm to corroborate the existence of "good." And with the novel's rich symbolic possibilties simultaneously truncated through allegory, we last see her as the guardian of Hollingsworth and, ironically, as the agent of his conversion from a man of passionate, if monomaniacal, conviction to a mellowed but defeated nonentity. In a book where all the principal figures experience but varying degrees of disenchantment and loss, only Priscilla emerges with some semblance of fulfillment—yet, it is an insubstantial and largely unconvincing triumph of little more than an idealized wish-fulfillment fantasy.

The ultimate nature of the action likewise resists any attempt to claim Priscilla or the "white heroine principle" as really victorious —for even if viewed pragmatically, on a wholly naturalistic level, Hollingsworth's choice of Priscilla is not salutary. Though the facts are underplayed in the narrative, we learn that he actually chose Priscilla not because of any spiritual conviction, but, on the contrary, because of the material fact that she has become the heiress of Zenobia's patrimony:

"I have no concealments," said Hollingsworth.

"We shall see," answered Zenobia. "I would first inquire whether you have supposed me to be wealthy?"

"On that point," observed Hollingsworth, "I have had the opinion which the world holds."

"And I held, likewise," said Zenobia. "Had I not, Heaven is my witness, the knowledge should have been as free to you as me. It is only three days since I knew the strange fact that threatens to make me poor; *and your own acquaintance with it, I suspect, is of at least as old a date.* . . . You are aware, too, of the disposition which I purposed making of the larger portion of my imaginary opulence. [Italics added.]

Immediately afterwards, Zenobia asks Hollingsworth if he loves Priscilla:

---

memory, and could now reproduce it as freshly as if it were still before my eyes. Of all modes of death, methinks it is the ugliest. Her wet garments swathed limbs of terrible inflexibility. *She was the marble image of a death-agony.* Her arms had grown rigid in the act of struggling, and were bent before her with clenched hands; her knees, too, were bent, and— thank God for it!—in the attitude of prayer. Ah, that rigidity! It is impossible to bear the terror of it" (italics added).

"Had you asked me that question a short time since . . . I should have told you—No! My feelings for Priscilla differed little from those of an elder brother, watching tenderly over the gentle sister whom God has given him to protect."

"And what is your answer now?" persisted Zenobia.

The plain implication that he loves Priscilla because she now has Zenobia's wealth is ratified in the next to last chapter, where Coverdale will not allow the matter to rest: "After all the evil that he did, are we to leave him thus, blest with the entire devotion of this one true heart, *and with wealth at his disposal. . . .*" [Italics added.] At the very least, Hollingsworth's decision appears to be motivated by the material, not the spiritual, and as such contradicts the critical disposition to see Priscilla's virtue as victorious. Furthermore, we must take Hollingsworth's final pathetic degeneration as either the consequence of his decision or as a statement of the results attendant upon making Lord Jim's choice: "He goes away from a living woman to celebrate his pitiless wedding with a shadowy ideal of conduct."[7]

In either case, Zenobia's defeat is intolerable because Priscilla's success offers no satisfactory tragic resolution, if as finally conceived she is intended as a counterpoise. Only Coverdale's love could be seen as symbolically the love of the good, and certainly he is not to be trusted either as narrator or as emotional touchstone. He chooses Priscilla not because she is better than Zenobia, but because he too is afraid of Zenobia's power; his choice appears negative rather than positive, and if he has virtue, it is "cloistered and fugitive." Thus Priscilla's charismatic potentialities are severely restricted; though she can "save" the chastened Hollingsworth, she can do nothing to save Zenobia from complete physical and spiritual annihilation, and Coverdale from a life of Prufrockian[8] aridity. As the price of maintaining the reality of good, the result is, at best, a bitter and Pyrrhic victory.[9]

Despite its architectonic failure, which results from Hawthorne's inability to sustain the perilous luxury of ambivalence employed during the first half of the novel, *The Blithedale Romance* is in many respects a profound, compelling, and surprisingly modern work of art. When Hawthorne does, however, start more rigidly to dichotomize his scheme into a morality play, the book degenerates into a strained and foggy quasi-allegory which neither clarifies the early symbolic ambiguity nor grows from the terms of its action.

7. Lord Jim is the title character in a novel (1900) by Joseph Conrad about a young man driven to self-destruction by his inability to fulfill the role he has envisaged for himself. [*Editors.*]

8. In "The Love Song of J. Alfred Prufrock" (1915), T. S. Eliot portrays a lonely, romantic figure whose diffidence and moral timidity exile him from any kind of emotionally vital life. [*Editors.*]

9. A victory won with very heavy losses, such as the victory of Pyrrhus (319–272 B.C.), King of Epirus, over the Romans at Asculum in 279 B.C. [*Editors.*]

NINA BAYM

The Blithedale Romance: A Radical Reading†
* * *

The trip to Blithedale Farm is Coverdale's attempt to find a
purpose. The narration chronicles the failure of his inner exploration. In the opening chapters he undertakes the familiar journey
into the self in search of one's inner core, the struggle to make
contact with the sources of life and energy within and to return to
the surface, refreshed and rejuvenated. In Boston Coverdale enjoys
the "sweet, bewitching, enervating indolence" of a genteel bachelorhood, parcelling out the social days among "my pleasant bachelor-
parlor, sunny and shadowy . . . ; my centre-table, strewn with books
and periodicals; my writing-desk, with a half-finished poem in a
stanza of my own contrivance; my morning lounge at the reading-
room or picture-gallery; my noontide walk along the cheery pavement, with the suggestive succession of human faces, and the brisk
throb of human life, in which I shared; my dinner at the Albion . . . ;
my evening at the billiard-club, the concert, the theatre, or at
somebody's party, if I pleased." This pleasant life lacks vigor; in its
atmosphere of tepid hedonism, art is but another languid pastime.
Coverdale leaves it behind to liberate and test his talent. He wants
to become a poet, "to produce something that shall really deserve to
be called poetry—true, strong, natural, and sweet."

The withdrawal and search are symbolized in two parallel ways,
which may be distinguished as the public and private, or outer and
inner dimensions of Coverdale's quest. The movement from Boston
to Blithedale supplies an outer form for the journey, which is paralleled on the inner stage by a movement from Priscilla, the Veiled
Lady (the Spiritual Ideal: Love and Art in genteel society), to
Zenobia. Boston represents the prison of institutions and conformity.
Leaving the city with other members of the community, Coverdale
notes "how the buildings, on either side, seemed to press too closely
upon us, insomuch that our mighty hearts found barely room
enough to throb between them. The snowfall, too, looked inexpressibly dreary, (I had almost called it dingy,) coming down through
an atmosphere of city-smoke, and alighting on the sidewalk, only to
be moulded into the impress of somebody's patched boot or over-
shoe." And Coverdale draws a fine transcendental moral from his
observations: "thus, the track of an old conventionalism was visible
on what was freshest from the sky."

† From *Journal of English and Germanic Philology*, 67 (1968), 545–69. The author's notes have been renumbered, and some have been expanded or omitted by
the editors of this Norton Critical Edi-
tion.

352 · *Nina Baym*

Blithedale, in contrast, is a radical community which aims, in an atmosphere of informality and innovation, to establish forms of labor and of love which will express and liberate, rather than inhibit and distort, the human spirit. It hopes to restructure human relationships around the principle of "familiar love" and to "lessen the laboring man's great burthen of toil." Life is to be "governed by other than the false and cruel principles, on which human society has all along been based." Coverdale is not deeply interested in the community's economic aims, for as a man of means he feels little tie to the working classes. Yet he recognizes a common interest, since work and leisure are both socially controlled activities. As for the aim of more natural and loving relationships between human beings, Coverdale has his version of that goal as well. The springtime in which Coverdale leaves for Blithedale symbolizes (as has often been noted) the rejuvenating and regenerating purposes of his withdrawal from society, as well as the optimism implicit in his quest. The severe snow he encounters represents the necessary death of the social self prior to spiritual rebirth. He contracts a bad cold, and points out that its severity is directly due to the "hot-house warmth of a town-residence and the luxurious life in which I indulged myself."[1] Recovering, he rejoins the community on May Day, exulting in the belief that he has been reborn.

My fit of illness had been an avenue between two existences; the low-arched and darksome doorway, through which I crept out of a life of cold conventionalisms, on my hands and knees, as it were, and gained admittance into the freer region that lay beyond. In this respect, it was like death. And, as with death, too, it was good to have gone through it. No otherwise could I have rid myself of a thousand follies, fripperies, prejudices, habits, and other such worldly dust as inevitably settles upon the crowd along the broad highway, giving them all one sordid aspect, before noontime, however freshly they may have begun their pilgrimage, in the dewy morning. The very substance upon my bones had not been fit to live with, in any better, truer, or more energetic mode than that to which I was accustomed. So it was taken off me and flung aside, like any other worn-out or unseasonable garment; and, after shivering a little while in my skeleton, I began to be clothed anew, and much more satisfactorily than in my previous suit. In literal and physical truth, I was quite another man.

Obviously, Coverdale thinks his struggle is over. In truth it is about to begin. Recognizing only external obstacles, Coverdale has naïvely imagined that removal from society would be sufficient to liberate

1. There is an interesting and close analogy in the literal use of hot and cold to define conditions of life, and the identification of the overly social life with overheating, to the first chapter of *Walden*. That first chapter had been in existence, in varied forms, for several years, and there is no reason why Hawthorne might not have known it.

the powers of self. He is as yet unaware that inhibiting forces exist within as well as without.[2] His innocence is paralleled by the community's here, for it believes in the possibility of reform without revolution.

The true, deep aim of Coverdale's quest is private; he wants to tap the soul's reservoir of energy, to make contact with its passionate, creative, active principle. This principle underlies, or animates, all forms of human self-expression whether in work, love, or play. It is the source of all impulsive, creative, and passionate activity; hence sexual and poetic energy are but varying forms of the same drive and, consequently, Zenobia, who unites in her person sex, art, and nature, is its perfect symbol. Of course, in addition, she is politically radical. Though the life-principle is not inherently or originally political, it inevitably comes in conflict with society because it is continually asserting the primacy of self and activity over institutions and stability. Society, whose necessary goals are permanence and control, forces this romantic energy into the mold of rebellion.[3] Zenobia, from society's point of view, is morally suspect, as is the energetic and passionate principle she represents. She is the real aim of Coverdale's search, and that is why she is waiting to greet him at Blithedale, and why in comparison to her the rest of the enterprise pales and looks unreal, becomes "a masquerade, a pastoral, a counterfeit Arcadia." She, and not the community, represents the reality Coverdale is seeking.

In this symbolic function, Zenobia is the creative energy both of nature and the self; without committing himself quite to a transcendental view of the unity of all things Hawthorne does at least imply a relation between nature and the creative self. But Zenobia's role is not by any means encompassed in this dual function; she is also, most impressively and concretely, a woman, and Hawthorne outperforms the feminists in the decisive way in which he links the liberation and fulfilment of the male to his understanding of and relation to woman. Not the threatening dark lady of the post-Victorians, nor even the ambivalently conceived symbol of experience, both fascinating and frightening, in Philip Rahv's famous formulation,[4]

2. Roy R. Male, in *Hawthorne's Tragic Vision* (Austin, 1957), defines the theme of *The Blithedale Romance* as Hawthorne's criticism of the "recurring American efforts at transformation without tragedy" (p. 139). The tragedy Male has in mind is the unavoidable tragedy of original sin; man may hope to be redeemed, but cannot hope to avoid sin and suffering.
3. Irving Howe, in *Politics and the Novel* (New York, 1957), I believe, reverses the causal order when he says that Zenobia's sexuality is related "both in its power and its limits, to her political boldness. . . . Zenobia's intellectual and political audacity makes possible a new kind of personal freedom" (p. 171). Zenobia's political attitudes are consequence, not cause, of her personal freedom.
4. Philip Rahv, "The Dark Lady of Salem," *Partisan Review*, VIII (1941), 362–81. Rahv accepts Coverdale as a Paul Pry. The essay's greatest contribution to an understanding of *The Blithedale Romance* is its perception that Coverdale, when he claims to be in love with Priscilla, is lying. "It is evident on every page that the only genuine relationship is that of Coverdale to Zenobia" (p. 377).

354 · Nina Baym

Zenobia is simply, as Coverdale says, "a magnificent woman." She is a depiction of the eternal feminine as earthy, maternal, domestic, natural, sensual, brilliant, loving, and demanding, and is described mainly in images of softness, radiance, warmth, and health, none of which are even slightly ambivalent or ambiguous in their emotional import. Her voice is "fine, frank, mellow," her hand "very soft and warm," and her smile "beamed warmth upon us all." Her laugh is "mellow, almost broad," her modes of expression "free, careless, generous." Coverdale summarizes by saying that "we seldom meet with women, now-a-days, and in this country, who impress us as being women at all; their sex fades away and goes for nothing, in ordinary intercourse. Not so with Zenobia." Later he is to become rhapsodic remembering the "native glow of coloring in her cheeks, and . . . the flesh-warmth over her round arms, and what was visible of her full bust." Von Abele points out that Zenobia is linked with the domestic Phoebe Pyncheon in that both are characterized in sun metaphors;[5] seeing her as a sun-ripened Phoebe will perhaps save us from being "morbidly sensitive" about Zenobia, a state which Coverdale, when he feels it, attributes to his "illness and exhaustion" and not to sinister qualities in the lady herself.[6]

Two aspects of Zenobia do not fit the unambiguous picture I am presenting here: first, her feminism and, second, the exotic flower, daily renewed, which she wears in her hair. Unquestionably Hawthorne does not think much of Zenobia *as a feminist*. "Her poor little stories and tracts never half did justice to her intellect," he says, praising the intellect even as he deprecates the form it has found to express itself. "I recognized no severe culture in Zenobia; her mind was full of weeds. It startled me sometimes, in my state of moral, as well as bodily faint-heartedness, to observe the hardihood of her philosophy; she made no scruple of oversetting all human institutions, and scattering them as with a breeze from her fan." Zenobia is uncultured because culture is a matter of society, institutions, and the past. True original energy is, by its nature, somewhat barbaric: Walt Whitman was shortly to dramatize this point.[7] Under the pressure of historical circumstances, Zenobia has become

5. Rudolph Von Abele, *The Death of the Artist* (The Hague, 1955), p. 78. [Phoebe is the heroine of *The House of the Seven Gables* (1851).—*Editors.*]
6. The fact that Zenobia assumes a name is often taken to indicate her lack of openness. But this interpretation doesn't hold up. To begin with, the name "Zenobia" is a true name for her in the sense that it expresses her character; she has chosen a name that reveals her, not one that hides her. Second, her real name is well known to all so that we must assume that "Zenobia" has not been adopted for purposes of escaping or hiding an identity.
7. In 1855 Whitman gave the world in *Leaves of Grass* a poetry which broke both with traditional form and subject matter. In "Song of Myself," the longest poem in the collection, written in what was later to be called free verse and including material which shocked contemporary readers, the poet promises "to speak at every hazard, / Nature without check, with original energy" (lines 12–13); having done so he characterizes his performance as a "barbaric yawp over the roofs of the world" (line 1334). [*Editors.*]

a female pamphleteer. The role is inherently unworthy of her (her true place is in a timeless natural setting such as Blithedale aspires to be), but it is the best she can do in a society that offers woman no worthy roles at all. Lastly, Coverdale's references to his own faint-heartedness make clear that Zenobia's "hardihood" is not being criticized; on the contrary, she illuminates Coverdale's feebleness.

For that hothouse flower Zenobia has had to suffer a great deal of critical abuse.[8] But when one reads that it was "so fit, indeed, that Nature had evidently created this floral gem, in a happy exuberance, for the one purpose of worthily adorning Zenobia's head," it is difficult to assert that it symbolizes sensual evil, or something unnatural. It *is* sensual, but neither evil nor unnatural. That is its point: it proclaims that Zenobia's nature is passionate as well as pastoral. It may frighten the sexually morbid, but in itself it is innocent. One may hazard that what Hawthorne is trying to do here is precisely to reinstate sexuality as a legitimate and natural element of femininity—and, by implication, of maleness. It will be a sign of Coverdale's "recovery" when his feelings about Zenobia no longer embarrass him. And because, in Zenobia, all kinds of passionate and creative energies have united in a fundamental Eros,[9] we can say that Coverdale's freedom depends on his ability to accept woman in her totality. The major block to Coverdale's release of energies is—because these energies are passionate—his inability to acknowledge passion as an element of human character. It is about Zenobia, and not Priscilla, that he ought to be writing poems; then he would be doing something more than contriving stanzas. Art is passionate and it celebrates passion; rejecting this truth, Coverdale is incapable of mature artistry and must remain a childish man, an ineffectual "poetling" (to borrow Whitman's phrase). Until man becomes able to accept the fact that the source of his strength is "erotic" (in the large sense of the term) he will be unable to draw on it. The narrative of *The Blithedale Romance* demonstrates Coverdale's incapacity. The ability freely to accept the

8. The most curious interpretation of the flower is that introduced by Newton Arvin, who says that it symbolizes Zenobia's desire to compete with men! *Nathaniel Hawthorne* [New York, 1929], pp. 197–99). Symbols may be forced in all directions, but there must be a shred of relation retained between tenor and vehicle. A hothouse flower simply cannot be used to represent something mannish. R. H. Fogle, in *Hawthorne's Fiction: The Light and the Dark*, revised ed. (Norman, 1964), takes a common view when he says that the flower symbolizes Zenobia's pride; Coverdale says so too at one point. Yet the problems of this reading can be seen in the result: "one might say that she falls because she is perfect and ripe for destruction. . . . Thus richly endowed, in her pride she fails to sacrifice to the infernal Gods, who love humility in men" (p. 173). The problem is not whether Zenobia is proud, but how Zenobia's pride is regarded. Fogle *thinks* he is taking the traditional view of Hawthorne; but in the traditional view, gods are not infernal. Even Von Abele, the most perceptive of Hawthorne's critics, says that the flower because it is an exotic is "a forced bloom bred by man for his lust's pleasure" (p. 80).

9. Sensuous love. [*Editors.*]

woman is frequently the test of a man in Hawthorne's writings—
one which he invariably fails.[1]

The relation between Coverdale and Zenobia begins auspiciously,
as they sit together beside the blazing kitchen fire. But the fire is
only of brush-wood; its energy will not endure. Were Coverdale the
man so easily to solve his problems, he would not have needed to go
to Blithedale to confront them. Silas Foster (the story's chorus)
predicts the fire's imminent death, and then a knock on the door
announces the arrival of Hollingsworth and Priscilla, who will put
out Blithedale's fires permanently by killing Zenobia. Zenobia is
soon laughingly to forecast her own doom when she calls Hollingsworth the "sable knight" and Priscilla the "shadowy snow maiden
who . . . shall melt away at my feet, in a pool of ice-water, and give
me my death with a pair of wet slippers." Priscilla and Hollingsworth are heavily veiled, and the veiling both obscures and yet
displays the hidden beings beneath. Priscilla's cloak hides everything
of her person except its all-important insubstantiality; Hollingsworth in his snow-covered coat looks like a polar bear. Hollingsworth is continually portrayed in images amalgamating fire and ice.
He is a polar animal, an iron savage. The imagery of iron and of
cold is clear enough, defining Hollingsworth as severe, rigid, and,
except on his one topic, unpassionate. The iron metaphors fore-
shadow his eventual appearance as a Puritan judge, for Hawthorne's
Puritans are always iron men.[2] In *The Blithedale Romance* we also
find iron imagery applied to society. The point of the animal imagery is that Hollingsworth, although he does not know it, derives his
energies from the savage core of his nature just like everyone else.
The high morality of his philanthropy encourages a fatal delusion,
fatal because when in his ignorance he repudiates Zenobia he destroys himself.

But at the moment of his entrance into the novel this debacle lies
in the future, and Hawthorne concentrates on delineating the man
of iron in his frowning and yielding faces, faces which make him
appear, falsely, to be a *loving* man of iron. Hollingsworth immediately displays his two faces; one, turned upon Priscilla, "looked
really beautiful with its expression of thoughtful benevolence." The
other, turned to Zenobia (who has just repulsed Priscilla's overly

1. Traditional interpretations have it, of course, that he successfully overcomes the temptation embodied in the woman.
2. This fact was first observed by Q. D. Leavis in "Hawthorne as Poet," *Sewanee Review*, LIX (1951), 179–205, 426–58. This article, in ways a milestone in Hawthorne criticism, shows very clearly how reluctant critics are to follow the romantic implications of their own analyses. Thus, having fully discussed the meanings of the iron men in "The MayPole of Merry Mount," Mrs. Leavis goes on to say *without any evidence* that there is "no doubt" that the May Lord and May Lady entered into a finer bond when they joined the community of iron men— and were married in the ceremony of the iron men's church—no doubt, that is, in Hawthorne's mind. But Mrs. Leavis' own discussion of iron imagery has established the doubt, beyond question.

emotional approach to her), is "stern and reproachful; and it was with that inauspicious meaning in his glance, that Hollingsworth first met Zenobia's eyes, and began his influence upon her life."[3] The outcome of the story is foreshadowed in these first glances, but Coverdale is long reluctant to accept what he has seen. Against all testimony, Hollingsworth's included, he persists in imagining that Hollingsworth is a benign and loving parent, a kind and tender priest who will remain noncompetitively on the sidelines and bless all the participants in the action.

In relation to Coverdale, Hollingsworth's role is very complicated. He is an alter ego, an admired version of the self, energetic, forceful, attractive, and purposeful to an extreme. He is also a father figure, rival and judge of the self. Perhaps we may infer from this coincidence of roles that Coverdale's weaknesses derive from the simple fact that he has too much respect for authority. Thus the alter ego is authoritarian. Coverdale supposes that the father within the self will rejoice at the son's maturity; he supposes that the father is an admirable model, a great emancipator. He assumes that his admiration for Hollingsworth as an individual will be reciprocated in kind. But Hollingsworth is a jailor who admires nothing in individuals, and desires nothing but their submission. He must dominate, and his morality serves his tyranny. His pretensions to being a romantic are "hollow" (Hollingsworth—Hollow-worth?). His nature does not change in the course of the novel, but Coverdale's perception of him alters. More accurately, Coverdale comes to accept what he has already perceived but refused to credit.

From the first he knows that Hollingsworth's "heart . . . was never really interested in our socialist scheme, but was forever busy with his strange . . . plan." Why then has he come to Blithedale? Coverdale thinks at first it is because, an outcast himself, he feels at home among outcasts. But this is wrong; Hollingsworth has come, as Howe puts it, to "bore from within." His motive is acquisition of the Blithedale property for his own uses. He wants to inspect it and to establish through Zenobia the means of acquiring the land if he fancies it. This means that his relation with Zenobia lacks, on his side, passion. "In the case of both his initial commitment to Zenobia and his later courting of Priscilla, Hawthorne suggests that his motive is purely economic; he is chasing Old Moodie's brother's fortune from one inheritrix to another."[4] Apparently, Hollingsworth rescues Priscilla from the clutches of Westervelt, after having connived in returning her to the magician, not because he has had a

3. A recent article of great interest, "Some Rents in the Veil: New Light on Priscilla and Zenobia in *The Blithedale Romance*," by Allan and Barbara Lefcowitz (*Nineteenth-Century Fiction*, XXI, [1966], 263–75), clarifies Zenobia's behavior in this scene. She, as well as Coverdale, thinks Priscilla is a prostitute.
4. Von Abele, p. 76.

crisis of conscience, but because he has learned about the reversal of fortune. "It is only three days," Zenobia says to Hollingsworth at her "judgment" scene, "since I knew the strange fact that threatens to make me poor; and your own acquaintence with it, I suspect, is of at least as old a date." This scene of repudiation takes place two nights after Coverdale has witnessed the rescue of Priscilla.

Hollingsworth wants the Blithedale property as the ground for his reform school. The contrast with Blithedale's purposes could not be more complete, and indeed his plans require dispossessing the Blithedalers as a preliminary. Far from envisioning a free relation between man and nature, Hollingsworth's scheme involves shutting man away from nature in an institution—a building—which conforms not to the spirit of the individuals within it, but to *his* spirit. Forever busy planning his structure to the last detail, his goal of a solid material edifice represents a negation of the organic ideal, in which shape flows from within and is never perfected, remaining sensitive to inner flux. While the Blithedalers are programmatic nonconformists who tolerate all styles of life—"whoso would be a man, must be a noncomformist"—Hollingsworth would impose, through his institution, a conforming sameness on individuals. He would not encourage people to grow in their ways, but force them to grow his way. Thus, he is not a romantic gone wrong, but a false reformer. We should not forget how the Transcendentalists detested philanthropists. A man like Thoreau, for example, would never for a moment have been deceived about Hollingsworth's true nature: "if I knew for a certainty that a man was coming to my house with the conscious design of doing me good, I should run for my life . . . for fear that I should get some of his good done to me,—some of its virus mingled with my blood."[5] Hollingsworth's vision denies the human freedom on which Blithedale is based and rejects the fundamental transcendental tenet, belief that man is divine and that therefore all men must treat each other as gods. Lastly, accepting as it does social judgments of morality and guilt, Hollingsworth's scheme to reform criminals perpetuates the social definitions of human nature that the romantic soul rejects. In sum, Hollingsworth does not represent a corrupted extreme of romantic libertarianism. He is the opposite principle, the spirit of authoritarian domination.

In Blithedale he is a true subversive, in a manner only superficially depicted by his maneuvering with respect to the Blithedale property. He brings to the farm the very principle it has been established to escape—subordination of the individual to the state. Hollingsworth is not, however, an obvious representative of mid-

5. From the "Economy" chapter of *Walden* (1854), where Thoreau points out the dangers of philanthropy (a "greatly over-rated' virtue) to the true renovation of man and society. [*Editors*.]

century Boston. Boston in fact sees him as just another amusing romantic, for from its complacent middle ground all varieties of extremism look alike. Boston is certainly far more "liberal" than Hollingsworth, having leavened its Puritan heritage with a certain amount of hedonism. But Blithedale recognizes no distinction between Boston 1640 and 1840, because to it all societies which exist on inhibition or exploitation to any degree are evil. Although Hollingsworth is anachronistic in genteel Boston, from the vantage point of the community he is the spiritual core of society. If Boston is blind in failing to see that Hollingsworth is totalitarian rather than anarchistic, Blithedale may be equally myopic in refusing to distinguish better and worse among bad societies. The Blithedalers cannot consider the possibility that society may inherently be founded on repressive principles: this goes counter to all their aspirations. And Hawthorne, though he shows the disintegration of the community, does not seem to be demonstrating thereby that the Blithedalers are mistaken in their hope that society *need* not be founded on repression. He is showing something else—that repression is impossible to escape, rather than that it is functional. The Blithedalers may be foolish and naïve but they represent the only truly moral point of view in the book. The view of authority, as personified in Hollingsworth, is a romantic view: authority is tyranny.

The plot of the novel shows how Hollingsworth uses the power which has been granted to him by the other characters, to destroy. The crux of the plot is his choice between two women; the surface reason for his choice is money. Having no sense of the women as people, he is unaware of the meanings of his choice in terms of the book's larger logic. One might ask, indeed, whether Hawthorne's plotting is not irrelevant and mechanical here. Of course it says something about Hollingsworth, that he makes his choice solely on economic grounds. It points up his lack of passion, reinforces his image as a man of institutions, concerned with things, substances, mass, power, money. Too, the disparity between the reason for his choice and the line of moral righteousness with which he dismisses Zenobia—his complete failure to see that in manipulating human passions he has done something deeply wrong—makes an acerbic comment on society's moralism. Hollingsworth's sanctimonious morality is no more than rationalization; yet, like society, Hollingsworth has the power to make his moral judgments stick.

The rerouting of the fortune from Zenobia to Priscilla is also of significance. Though Zenobia, for most of the book, is the wealthy sister, the depiction of her does not utilize money for its effect. Her richness is all of body and spirit. She dresses in homely, dateless rustic garb and is continually portrayed in natural images—even the

why then is Zenobia attracted to Hollingsworth

hothouse flower is real. She operates in a frame independent of money. This is not true of Priscilla, who has been deformed by poverty. Whether one thinks of her as the seamstress or as the Veiled Lady, one finds her intimately connected with economic questions, servant to an environment that demands artifice. As a seamstress she makes one highly specialized luxury item, a finely wrought silk purse. Whether this product has sartorial or sexual meaning, it is created for a jaded market. As the Veiled Lady, Priscilla herself is artifice: Hawthorne brings this out quite clearly in the Boston scenes of the novel, where the two women undergo striking transformations. Zenobia, though beautiful as ever, seems curiously artificial and dead despite the amazing luxury of her dress, perhaps because of it. The hothouse flower has been replaced by a jewel, and this metamorphosis signifies the way, in an artificial context, her attractions seem unnatural. Coverdale, talking to her, cannot rid himself of the sensation that she is acting a part.

In contrast, pallid Priscilla comes to life. In the city she is in her element. Although Coverdale asserts that her beauty is so delicate that "it was safest, in her case, to attempt no art of dress," he declares in the next breath that her marvellous perfection is due to consummate art. "I wondered what Zenobia meant by evolving so much loveliness out of this poor girl." As a result of this art, Priscilla has become a symbol of matchless purity and innocence. But it takes the city to bring her meaning out. "Ever since she came among us, I have been dimly sensible of just this charm which you have brought out. But it was never absolutely visible till now." And Coverdale then expresses the book's most bitter paradox. "She is as lovely," he proclaims, "as a flower." In other words, Priscilla is the true artificial flower of the book, the flower that appears natural in the city, the domain of repression and artificial pleasures. Zenobia's flower, in the distorting glass of civilization, looks fake. She does not belong here, but Priscilla fits in.

The point of this is that, as money is intricately and intimately bound into the fabric of society, and as Priscilla is a creature of society and Zenobia is in revolt against it, the money *belongs* with Priscilla. "The upshot of the fable is that Priscilla's conformism triumphs, but Zenobia's rebellion destroys her."[6] Moodie's decision to redirect the fortune, appropriately enough, stems from Zenobia's failure properly to treat Priscilla as a sister. There is every indication that he has insinuated Priscilla into Blithedale just *as* a test of Zenobia. To accept Priscilla is, for Zenobia, to accept the very shape of womanhood she is in rebellion against, society's version of the feminine. She loses her fortune, then, because she refuses to surrender on society's terms. The wrath of society, relayed to her by

6. Von Abele, p. 80.

Hollingsworth, who acts (as he has acted in bringing Priscilla to Blithedale) as Moodie's surrogate, is inevitable.[7]

The money motif, then, plays an important clarifying role, elucidating relations between symbols and reinforcing the contrast between Zenobia and Priscilla. It is often said that Zenobia is Eros and Priscilla Agape, where the terms are understood in their Neoplatonic[8] sense of earthly versus spiritual love. If we take Eros in its more contemporary sense, it must be opposed not to Agape, but to Thanatos,[9] and that indeed is what Priscilla represents. Where Zenobia is the life force, capable of good, capable of evil but above all simply a reservoir of energy striving to realize itself, Priscilla is spirituality opposed to life: love without passion, art without energy, woman without body. * * *

As Zenobia is the natural and eternal woman, Priscilla is the woman in history, distorted by her social role and misrepresented by the ideals derived from her. She is considered an inferior being, subjected, exploited, and yet idealized. The ideal is pernicious because it derives from woman's subjected state and ultimately ennobles the condition of slavery. As seamstress Priscilla represents the whole range of exploited feminine roles in society, all of which, from wife to prostitute, were viewed by feminists as examples of economic subjection of woman to man. As the Veiled Lady, Priscilla stands for the feminine ideal. Just as Zenobia projects a part of Coverdale's personality, Priscilla too represents part of Coverdale, but here there is a divergence in the parallel because Priscilla is less an active force than a channel for forces. The true opposition, in terms of Coverdale's psyche, is between Zenobia and Hollingsworth, but Priscilla *plays the role* of Zenobia's anti-self. This is entirely appropriate to Priscilla's status as a medium. "I am blown about like a leaf. . . . I never have any free will."

The various meanings of Priscilla are centered on her role as woman in the city. This presentation has always struck readers as the most "incoherent" part of the book; first, because it is hard to grasp the interrelatedness of her two incarnations, let alone to interpret the obscured meanings of the Veiled Lady. Second, according to whether Priscilla is viewed as herself the most abject victim of social tyranny, or as an agent in the service of that tyranny, the point of view toward her changes radically. In the first instance she is an object of almost bathetic compassion, but as an agent she is

7. What is the meaning of Moodie, the shy derelict with the eye patch, much in the public eye and yet seldom seen, who sits obscurely in the bushes when he visits Blithedale and is fed like an "enshrined and invisible idol"? Father of Zenobia and Priscilla, manipulator of fortunes, he must be one of the book's "infernal" deities, to whom Zenobia neglects to sacrifice. The trinity is completed (blasphemously) by Westervelt and the dove, Priscilla.
8. A third century A.D. philosophical system derived from Plato and oriental mysticism. [*Editors.*]
9. Death. [*Editors.*]

362 · Nina Baym

regarded with fear, distrust, and repugnance. Priscilla the seamstress is rendered almost entirely in images of feebleness, illness, and furtiveness. She is physically almost a cripple—notice her limping run—and though dexterous with her needles is clumsy in all other ways. Domestically inept, incapable of assuming any of the farm chores, she is permitted to run about like a child and is generally regarded as a case of arrested development. She has little in common with the blond maidens of Hawthorne's other novels, possessing neither the sunny domestic girlishness of Phoebe nor the polar, vestal inflexibility of Hilda. She is simply a victim, her physical and mental debilitation directly caused by the conditions of her exploited life. Hawthorne's picture of her approaches the grotesque, but is counterbalanced by stress on her gentleness, her timidity, her original sweetness of nature, and a quite striking and significant animal wildness that develops as she recovers at Blithedale.

Coverdale's imagination is much taken up with the spectacle of her frailty, but, as he himself has to admit, Priscilla is mostly a shadowy background for his own fantasizing, a void for the poet to decorate. She is, in fact, a fine subject for the kind of poetry Coverdale writes. The poetic impulse to idealize the vapid leads, inevitably, to vapid poetry. Moreover, the celebration of feebleness and frailty turns these qualities into admired attributes, and thus the genteel poet does his part in maintaining the status quo by praising it. It is hard to shake the appealing image of Priscilla out of the heart, but there is no hope for man or woman unless she is dislodged. The condition of woman in the nineteenth century, in a word, is slavery.[1] Hollingsworth's response to the idea of an alteration in her status is appropriately ferocious.

1. The question of Hawthorne's views about Margaret Fuller have long bedeviled the discussion of his feelings about Zenobia and women's rights. Despite the fact that Priscilla is specifically, and rather elaborately, linked to Margaret Fuller in the novel, critics have insisted that she is the source for Zenobia, because Zenobia like Miss Fuller is a feminist residing at a Utopian community. But the two women share no traits.

Hawthorne did not like Margaret Fuller. He thought she was intellectually pretentious; her vast reading had neither improved nor disguised a fundamentally mediocre and conventional mind. Such criticism is not applicable to Zenobia. Her intellect may not be most fitly expressed in literature, but it is unquestionably fine. Secondly, Hawthorne objected violently to what he interpreted as a false spirituality in Margaret Fuller—surely not a claim one can bring against Zenobia! A reading of *Woman in the Nineteenth Century* reveals that Margaret Fuller accepts an ideal of femininity as spiritual and noncorporeal. She discusses—or pretends to

discuss—the entire context of woman in the world and in her relations to men, without once referring to sexuality except in such phrases as "mists of sensuality" which imply that the ultimate relations between men and women should be sexless. She images the ideal relation between the sexes as that between father and daughter, mother and son, or brother and sister. There is no place for Zenobia there! Lastly (and this will surprise a reader who moves from Hawthorne to Fuller), she talks a good deal about the "electric" nature of woman's intelligence, a belief in which makes her take mesmerism quite seriously. "To this region, however misunderstood, or interpreted with presumptuous carelessness, belong the phenomena of magnetism, or mesmerism" ([London, 1850], p. 97). Here, if anywhere, is her link to *The Blithedale Romance*, and here is the explanation of her tie to Priscilla. If Hawthorne is saying anything about Margaret Fuller here, it is that her feminism is false, for it leads to Priscilla-worship, idealizes a hideous exploitation as an example of spirituality.

Her place is at man's side. Her office, that of the Sympathizer; the unreserved, unquestioning Believer . . . the Echo of God's own voice, pronouncing, "It is well done!" All the separate action of woman is, and ever has been, and always shall be, false, foolish, vain, destructive of her own best ⸉and holiest qualities, void of every good effect, and productive of intolerable mischiefs! Man is a wretch without woman; but woman is a monster . . . without man, as her acknowledged principal! As true as I had once a mother, whom I loved . . . if there were a chance of their attaining the end which these petticoated monstrosities have in view, I would call upon my own sex to use its physical force, that unmistakable evidence of sovereignty, to scourge them back within their proper bounds!

The reference to physical force as evidence of sovereignty reveals Hollingsworth more clearly than ever, and indicates as well how true it is that woman is a slave in his system, rhetoric notwithstanding. His words strike Coverdale as "outrageous," the "very intensity of masculine egotism," which "deprived woman of her very soul, her inexpressible and unfathomable all, to make it a mere incident in the great sum of man." Coverdale does not recognize in his own alternate version of the ideal relations between woman and man an equal, if less savage, egotism, and he is piqued by the indifference with which his declamation in favor of women is received by Zenobia and Priscilla.[2] And he is wrong when he interprets Zenobia's words, "Let man be but manly and god-like and woman is only too ready to become to him what you say," as her submission to Hollingsworth's views, for her qualification is vital. Except as man takes woman as a free spirit, equal to his own and with the same rights, he is not manly or godlike.

Priscilla, the "gentle parasite," the "type of womanhood, such as man has spent centuries in making it," rewards Hollingsworth for his defense of slavery with a "glance of . . . entire acquiescence and unquestioning faith." In her approbation it is clear that she and Hollingsworth belong together, and as they entered the novel together so they will leave it. Though she adores him, Priscilla can never be Hollingsworth's wife or friend. In the beginning she is his child, and at the end she is his nurse. And she is fulfilled in her role as caretaker and guardian to the broken Hollingsworth, thus literally realizing the idea that a degrading conception of woman implies

Margaret Fuller, more than she realizes, is a pathetic victim of society; her feminism has not succeeded in freeing itself from the conditions it rebels against. What Hawthorne says is that Margaret Fuller was a far more ordinary person than she supposed herself to be; but he says over and over again that Zenobia is extraordinary.

2. Coverdale's ideal woman is Mary, the mediating mother; his mind is engaged with the relation between father and son, and he subordinates the woman into this primary relationship. His system certainly does not allow for assertions of freedom by woman. Perhaps Hawthorne feels that *all* the ideals, in this situation, are social products and hence corrupted.

a degradation of man. If man idolizes a crippled spirit, he will cripple his own. Man "is never content," Zenobia comments, "unless he can degrade himself by stooping towards what he loves. In denying us our rights, he betrays even more blindness to his own interests, than profligate disregard of ours." Expanded to cover all the meanings of Zenobia's presence in the book, her remark can stand as the novel's epigraph; yet even she does not fathom the depths of that blindness.

These matters are recapitulated on a much more intimate and—given the temper of the times—dangerous level in the story of the Veiled Lady. When Priscilla is not making purses she is performing on the stage as the subject of Westervelt's mesmeric powers. In these appearances she wears a many-layered, gauzy white veil. The Veiled Lady is the Victorian ideal of womanhood as a spiritual (noncorporeal) being, carried to an extreme and implicating in its extremity the basest kinds of human emotions. Though she is proclaimed as a being almost entirely spiritual, she is in fact a "possessed" creature owned and exploited by Westervelt. She is in a position which denies her spiritual nature even while pretending to demonstrate it. The particular being in whose service she performs is a cosmopolitan devil, his name implying his worldliness. Like Moodie, another urban figure, he lives off the proceeds of his exploitation; but where the one employs her physical talents, the other employs her very soul. As a cosmopolitan charlatan, he caters to a curious set of prurient and voyeuristic tastes in the audience, which comes to see purity violated, modesty exhibited. F. O. Matthiessen spoke of Hawthorne's Hilda as performing a kind of spiritual striptease—the phrase is even more aptly applied to Priscilla, for the veil functions largely to excite the viewers' interest in what it conceals. The Veiled Lady titillates even as she appeals to an ideal of feminine purity. On the one hand, talk of purity "veils" what is actually taking place; on the other, the purity itself contributes to the excitement of the display.

The veil, along with the references to Priscilla's insubstantial frame, and metaphors of shadows and melting snows, and contrasts to Zenobia's ample proportions, goes far to suggest that in this ideal of spirituality a crude equation has been made with lack of body. As woman is *literally* less and less physical, she is more spiritual, as though these were quantitative matters. To deny the flesh is to deny the emotions flesh arouses, and this ideal indeed denies the normality of sex. Zenobia's flower becomes a jewel in Boston because society considers sex unnatural. Westervelt's game inhibits the acceptance of sex as normal by holding up a flesh-denying ideal of purity. Simultaneously he controls his audience's emotions through participation in an act of ritual violation of that very ideal. Yet, the denial of sex is not Westervelt's ultimate goal; he is aiming to suppress the radical Eros itself, in its totality. Ideally, he would use Zenobia to deny herself; failing that, he seeks to blot her image out of the hearts of men by polluting it. The Veiled Lady's exhibitions are cathartic spectacles to draw off and channel threatening emotions; they are rituals of socialization.

Westervelt is a hideous creation, and he exists somewhere in the deepest layers of Coverdale's mind. Coverdale meets him in the forest, always Hawthorne's locale for the soul's profundities. In Coverdale's mind he operates as the demon of sexual cynicism and fear, the internalization of society's life-denying strategies. "The Professor's tone represented that of worldly society at large, where a cold scepticism smothers what it can of our spiritual aspirations, and makes the rest ridiculous. I detested this kind of man, and all the more, because a part of my own nature showed itself responsive to him." Westervelt within the psyche tarnishes the images of all women; he is the principle of "dirty-mindedness."[3] Zenobia, too, has been in bondage to him, and in a sense always will be so; but at the same time she has fundamentally escaped him. The two seem to occupy separate spheres. They cannot touch. In the forest Coverdale notices that "as they passed among the trees . . . she took good heed that even the hem of her garment should not brush against the stranger's person." Watching them again at the boarding house, he observes that "it still seemed to me, as on the former occasion, that Zenobia repelled him—that, perchance, they mutually repelled each other—by some incompatibility of their spheres." A key contrast between the two is made in terms of heat and coldness, so that Westervelt's deviltry is linked to all the other images of rigidness and coldness in the book, to the rigid, passion-repressing, "puritannical" part of the personality.

Finally, the combination of Veil and Devil suggests that the Lady may even be a delusion, conjured up to deflect men from true ideals, such as (perhaps) those embodied in Blithedale and its resident goddess. This delusory ideal, though it promises fulfillment, in fact means incompleteness for man and woman. So we have seen,

---

3. At the same time Westervelt, like many another demon, functions to utter certain truths that Coverdale no more than any social being of his time could admit to entertaining. Thus, although he is the mesmerist who works Priscilla's spiritual powers, he derides her spirituality to Coverdale. "Some philosophers choose to glorify this habit of body by terming it spiritual; but, in my opinion, it is rather the effect of unwholesome food, bad air, lack of out-door exercise, and neglect of bathing, on the part of these damsels and their female progenitors; all resulting in a kind of hereditary dyspepsia." Thoughts like these are obviously forbidden; having thought them, Coverdale will be anxious to disown them. Westervelt's habit of uttering truths should not blind us to his diabolical nature, nor should his nature make us assume that he can only tell lies.

Through Westervelt there is an interesting link, to my knowledge unnoticed, between James and Hawthorne. Much has been written about the influence of Hawthorne on James, and *The Blithedale Romance* is generally accepted as an influence on *The Bostonians*. But the funeral scene of *The Blithedale Romance*, in addition, where the demon lover is interrogated by the narrator and gives certain answers about the nature of the dead woman, is strikingly similar to the one in *Daisy Miller*.

and so Zenobia tries to imply in her "Legend of the Silvery Veil" (Chapter XII, the middle of the book). Theodore, sneaking into the Veiled Lady's dressing room for a peep, is asked for a kiss by the shadowy figure. The idea repels him; he imagines all kinds of horrors beneath the veil, and refuses the request. Failing to accept the physical side of relations between the sexes, he forfeits his opportunity to set the Veiled Lady free. She sorrowfully disappears, but not before Theodore has seen her lovely face, the memory of which is to haunt him for the rest of his life and make his existence seem unsubstantial. In this story, Zenobia is actually assimilating the Veiled Lady to herself: insofar as the Veiled Lady is a girl or woman, she must be treated as a being of flesh and blood. Life is "realized" only in the flesh. Priscilla is imprisoned in the "ideal" which men like Theodore and Coverdale have imposed on her. The ideal keeps people dead, keeps them forever unrealized, makes a society of phantoms no more real than the Lady herself.

Priscilla in Blithedale, then, is enormously dangerous, but only Zenobia sees it. From the beginning her energies are absorbed in attempting to detach Priscilla from Hollingsworth, so that there may be a longed-for union of the forces of passion and control, a union that might make a whole, vigorous self. Zenobia's strategy, since she is incapable of artifice, consists largely in contrasting Priscilla's physical meagerness to her own full womanhood. The tactic is self-defeating, for the more Zenobia demonstrates the nature of her rival, the more she calls up the prior socio-moral commitments of the men. However pathetic Priscilla, in the fragility of her physical frame, may appear to be, and however she is an exploited slave in her relation to men, she is not helpless in a battle against Zenobia. Men will fight to the death to defend her as a slave. In this sense, both the men in the story are on her side, and Zenobia succeeds only in aligning the men against her. Increasingly she defines the conventional polarity of pit and pedestal and puts herself in the pit. The more the contrast between the Boston and Blithedale women is clarified, the more uncomfortable Coverdale becomes and the more angry Hollingsworth. In the long run, Hollingsworth is immune to Zenobia because she stands for the romantic individualism and freedom he so abhors. In the long run, too, Coverdale cannot overcome his attachment to genteel poetry and the genteel way of life to serve the romantic muse.

Thus, in full season, the adventure at Blithedale leads to a polarization of forces so extreme that even the earlier anxious moments at the farm can be remembered as harmonious. Acting under a confluence of forces, Hollingsworth takes on his core identity as Puritan judge and condemns Zenobia. His action signifies, on all levels of her meaning, her death. As the life force, she has been put down; as woman, she has been denied a place in a world administered by men. She kills herself, as she must, but the marble imagery of the scene by the rock shows that she is, before her suicide, already dead. With her death Blithedale, too, dies for Coverdale; his chance is finished. He returns to Boston in desolation, looking ahead to an empty future, from the vantage point of which only these months at the farm will appear to him to have been "real." He leaves Blithedale not a new man but a mutilated one. His inner quest has ended in catastrophe because he has proven too weak to become free.

The destruction of Hollingsworth is particularly interesting. From the social vantage point, he has triumphed, but as an aspect of Coverdale he must go down to destruction with the rest of the personality. It has been his supreme folly to imagine that he has acted as an "inspired" man; acted, that is, on energy supplied from higher sources. But it seems as if he too has ultimately derived his powers from Zenobia, as though she were the book's true sun, its sole source of energy. Casting out Zenobia, Hollingsworth inadvertently casts out his own vitality and thus ruins himself. He makes himself into a fit mate for Priscilla, and is seen some years later showing a "childlike, or childish, tendency to press close, and closer still, to the side of the slender woman whose arm was within his."

His act demonstrates that it is necessary, for the life of the organism, that the punishing tendencies of the soul be checked, for if left free they will crush it. The controlling forces within must themselves be controlled, because they will not control themselves; on the contrary, interpreting themselves as transmitters of the divine, they will brook no restraint. The goal, presumably, is in some kind of harmony in the consciousness between energy and restraint, but such a mediating force as is required Coverdale cannot supply. Agonizedly, he watches the drama of his fragmenting psyche, but cannot impress himself on the warring forces. Eventually he witnesses his own collapse.

Undoubtedly books have been written on the complementary theme, the dangers to the personality when the passionate energies are given free rein, rather than when the punishing and repressive capacities are released unhindered. But *The Blithedale Romance* is not such a book. We cannot even hypothesize, after reading it, what Hawthorne would "do" with the theme of complete self-expression, because this novel is about the murder (and suicide) of self-expressive energies in the soul. Utopias do not work because they never succeed in freeing themselves from the many subtle pressures of the society they think to leave behind.[4] Indeed, the judging core of the

4. On the surface level of the book, as Howe has noted, there is a similar failure to shake off social dependence; for Blithedale "by virtue of being subject to the demands and pressures of the market . . . becomes a competitive unit in a competitive society" (p. 169).

personality, an anarchic and intemperate concentration of inhibiting forces, is far more severe when it is not muffled by the easygoing life of Boston which, if it inhibits the passions, also inhibits their punishment. We cannot see *Blithedale* as a book saying that society does well insofar as it controls the passions, on the assumption that without control the soul is a passionate and evil anarchy. We have to see Hawthorne saying, rather, that insofar as society seeks to eliminate the passions altogether it seeks its own eventual suicide: there is no society without people, and there are no people without passion. What Hawthorne's hero might do if he were free, one does not know, because he cannot free himself.

HYATT H. WAGGONER

[Fire and Veils: The Texture of *The Blithedale Romance*] †

* * *

3

The texture of *The Blithedale Romance* is remarkably rich and interesting, even for Hawthorne. Two main streams of imagery clarify, reinforce, and expand the themes suggested by the name symbolism. In the early chapters fire imagery is dominant. Hawthorne insists on it so much, in fact, that at the beginning of chapter four he apologizes for "harping on it." But the imagery of masks, veils, and disguises, though subordinate to the fire imagery in most of the opening chapters, is introduced earlier. It is doubly present in the first sentence of the first chapter, explicitly in the reference to the Veiled Lady and implicitly in the reference to Moodie; and thereafter it dominates the chapter. It is apparent * * * in the name of the narrator. And it finally overshadows the fire imagery. Both it and the fire imagery are enriched by being associated with other image patterns, but the two of them are so much more frequent and emphatic than the others that they establish the pattern within which all the images have their place.

Readers often find Hawthorne's first chapter puzzling and unsatisfactory. He devotes it to introducing, first, the Veiled Lady, who except for Coverdale is the first character to appear, and second, old Moodie, whose name supplies the chapter with its title. Toward the end of the chapter we hear of Zenobia. One of the peculiarities of the chapter for the modern reader is that it is devoted to introducing three people of whom only one, Zenobia, is apparently a character

† From Hyatt H. Waggoner, *Hawthorne:* Mass.: Harvard University Press, 1963), *A Critical Study*, rev. ed. (Cambridge, pp. 188–208.

of any consequence in the novel. I say "apparently" because we eventually discover that the Veiled Lady is really Priscilla and old Moodie is the father of both Priscilla and Zenobia. But by the time we discover this we are likely to have ceased to care, for the "mysterious" aspects of Hawthorne's plot are certainly not likely to hold our attention long today. Is this chapter then, we wonder, simply a rather extreme example of the trouble Hawthorne often had with the mechanics of his stories?

I think we may assume that Hawthorne felt he was gaining a valuable addition to suspense by this device of introducing characters whose identity remains hidden. But the chapter served Hawthorne in another way, and for us this is surely the more important. It introduces and places in the foreground of our attention veil and fire images. And it is typical of Hawthorne that the images which will be the chief carriers of the theme grow out of the plot, which thus functions symbolically even though it remains clumsily contrived and Gothic on the literal level.

The introduction of a mysterious Veiled Lady in the first chapter of a work that is to be full of disguises is obviously appropriate, but the thematic function of the chapter does not end there. Old Moodie, too, wears his own kind of veil. "He was a very shy personage, this Mr. Moodie." He wears a patch over one eye, and he never, as Coverdale immediately notices, reveals more of himself than is absolutely necessary. When he visits Blithedale and eats lunch in the field with Hollingsworth and Coverdale, he eats "with" them but not in sight of them, for he manages to sit so that a screen of leaves hides everything about him but his shoes. When he follows the two to the farmhouse he walks behind Hollingsworth so that Hollingsworth "could not very conveniently look him in the face." Coverdale notes that he gave the impression of "hiding himself behind the patch on his left eye." At the funeral of Zenobia he keeps his face "mostly concealed in a white handkerchief." He is as much a veiled character as the Veiled Lady and more obviously so than Coverdale.

The only other character introduced in the first chapter is Zenobia, and from what we learn of her later we first get the impression that she is unlike Coverdale, Moodie, and the Veiled Lady in being quite lacking in a veil. (Coverdale pictures her once lacking not only a veil but any other sort of drapery or covering.) She does not share Moodie's tendency to hide behind bushes or Coverdale's to peer out of thickets or into windows; she seems in fact to Coverdale to be rather immodestly open in her manner, disturbing him with her frank acknowledgment of her womanliness. Yet there is one secret she will not reveal, the secret of her very identity. So it is that Coverdale remarks to Moodie in the first chapter that "Zenobia . . . is merely her public name; a sort of mask in which she comes before the world . . . a contrivance, in short, like the white drapery of the Veiled Lady, only a little more transparent." Every character in the first chapter, then, wears his mask. When finally we discover that Priscilla is the Veiled Lady and half-sister of Zenobia, we realize that these two who are so unlike in almost every respect are connected in a significant way: one wears a veil by choice, the other by necessity. It is not difficult, knowing Hawthorne, to guess which will serve as heroine.

But we are not quite through with this first chapter yet. When Coverdale replenishes his fire we have the unobtrusive beginning of a chain of fire imagery that does not cease until the end of the romance. Thus the opening chapter does in fact accomplish a good deal: it introduces all but Hollingsworth among the principal characters and it first states the leading images. The distance between this and the opening chapters of *The Scarlet Letter* and *The House of the Seven Gables* is after all not so great as it at first seems.

After this Hawthorne never lets us forget for long the theme signalized by the veil imagery. We are reminded of it on some thirty-five of the subsequent pages. But to say that we are "reminded" is not to convey adequately what is really going on. For the veil is not a static or allegorical symbol, and the first chapter merely introduces it, it does not define it. Twenty-two of the twenty-nine chapters develop the theme explicitly, and all of them, of course, do so implicitly.

Coverdale, for instance, journeys to Blithedale in a snowstorm that veils the "conventionalism" of the world against which Blithedale is a protest. Zenobia wears her unnatural flowers, which Coverdale decides are a "subtile expression" of her character. Westervelt hides his true character behind a false laugh and false teeth: his laughter, "brief, metallic," reveals that his "remarkably brilliant" teeth are "a sham." Coverdale feels "as if the whole man were a moral and physical humbug; his wonderful beauty of face, for aught I knew, might be removable like a mask." Even the pair of spectacles Westervelt later puts on are masking devices: they "so altered the character of his face" that Coverdale "hardly knew him again." The reformers spend an evening at charades and Zenobia remarks that the identity of the actors is too apparent through their improvised disguises. Later the whole company, with the exception of Coverdale, put on masks and play at being Arcadians. Coverdale does not need a mask. He remains hidden as usual even without one, peering at the others through the leaves and later retreating, when he is discovered, to his "bower," from which he observes Priscilla, Zenobia, and Hollingsworth without disclosing his own presence. Everyone at Blithedale except Silas Foster, the hired farmer, has a mask, veil, or disguise on at some time in the story.

4

The fire imagery is only slightly less prominent than that of veils, masks, and disguises. Chapter one closes with Coverdale building up his fire. Chapter two opens with his admission that he is not likely ever again to know so cheery a blaze as that which he remembers from his first day at Blithedale. The remainder of the chapter develops the implications of this initial imagery. The fire that first day warmed the heart as well as the body. The cheer it provided in contrast to the cold outside strengthened Coverdale and his companions in their hope that here they might begin "the life of Paradise anew." After sèveral reminders of the presence of the fires in chapter three, chapter four turns again to extended treatment of the subject. The great old kitchen fireplace, with its "cavernous" opening, is now described. The fire that burns in it is very cheery, but it is not such as any real farmer would build: it is too large to be perfectly natural even in such a fireplace, and, as Silas Foster sardonically points out, it is built of brushwood, which burns very brightly but will not last.

Silas Foster's doubt about the permanence of the fires at Blithedale is paralleled by Priscilla's inability to be warmed by them. She finds "the sense of vast, undefined space, pressing from the outside against the black panes of our uncurtained windows . . . fearful . . . The house probably seemed to her adrift on the great ocean of the night." And so it was later to seem to Coverdale. Very soon after arriving, indeed, he was forced to go shivering to his "fireless chamber" with a cold in the head.

While Coverdale is still confined to his sickbed, Hollingsworth builds a fire to warm the room, and it is very welcome to the sufferer from cold. Yet "there never was any blaze of a fireside that warmed and cheered me, in the down-sinkings and shiverings of my spirit, so effectually as did the light out of those eyes, which lay so deep and dark under his shaggy brows." When it becomes clear to Coverdale later that his friend has given way to "the terrible egotism which he mistook for an angel of God," the light that warms disappears. Coverdale is left thereafter with more cause than ever to deplore the coldness of his own heart. His "cold tendency," which has gone far as he thinks toward "unhumanizing" him, leads him to want fires everywhere, even when he does not need them: "Summer as it still was, I ordered a coal-fire in the rusty grate, and was glad to find myself growing a little too warm with an artificial temperature." The cold from which Coverdale suffered was more internal than external. Like that of Gervayse Hastings in "The Christmas Banquet,"[1] it was the cold that proceeds from a frozen heart.

Several other image patterns are related, some obviously and

1. The central figure in Hawthorne's 1844 tale, doomed to be incapable of feeling any emotion at all. [*Editors.*]

some obscurely, to the veil and fire clusters. It has already become clear how coldness comes in as the counterpart of the fires and warmth, and how these two lead naturally, as always in Hawthorne, to heart imagery. These four, veil and fire, coldness and the heart, take on added meaning in their relationships with the iron imagery associated with Hollingsworth, the flower imagery and the frequent allusions to the theater and acting associated with Zenobia, the images of laughter that make an interesting connection between Westervelt and Coverdale, and the images of dreaming that are associated with Coverdale alone. And all these running metaphors are tied in with the frequent allusions to Eden, Arcadia, and Paradise. Some, like the iron imagery that helps to characterize Hollingsworth, grow naturally out of the main image patterns, extending and reinforcing them; others, like the flower imagery associated with Zenobia, serve to qualify or counter the suggestions of the dominant images. Though each of these might profitably be given separate treatment, I shall comment on only two of them, the heart and cold clusters, which may be treated together.

The cold is at first external. We see it in a set of pure images which at first reading have no obvious metaphorical force: Coverdale and his friends begin their enterprise in a snowstorm, and as they gather around their fires the cold seems to press in from without. Then, following a brief spring and summer which some of the less perceptive of the utopians seem to expect to last forever, Coverdale returns to the farm in the fall. Once again the weather is cold, but by now the metaphorical implications are clearer, so that the images are like those I called "mixed" in *The Scarlet Letter*: Coverdale finds the "ice-temper" of the air invigorating because he is experiencing a momentary resurgence of faith. When his heart is warm, he can defy, or even enjoy, the outer cold. And what is implicit here, the uniting of the streams of heart, fire, and cold imagery, is also made explicit. Zenobia is talking to Priscilla about the latter's probable future as Hollingsworth's wife:

> "Poor child! Methinks you have but a melancholy lot before you, sitting all alone in that wide, cheerless heart, where, for aught you know,—and as I, alas! believe,—the fire which you have kindled may soon go out. Ah, the thought makes me shiver for you! What will you do, Priscilla, when you find no spark among the ashes?"

We were prepared for "that wide, cheerless heart" by the descriptions of the kitchen hearth, with its "old-fashioned breadth, depth, and spaciousness," much earlier. We see now that the hearth has been a symbolic heart all along. And the brushwood fires prepared us for the ardor which Priscilla has awakened in Hollingsworth and which Zenobia believes is bound to be short-lived. We can now see that the groundwork for all this was laid as early as the first chapter and elaborated in the meditation of Coverdale which opens chapter two:

> There can hardly remain for me (who am really getting to be a frosty bachelor, with another white hair, every week or so, in my mustache), there can hardly flicker up again so cheery a blaze upon the hearth, as that which I remember . . . at Blithedale. It was a wood-fire, in the parlor of an old farm-house, on an April afternoon, but with the fitful gusts of a wintry snow-storm roaring in the chimney. Vividly does that fireside re-create itself, as I rake away the ashes from the embers in my memory, and blow them up with a sigh, for lack of more inspiring breath. Vividly, for an instant, but, anon, with the dimmest gleam, and with just as little fervency for my heart as for my finger-ends! The staunch oaken logs were long ago burnt out. Their genial glow must be represented, if at all, by the merest phosphoric glimmer, like that which exudes, rather than shines, from damp fragments of decayed trees, deluding the benighted wanderer through a forest. Around such chill mockery of a fire some few of us might sit on the withered leaves, spreading out each a palm towards the imaginary warmth, and talk over our exploded scheme for beginning the life of Paradise anew.

* * *

FREDERICK C. CREWS

Turning the Affair into a Ballad†
* * *

* * * *The Blithedale Romance* is, in an almost incredibly cryptic way, an intelligible product of the obsessed Hawthorne whose private themes have become so predictable. I believe we can justify the supposition that Hawthorne, finding his literal plot hopelessly distorted by irrational fantasy, turned the book into a self-critical comedy by attributing that distortion to his narrator. Like James in *The Sacred Fount*, perhaps, he partially rescued a doomed story by stressing the principle of self-delusion inherent in the narrator's— and ultimately in his own—prying concern with other lives. In neither case is the irony sufficiently unambiguous or sufficiently discernible to the reader; the most we can say is that it is consistently available to close scrutiny.

Certainly it is difficult to take the bewildering "romance" among Hollingsworth, Zenobia, and Priscilla as the heart of the book as it now stands. No narrator ever had worse luck than Coverdale in

† From Frederick C. Crews, *The Sins of the Fathers: Hawthorne's Psychological Themes* (New York: Oxford University Press, 1966), pp. 194–212.

learning the most essential facts about the figures whose story we are supposed to enjoy. Late in the plot he summarizes the points he has yet to settle, and indeed will never get straight at all: "Zenobia's whole character and history; the true nature of her mysterious connection with Westervelt; her later purposes towards Hollingsworth, and, reciprocally, his in reference to her; . . . the degree in which Zenobia had been cognizant of the plot against Priscilla, and what, at last, had been the real object of that scheme." Most of the important scenes he describes, furthermore, are observed from an inconvenient distance, or are not observed at all. Two of his chapters—Zenobia's legend of the Veiled Lady and the autobiography of her father, old Moodie—are imaginative reconstructions of someone else's words, and for the most crucial meeting of Hollingsworth, Zenobia, and Priscilla he arrives "half-an-hour too late."

These puzzling difficulties become significant when we realize that Hawthorne, and indeed Coverdale himself, have taken considerable pains to suggest that the story as we read it is not to be altogether trusted.[1] Repeatedly the narrator warns us that his descriptions may interest us not merely for their element of truth but "as exemplifying the kind of error into which my mode of observation was calculated to lead me." As soon as we put a friend under our microscope we "insulate him from many of his true relations, magnify his peculiarities, inevitably tear him into parts, and, of course, patch him very clumsily together again. What wonder, then, should we be frightened by the aspect of a monster, which, after all—though we can point to every feature of his deformity in the real personage—may be said to have been created mainly by ourselves!" This is, to be sure, a familiar Hawthornian paradox, but in *The Blithedale Romance* it appears to have been carried to a logical extreme. For Coverdale not only takes poetic liberties with the events he is narrating; he represents himself as having known how they would turn out before they occurred. His dreams and fantasies at Blithedale, if they had been recorded, "would have anticipated several of the chief incidents of this narrative, including a dim shadow of its catastrophe." It is impossible to say whether Coverdale has really had foreknowledge or has seriously altered the facts in recounting them; the only certain point is that we are meant to see some degree of correspondence between his tale and the secret inclination of his mind. From both ends of the plot—in apparent foreknowledge and in narrative distortion—Coverdale shows us the condition of a man in the grip of some private symbolism.

Whatever the basis of Coverdale's obsession, the form it takes is

---

1. Some of the evidence for this and following statements may be found in my article, "A New Reading of *The Blithedale Romance*," *American Literature*, XXIX (May 1957), 147–70. My present view of the book, however, differs from the conclusions reached there.

literary. He imagines that his part has been "that of the Chorus in a classic play, which seems to be set aloof from the possibility of personal concernment, and bestows the whole measure of its hope or fear, its exultation or sorrow, on the fortunes of others, between whom and itself this sympathy is the only bond." Such aloofness is not to be confused with indifference; Coverdale is saying that he will allow his hope and fear to be expressed through his set of "characters." Indeed, that is just what he calls them—"these three characters . . . on my private theatre." If in real life he is "but a secondary or tertiary personage" with his friends, and if "these three had absorbed [his] life into themselves," he at least has the artistic luxury of contemplating their worthiness for a "sufficiently tragic catastrophe." "After all was finished," he thinks with satisfaction, "I would come, as if to gather up the white ashes of those who had perished at the stake, and to tell the world—the wrong being now atoned for—how much had perished there which it had never yet known how to praise." Though "real life never arranges itself exactly like a romance," this is precisely what Coverdale has hoped to make of it—a Blithedale Romance. The abandonment of this hope, after it has been smashed by a real-life tragedy with no literary trimming, constitutes the true resolution of Hawthorne's plot.

To state the case in this manner is perhaps to underrate the obvious intellectual content of *The Blithedale Romance*; as most critics have chosen to emphasize, the book is Hawthorne's *apologia*[2] for leaving Brook Farm and scorning its visionary ideals. I am certainly willing to believe that this was an important part of his intention when he began writing, but with Hawthorne self-justification invariably verges into self-criticism. What we in fact find in *The Blithedale Romance* is not so much a theoretical refutation of utopianism as an implied confession that the Hawthorne-Coverdale temperament is unsuited for real enterprises of any sort, whether spiritual or practical. One can abstract Coverdale's negative pronouncements about Blithedale into a body of social theory only by ignoring the intemperate sarcasm with which those pronouncements are delivered and the retractions that speedily follow them. Coverdale himself is aware, as Hawthorne's critics are often not, that all his contradictory opinions are dictated by his excessively self-conscious efforts to achieve a steady relation to his three "characters."

In order to understand Coverdale's complex situation it is not enough to see that he wants his three friends to act out a ready-made romance. Like other artist-heroes in Hawthorne's work he has a private failure of emotional capacity at the base of his need for aesthetic distance. He is the Hawthornian artist *par excellence*: a

2. A formal spoken or written defense. [*Editors.*]

poetaster and a retiring bachelor whose emotions can be clearly expressed only within a womblike woodland "hermitage" where the voluptuous entanglement of vines and trees is conducive to spying at secret *rendezvous* and daydreaming about artistic and erotic successes that will never be realized. "Had it ever been my fortune to spend a honey-moon," he explains, "I should have thought seriously of inviting my bride up thither"—namely, into "a hollow chamber, of rare seclusion . . . formed by the decay of some of the pine-branches, which the vine had lovingly strangled with its embrace." And yet the speaker of these lines—eloquent as they are in declaring his oneness with the sexual eccentrics who dominate Hawthorne's tales—tells us, when his "romance" has collapsed, that he was in love with Priscilla all along. Whether or not we are prepared to take the statement at face value, its insertion at the last possible moment is characteristic of the erotic furtiveness which pervades the narrative.

Thus we cannot rest content with the view of Coverdale adopted by Hollingsworth, who accuses him of feigning interest in utopianism only because "it has given you a theme for poetry," nor with the similar charge brought by Zenobia: "You are turning this whole affair into a ballad." These are half-truths which exaggerate the definiteness of Coverdale's intention and the steadiness of his aesthetic detachment. The cumulative evidence of Coverdale's own statements suggests that he cannot decide whether to win his companions' affection or to pry coldly into "the secret which was hidden even from themselves." Generally speaking, what happens in the plot is that Coverdale, harboring this uncertainty of purpose, half-intentionally alienates all three of his potential intimates and is thus driven increasingly into the role of literary snoop. Hollingsworth, Zenobia, and Priscilla become, no longer human companions, but "goblins of flesh and blood" from whom he would like to escape— but from whom he simultaneously wants to extort "some nature, some passion, no matter whether right or wrong, provided it were real." And correspondingly, his fantasies become at once more destructive and more literary as he is continually rebuffed. Well before the real tragedy of the book occurs, Coverdale

> began to long for a catastrophe. If the noble temper of Hollingsworth's soul were doomed to be utterly corrupted by [his] purpose . . . ; if the rich and generous qualities of Zenobia's womanhood might not save her; if Priscilla must perish by her tenderness and faith . . . ; then be it so! Let it all come! As for me, I would look on, as it seemed my part to do, understandingly . . . The curtain fallen, I would pass onward with my poor individual life, which was now attenuated of much of its proper substance . . .

This vengeful daydream recalls the consolations of other embittered artists in Hawthorne's fiction. Having survived his indifferent friends and emptied himself of concern for them (even at the price of losing all further meaning in his life), Coverdale will have the luxury of contemplating their doom "reverently and sadly."

Though it is impossible to draw a point-by-point comparison between the actual course of events and Coverdale's fantasies, we can observe that the real calamity of the plot makes Coverdale profoundly ashamed of those fantasies. This may suggest that something more is involved than mere disappointment of the wish to win Priscilla. Like some previous heroes Coverdale is made to feel guilty, or at any rate chastened, about a death he has not caused but has hazily "foreseen" in fantasy. It seems plausible to assume that one component of his feelings toward Zenobia—namely, the anxiety that has made the pale Priscilla a safer object of desire—has found the thought of her removal advantageous. Or we could surmise, with equal likelihood, that it is Hollingsworth, his rival for the affection of both women, against whom Coverdale's aggressive prophecies have been intended. In either case Coverdale has indeed anticipated "a dim shadow of the catastrophe" of his Blithedale Romance, and is jolted by the shocking explicitness of that catastrophe when it occurs.

Coverdale himself has no clear idea of why Hollingsworth, Zenobia, and Priscilla together are more meaningful to him than his relation to any one of them individually. And yet our awareness of the fantasies chronically harbored by Hawthorne's escapists may make us attentive to some revealing clues. Hawthorne and Coverdale have virtually begged us to see the story of Coverdale's friends —not just his attitude toward it, but the bare facts of the story itself—as indicative of the inmost tendency of his mind. That story, we must emphasize, is intricately involved in family matters of a vaguely guilty nature. The sexual rivals, Zenobia and Priscilla, turn out to be half-sisters. Their remorseful benefactor, old Moodie, is revealed to be their common father, who has neglected the child he loved best in order to live vicariously in the other child's splendor. The devilish mesmerist Westervelt, the touchstone of evil in *The Blithedale Romance*, is said to be Zenobia's former husband. He is thus related, however remotely, to the Priscilla who is perhaps turned over to his mesmeric power through the contrivance of Zenobia herself—a fine example of Hawthornian family co-opera-tion. Priscilla's rescue in turn is effected by the noble Hollingsworth, who, though he has hitherto loved her like "an elder brother," promptly marries her.[3]

3. Even the nature of Priscilla's affection for Zenobia seems a bit perverse if we follow the implications of Hawthorne's imagery: "Priscilla's love grew, and

These facts alone cannot be called proof that the furtiveness and ambivalence of Coverdale's attitudes may be related to a preoccupation with incest. Yet that speculation begins to seem more respectable as we examine the specific feelings his three friends arouse in him. The brash and bosomy feminist Zenobia, Coverdale's first and most deeply engaging figure of challenge, incites anxiety and defensive sarcasm by flaunting her sexuality before him. Her provocative language forces him to picture "that fine, perfectly developed figure, in Eve's earliest garment"—a vision not entirely welcome to a nature like Coverdale's. The significant fact, however, is that he can scarcely accept the blatantly obvious fact of her sexual experience, but must dwell on the question with prurient concern: "Pertinaciously the thought—'Zenobia is a wife! Zenobia has lived, and loved! There is no folded petal, no latent dew-drop, in this perfectly developed rose!'—irresistibly that thought drove out all other conclusions, as often as my mind reverted to the subject." This dainty pornography is continually rejected as "a masculine grossness—a sin of wicked interpretation, of which man is often guilty towards the other sex." The absurdity of such scrupulous fancies is diminished if we bear in mind that Zenobia is, for Coverdale's mind, less an individual person than "womanliness incarnated," and that his view of this womanliness is rather that of a scandalized son than a sophisticated bachelor. * * * Coverdale has not yet forgiven womankind for its deviation from the maternal ideal.

If Zenobia is to this extent eligible for sentiments that should properly attach themselves to a mother, Hollingsworth is more easily recognized as a version of the Hawthornian father. Though Coverdale is forced to respect him and yearn for his affection, the physically imposing, fiercely stern and fanatical Hollingsworth drains life from everyone who must live under his authority, and more particularly usurps all the feminine sympathy that Coverdale himself seeks. In retrospect it seems inevitable that he must eventually appear to Coverdale in the stereotyped role of the Hawthornian father, as "the grim portrait of a Puritan magistrate, holding inquest of life and death in a case of witchcraft." The transformation has been anticipated since Coverdale's first confession that he feels a need to exaggerate Hollingsworth's awesomeness: "In my recollection of his dark and impressive countenance, the features grew more prominent than the reality, duskier in their depth and shadow, and more lurid in their light; the frown, that had merely flitted across

---

twined itself perseveringly around this unseen sister; as a grape-vine might strive to clamber out of a gloomy hollow among the rocks, and embrace a young tree, standing in the sunny warmth above." The echo of Coverdale's "per-fectly inextricable knot of polygamy" in his tree-vine hermitage casts a metaphorical suspicion of fixated emotion even on the vapid Priscilla—or perhaps merely on Coverdale's interest in her.

his brow, seemed to have contorted it with an adamantine wrinkle."
Here we are observing Coverdale in the process of creating a bogey-
father, a devil; and significantly, the true "devil" of *The Blithedale
Romance*, Westervelt, is held responsible for having destroyed
Zenobia's much-lamented innocence.

As for Priscilla, she is literally a sister, she looks like a sister, she
is loved like a sister by Hollingsworth, and she inspires protective
brotherly feelings—mixed with an erotic desire which is confessed
later—on Coverdale's part. The shunting of that desire from
Zenobia to her is nothing more than what is demanded by Freudian
logic and Hawthornian precedent. Her integral role in Coverdale's
fantasy-family is indicated by his most revealing dream: "Hollingsworth and Zenobia, standing on either side of my bed, had bent
across it to exchange a kiss of passion. Priscilla, beholding this—for
she seemed to be peeping in at the chamber-window—had melted
gradually away, and left only the sadness of her expression in my
heart." The reader who doubts that Coverdale has unconsciously
cast himself as a son must wonder why this dream depicts Hollingsworth and Zenobia in the unorthodox erotic pose of bending across
Coverdale's bed. And all readers must surely note the moral ambiguity of the wish expressed in the dream. Priscilla is meant to be
disillusioned by the sexual passion which she has discovered in her
elders, yet Coverdale's own intentions toward her, as we later discern, are those of a lover. As in the unfinished romances, where real
brothers and sisters are forever about to become lovers or spouses,
the image of Priscilla-detached-from-Hollingsworth melts away before its purpose in Coverdale's mental scenario becomes too plain.

In all this, it may be objected, there is no compelling evidence
that Coverdale's hesitant designs on Priscilla, and more distantly on
Zenobia, are incestuous in quality. I agree. What we find is, on one
side, an extraordinary deviousness in his approach to both women,
and on the other a configuration of attitudes which, if discovered in
a real neurotic, would point to incestuous fixation. A man of mature years who dwells with awe and titillation on the possibility that
a mature woman may not be virginal, who must suppose that her
experience has been at the hands of a fiendish seducer, who hopes
for the love of a sexless girl but can do nothing to win her, and who
turns his sexual rival into an imaginary paternal tyrant—such a
man may justly be called a casualty of Oedipal strife.[4] The real
difficulty in applying this reasoning to Coverdale is that the literal
reality surrounding him conforms so well to his apparent fixation.
We must assume, as so often in the past, that the obsession of *The*

4. In Greek legend, Oedipus is the King
of Thebes who unwittingly kills his father
and marries his mother; in psychoanaly-
sis, then, Oedipal strife involves the unconscious tendency of a child to be attached to the parent of the opposite sex
and to feel hostility toward the other parent. [*Editors.*]

Blithedale Romance is jointly owned by the hero and the author. And this assumption is necessary anyway if we are to accept without astonishment the intricacy and secrecy of self-debate in this book. If Hawthorne has blurred all his portraits except Coverdale's, backed away from the simplest explanations of fact, exploited literal scenes for a cabalistic meaning that is lost upon the reader, and included episodes that make virtually no sense apart from such meaning, then we must infer that Hawthorne as well as Coverdale is at the mercy of unconscious logic.

* * *

KELLEY GRIFFITH, JR.

Form in *The Blithedale Romance*†

Most of the unfavorable criticism of *Blithedale* has centered on * * * problems of form. This criticism usually sees Blithedale as a "satire" of Brook Farm and holds that because Hawthorne could not maintain the satiric point of view, the book fails structurally.[1] Other critics, however, take an approach that helps make the form of *Blithedale* a unified whole. Their understanding is that Coverdale is central to the meaning and form of the book—that the actions and opinions of the characters (including Coverdale) must be seen as reflected off Coverdale's mind and not Hawthorne's. The form through which Hawthorne works in *Blithedale*, therefore, is entirely dependent on the very restricted point of view of Miles Coverdale, not on the omniscience of Hawthorne. Some critics have rejected this understanding because of the autobiographical overtones of the book.[2] Yet the critics who see Coverdale as the book's central focus agree that Hawthorne detached himself from Coverdale through irony. Granted, Hawthorne puts some of his Brook Farm notes into Coverdale's mind, but Coverdale is a fully drawn character apart from the author. At most, Coverdale is an objectified "part" of Hawthorne's psyche. He is what Hawthorne "might have become" had he not done this or that, but he is not the complete Hawthorne.[3]

† From *American Literature*, 40 (1968), 15–26.

1. See Robert C. Elliot, *"The Blithedale Romance," Hawthorne Centenary Essays*, ed. Roy Harvey Pearce (Columbus, Ohio, 1964), p. 111; Mark Van Doren, *Nathaniel Hawthorne* (New York, 1949), pp. 188–191; Hyatt H. Waggoner, *Nathaniel Hawthorne* (Minneapolis, 1962), pp. 41–42.

2. Van Doren, p. 189.
3. See Roy R. Male, Jr., "Toward *The Waste Land:* The Theme of *The Blithedale Romance," College English*, XVI, 278, 295 (Feb., 1955); Frederick C. Crews, "A New Reading of *The Blithedale Romance," American Literature*, XXIX, 149, 169 (May, 1957); William Hedges, "Hawthorne's *Blithedale:* The Function of the Narrator," *Nineteenth-*

I

Understanding Coverdale's character makes possible a new view of the form of *Blithedale*. Just as Hawthorne is not Coverdale, the erratic structure of Coverdale's narrative relates to Coverdale's personality, not Hawthorne's. In other words, Hawthorne purposely distorts the narrative in order to indicate Coverdale's state of mind. In this way, he works through the mind of a highly sensitive, ironical, intelligent, though disturbed mind much the way in which James works through Lambert Strether's or Sterne through Tristram Shandy's.[4] And, as Roy Male astutely observes, Hawthorne's Coverdale is a prefiguration of the modern self-conscious narrator, a nineteenth-century Jack Burden or Prufrock.[5]

The form Hawthorne uses for the book, consequently, cannot be defined in traditional structural terms. The plot does not proceed logically simply because Hawthorne did not intend for it to do so. The form of *Blithedale*, rather, is like that of an interior monologue, which represents the narrator's illogical thought processes and his attempts to shift events in his mind until he can settle on an arrangement satisfactory to himself.

An author may use many devices to give form to an interior monologue. Hawthorne's most consistent device—the device that gives form to the entire book—is dream. Daniel Hoffman has already noted Hawthorne's connection of dream with a stream-of-consciousness quality in *Blithedale*. "We can never be certain," he says, "whether Miles Coverdale is reporting what he has actually seen and heard, or what he has dreamed. Parts of the book indeed seem to rely on, to create, a stream-of-consciousness narration."[6] He further notes Hawthorne's own comment in the Preface that the Brook Farm experience seemed like a "day-dream, and yet a fact" to him: "In his romance," Hoffman says, "he has Miles Coverdale treat Blithedale as though it were both. . . . The facts and the dreams appear inextricably intertwined."[7]

Crucial in the form that Coverdale's dreams give *Blithedale* is the division of the book into halves. In the first half (up to Chapter xv), the narrative moves logically. Except for the Veiled Lady

Century Fiction, XIV, 303–304 (March, 1960); F. O. Matthiessen, *American Renaissance* (New York, 1941), pp. 229, 297; William O'Connor, "Conscious Naiveté in *The Blithedale Romance*," *Revue des Langues Vivantes*, XX, 44–45 (Feb., 1954).

4. Matthiessen, p. 297. [Lambert Strether is the main character in Henry James's *The Ambassadors* (1903); Tristram Shandy is the main character in *The Life and Opinions of Tristram Shandy, Gent.* (1759–67), a novel by Laurence Sterne. *Editors.*]

5. Male, *Hawthorne's Tragic Vision* (Austin, Tex., 1957), pp. 150–51. [Jack Burden, in describing the career of Willie Stark, a Southern politician, chronicles the story of his own moral life in Robert Penn Warren's *All the King's Men* (1946); Prufrock, in T. S. Eliot's dramatic monologue, "The Love Song of J. Alfred Prufrock" (1915), describes the psychological impasse of his life. (*Editors.*)]
6. Daniel Hoffman, *Form and Fable in American Fiction* (New York, 1961), p. 217.
7. Ibid.

legend and the sporadic appearances of Old Moodie, the reader can accept the events as reasonable enough. The second half, however, is extraordinary for its chaotic ordering of incidents and its refusal to fructify many of the crucial developments of the first half. The reason for this difference between the halves lies in Hawthorne's use of Coverdale's dreams. The first half we can accept for the most part as real; the second half we may see for the most part as dream—as a mirror of what Coverdale has seen and thought in the first half and of what he *in fact* learns after he leaves Blithedale.

Hawthorne's treatment of dream in *Blithedale* is complex and entangled with his major themes. He presents at least three types of dreams, all of which contain elements of one another, all of which represent the unreal or an imaginative reworking of the real. First, there is the "dream" of bringing about a utopia (Chapter III is named "A Knot of Dreamers"). This "dream" Hawthorne connects with the Puritan "dream" of establishing an ideal Christian society in the New World. Second, there is the "dream" created by the imagination and memory, which solidifies in the work of art, itself a "dream." The work of art seems equivalent to the stocking Mrs. Foster knits in Chapter V: she sits asleep yet keeps her needles moving; thus she foots the stocking "out of the texture of a dream." Finally, there is the dream one has when asleep. Coverdale has several vivid dreams of this sort. All of these dreams integrate with the veil and mask imagery that recur in the book and with the basic questions in Coverdale's mind as to what is real and unreal, how to get at the real, and how to represent the real (life) and the unreal (art).

The dreams Coverdale has when asleep and the "dreams" of his imagination figure prominently in the structure of the book. In them, Hawthorne creates the stream-of-consciousness narration that throws the second half out of phase with the first. All of the dream references in the first half, however, make the second half plausible. Following Hawthorne's own statement in the Preface that Brook Farm was "essentially a day-dream," Coverdale at the beginning pictures the Blithedale utopians as daydreamers. Through the dimness of his memory he creates dream-like characters: Zenobia appears "like a ghost, a little wanner than the life" and Priscilla is otherworldly. Coverdale's imagination is hyperactive. He constantly changes reality to something else. His imaginative gift he protects and nurtures and equates with his individuality: "Unless renewed," he says, "by a yet farther withdrawal [than Blithedale] towards the inner circle of self-communion, I lost the better part of my individuality." At his hermitage, which symbolizes withdrawal within himself, he decks Priscilla out with "fancy-work" and flings her an imaginary message. Hawthorne equates Coverdale's fits of imagination with a dream state. The reader may justifiably wonder how much of Coverdale's version of meeting Westervelt in the woods can be trusted. Coverdale goes into the woods to enjoy one of his self-contemplative moods "with my heart full of a drowsy pleasure." While walking, Coverdale fails to notice Westervelt, who manages to pass him by "almost without impressing either the sound or sight upon my consciousness." When they do meet, Westervelt has "almost the effect of an apparition," is a "spectral character." Later, at Eliot's Pulpit, Coverdale wonders if Westervelt were a goblin, "a vision that I had witnessed in the wood." Hawthorne also in the first half establishes the fact that Coverdale can dream fantastically when asleep. The night he falls ill, he has "half-waking dreams" that in his belief "would have anticipated several of the chief incidents of this narrative, including a dim shadow of its catastrophe." He views life through a "mist of fever" and sees Zenobia as an enchantress, whose "flower in her hair is a talisman": "if you were to snatch it away, she would vanish, or be transformed into something else." Zenobia calls this an "idea worthy of a feverish poet."

II

The first half of *Blithedale* then, is a fairly accurate telling of what Coverdale experiences at Blithedale Farm, but Hawthorne strews it with references to dream, and he establishes the fancifulness of Coverdale's mind and Coverdale's ability to dream psychic dreams. The second half, on the other hand, is literally a different story. The key chapter, the one that sets up the dream, stream-of-consciousness method, is Chapter XVI, "Leave-Takings." Hawthorne first indicates Coverdale's state of mind. Coverdale says that his change of attitude toward Blithedale was "dreamlike and miserable." He explains that at Blithedale he had lost a sense of the "existing state of the world." Of late he has felt that "everything in nature and human existence was fluid, or fast becoming so; that the crust of the Earth, in many places, was broken, and its whole surface portentously upheaving; that it was a day of crisis, and that we ourselves were in the critical vortex. Our great globe floated in the atmosphere of infinite space like an unsubstantial bubble." He wants to go back for a while to "the settled system of things." Zenobia in telling him goodbye refuses his help and says: "It needs a wild steersman when we voyage through Chaos! The anchor is up! Farewell!" Coverdale in turn tells Priscilla that he has a "foreboding that, were I to return even so soon as tomorrow morning, I should find everything changed." Of the principal characters, therefore, Zenobia and Coverdale are in a frenzied state of mind. The world for them has turned topsy-turvy. The second half of *Blithedale* will indeed be a voyage through chaos—*mental* chaos. And from this point on, the anchor is up.

Hawthorne next, in the last incident of the chapter, hints how he will take the reader on this voyage through chaos. Coverdale visits Silas Foster's four pigs and describes them as "the very symbols of slothful ease and sensual comfort." These "greasy citizens" "stifled, and buried alive" as they were in "their own corporeal substance," were "sensible of the ponderous and fat satisfaction of their existence": "Peeping at me, an instant, out of their small, red, hardly perceptible eyes, they dropt asleep again; yet not so far asleep but that their unctuous bliss was still present to them, betwixt dream and reality." In the following chapter, this piglike state is exactly the state that Miles Coverdale falls into when he settles in his hotel room. He orders a coal fire (in summer) and is "glad to find myself growing a little too warm with an artificial temperature." He begins to lose perspective: "At one moment, the very circumstances now surrounding me—my coal fire, and the dingy room in the bustling hotel—appeared far off and intangible. The next instant, Blithedale looked vague, as if it were at a distance both in time and space, and so shadowy, that a question might be raised whether the whole affair had been anything more than the thoughts of a speculative man. I had never before experienced a mood that so robbed the actual world of its solidity." Nonetheless, he will "enjoy the moral sillabub [of the mood] until quite dissolved away," just as the pigs might enjoy their evening meal.

Coverdale says that he spent the next few days in this mood, "in the laziest manner possible," reading a book that had a "sort of sluggish flow, like that of a stream in which your boat is as often aground as afloat." After visiting the theater one night, he sleeps and dreams about Hollingsworth, Zenobia, and Priscilla: "It was not till I had quitted my three friends that they first began to encroach upon my dreams." Supposedly he wakens from his dream, but the same dream mood, "one of those unreasonable sadnesses that you know not how to deal with, because it involves nothing for common-sense to clutch," lingers in his mind. His feelings of guilt well up within him that he left Blithedale too soon and resigned his friends "to their fate." Looking out the window, he sees Zenobia and Priscilla in the boarding house across from his hotel. The description of this discovery coincides with his mood. Coverdale says that he saw "with no positive surprise, but as if I had all along expected the incident" that the girl was Zenobia. Such expectancy and lack of surprise would be probable in a dream but hardly so in real life. Also, he sees Zenobia "like a full-length picture," as if she were appearing in the cinemascope of his mind rather than in a real boarding-house window.

This dream mood of Coverdale's, which, like the pigs', is between dream and reality, between sleeping and waking, pervades the entire sequence of events from his discovery of Zenobia in the boarding house (Chapter XVIII) to his falling asleep at Eliot's Pulpit after Zenobia's confrontation with Hollingsworth, near the end of the book (Chapter XXVI). Much, if not all, of what Coverdale reports between these chapters may be seen as dream or half-dream. This dream sequence proceeds in episodes.

The first episode begins with Coverdale's discovery of Zenobia and Priscilla in the boarding house. When Zenobia pulls down the curtain to cut off Coverdale's view, he reviews the moral question of his voyeurism, and suggests that if he had to be judge as well as witness to the events of Zenobia's and Hollingsworth's lives, he would pass down a just sentence yet would be mindful of his love for them and their good qualities. This prefigures the sequence at Eliot's Pulpit when Zenobia calls him "Judge Coverdale" and asks him to pass sentence on her and Hollingsworth. When Coverdale visits Zenobia's drawing room, the event is dream-like. The brilliancy of the room dazzles him: "it struck me that here was the fulfilment of every fantasy of an imagination, revelling in various methods of costly self-indulgence and splendid ease. Pictures, marbles, vases . . . and the whole repeated and doubled by the reflection of a great mirror, which showed me Zenobia's proud figure, likewise, and my own." Ironically, he tells Zenobia that the Blithedale days seem to him "like a dream," and Zenobia chides him for converting the past into a dream. He describes Priscilla as a dream-like figure, whose pure white dress "seems to be floating about her like a mist." To complete the dream aura, Coverdale tells Priscilla, "everything that I meet with, now-a-days, makes me wonder whether I am awake. You, especially, have always seemed like a figure in a dream—and now more than ever." Priscilla counters with the comment that Zenobia is much more like a dream than she is. Westervelt, the "spectral figure" of the first half, appears and takes the two "dreams" away. The title of the chapter is aptly "They Vanish."

The next episode in the dream sequence is Coverdale's meeting with Old Moodie. The saloon contains art works which either idealize reality or overemphasize it. It contains topers who seek rejuvenation through the dream state brought on by alcohol. The most unreal aspect of the saloon is the fountain, whose coral and rock-work and fishes are "like the fanciful thoughts that coquet with a poet in his dream." Old Moodie glides "like a spirit, assuming visibility close to your elbow." "His existence," says Coverdale, "looked so colorless and torpid—so very faintly shadowed on the canvass of reality—that I was half afraid lest he should altogether disappear, even while my eyes were fixed full upon his figure." Old Moodie tells his story, with which Coverdale admits taking "romantic and legendary license," while both he and Coverdale are slightly inebriated. The legend elaborates both on Fauntleroy's shadowy character, pointing out that as "from one dream into another, Fauntleroy looked forth out of his present grimy environment, into that past magnificence," and on Priscilla's ghostly quality. Zenobia's diamonds produce the same sort of dream effect in Old Moodie's room that the fountain does in the saloon. Coverdale ends the episode by admitting fabricating both Old Moodie's meeting with Zenobia and his thoughts about his two daughters after Zenobia leaves.

The third event in Coverdale's dream sequence occurs in a lyceum several weeks after his meeting with Old Moodie. He reflects on how he has spent hours deliberating on his friends, "and rendering them more misty and unsubstantial than at first, by the quantity of speculative musing, thus kneaded in with them. Hollingsworth, Zenobia, Priscilla! These three had absorbed my life into themselves." He then tells of finding Hollingsworth at the lyceum awaiting the appearance of the Veiled Lady. The incidents that Coverdale describes and his own actions are strange. He puts his mouth close to Hollingsworth's ear, addresses him in a "sepulchral, melodramatic whisper," and asks where Zenobia is. Skeptic though Coverdale is when awake, he finds himself believing horrible things about what one can do to another's soul. Hollingsworth gives a "convulsive start" when Coverdale asks what he has done with Priscilla. The Veiled Lady, that legendary figure from the first half of the book, appears like a "disembodied spirit." Finally, Hollingsworth calls Priscilla away, who gives a shriek, "like one escaping from her deadliest enemy."

The fourth episode in Coverdale's dream sequence contains the most dream-like chapter of all, "The Masqueraders," and sets the scene for Zenobia's death. It begins with Coverdale's going back to Blithedale and, again, brooding about his three friends: "Hollingsworth, Zenobia, Priscilla! They glided mistily before me, as I walked." And, again, he feels guilty about his role in their affairs. He cannot, as he walks, believe that Blithedale and the events of the summer have been real, and he asks the question that constantly plays on his mind, What is reality? He begins to catch glimpses of Blithedale Farm, saying, "That, surely, was something real." He reviews the "ominous impressions" that he has had since the end of the first half: "For, still, at every turn of my shifting fantasies, the thought stared me in the face, that some evil thing had befallen us, or was ready to befall." As he passes on in his trip back to Blithedale, he reviews meaningful places and things. He comes to the place in the river where Zenobia will drown. He rests for a moment in his hermitage. He gets angry at cows he has milked, who refuse to recognize him. And he comes on all of the Blithedale utopians, who are nightmarish in their attire and actions: "I saw a concourse of strange figures beneath the overshadowing branches; they appeared, and vanished, and came again, confusedly, with the streaks of sunlight glimmering down upon them." Instead of acting as his friends, they dance to "the devil's tune" and chase Coverdale: "The whole fantastic rabble forthwith streamed off in pursuit of me, so that I was like a mad poet hunted by chimaeras." As he runs from them, he stumbled over some dead logs and conjures up the "long-dead woodman, and his long-dead wife and children, coming out of their chill graves, and essaying to make a fire with this heap of mossy fuel!" He wanders from this spot "quite lost in reverie," neither knowing nor caring where he is going, when "a low, soft, well-remembered voice" calls to him. Another voice speaks and seems almost the voice of judgment, calling Coverdale to the Final Reckoning: "Miles Coverdale! . . . Let him come forward, then!"

Finally, in the last episode of the dream sequence, Coverdale finds himself confronted with his three friends at Eliot's Pulpit. There Zenobia taunts him about "following up" on his game, "groping for human emotions in the dark corners of the heart." He witnesses Zenobia's judgment of Hollingsworth, which is a repetition of his own opinions formed in the first half of the book, and the revelation of Zenobia's undefined offense against Priscilla, also which he has suspected since the first half. Zenobia calls Blithedale a "foolish dream," and after she leaves the spot Coverdale is "affected with a fantasy that Zenobia had not actually gone, but was still hovering about the spot, and haunting it." In a state of mental exhaustion, Coverdale sleeps and has a dream that "converged to some tragical catastrophe." His awakening confronts him face to face with the event that, far from being dream, is stark, brutal reality—Zenobia's death and the discovery of her body in the river.

All of these dream episodes, with the exception in part of the meeting with Old Moodie and with the Fauntleroy legend, follow a pattern that evolves from the first half of the book. The pattern begins first with Coverdale brooding, even "dreaming" about Hollingsworth, Zenobia, and Priscilla, something he did from the early chapters of the first half. Second, as he works them up in his imagination, he brings in his own guilt resulting from his moral obligation to them (he leaves them to their fate at the end of the first half) or from the questions relating to his art (he is a voyeur from the first). Third, he questions the value of Blithedale utopianism (often satirizing it, as in the lyceum incident, where Westervelt offers his version of utopia), and wonders what is reality—whether the events of the past, if not the present, are all dream. Both of these he does throughout the first half. Finally, he reiterates his judgment of Zenobia and Hollingsworth for taking advantage of

Priscilla. This judgment brings on his sense of foreboding, a foreboding that he began to have when he first suspected Hollingsworth's character.

The episodes in the dream sequence, therefore, are a stream-of-
consciousness, dream mirror of the events in the first half of the
book. But because they bring the Priscilla-Hollingsworth-Zenobia
relationship to a crisis, they are also reflections of facts that Coverdale has found out in "waking moments" since the first half, facts
that Coverdale chooses to leave hazy but which have enough significance to bring on the catastrophe that ends the book. The reader, of
course, can never know specifically what these facts are because we
see them only through the distorted medium of Coverdale's dreams.

Seeing how dream molds the form of *The Blithedale Romance*
introduces numerous new possibilities in interpreting this enigmatic
novel of Hawthorne's. It possibly brings the book into another
genre, the dream allegory. *The Blithedale Romance* resembles Bunyan's *Pilgrim's Progress*,[8] the one dream allegory that Hawthorne
knew best, more than it resembles any other book. The pilgrim
imagery throughout the book, like the dream imagery, is manifest,
and just like the narrator of *Pilgrim's Progress*, Coverdale seems to
"dream a dream" of allegorical significance.[9] Although as the central "pilgrim" of the book he has not reached the Celestial City, he
at least can face his moral problems, write them out for all to see,
and admit the one thing that will throw light on the most morally
agonizing event in his life. *Blithedale*, in fact, is Coverdale's attempt
to purge through art, through allegory, the guilt and suffering from
his soul. His confession of love for Priscilla is not a confession of
love for a human being (for Coverdale is most obviously drawn

8. In *Pilgrim's Progress* (1678–84), John
Bunyan, English religious writer and
preacher, describes the journey of the
God-fearing on the road to salvation.
[*Editors.*]
9. There are numerous uses of pilgrim
imagery in *Blithedale*. As Coverdale con-
valesces from his illness, for example, he
reads Emerson, Carlyle, and George
Sand, who, he says "were well adapted
. . . to pilgrims like ourselves." He emphasizes his own pilgrim role in Chapter
XVI when he says that after he has trav-
eled and "the colonists of Blithedale have
established their enterprise on a permanent basis, I might fling aside my pilgrim-
staff and dusty shoon, and rest as peacefully here as elsewhere."
In the second half of the book, the
main characters take on a significance
more specifically allegorical than in the
first half. Priscilla seems to represent a
choice not only for Hollingsworth but
also for Coverdale. She symbolizes a
way of life and a way of art, not altogether wholesome, for Coverdale. William
O'Connor is possibly right when he suggests that Priscilla may stand for the
otherworldly values of transcendentalism
(op. cit., p. 44). Certainly Hawthorne
takes a healthy swipe at transcendentalism through Priscilla when Westervelt
says that the limitations of time and space
have no existence within Priscilla's veil:
"This hall," he says, "—these hundreds
of faces, encompassing her within so narrow an amphitheatre—are of thinner substance, in her view, than the airiest vapor
that the clouds are made of. She beholds
the Absolute!" How very like Emerson
that sounds! Priscilla's antagonist, Hollingsworth, the pilgrim similar to the
Apostle Eliot, is condemned at Eliot's
Pulpit to the fate that supposedly the
Apostle avoided: "I see in Hollingsworth,"
Coverdale says, "an exemplification of the
most awful truth in Bunyan's book of
such;—from the very gate of Heaven,
there is a by-way to the pit!"

physically and emotionally to Zenobia) but love for the way of life and art that she allegorizes in his imagination.

But more important, Hawthorne's use of dream in *Blithedale* makes the book—and thus Hawthorne—more meaningful for us today. Lionel Trilling's strictures that Hawthorne does not, like Kafka,[1] set the reader free from the restrictions of reality appear invalid. Kafka, Trilling says, is aesthetically successful because his imagination deals only with subjective reality: "Like the dream, it confronts subjective fact only, and there are no aesthetically unsuccessful dreams, no failed nightmares." On the other hand, Hawthorne's "too limited faith in the imagination" makes him insist "that the world is there, that we are dependent upon it": "At his very most powerful, Hawthorne does not interpose his imagination between us and the world; however successfully he may project illusion, he must point beyond it to the irrefrangible solidity."

Yet the second half of *Blithedale is* dream. In it Hawthorne does "interpose his imagination between us and the world"; he sets the reader free from objective reality and sends him floating down the stream of Coverdale's chaotic conscious. As Zenobia says, the anchor is up!

Dream, consequently, does more than harmonize the disparate structural elements of *The Blithedale Romance* into one unified whole; it makes the book relevant in a century influenced by Kafka, Joyce, and Eliot.[2]

LOUIS AUCHINCLOSS

The Blithedale Romance: A Study of Form and Point of View†

* * *

I remember, many years back, when I read *The Blithedale Romance* for the first time, that I thought it was one of the clumsiest uses of narration that I had ever come across. I think it strikes many first-time readers this way. It starts off by doing precisely what narrator novels are supposed not to do: it mystifies the reader. Instead of being able to rely on the "I" character to give one

1. Franz Kafka (1883–1924), Austrian poet and writer of surrealistic psychological and philosophical fiction. [*Editors.*]
2. James Joyce (1882–1941), Irish poet, novelist, and dramatist; author of the novels *A Portrait of the Artist as a Young Man* (1916), *Ulysses* (1922), and *Finnegans Wake* (1939). Thomas Stearns Eliot (1888–1965), American-born British poet and essayist, author of *The Sacred Wood* (critical essays, 1920), *The Waste Land* (poem, 1922), *Murder in the Cathedral* (play, 1935). [*Editors.*]
† From *Nathaniel Hawthorne Journal* (1972), 53–58.

accurate data, one has to examine everything he says for a further meaning. This atmosphere of partial disclosure is set with his very name—*Cover*dale. In the first chapter he talks to Old Moodie who is wearing a patch over one eye, and reference is made to a lady who is veiled and to another called Zenobia, but whose name is a *pseudonym*. All that seems to occur in this chapter is that the narrator refuses to undertake a mission, the nature of which Old Moodie refuses to disclose. Kafka himself could not have opened a tale with less information conveyed.

Thereafter the mystifications proliferate. Coverdale has been to the Veiled Lady to inquire as to the success of the Blithedale experiment. He tells us that her response unveiled itself—with true sibylline stamp—to a variety of interpretations "one of which has certainly accorded with the event." Nowhere in the novel are we told what that response was or what event it accorded with.

When Coverdale meets Zenobia at Blithedale he observes that she makes the whole heroic enterprise show like a counterfeit Arcadia. He tries to analyze this impression but with no success. Is it because Zenobia has come to Blithedale only with a purpose of following Hollingsworth, a man whom she has heard lecture but whom she has never met? Has she already fallen in love with him?

When Priscilla comes to Coverdale's room in Blithedale to bring him a letter from the famous Margaret Fuller, he notices a resemblance in Priscilla to Miss Fuller. What is the point of this? Priscilla would seem, in character at least, to be the very opposite of Margaret Fuller. Is it a device to put the reader off the track of Margaret Fuller's actual resemblance to Zenobia? Or is it to prepare us for Zenobia's death by drowning? Presumably every reader of the time would know that Miss Fuller had met her own end that way, although not, of course, by suicide.

If we are not sure why Zenobia comes to Blithedale, we are equally uncertain as to Hollingsworth's motive. Coverdale suggests that it may have been to dwell with people who are in dissent, as Hollingsworth is, with the world. But is it not also possible that he may have come to solicit Zenobia's money for his enterprise or even to look over the farm which, as it turns out later, he wants as a site for his institute? We never know to what extent he is using his own personal attraction as a means of prying money out of Zenobia or even to what extent he has been prepared to sacrifice Priscilla to the greater goal of obtaining Zenobia's funds.

Nor do we know how Hollingsworth has been able to trace Priscilla to the Veiled Lady or why he finally turns up at the same performance attended by Coverdale where he liberates her from the spell of the magician.

When Coverdale returns to Blithedale, he discovers that Zenobia has been stripped of her fortune. We may presume that old Moodie has taken legal action to recover his inheritance as a revenge on Zenobia for having turned Priscilla over to Westervelt, but we never *know* this. If Moodie gives the money to Priscilla what does she do with it? She and Hollingsworth are last seen living in modest circumstances.

Most mysterious of all is Coverdale's famous final assertion that all the while he has been in love with Priscilla. Are we meant to believe this? Are we meant to believe that *he* believes it? Why has his preoccupation been entirely with Zenobia, whom he keeps visualizing stripped of her clothes?

As if to prepare us for all these confusions, Coverdale puts us early on notice that he is not a reliable reporter. As soon as he has established his own primary concern with the Zenobia-Priscilla-Hollingsworth triangle—as soon, that is, as he has set this up as the principal subject of his story—he proceeds to accuse himself of a bad habit of exaggeration. Furthermore, Zenobia and Hollingsworth both denounce his quality of intellectual detachment. They would obviously be totally dissatisfied with any assessment of their lives made by Coverdale. Whom, then, are we to believe? What is Hawthorne up to? Is it just a literary game?

Far from being a literary game, I believe that Hawthorne, in putting this novel together, was engaged in the most serious enterprise of his literary career. In all of his books and throughout his life he was obsessed with the problem of the detached soul, of the man who saw but did not fully feel—of the *voyeur*. In Miles Coverdale he created a character whose function is to make the reader feel the experience of living a half life as Hawthorne himself felt it, and as he may have suspected that most men felt it. The very success which he achieves makes the book difficult to read. Indeed, it makes it in places an almost disagreeable experience. I find a stifling quality in the novel which makes me keep wishing to put it down. The atmosphere in which the characters are drenched is dream-like and frustrating. One keeps reaching and reaching as the truth keeps eluding one's grasp. But Coverdale, I am convinced, is never deliberately seeking to hoodwink the reader. He is attempting to describe the world as it impresses itself on his senses rather than to pass on mere intellectual conclusions from observed facts. Thus he is never allowed to tell us of events which he has learned of second-hand. He must allow us to make our own inferences from the facts as they appeared at first instance to him. The process moves us gradually *into* Coverdale's mind so that we share in his sensations. This takes considerable treatment.

In order to convey Miles Coverdale's peculiar sense of how the activities of other and (at least to his way of thinking) greater, souls appeared to him, Hawthorne has adopted an interesting technique. The book is told by a narrator, but the reader learns only such things as he would have learned had he been present with the narrator *as* the episodes occur. He is not given any information existing in Miles Coverdale's mind independently of what he and Coverdale jointly see and hear. He may, however, share with Coverdale knowledge of public events, and two of the characters of the novel, Zenobia and Hollingsworth, are represented as being in the public eye. And, of course, he may learn facts *with* Coverdale, as both observe them for the first time. Let us see this technique at work.

In the first chapter, Coverdale tells the reader that he has had a response to his inquiry from the Veiled Lady, but he does not reveal what that response was. This is because the episode occurred before —if only just before—the action of the novel commences.

The first character we meet is Old Moodie, but we are not told that he makes his living by selling purses which his daughter has made (a fact which Coverdale knows) because he is not in the act of selling purses when the reader first observes him. When he later sees Priscilla engaged in making a purse, and when Old Moodie comes to inquire about her in Blithedale, he at last makes the connection. But by the time he makes it, the author is almost impatient with him. Coverdale asks Old Moodie to tell him about the maker of the little purses, and Hollingsworth interrupts with the retort: "Why do you trouble him with needless questions, Coverdale? You must have known, long ago." In this curious fashion Coverdale takes the blame for the reader's slowness in catching up with him. It creates a sense of intimacy between reader and narrator.

When Zenobia first appears, Coverdale speculates that she will turn their serious enterprise into a masquerade. Why? Her next speech reveals the answer to the reader. She has not come to Blithedale because of its ideals but merely to be close to Hollingsworth. Here is an example of the reader and Coverdale receiving an important impression together.

When Coverdale reveals information that he has obtained before the action commences and independently of what he and the reader have observed together, such as the fact that Hollingsworth was once a blacksmith, he is careful to add "as the reader probably knows." *Why* should the reader probably know? Because Hollingsworth, like Zenobia, is a public figure whose career is partially known to the reader as it is partially known to Coverdale.

When Coverdale first meets Professor Westervelt in the woods, he fails to recognize him, although it later turns out that Westervelt is the impresario who directs the Veiled Lady, and we know that

Coverdale has been present at one of these performances. Is Coverdale fooling the reader here? No. It is perfectly clear that Coverdale does *not* recognize Westervelt. Recognition only comes towards the end of the novel when Coverdale attends another performance of the Veiled Lady and sees a bearded man in Oriental costume, and realizes that this is Westervelt in disguise and that it is the third time that he has seen him. This is the point where the reader and Coverdale at last achieve a union of knowledge about Zenobia, Hollingsworth and Priscilla, and from here on they merge into the observer. The effect of this union is to give a tremendous impact to the "trial scene" when Zenobia and Hollingsworth have their final, shattering confrontation. There are still things that the reader does not know, but Coverdale does not know them, either, which makes them seem even darker and more mysterious. Who has taken away Zenobia's wealth? Why has it not been given to Priscilla? To what extent was Hollingsworth guilty of subjecting Priscilla to the evil influence of Westervelt?

The subtlety of Hawthorne's technique was never fully appreciated by Henry James although the latter professed to admire him. James found him a good deal simpler as a technician than we find him today. But consider what Hawthorne has done to us through the character of Coverdale. By establishing a relationship between the reader and the narrator whereby they start knowing certain facts available to the general public and learn other facts together by watching the action unfold until the point where the reader has finally enough facts to be able to deduce all the other facts previously known by the narrator, Hawthorne is able to bring his reader gradually around to the narrator's point of view until there is a kind of explosion of recognition at the point where fusion is complete. At this point the verisimilitude is intensified by the fact that there still remain elements in the story unknown to both reader and narrator.

What Hawthorne achieves by the use of the double vision of the reader and Coverdale is that he can thus offer the reader the experience of a gradual fusion with his narrator. One has something of the impression, in reading the book, of actually turning into Coverdale. It is by no means always an agreeable experience. The isolation of the narrator seems at times an individual complaint, at times a universal one and at times something that the reader alone shares guiltily with him. Coverdale says: "In the midst of cheerful society, I had often a feeling of loneliness." He is always intensely aware of his habit of standing outside the course of human events as a mere spectator, but he desperately tries to justify his role as that of a loving and deeply concerned observer. He even, in one passage, goes so far as to place himself in the position of an inquisitor who, having burned his victims, i.e., Zenobia and Hollingsworth, searches

lovingly among the ashes for relics which, now that their sin has
been expiated, will become objects to be venerated. But the reader
never becomes Coverdale to the extent of believing this, for Coverdale never quite believes it himself. When Zenobia denounces his
habit of spying as "a cold-blooded criticism, founded on a shallow
interpretation of self-perceptions, an irreverent propensity to thrust
Providence aside and substitute oneself in its awful place," the
reader not only agrees with her, but he feels something like guilt at
having spied on Zenobia with Coverdale.

The narrator's final revelation that all along he has been in love
with Priscilla has caused a great deal of speculation. Philip Rahv
has gone so far as to say that it is not to be believed. It is perfectly
clear to Rahv that Coverdale all along has been in love with
Zenobia and that the pale and ineffectual Priscilla could never have
aroused so much emotion. But I cannot agree. To me this final
revelation is meant to relate directly back to the unanswered prediction of the Veiled Lady. The tragedy of Coverdale is always to
overlook what is directly his own concern in favor of living vicariously in the lives of others. He will not engage in life; he will not
risk himself. Zenobia's fable of Theodore who refused to kiss the
Veiled Lady until he had first raised her veil and thus lost her
forever is directly applicable to Coverdale. Both Hawthorne and
Zenobia intend it so. Coverdale has ignored Priscilla in his fascination with Zenobia and Hollingsworth. But the loss is not his alone.
Hawthorne is making a further point that the *voyeur* can do actual
harm to others as well as to himself. Had Coverdale paid more
attention to Priscilla when he first spotted her resemblance to Margaret Fuller, had he recognized that this was the signal of his own
original attraction, he might have removed Priscilla from the drama,
and Zenobia and Hollingsworth might then have worked things out
for themselves. Zenobia herself makes this point passionately at a
later point when she rebukes Coverdale for overlooking Priscilla.
The final twist of the ending is that the detached observer helped to
cause the tragedy that he thought he was only observing.

I might make an observation, in closing this analysis of the novel,
about the use which Hawthorne makes of the contrast between
country and city which permeates the whole book. The city is the
natural environment for the *voyeur*, who, like Coverdale, can watch
the goings on of his neighbors by peering from his back window
into their back windows. The city is the best place for Coverdale to
live so long as he cannot transcend his own spiritual limitations, and
he is able to find considerable contentedness, even occasional happiness, in its crowded life of restaurants, bars, theatres and auction
galleries. But the country, which must always beckon him, represents the two aspects of life where he constantly fails: the idealistic
aspirations of men as exemplified in the Blithedale experiment and

the love of men and women as exemplified by Hollingsworth, Zenobia and Priscilla. Coverdale sympathizes with the Blithedale experiment, but he has a mind and temperament that must always keep turning to the inevitable failure of such schemes. In similar fashion, he would like to be able to give himself to an inspiring passion but he cannot do so. He must fancy himself attracted by Zenobia because he knows her affections are already engaged, and he must not see his love for Priscilla until after she is married to another man. In this way he must always guard himself from any wholehearted participation in the life of the heart or in the life of the mind.

JAMES H. JUSTUS

Hawthorne's Coverdale: Character and Art in *The Blithedale Romance*†

* * *

II

It is curious that *Blithedale* is such a dispassionate document. Despite its subject, it lacks the fire and thunder appropriate to the widespread hyperbolism of reformist New England. Hollingsworth's moral enthusiasm before his break with Coverdale is low-keyed for a man who is described as "forever fiddling on a single string," and the early Zenobia is as much a chattering dilettante as Coverdale. It is almost as if Hawthorne had taken the fervent reformers of his time, who from most accounts turn out to be impassioned creatures of both mind and tongue—almost their own caricatures of re-formers—and scaled them down into characters less sensational, less melodramatic, less visceral than their general counterparts in real life.

One critic believes that Hollingsworth is "an unimpressive monomaniac" and Zenobia is "an unconvincing feminist" because of Hawthorne's inept characterization.[1] More to the point is Haw-thorne's necessity for giving over the duties of characterization to his artist-narrator, whose skill at painting such portraits is not equal to the bias which nourishes them. Hawthorne's subject of course is not reform, and Miles Coverdale is not the spokesman for a specific reform movement. Yet Coverdale is convincing in his revealed ambivalences toward reform and reformers; his earlier faint praise of Hollingsworth and his admiration for the New Woman cannot

† From *American Literature*, 47 (1975), 21–36. The author's notes have been re-numbered and some have been omitted.

1. Rudolph Von Abele, *The Death of the Artist: A Study of Hawthorne's Disinte-gration* (The Hague, 1955), p. 83.

conceal Coverdale's perverse psychic thrill in seeing both finally get their comeuppance. In this complex work, the nature of reform and the nature of the narrator are mutually reinforcing aspects of Hawthorne's vision.

As a document, *The Blithedale Romance* directly confronts the question, livelier perhaps in antebellum Massachusetts than elsewhere, of "How shall a man live?" It exploits the competing claims for saying how, from such pseudo-sciences as mesmerism and spiritualism to such serious concerns as social theory and humanitarianism. Indeed, it touches upon choices demanded by a reformist culture: material grubbing or spiritual transformation? labor or leisure? commerce or art? urban or rural values? patchwork revision or radical reform? dilettantism or ideology? The generating energies in this narrative emerge from what Hawthorne's Concord neighbor Emerson referred to variously as "The Present Age," "The Times," or "The Mind and Manners of the XIX Century." Here, the truths of the human heart are tested by the explicitly social and cultural ferment of reform, the most characteristic signature of American life in the 1840's and 1850's. In no other of his fictions does Hawthorne encompass such a remarkable spectrum of life-styles of his time; *Blithedale* is his "Mind and Manners of the XIX Century," his one romance that at least aspires to the form of the novel.

The pivot in this romance-novel is Coverdale. The bits and pieces of the story of the Blithedale brotherhood form the substance of Coverdale's story; these same bits and pieces, augmented by the ramifying implications of the urban past and the conflict of influences both personal and ideological in Coverdale,[2] form the substance of Hawthorne's story. If Coverdale is an embarrassingly peripheral actor in the romance of Blithedale, Hawthorne makes him the leading performer in *The Blithedale Romance*. That Coverdale, as narrator, is not entirely to be trusted in the tale he tells is by now generally accepted, but Coverdale's limitations follow from the contextual fact that the elusive and disjointed events which Coverdale relates are totemistic events whose importance lies in the valuations he puts on them.[3] The character of this narrator finally cannot

2. Leo B. Levy is the only critic to stress societal change as an important context for the fate of Hawthorne's characters. Coverdale, he observes, stands midway between the forces of a newly mechanized society and an older rural America. See "*The Blithedale Romance*: Hawthorne's 'Voyage Through Chaos,' " *Studies in Romanticism*, VIII (Autumn, 1968), 1–15.

3. In "A New Reading of *The Blithedale Romance*," *American Literature*, XXIX (May, 1957), 147–170, Frederick C. Crews finds Coverdale a morally deficient narrator; in *Sins of the Fathers*, he finds crippling Oedipal compulsions as well. William Hedges argues for a Coverdale

who learns from his experiences in "Hawthorne's *Blithedale*: The Function of the Narrator," *Nineteenth-Century Fiction*, XIV (March, 1960), 303–316. Kelley Griffith, Jr.'s "Form in *The Blithedale Romance*," *American Literature*, XL (March, 1968), 15–26, and Nina Baym's "*The Blithedale Romance*: A Radical Reading," *JEGP*, LXVIII (Oct. 1968), 545–569, are the two most pertinent studies which concentrate on the narrator as Hawthorne's subject. See also Louis Auchincloss, "*The Blithedale Romance*: A Study in Form and Point of View," *Nathaniel Hawthorne Journal*, II (1972), 53–58.

be abstracted from the form which he encloses (the story he tells), but, more crucially, he cannot be abstracted from the form which encloses him (the story which Hawthorne tells).

Whereas this minor New England poet writes of a failed communal enterprise, Hawthorne writes of a failed human being—and does so both as romancer and novelist. Coverdale explores the weaknesses of egotists, faithless lovers, proud businessmen brought low, females both liberated and parasitic, grubby Yankee farmers, and spiritualist charlatans, all of whom undercut the high purposes of Blithedale; Hawthorne explores the process by which a man who shrinks from the taint of human imperfection dooms himself irrevocably to a life of sterile complacency.

The mannerisms which so annoy Coverdale's friends are not only the traits of a self-indulgent Boston gentleman; they are also symptoms of an unfulfilled poet whose life in the city has been as comfortably conventional as his verse. Psychologically, Coverdale is never far away from his urban quarters, which he alludes to several times, and the society which shapes his tastes and values. If his good life suggests dilettantism, the tenacity with which he mentally clings to it suggests the need for emotional anchoring. His bout of chills and fever at Blithedale, following his exposure to the unseasonable weather, is a physical equivalent of the emotional strain involved in the transition. In a new and untried society, he recalls the stable charm of what he has left behind:

> My pleasant bachelor-parlor, sunny and shadowy, curtained and carpeted, with the bed-chamber adjoining; my centre-table, strewn with books and periodicals; my writing desk, with a half-finished poem in a stanza of my own contrivance; my morning lounge at the reading-room or picture gallery; my noontide walk along the cheery pavement, with the suggestive succession of human faces, and the brisk throb of human life, in which I shared; my dinner at the Albion, where I had a hundred dishes at command . . . ; my evening at the billiard-club, the concert, the theatre, or at somebody's party, if I pleased:—what could be better than all this?

The man whose comfort is made secure by "a good fire burning in the grate" and a closet stocked with champagne and claret must adjust to plain tea from "earthen cups" before a more unrestrained fire of peat, pine, and oak in a country fireplace.

III

Miles Coverdale begins his last chapter with a conventional tack: "It remains only to say a few words about myself." What follows, however, is gratuitous, since the entire story has been more a self-dramatization than an account of a failed communal experiment. What the reader learns of the founding and disbanding of Blithedale is thin, curiously inert, generalized; any sense of a thickly textured life comes primarily from the minutely recorded stages of the narrator's personal relationships.

Amiable as he is, Coverdale displays revealing deficiencies both as a man and as an artist, and those deficiencies matter. While Hawthorne was always too ambivalent about the artist ever to equate the good man and good artist, both kinds of flaws in Coverdale coincide in such a way that they not merely round out the portrait of one character but also signal Hawthorne's abiding interest in both the implications of the cold heart in human affairs and in the possibilities and limitations of art. From his own account, two aspects of Coverdale can be isolated for analysis without damaging the overall texture of his narrative: his attitude toward Hollingsworth (which suggests his frailty as a man) and his use of Zenobia as symbol (which establishes the aesthetic boundaries of his art). Coverdale's judgment that he has made "but a poor and dim figure in [his] own narrative," like so many evaluations which he makes earlier, is untrue. Though the springs of action for most of the principals in the story remain hidden, those of Coverdale do not. For all his flaws he is the most familiar, the most knowable character in the book.

Coverdale's declaration of love for Priscilla at the end of his narrative may not be as jejune as earlier readers took it to be, but it indicates a spiritual impoverishment more profound than some readers now are willing to grant.[4] Prior to his "Confession," Coverdale gives no indications that he looks upon the seamstress as anything more than a vacuous encumbrance, a patronizing attitude betraying a social and intellectual snobbery. Throughout the narrative, however, he has been attracted to both Zenobia—for her sexuality, her intelligence and passion, and her "mystery"—and Hollingsworth—for his masculine authoritativeness and his magnetism; he has even been drawn briefly, Coverdale admits, to the despicable Westervelt. But all are finally irrelevant in the matter. "Miles Coverdale's Confession" covertly acknowledges an inability to love, a radically disabling flaw which cripples him both as man and artist. His unimpressive substitutes for love, on which he expends considerable energy, are a peevish antipathy for masculine power and an exaggerated emphasis on feminine passion. Those substitutes are a direct outgrowth of his disappointing relationships with Hollingsworth and Zenobia.

Critics usually take Hollingsworth's scheme to rehabilitate criminals at face value (which is to say at Coverdale's valuation)—at best a single-minded, abstract, "partial" reform of the kind which both

4. Ellen Morgan for example, argues convincingly that Coverdale's passion for Zenobia is psychologically displaced by Priscilla in the "confession," but concludes curiously that Coverdale is "finally not a failure, but . . . a man capable of a profoundly moving lover's obsession." See "The Veiled Lady: The Secret Love of Miles Coverdale," *Nathaniel Hawthorne Journal* (1971), 169–81.

Emerson and Hawthorne distrusted, and at worst one that is gran-
diose, self-serving, dishonest, and possibly illegal. Although Hollingsworth's language in Chapter 15 is egocentric and absolutist, as
befitting the radical reformer, much of the extremist tone is a result
of Coverdale's mediating consciousness. After Hollingsworth rejects
Coverdale's proposal to put some of Fourier's principles to work at
Blithedale, Coverdale uses the incident to charge his friend with a
lack of "real sympathy with our feelings and our hopes"; and he
characterizes Hollingsworth's philanthropic reform with such terms
as "one channel," "prolonged fiddling upon one string," and "his
lonely and exclusive object in life." But Hollingsworth rejects the
Fourieristic system because he believes it to be based on "the selfish
principle—the principle of all human wrong, the very blackness of
man's heart, the portion of ourselves which we shudder at, and
which it is the whole aim of spiritual discipline to eradicate."

And though his own scheme may be overly sanguine, its principle
is unselfishness.[5] It concerned, Coverdale reports, "the reformation
of the wicked by methods moral, intellectual, and industrial, by the
sympathy of pure, humble, and yet exalted minds, and by opening
to his pupils the possibility of a worthier life than that which had
become their fate." Since even in the narrator's paraphrase the
project sounds more admirable than heinous, to discredit it Coverdale falls back on what "most people thought": that it was "impracticable." But Hollingsworth rightly assesses the impracticable-
ness of Blithedale, which is, he says, "a wretched, unsubstantial
scheme . . . on which we have wasted a precious summer of our
lives." As reforms go, Hollingsworth's is considerably more tangible
and less self-serving than the Blithedale experiment, which Coverdale defends in language that betrays an unsupportable position
even as it reveals the abstraction of his commitment.

The man who in April calls Blithedale a "counterfeit Arcadia"
and who with his "customary levity" admits that he has little purpose in life other than to "make pretty verses, and play a part, with
. . . the rest of the amateurs, in our pastoral," is the same man who in
August exclaims that the community is now "beginning to flourish."
Hollingsworth disagrees: "It is full of defects—irremediable and
damning ones!—from first to last, there is nothing else! I grasp it in
my hand, and find no substance whatever. There is not human
nature in it!" Coverdale's adherence to the idealism of Blithedale is
escapist, and Hollingsworth's invitation to "strike hands" with him
promises this minor poet no more "languor and vague wretchedness"
but "strength, courage, immitigable will—everything that a manly

5. Zenobia's evaluation of Hollingsworth
("It is all self!"), though understandable,
is not necessarily the complete story;
moreover, the rage is directed toward
Hollingsworth the man and would-be husband rather than Hollingsworth the philanthropist.

and generous nature should desire!" From Coverdale's perspective, the temptation is evil, but from the reader's it has all the marks of a healthy alternative for "an indolent or half-occupied man."

What Hollingsworth offers to Coverdale is what Coverdale, given his coldness and abstraction, cannot accept: a tangible brotherhood, disinterested devotion, generous cooperation, purpose, and above all, love. Coverdale admits, "I stood aloof." It is the stance that damns. Blithedale is a sham, but as long as it is detached from what Hollingsworth calls "human nature," as long, that is, as it is safely idealized, Coverdale can pretend to a new life of courage and purpose. A few days after the "crisis" in the potato patch, Coverdale, with "intolerable discontent and irksomeness," lays down his hoe, says farewell to the pigs, and takes his first leave of Blithedale.

If Coverdale's failure as a man is crystallized in his "tragic passage-at-arms" with Hollingsworth, his failure as an artist is confirmed by his last meeting with Zenobia, a scene marked by his inability to redeem his superficial and derivative art with insight and charity. After Hollingsworth's rejection of Zenobia, only Coverdale witnesses her convulsive weeping. Regaining her composure, she adopts what is by this time her usual brittle and deflating attitude toward him: "Ah, I perceive what you are about! You are turning this whole affair into a ballad. Pray let me hear as many stanzas as you happen to have ready!" The words are an echo of her remark to Coverdale on their first evening, when he surmises that Priscilla has come to join the community to pay homage to the well-known feminist. "Since you see the young woman in so poetical a light," Zenobia says, "you had better turn the affair into a ballad." After projecting a romantic literary ballad, which becomes a fanciful condensation of the narrative of *Blithedale*, Zenobia turns from fanciful chatter to a more down-to-earth explanation. By "tokens that escape the obtuseness of masculine perceptions," she declares Priscilla not a death-dealing snow-maiden but a poor seamstress from the city come for "no more transcendental purpose" than to do Zenobia's miscellaneous sewing. The "affair" which might be turned into a ballad is not one of thwarted sexual love between an exotic woman and a rugged philanthropist, but a sisterly love that carries with it moral responsibility. If it is a kind of love which lies beyond Coverdale's "obtuse" perceptions, its violation of course lies even further. By her betrayal of Priscilla, Zenobia sins against the human heart in ways far more serious than her frustrated passion for Hollingsworth could ever do. That remorse over her betrayal of Priscilla for her own gain (love, money, or both) might have impelled her to take her own life never occurs to Coverdale.

The repartee between Zenobia and Coverdale on her final evening is a grim replay of this earlier scene, and her manner is an intensi-

fied version of her earlier bantering and edged wit. She utters a
"sharp, light laugh." She ranges from mild irony to scornful sarcasm to haughty solemnity to calm security; but throughout the
exchange, Coverdale notes that she is also "laughing" or "smiling"
and remarks on the strange way in which her mind seemed "to
vibrate from the deepest earnest to mere levity." It is clearly the
portrait of a woman only partly in control of her emotions; but it is
also a glimpse of a woman sufficiently alert to her confidant's limitations to allow him (indeed, to encourage him) to interpret her grief
as simplistically as he, with his "obtuseness," is inclined to do. Thus,
Zenobia collaborates with Coverdale on a little ballad about herself,
the point of which is the way the world conspires against the
woman "who swerves one hair's breadth out of the beaten track."
Coverdale interprets this specifically as Zenobia's love for Hollingsworth and generally as the dangers of the passions which overcome
the intellectual, liberated woman. Though he protests that her interpretation has "too stern a moral," it is nevertheless the one he
adopts.

If the moral is "too stern," it is also irrelevant. *The Blithedale
Romance* is remarkably free of evidence that the world punishes
this feminist for her activities. As in other works of Hawthorne, the
source and means of punishment here are more profoundly spiritual
than those at the service of the world. (The same is true for Hollingsworth, whose public scheme for the reformation of criminals
must be painfully internalized to cope "with a single murderer.")
Though we hear much of Zenobia's activism in the cause of wom-
en's rights—which would presumably distort her humanity just as
Hollingsworth's philanthropy is said to distort his—what Hawthorne dramatizes is feminine spirit, not ideological advocacy. And
in the most explicitly "feminist" chapter in the book, "Eliot's Pulpit," Zenobia's statements on women's rights pale into vagueness
when set beside Coverdale's own conciliating, extravagant vision of
a matriarchy in which the submissive male "would kneel before a
woman-ruler!"

Coverdale's limited understanding of both friends is betrayed by
his language. Hollingsworth's challenge provokes Coverdale to self-
torturing envy. Whereas in the earlier chapters the narrator speaks
merely patronizingly of his friend, after "A Crisis" he drops even
the pretense of good will. The diction grows excessive, even viru-
lent: *odious, loathsomeness; great, black ugliness of sin; trample on
considerations; squalid.* After Zenobia's death, his conduct toward
Hollingsworth is dictated by what Coverdale believes to be "all the
evil" of which the philanthropist is guilty; his taunts are those of a
harpy. Coverdale's "ballad" about Zenobia, the kind which might
have reclaimed a genteel, minor Romantic, turns out to be simply

another work about the passionate heroine who, "defeated on the broad battlefield of life," falls on "her own sword, merely because Love had gone against her." Even Westervelt, at her grave, knows better than this. The world, concludes Coverdale, should throw open "all its avenues to the passport of a woman's bleeding heart." The vision is derivative just as the language which describes it is shabby. But Coverdale's failure of perception here, antecedent to his failure as artist, should come as no surprise. Much earlier, with his narrator's arrival at Blithedale, Hawthorne has prepared the reader for this moment. His new friends, particularly Zenobia, understand that Coverdale will be poet in residence, which means a continuation of his role as romantic poet now put to the service of the brotherhood; Coverdale, however, apparently expects that his new life will be the source for an art that will be qualitatively different from his previous work.[6] Perhaps now, he says to Zenobia, he will write something deserving the name of poetry—"true, strong, natural, and sweet, as is the life which we are going to lead—something that shall have the notes of wild-birds twittering through it, or a strain like the wind-anthems in the woods." If this remark does nothing else, it establishes Coverdale as a thoroughly undistinguished talent of Mainstream Romantic. Although Hawthorne protects his readers from knowing at first hand any of his protagonist's productions, the implications are clear. The new experience should result in work more ambitious and more significant than the mechanical competence which finally attracts the attention of Rufus W. Griswold.[7] Now to be tested are the depth and breadth of Coverdale's artistic powers, and the crucial question has implications both personal and aesthetic. Can this creator of trivial art show himself to be more than trivial? Can he in fact create something better than trivial art? The results are not promising. If there is tragedy attendant upon Zenobia's fate, it takes shape, outside and beyond the range of Coverdale's perceptions. If there is tragedy attendant upon Hollingsworth's abortive scheme for the reformation of criminals, its resonances are heard despite Coverdale's assessment of the man.

Coverdale's "romance," then, is one of the thinner kinds. It is compounded of soaring passions—most of them misdirected and coming to grim fruition. Two linked ironies emerge—that a self-confessed idler whose lack of purpose has rendered his life "all an emptiness" should denounce and hound someone else whose errors have dried up his "rich juices," and that the rich potentialities of artistic renewal should wither to the point where Coverdale can

6. Terence Martin stresses the narrator's search for a role, a search seen largely in theatrical imagery that reinforces the position of Coverdale as spectator. See *Nathaniel Hawthorne* (New York, 1965),

pp. 151–157.
7. A famous nineteenth-century anthologist of poetry; see note 1, p. 226. [*Editors.*]

divert the tragedy of Zenobia into conventional nineteenth-century melodrama.

IV

The Blithedale Romance stands as its own critique of Coverdale. As a memoir, it contains the testing of himself as a man; the memoir itself is the test of Coverdale the artist. He fails the first test, and only ironically does he pass the second. A bittersweet narrative, not wind-anthems or onomatopoetic songs about twittering birds, is Coverdale's ultimate response.

If Coverdale's focus in his narrative is blurred by a multiplicity of subjects (Hollingsworth, Zenobia, Old Moodie, his own routine urban life as well as his one ambivalent adventure in communal living), Hawthorne's focus on Coverdale is as sharp, intense, and composed a bit of portraiture as that provided by other first-person narratives of the nineteenth century. One of the remarkable accomplishments of *Blithedale* is Hawthorne's novelistic exploration of a theme most commonly seen in those tales written as romances, allegories, or exempla. Coverdale, a man whose emotional deficiency isolates him from the human mainstream, joins the ranks of Wakefield, Ethan Brand, Roger Chillingworth, Aylmer ("The Birthmark"), and Giovanni ("Rappaccini's Daughter");[8] but unlike them, he seems to exist in an actual and multidimensional society which asserts its own claims beyond the rather rigid ones he chooses to acknowledge. Hawthorne allows his protagonist entry into a wide area of contemporary life, the pleasing urbanities of society in the city, the not-so-pleasing physical demands of life in the country, the low-powered lyceum entertainments in the villages. Though in writing his memoir Coverdale thinks and acts as the romancer, Hawthorne renders the context in which Coverdale moves with the kind of circumstantial detail, the observations of commonplace reality, which occur more often in Hawthorne's notebooks than in his fiction.

Readers find Coverdale as unsatisfactory as do most of his fellow participants in the Blithedale brotherhood, and for much the same reasons: his reticence to commit himself humanly to others and his dilettantish curiosity. Both his reticence and his curiosity are expressions of a man whose frustrated search for meaning leads him

8. These are some of Hawthorne's failed human beings. The title character of "Wakefield" (1835), for over twenty years, lives in secret a street away from his wife and home; the title character of "Ethan Brand" (1850) engages in a monomaniacal search for the unpardonable sin, which severs him from "the magnetic chain of humanity" and turns his heart to marble; Roger Chillingworth pursues revenge in *The Scarlet Letter* (1850), becoming a nihilistic fiend; Aylmer, the scientist in "The Birthmark" (1843), is so repelled by the blemish on his wife's otherwise beautiful face that he experiments with methods of erasing it until he kills her; Giovanni, the young medical student in "Rappaccini's Daughter" (1844), because he cannot believe that his lover is spiritually pure despite her literal poisonness, complies in her death. [*Editors*.]

to the dubious comfort of "conjectured" reconstructions of events and their significance.

Coverdale's insufficiency as man or artist cannot be justified or wished away, but lurking about this narrator is something more than mere obtuseness or inexcusable behavior. Many of Hawthorne's protagonists—saints and sinners alike—suffer from spiritual rigidity, obsessiveness, isolation, and the cold heart which threatens their moral survival; but unlike most of them, Coverdale displays a sense of humor, a tonic irony directed toward himself as well as others, a distancing perspective which permits disclosure of those ambivalences pulling him from one inadequate footing to another. With these characteristics Hawthorne extends the complexities only suggested by his customary quasi-allegorical figures into a narrator more fictively realistic. The gain is substantial. For this character whose dilemma is neither so domestic as Wakefield's nor so apocalyptic as Ethan Brand's, Hawthorne succeeds in projecting a situation that is understated, bland, and modern in its horror onto a consciousness singularly unequipped to perceive the horror. That very disparity allows Hawthorne to lavish his full creative attention on a character who, despite an irritating and acerbic ineffectuality, stands revealed as pathetic.

For all the annoying complacency in which he cloaks himself, Coverdale still possesses a certain frail honesty which makes his failures humanly, even poignantly, understandable. The reader is not surprised, for example, when he asserts, on practically the last page of his narrative, that he would still be willing to die for a just cause provided "the effort did not involve an unreasonable amount of trouble," because this is precisely the attitude he reveals in Chapter I, when he expresses a willingness to do Old Moodie a favor if it involves "no special trouble" to himself. Early or late, Coverdale never disguises his arid emotions. What gives this account both its chill and its pathos is the realization that at its end nothing has changed. Even more pathetic, however, is the realization that Coverdale fails to understand his limited nature; his experiences, though traumatic, contribute nothing to his potential self-knowledge. It is a horrifying self-portrait of a man whose divided sensibilities are never harmonized, whose purposelessness is never replaced by purpose, and whose inability to love continues to be trivialized by fantasy.

Except for the final chapter, Coverdale seems not to see his narrative as a confession. But in its larger perspective, Hawthorne surely means for his readers to see it as such. This protagonist is not an Underground or Superfluous Man. Those Russian figures, alive as they are to every suggestion of suffering, grope messily and blatantly for some meaning to their separated lives. Coverdale, however, covers his tracks, throwing off pursuit by the civility of his personality, and presumes that sicknes is to be found in souls other than his own. His document, for all its veneer of control and self-sufficiency, is confessional, and its complexity comes not from Coverdale's bland exposition but from Hawthorne's manipulation of his narrator's character.

The key to that character is Coverdale's idealism. Behind the aloofness, behind the witty and abrasive language, stands the man of good will who insists that the ideal represented by the Blithedale experiment is one to which he once genuinely subscribed. Moreover, at the end of the narrative he strongly suggests that of that little band of reformers, only he has remained faithful to its high undertaking. The adventure is a crucial one for Coverdale; and both the substance and the style of his account bespeak the poignant efforts of a man struggling to redeem himself morally and aesthetically. Alone of the major characters, including even the frail and ill-used Priscilla, Coverdale engages in no real deceptions, has no past worthy of concealing, offers no covert reformist schemes as alternatives to the community; but despite those admirable, if negative, virtues, he is concerned exclusively with ideal relationships. He is unprepared to accept, or at first even to acknowledge, the imperfect human context in which the ideal must realize itself if it is to realize itself at all. The idea of brotherhood, like a high and certainly cloudy romance, continues to attract him more than a decade after the collapse of Blithedale. As Hawthorne makes clear, however, the *idea* of brotherhood is not sufficient for redemption. Hollingsworth and Zenobia come to experience the full human implications when idealism and factuality clash, which is another way of saying that they attain a tragic self-awareness denied Coverdale.

Coverdale's very inability to do full justice to his Blithedale fellows ironically allows a self-concentration—the disclosure of character broader and richer than is possible in the portrayal of Hollingsworth, Zenobia, and Priscilla. Hawthorne's choice of a first-person narrator provides an obvious but functional hiatus of information at several crucial moments throughout the narrative. Zenobia, for example, tells Coverdale that he has returned to Blithedale "half an hour too late" to witness a climactic scene between her and Hollingsworth, and Coverdale with some chagrin admits the missed opportunity:

> And what subjects had been discussed here? All, no doubt, that, for so many months past, had kept my heart and my imagination idly feverish. Zenobia's whole character and history; the true nature of her mysterious connection with Westervelt; her later purposes towards Hollingsworth, and, reciprocally, his in reference to her; and, finally, the degree in which Zenobia had been cogni-

zant of the plot against Priscilla, and what, at last, had been the real object of that scheme. On these points, as before, I was left to my own conjectures.

Considering the consummate effectiveness of the final scaffold scene in *The Scarlet Letter*, it is somewhat surprising that Hawthorne should pass up an opportunity to dramatize what would normally have been its counterpart in this work. Technically, of course, Hawthorne limits himself: to supply information unavailable to Coverdale would violate point of view, even with the latitude generally enjoyed by the romancer. He as well as his narrator must remain content with Coverdale's "conjectures." But why should Hawthorne deliberately delay his narrator's arrival for the key scene thirty minutes too late? Dramatized or not, this is the climactic moment in the action, the moment from which Zenobia's death and funeral and Hollingsworth's remorse inevitably follow. A simple adjustment, coming so late in the narrative, would have necessitated no radical changes in plot progression or character development. The answer lies in consistency of characterization. If Hawthorne had finally given his narrator full access to those subjects about which he had been "feverish" for several months, a vital aspect of Coverdale's character—mischievous curiosity—would have been mitigated. By keeping Coverdale in ignorance Hawthorne maintains the careful ambivalence with which he imbues his narrator from the beginning. Disallowing him the final and most important revelations is a deft tactic. It not only sustains the too-little-too-late aspect of Coverdale with which the reader has come to be so familiar; it also marks an innovative imagination at work—in its tidy culmination, the romance form is in this case skewed just enough to deprive both narrator and reader of full gratification. Both must be content with the "conjectures" of one limited man whose partial view is not only self-evident but also self-admitted.

It is tempting to sympathize with Hollingsworth's impatience with Coverdale's fashionable airs or with Zenobia's exasperation when she accuses him of "Bigotry; self-conceit; an insolent curiosity; a meddlesome temper; a cold-blooded criticism . . . ; a monstrous scepticism. . . ." But the reader knows Coverdale better than his friends know him, and for all his flaws, he is not quite a monster.[9] He is, to be sure, a "frosty bachelor" who takes too keen an interest

9. It is surely a misplaced emphasis to suggest, as readers occasionally do, that Coverdale's speculative detachment destroys Blithedale and that his spoiler instincts aggravate and hasten the personal tragedies of Zenobia and Hollingsworth. The latter two characters pursue destruction out of the strength of their own wills. And common sense, as well as the logic of the narrative, says that Blithedale must fail with or without Coverdale. Its presumptuous example of the higher possibilities for living, directed at crass society at large, is articulated by physical withdrawal from that society (though, significantly, not to the point of disdaining agricultural competition).

in indulging his curiosity; and coupled to his ineffectual and rigid idealism is a mannered style which paradoxically establishes him as a frivolous dabbler among solemn socialists. When he is not being the abrasive wit, he is the moralistic meddler. His customary moral posture is a little silly, but, more important, it is also sad. It dooms him from any further emotional growth, either in or out of Blithedale. The personal renewal promised by the new life is aborted, and with it goes the chance for artistic renewal. Thus, Coverdale will recast his Blithedale experiences according to both what he knows (which is limited enough) and what he feels—pity and exasperation in dangerous proportions.

What Hawthorne achieves in this work is a sense of the human costs of failure, the pathos of weakness, without any diminishment of his own tough-minded standards for the conduct of life. In no other work does he succeed so well in dramatizing emptiness and purposelessness; in no other work does he sacrifice so many of the comfortable conventions of allegory or moral apologue or legend for the more difficult challenges of the realistic memoir, exchanging (in currently fashionable terms) telling for showing. Coverdale looks forward to James's emotional cripples (Marcher of "The Beast in the Jungle," Winterbourne of *Daisy Miller*, or Acton of *The Europeans*) and beyond them—to the desperate expatriates of Fitzgerald's and Hemingway's fiction and to the hollow men of Eliot's earlier poems.[1] In permitting Coverdale virtually to construct his self, his voice, his configuring nuances, Hawthorne releases the ironic possibilities of a narrating intelligence who unconsciously steps beyond the limits which, as a romancer, he consciously observes.

KENT BALES

The Allegory and the Radical Romantic Ethic of *The Blithedale Romance*†

* * *

Like all good allegories, *The Blithedale Romance* has a central, controlling image and a basic kind of relationship. As in most

1. Roy R. Male sees Coverdale as the fictive ancestor of such modern intellectuals as Prufrock and Robert Penn Warren's Jack Burden. See *Hawthorne's Tragic Vision* (Austin, 1957), pp. 151–55. John C. Stubb remarks that to achieve a fusion of the comic and the tragic, "Hawthorne had to invent the Jamesian narrator before James" (*The Pursuit of Form: A Study of Hawthorne and the Romance*, [Urbana, Ill., 1970], p. 136). See also Nicholas Canaday, Jr., "Community and Identity at Blithedale," *South Atlantic Quarterly*, LXXI (Winter, 1972), 30–39.

† From *American Literature*, 46 (1974), 41–53.

allegories, both image and relationship are double, providing simultaneously for mystery and clarity. *Blithedale's* image is woman in her two roles as Veiled Lady and Queen Zenobia, as Spirit and as Flesh or Nature; its relationship is a loving interdependence, "the blessed state of brotherhood and sisterhood." Priscilla and Zenobia are thus central to the allegory, for they are at once sisters and avatars of Veiled Lady and Queen. But just as they do not behave as loving sisters, they are not really (i.e., fully) Veiled Lady and Queen: Zenobia has chosen her name and role (her "real" name is well known, we are told); Priscilla's role has been forced upon her. Neither is "really" (i.e., "in life" or in the novel) what she "represents" in the allegory; indeed, Zenobia's name was conceived as "a sort of mask . . . , like the white drapery of the Veiled Lady. . . ." The role of Queen Zenobia incorporates Eve, Flora, and Pandora "fresh from Vulcan's workshop," but the woman Zenobia cannot live up to such models. Neither does Priscilla fulfill the role of Spirit: she is retarded in development for, as Zenobia points out, she has " 'been stifled with the heat of a salamander-stove, in a small, close room, and has drunk coffee, and fed upon dough-nuts, raisins, candy, and all such trash, till she is scarcely half-alive.' " Furthermore, her opinions prove to be as repressive as her environment has been. The sisters' failure to fulfill their allegorical roles does not invalidate the roles, however; the roles set the standard (impossibly high, to be sure), state the ideal. The allegory shows us these ideals; the novel shows us persons failing to fulfill them.

Since by supposed conviction and radical rhetoric all Blithedalers are brothers and sisters, Zenobia's deliberate cruelty to Priscilla violates the community ethic, a violation the worse because Priscilla is a blood sister. Another failure, of similar configuration though of different import, occurs when Coverdale and Hollingsworth fail to live as brothers. Hollingsworth is the complement to Coverdale, his mirror image. Coverdale's need to be completed points to the need for the Blithedale experiment, while the failure of Coverdale and Hollingsworth to get together defines the failure of the Blithedale experiment.

It is more than interestingly ironic, then, that Coverdale charges Hollingsworth with an "all-devouring egotism," for in that they are truly brothers—brother subversives. Philanthropists like Hollingsworth, Coverdale claims, "have an idol" which, while "they see only benignity and love, is but a spectrum of the very priest himself, projected upon the surrounding darkness." Hawthorne projects, through Coverdale's narrative, a like image and judgment of him. Hiding himself in his rotten tree hermitage, Coverdale thinks himself Nature's idol, worshipped by her in sending incense "as if I had been an idol in its niche." Like the temples of Spenser's *Faerie*

Queene,[1] this temple to self forms an allegorical core, but the core, like the man who fancies himself a god in it, is rotten. Thus, where Hollingsworth's egotism is active and "devouring," Coverdale's is passive. " 'It is all self!' " as Zenobia bitterly says of Hollingsworth. One self loves action, the other ease; one is a self-made man, the other a man of means; one thinks morally, the other aesthetically; one's will is set on gaining an end, the other's will is set on protecting its gains. Each tendency, by its exaggeration, is monstrous and vicious, an insight partially gained by Coverdale in retrospect: "As Hollingsworth once told me, I lack a purpose. How strange! He was ruined, morally, by an overplus of the very same ingredient, the want of which, I occasionally suspect, has rendered my own life all an emptiness." Could the selves have been merged, the balance struck, these brothers would no longer have been monstrously selfish and, microcosmically, the Blithedale experiment would have been on the way to success.

Such individual wholeness, the original state of the "god in ruins"[2] that Emerson and other romantic writers tried to realize with their art, has been described by psychiatrist Kenneth Keniston:

> . . . human wholeness means a capacity for commitment, dedication, passionate concern, and care—a capacity for whole-heartedness and single-mindedness, for abandon without fear of self-annihilation and loss of identity. In psychological terms, this means that a whole man retains contact with his deepest passions at the same time that he remains responsive to his ethical sense. No one psychic potential destroys or subverts the others: his cognitive abilities remain in the service of his commitments, not vice versa; his ethical sense guides rather than tyrannizing over his basic passions; his deepest drives are the sources of his strength but not the dictators of his action.[3]

Blithedale was formed to help each member regain this state, and the possession of it is the greatest positive value in *The Blithedale Romance*. Consequently, it lies at the core of *Blithedale*'s two basic allegories, the normative allegory that sets *Blithedale*'s values in the context of the world's, and the psychological allegory that defines and explores the divided consciousness. In this second allegory, much as in the *psychomachia*[4] of earlier allegories, the separate characters of *Blithedale* are parts or tendencies of a single consciousness, so that "getting together" the Blithedale community successfully is analogous to "getting together" the individual self.

The allegory is most stridently normative when it seems the most arbitrarily formed, the most willed. "Zenobia's Legend" and "Faun-

1. Allegorical epic-romance (1589–96) by Edmund Spenser. [*Editors.*]
2. From "Prospects," in *Nature* (1836), by Ralph Waldo Emerson. [*Editors.*]

3. *The Uncommitted: Alienated Youth in American Society* (New York, 1965), pp. 441–42.
4. Soul-conflict. [*Editors.*]

tleroy" present the greatest digressions from realism, and they most
resemble the kind of tale within a tale by which Spenser defined the
central issue of each book of Hawthorne's beloved *Faerie Queene*.
The first of these chapters defines Coverdale's failure, the second
defines the world's and Blithedale's failure to incorporate Spirit, to
achieve whole rather than compartmentalized lives.

Like the keystone of an arch, "Zenobia's Legend" is physically
and necessarily central. After it, the plot declines to its terrible
denouement, while surrounding it we have the two most important
subsidiary emblems of the book: "Coverdale's Hermitage" of vine-
embraced tree, and "Eliot's Pulpit," the earth-embedded rock that
symbolizes Hollingsworth's Antaeus-like[5] strength. In Zenobia's
legend of Theodore's encounter with the Veiled Lady, Theodore
fails the basic test of the fairy tales: asked to express his trust with a
kiss, the act that invariably turns frogs into princes, hags into princesses, he refuses. As a man of common sense, a skeptic, he insists
on a look at the lady's face—no leaper he! "His retribution was, to
pine, forever and ever, for another sight of that dim, mournful
face—which might have been his life-long, household, fireside joy—
to desire, and waste life in a feverish quest, and never meet it
more." Since Coverdale professes poetry, we might expect him to
place more faith in literary precedent than Theodore does, but his
actions throughout suggest that he has tried to lift the veil rather
than kiss through it. At the outset he is cool to Moodie's request for
help, which would have given him Priscilla's guardianship had he
responded more sympathetically; he immediately answers Zenobia
that he will never be " 'guilty' " of favoring her " 'with a little more
love than one can conveniently dispose of' "; he pays no heed to
Hollingsworth's plea not to " 'forsake' " him. His love of prying is a
corollary to this reservation of love and commitment: when caught
peeping and identified by Diana as " 'some profane intruder,' " he
has been imitating the stealth of Theodore in attempting to penetrate the "mystery" of the Veiled Lady with "a hostile, or, at least,
an unauthorized and unjustifiable purpose." Also like Theodore,
whose "medium" is wine, Coverdale has no higher afflatus. For a
poet he is remarkably hostile to mystery, incapable of the imaginative flights displayed by Zenobia in her legend (which, like the wine
of true inspiration or the water of Pieria's spring,[6] "came bubbling
out of her mind" and by Hollingsworth in his impromptu sermons
from Eliot's Pulpit (which are so inspired as to be "in a strain that
rose and fell as naturally as the wind's breath").

In these respects he is simply a man of the world, and it is the

5. In Greek mythology, Antaeus was a
giant wrestler who was invincible as long
as he was touching his mother, the earth.
[*Editors.*]

6. A spring in Pieria, a region in ancient
Macedonia where the Muses were wor-
shiped. [*Editors.*]

nature of this worldliness that Old Moodie's tale of "Fauntleroy" discloses. An ordinary sensual man, rich for part of his life, poor for the rest (hence "ordinary" in that he experiences and represents all of society, as well as youth and age), has two daughters, one naturally gifted with beauty and artistic talent, one preternaturally gifted with spiritual insight. The beauty is rich, the psychic one poor, but they share relations with another, "marvellously hand- some" man. Representative of the Western World, as the name he bears elsewhere in the romance tells us, Westervelt's stylish appear- ance and good looks put a new face on the old enterprise of Wes- tern Civilization. (Beneath this "mask" he may be a "wizened elf" or the Devil himself.) Zenobia's powers give her a measure of freedom from him, or at least a license to move largely as she wishes; but Priscilla is his slave, a spiritual prostitute—for Western Civilization has nothing better to do with Spirit than to convert it to gold. Her father concurs in this exploitation because he profits from it, just as he does from her skill as a seamstress. He is ashamed, to be sure— he now lives in shame, as he had lived in pride when wealthy. Then—and this is outside the "legend" but clear from the opening chapters—the Blithedale experiment offers a way apparently differ- ent from the way of the world. Moodie, true to his name, sends Priscilla there to be rehabilitated and to expend her spirit on the great "love" of her life, the "idea" of sisterhood. Once in this mood, Moodie commits himself fully: he will disinherit Zenobia if she does not conform. He is true to his word, and within a few chapters Zenobia is dead. This radical divorce of Nature and Spirit, of form and idea, of body and soul is directly the result of Moodie's one- eyed vision: he cannot conceive of shared wealth. In this mood compromise, an integration of interests, is impossible.

Zenobia's death brings about the death of Blithedale. It is appro- priate, for she was its queen, her most questionable actions quickly accepted by the community. Even when she terrifies Priscilla into a faint, the Blithedalers think it "a very bright idea of Zenobia's, to bring her legend to so effective a conclusion." At the outset she treats Silas Foster more like an innkeeper or servant than a brother and throughout asserts her sense of superiority to all but Hollings- worth. Her actions, and the Blithedalers' acquiescence in them, give the lie to their profession of egalitarian principles. In turning to Nature (and Zenobia, who greets them all, surely represents this choice), they by and large neglect Spirit. Yet there is at the outset a possibility that Spirit can grow to rival Nature, for Spirit in the person of Priscilla begins to flourish in the relatively greater sympathy for it that Blithedale affords. But Spirit is immature, scarcely formed—or reformed from the malformation that the world has forced on it. Before it can mature and stand as an equal in strength and beauty to the rival sister, before a dialectical tension between Spirit and Nature can develop that will convert hierarchy into democracy, a choice is forced.

Blithedale's choice of Priscilla, of Spirit, seems motivated from without: it is made theatrically, almost ritually. Hawthorne is careful to have Coverdale establish the broadly representative nature of the worldly audience and the modern typicality of its setting in a suburban New England village's lyceum-hall.[7] In this Vanity Fair[8] Westervelt, with Priscilla once again apparently in his power, is exhibiting her as the Veiled Lady and claiming absolute dominion over her. " 'Nor does there exist the moral inducement, apart from my own behest, that could persuade her to lift the silvery veil, or arise out of that chair' " he boasts; and as if on cue Hollingsworth mounts the platform to accept the challenge. When Priscilla throws off her veil and runs to Hollingsworth's protecting arms, she becomes Hollingsworth's (and through him, Blithedale's), and he hers. (Coverdale likewise finally confesses that he has been in love with Priscilla.) The choice involves rejecting Nature—the supposed alternative of natural, sensuous, sensual pleasure that Zenobia symbolizes—for the still untested virtues of Spirit. Instead of carefully nurturing Spirit in company with Nature, the Blithedalers adopt the single vision of the world and become shallow ideologues, "lapsing into Fourierism" as Coverdale puts it. Instead of continuing the anarchist experiment they began, they turn to blueprint socialism. In closing all options but one, they prove that their spirit, like the world's, occupies a very narrow house.

Thus trust and faith, sharing and inclusiveness are the values established by these legends. The inclusiveness, however, is not that of liberal society that permits—in the name of freedom—the painful separation of rich and poor that Moodie has experienced. (This is Coverdale's society, and his affection for the pigs at Blithedale surely is meant to signal his agreement with it and the "Pig Philosophy" that Carlyle saw as its apology.)[9] Nature and Spirit too must be included and include each other in this Emersonian world where apparent contradictions are made complementary by love and trust, so that community and communitarians incorporate or "have" both Priscilla and Zenobia. Two threats to these values are personified by Westervelt and Old Moodie. The first mixes skepticism that reform is possible or necessary with a cynicism that establishes his relation-

7. Lecture hall. [Editors.]
8. From Pilgrim's Progress (1678–84) by John Bunyan (1628–88), in which there was always a fair going on in the town of Vanity; hence, symbolic of worldly folly and frivolity. [Editors.]
9. In Thomas Carlyle's Past and Present (1843), the feudal aristocracy of the twelfth century is compared favorably to the capitalistic system of nineteenth-century England. In the earlier society, "even a Gurth born thrall of a Cedric lacks not his due parings of the pigs he tends"— that is, though the peasant belongs to a master, he gets his share of the profits of the butchered pigs. [Editors.]

ship to the whole affair of the apple. (As Old Nick[1] in modern dress he represents the possibility of original sin—or, more appropriately, the paralyzing *belief* in original sin.) The second, Moodie's demand that Blithedale conform to his stereotype of reform, urges a choice of the "spiritual" mode of life prematurely and in violation of Blithedale's experimental nature.

* * *

1. The devil. [*Editors.*]

Bibliography

The bibliography which follows is highly selective and does not include items which have been excerpted in the body of the book, since full bibliographical information has already been given. The most complete bibliography of Hawthorne is *Nathaniel Hawthorne: A Reference Bibliography, 1900–1971*, compiled by Beatrice Ricks, Joseph D. Adams, and Jack O. Hazlerig (Boston: G. K. Hall, 1972). Other convenient checklists of *Blithedale* criticism are in Maurice Beebe and Jack Hardie, "Criticism of Nathaniel Hawthorne: A Selected Checklist," *Studies in the Novel*, 2 (1970), 519–87, and Buford Jones, *A Checklist of Hawthorne Criticism, 1951–1966* (Hartford, Conn.: Transcendental Books, 1967).

Arvin, Newton. Hawthorne (Boston: Little, Brown, 1929; repr. New York: Russell & Russell, 1961), pp. 196–202, 209–19.
Bales, Kent. *"The Blithedale Romance*: Coverdale's Mean and Subversive Egotism," *Bucknell Review*, 21, iii (1973), 60–82.
Bewley, Marius. *The Complex Fate* (New York and London: Chatto & Windus, 1952), pp. 11–30.
———. *The Eccentric Design* (New York: Columbia University Press, 1959), pp. 147–60.
Birdsall, Virginia Ogden. "Hawthorne's Fair-Haired Maidens: The Fading Light," *PMLA*, 75 (1960), 250–56.
Canaday, Nicholas, Jr. "Community and Identity at Blithedale," *South Atlantic Quarterly*, 71 (1972), 30–39.
Cargill, Oscar. "Nemesis and Nathaniel Hawthorne," *PMLA*, 52 (1937), 848–62.
Carpenter, Frederick I. "Puritans Preferred Blondes: The Heroines of Melville and Hawthorne," *New England Quarterly*, 9 (1936), 253–72.
Chase, Richard. *The American Novel and Its Tradition* (Garden City, N.Y.: Doubleday, 1957), pp. 82–7.
Crews, Frederick C. "A New Reading of *The Blithedale Romance*," *American Literature*, 29 (1957), 147–70.
Cronin, Morton. "Hawthorne on Romantic Love and the Status of Women," *PMLA*, 69 (1954), 89–98.
Davidson, Frank. "Toward a Re-Evaluation of *The Blithedale Romance*," *New England Quarterly*, 25 (1952), 374–83.
Dennis, Carl. *"The Blithedale Romance* and the Problem of Self-Integration," *Texas Studies in Literature and Language*, 15 (1973), 93–110.
Doubleday, Neal F. "Hawthorne's Criticism of New England Life," *College English*, 2 (1942), 648–53.
Elliott, Robert E. *"The Blithedale Romance,"* Hawthorne Centenary Essays, Roy Harvey Pearce, ed. (Columbus: Ohio State University Press, 1964), pp. 103–17. Repr. *The Shape of Utopia* (Chicago: University of Chicago Press, 1970).
Erlich, Gloria C. "Deadly Innocence: Hawthorne's Dark Women," *New England Quarterly*, 41 (1968), 163–79.
Flint, Allen. " 'Essentially a Day-Dream, and Yet a Fact': Hawthorne's *Blithedale*," *Nathaniel Hawthorne Journal* (1972), 75–83.
Fogarty, Robert S. "A Utopian Literary Canon," *New England Quarterly*, 38 (1965), 386–91.
Fogle, Richard Harter. *Hawthorne's Fiction: The Light and the Dark* (Norman: Oklahoma University Press, 1952; rev. ed. 1964), pp. 140–61.
———. *Hawthorne's Imagery: The "Proper Light and Shadow" in the Major Romances* (Norman: Oklahoma University Press, 1969), pp. 92–124.
———. "Priscilla's Veil: A Study of Hawthorne's Veil Imagery in *The Blithedale Romance*," *Nathaniel Hawthorne Journal* (1972), 59–65.
Folsom, James K. *Man's Accidents and God's Purposes: Multiplicity in Hawthorne's Fiction* (New Haven: College and University Press, 1963), pp. 147–51.
Fossum, Robert H. *Hawthorne's Inviolable Circle: The Problem of Time* (Deland, Fla.: Everett/Edwards, 1972), pp. 140–49.
Gollin, Rita K. "Dream-Work in *The Blithedale Romance*," *Emerson Society Quarterly*, 71 (1973), 74–83.

Gordon, Joseph T. "Nathaniel Hawthorne and Brook Farm," *Emerson Society Quarterly*, 33 (1963), 51–61.

Haraszti, Zoltan. *The Idyll of Brook Farm* (Boston: Public Library, 1937).

Hawthorne, Manning. "Hawthorne and Utopian Socialism: Two Letters Written to David Mack," *New England Quarterly*, 12 (1939), 726–30.

Hedges, William L. "Hawthorne's *Blithedale:* The Function of the Narrator, *Nineteenth-Century Fiction*, 14 (1960), 303–16.

Hilton, Earl. "The Body in Hawthorne's Fountain," *Papers of the Michigan Academy of Science, Arts, and Letters*, 52 (1967), 385–87.

Hirsh, John C. "The Politics of Blithedale: The Dilemma of the Self," *Studies in Romanticism*, 11 (1972), 138–46.

———. "Zenobia as Queen: The Background Sources to Hawthorne's *The Blithedale Romance*," *Nathaniel Hawthorne Journal* (1971), 182–90.

Hoeltje, Hubert H. *Inward Sky; The Mind and Heart of Nathaniel Hawthorne* (Durham: Duke University Press, 1962), pp. 380–95.

Hoffman, Daniel G. *Form and Fable in American Fiction* (New York: Oxford University Press, 1961; corrected ed., 1965), pp. 202–18.

Howard, David. "*The Blithedale Romance* and a Sense of Revolution," *Tradition and Tolerance in Nineteenth-Century Fiction*, David Howard, John Lucas, John Goode, eds. (London: Routledge & Kegan Paul, 1966), pp. 55–97.

Howells, William Dean. *Heroines of Fiction*, I (New York: Harper & Brothers, 1901), pp. 175–83.

James, Henry. *Hawthorne* (New York: Harper & Brothers, 1879), pp. 128–33.

Johnson, Claudia D. "Hawthorne and Nineteenth-Century Perfectionism," *American Literature*, 44 (1973), 585–95.

Jones, Buford. "The Faery Land of Hawthorne's Romances," *Emerson Society Quartely*, 48 (1967), 118–23.

———. "Hawthorne's Coverdale and Spenser's Allegory of Mutability," *American Literature*, 39 (1967), 215–19.

Joyner, Nancy. "Bondage in Blithedale," *Nathaniel Hawthorne Journal* (1975), pp. 227–31.

Kay, Donald. "Five Acts of The Blithedale Romance," *American Transcendental Quarterly*, 13 (1972), 25–28.

Kearns, Francis E. "The Theme of Experience in Hawthorne's *Blithedale* Romance," *History and Fiction; American Prose in the 19th Century*, Alfred Weber and Hartmut Grandel, eds. (Gottingen: Vandenhoeck and Rupert, 1972), pp. 64–84.

Lawrence, D. H. *Studies in Classic American Literature* (New York: Thomas Seltzer, 1923), pp. 148–62.

Leavis, Q. D. "Hawthorne as Poet: Part II," *Sewanee Review*, 59 (1951), 440–54.

Levin, Harry. *The Power of Blackness* (New York: Alfred Knopf, 1958), pp. 85–90.

Long, Robert Emmet. "The Society and the Masks: *The Blithedale Romance* and *The Bostonians*," *Nineteenth-Century Fiction*, 19 (1964), 105–22.

———. "Transformations: *The Blithedale Romance* to Howells and James," *American Literature*, 47 (1976), 552–71.

Magretta, Joan. "The Coverdale Translation: *Blithedale* and the Bible," *Nathaniel Hawthorne Journal* (1974), 250–56.

Male, Roy R. "Hawthorne's *The Blithedale Romance*," *Explicator*, 28 (1970), item 56.

———. "Hawthorne's Allegory of Guilt and Redemption," *Emerson Society Quarterly*, 25 (1961), 16–18.

———. "Hawthorne's Fancy, or the Medium of *The Blithedale Romance*," *Nathaniel Hawthorne Journal* (1972), 67–73.

Marks, Alfred H. "Ironic Inversion in *The Blithedale Romance*," *Emerson Society Quarterly*, 55 (1969), 95–102.

Martin, Robert K. "Hawthorne's *The Blithedale Romance*," *Explicator*, 28 (1969), item 11.

Martin, Terence. *Nathaniel Hawthorne* (New York: Twayne, 1965), pp. 145–59.

McCullen, Joseph T. "Zenobia: Hawthorne's Scornful Skeptic," *Discourse*, 4 (1961), 72–80.

McPherson, Hugo. *Hawthorne as Myth-Maker: A Study in Imagination* (Toronto: University of Toronto Press, 1969), pp. 146–58.

Minter, David L. "Definition of a Fictional Form: Hawthorne's *The Blithedale Romance*," *The Interpreted Design as a Structural Principle in American Prose* (New Haven: Yale University Press, 1969), pp. 137–60.

Montgomery, Judith H. "The American Galatea," *College English*, 32 (1971), 890–99.

Morgan, Ellen E. "The Veiled Lady: The Secret Love of Miles Coverdale," *Nathaniel Hawthorne Journal* (1971), 169–81.

Murray, Peter B. "Mythopoesis in *The Blithdale Romance*," *PMLA*, 55 (1960), 591–96. Repr. with revisions as "Myth in *The Blithedale Romance*," *Myth and Literature*, John B. Vickery, ed. (Lincoln: Nebraska University Press, 1966), pp. 213–20.

O'Connor, William Van. "Conscious Naiveté in *The Blithedale Romance*," *Revue des Langes Vivantes*, 220 (1954), 37–45. Repr. "The Narrator as Distorting Mirror," *The Grotesque: An American Genre and Other Essays* (Carbondale: Southern Illinois Press, 1962).

Pearce, Roy Harvey. "Day-dream and Fact: The Import of *The Blithedale Romance*," in *Individual and Community*, Kenneth H. Baldwin and David K. Kirby, eds. (Durham: Duke University Press, 1975), pp. 49–63.

———, ed. Introduction, *The Blithedale Romance* (Columbus: Ohio State University Press, 1964).

Poirier, Richard. *A World Elsewhere: The Place of Style in American Literature* (New York: Oxford University Press, 1966), pp. 115–24.

Porte, Joel. *The Romance in America* (Middletown, Conn.: Wesleyan University Press, 1969), pp. 125–37.

Ragan, James F. "The Irony in Hawthorne's *Blithedale*," *New England Quarterly*, 35 (1962), 239–46.

Randel, William Peirce. "Hawthorne, Channing, and Margaret Fuller," *American Literature*, 10 (1939), 472–76.

Rees, John O., Jr. "Shakespeare in *The Blithedale Romance*," *Emerson Society Quarterly*, 71 (1973), 84–93.

Rose, Marilyn G. "Miles Coverdale as Hawthorne's Persona," *American Transcendental Quarterly*, 1 (1969), 90–91.

Ross, Donald, Jr. "Dreams and Sexual Repression in *The Blithedale Romance*," *PMLA*, 86 (1971), 1014–17.

Rust, James D. "George Eliot on *The Blithedale Romance*," *Boston Public Library Quarterly*, 7 (1955), 207–15.

Rust, R. V. "Coverdale's Confession, A Key to Meaning in *The Blithedale Romance*," in *Literature and Ideas in America*, Robert Falk, ed. (Athens: Ohio University Press, 1975), pp. 96–110.

Sachs, Viola. "The Myth of America in Hawthorne's *The House of the Seven Gables* and *The Blithedale Romance*," *Kwartalnik Neo-filologeczny*, 15 (1968), 267–83.

Sams, Henry W., ed., *Autobiography of Brook Farm* (Englewood Cliffs, N.J.: Prentice-Hall, 1958).

Shroeder, John W. "Miles Coverdale as Actaeon, as Fannus, and as October: With Some Consequences," *Papers on Language and Literature*, 2 (1966), 126–39.

———. "Miles Coverdale's Calendar: or, A Major Literary Source for *The Blithedale Romance*," *Essex Institute Historical Collections*, 103 (1967), 353–64.

Smith, David E. "Bunyan and Hawthorne," *John Bunyan in America* (Bloomington: Indiana University Press, 1966), pp. 45–89.

Smith, Julian. "*The Blithedale Romance*—Hawthorne's New Testament of Failure," *Personalist*, 49 (1968), 540–48.

———. "Why Does Zenobia Kill Herself?" *English Language Notes*, 6 (1968), 37–39.

Sprague, Claire. "Dream and Disguise in *The Blithedale Romance*," *PMLA*, 84 (1969), 596–97.

Stanton, Robert. "Hawthorne, Bunyan and the American Romances," *PMLA*, 71 (1956), 155–65.

———. "The Trial of Nature: An Analysis of *The Blithedale Romance*," *PMLA*, 76 (1961), 528–38.

Stoehr, Taylor. "Hawthorne and Mesmerism," *Huntington Library Quarterly*, 33 (1969), 33–60.

Stubbs, John Caldwell. *The Pursuit of Form: A Study of Hawthorne and the Romance* (Urbana: University of Illinois Press, 1970), pp. 120–37.

Tharpe, Jac. *Nathaniel Hawthorne: Identity and Knowledge* (Carbondale: Southern Illinois University Press, 1967), pp. 125–33.

Turner, Arlin. "Autobiographical Elements in Hawthorne's *The Blithedale Romance*," *Texas Studies in English*, 15 (1935), 39–62.

———. "Hawthorne and Reform," *New England Quarterly*, 15 (1942), 705–11.

Van Cromphout, Gustaaf. "Blithedale and the Androgyne Myth: Another Look at Zenobia," *Emerson Society Quarterly*, 18 (1972), 141–45.

———. "Emerson, Hawthorne, and *The Blithedale Romance*," *Georgia Review*, 25 (1971), 471–80.

Van Doren, Mark. *Nathaniel Hawthorne* (New York: William Sloane, 1949), pp. 188–91.

Von Abele, Rudolph. *The Death of the Artist: A Study of Hawthorne's Disintegration* (The Hague: Nijhoff, 1955), pp. 71–83.

Warren, Austin. "Hawthorne, Margaret Fuller, and 'Nemesis,'" *PMLA*, 54 (1939), 615–18.

Whelan, Robert E. Jr. "*The Blithedale Romance:* The Holy War in Hawthorne's Mansoul," *Texas Studies in Literature and Language*, 13 (1971), 91–109.

Yates, Norris. "Ritual and Reality: Mask and Dance Motifs in Hawthorne's Fiction," *Philological Quarterly*, 34 (1955), 63–66.

NORTON CRITICAL EDITIONS